Yale Studies in Political Science, 11

David Horne, Editor

PUBLISHED UNDER THE DIRECTION OF
THE DEPARTMENT OF POLITICAL SCIENCE

THE LAWMAKERS

Recruitment and Adaptation to Legislative Life

by JAMES DAVID BARBER

GREENWOOD PRESS, PUBLISHERS
WESTPORT, CONNECTICUT

Library of Congress Cataloging in Publication Data

Barber, James David.
  The lawmakers.

  Reprint of the ed. published by Yale University Press,
New Haven, which was issued as no. 11 in Yale studies in
political science.
  Bibliography: p.
  Includes index.
  1. Politics, Practical. 2. United States--Politics
and government. 3. Politicians--United States.
I. Title. II. Series: Yale studies in political
science ; 11.
[JK1976.B3 1980]   328.73'07'3   79-26379
ISBN 0-313-22200-2 lib. bdg.

Reprinted with the permission of Yale University Press.

Reprinted in 1980 by Greenwood Press, Inc.
51 Riverside Avenue, Westport, CT 06880

Printed in the United States of America

10 9 8 7 6 5 4 3 2 1

For Edith N. and Daniel N. Barber

who made the laws for me

Preface

This is a study of politics as a personal experience of the politician. In writing it, I have tried to maintain a focus on the *political* significance of personality, the impact it has on the recruitment, adaptation, and performance of political leaders. Why are certain types of people especially attracted to political candidacy? How do their subsequent political experiences reward them? What tensions and anxieties do they encounter in their official roles? What effects do their patterns of personal adjustment have on the process of government decision-making?

My interest in seeking answers to these questions (and, I should add in haste, I am still seeking) arose from a concern and a paradox. The concern is that of democracy for leadership. Surely the major lesson to be derived from contemporary research on public opinion is that a great gulf exists between the strains and complexities of policy-making and the average citizen's political casualness. To say this is by no means to denigrate the people; perhaps the wonder is that in a time of relative peace and prosperity they take as much interest as they do. Their performance in choosing among candidates, in empowering and restraining and attending to leaders, has often been impressive. But they do not and cannot govern. If democracy succeeds in the United States, a very large portion of the credit must go to the activists, the opinion leaders, and especially the public officials who make the hard, intricate, fateful decisions of governance. To discover how and why they do so is a central concern of political science.

The paradox can be simply stated. Our culture defines politics as an arena of conflict, a battleground on which eager candidates struggle to win and keep office. Yet a look at the statistics of turnover—in Washington as well as in the state capitals—shows that whole regiments of officials, many of whom could easily retain their posts, desert them after a brief incumbency. Which picture is the more accurate: is public office a prize to be sought or a burden to be escaped? And if the answer is that it is a prize for some and a burden for others, what distinguishes these types from one another?

These are grand questions; this book is an empirical exploration of a few politicians, meant to suggest only tentative answers. It is based primarily on twenty-seven long private interviews, tape-recorded with the subjects' consent, with legislators serving their first session in the Connecticut House of Representatives. From these twenty-seven interviews, three are used to illustrate in detail each of four legislative types, labeled Spectators, Advertisers, Reluctants, and Lawmakers. These categories are described in the four central chapters. The data consist also of replies to two questionnaires (before and after the session), interviews with experienced legislators, direct observation of many committee meetings, caucuses, and plenary sessions, and official documents, newspapers, and books. But I have found the interviews with "freshmen" legislators—all elected at the same time, sharing a certain generational spirit—most revealing and useful. The methodological details are presented in a separate appendix. But it is important that the limitations of the evidence be clear from the first.

The book's theoretical framework is described in the first chapter, and the final chapter is given over to broader interpretations and speculations.

I owe a great deal to two friends who performed the ultimate scholarly favor—reading and criticizing the manuscript of this book in detail. Over a period of six years, as my teacher, adviser, and colleague, Robert E. Lane has given me more hours of his time, more good ideas, and more generous encouragement than I have deserved. For nearly as long a time, Fred I. Greenstein has shared with me his comprehensive knowledge of the professional literature, his incisive criticisms, and his good fellowship.

My interest in legislatures began in Herman Finer's classes. The particular subject of this book traces back to an article by Charles Hyneman. In the research planning stage, Allan P. Sindler, Duane Lockard, and Heinz Eulau made helpful suggestions. Comments by Peter B. Clark, Robert A. Dahl, Karl W. Deutsch, James W. Fesler, and Harold D. Lasswell helped me make a dissertation out of a collection of data. Philip E. Converse, Stanley Coopersmith, and Morton J. Tenzer took time to contribute thoughtful comments. Herbert

Jacob, Rufus Browning, and William Flanigan, fellow Yale graduate students, were my partners in hatching numerous ideas.

When the dissertation first arrived at Yale University Press in 1960, it was replete with information, adequate in organization, and about as readable as a telephone directory. Thanks to the detailed comments and wise advice of the editors, David Horne, Marian Neal Ash, and Ruth L. Davis, I have completely revised the text. I am especially grateful to Miss Davis for correcting many stylistic gaffes in the earliest manuscript. Subsequently Mr. Horne performed a deft and thorough job of editing the last draft. For additional help in preparing copy I am indebted to Veronica E. O'Neill, secretary of the Yale Department of Political Science, Ann Barber, Grace Stanley, Leah Lettes, Eve Cummings, Lavon Saunders, Joy du Trieuillé, Donna du Trieuillé, and Robert Bunselmeyer. Dorothy Ciosek of the Yale Computer Center assisted with some early calculations.

I am grateful to the Southern Fellowships Fund and the Samuel S. Fels Fund for generous financial support during the project's early years.

The many legislators, former legislators, and other officials who gave so freely of their time and thought have my heartfelt thanks. Anonymous in these pages, they will remain very real to me.

To my wife Ann for gay faith and dogged labor, and to my children for laughter and silence, I owe the deepest of debts. This book is dedicated to my parents who, since this day years ago, have guided and encouraged me.

J. D. B.

New Haven, Connecticut
July 31, 1964

Contents

The longer one frets with the puzzle of how democratic regimes manage to function, the more plausible it appears that a substantial part of the explanation is to be found in the motives that actuate the leadership echelon, the values that it holds, in the rules of the political game to which it adheres, in the expectations which it entertains about its own status in society, and perhaps in some of the objective circumstances, both material and institutional, in which it functions.

V. O. Key, Jr.

1. Politics as Recruitment

Now the number of mice is largely dependent, as
everyone knows, on the number of cats.

CHARLES DARWIN

Perhaps the survival of American democracy does not depend on recruiting the very best talents to government. But excellence in American government—the rationality of its decisions, the quality of justice
it dispenses, the timeliness of its actions—these things depend profoundly on the character of those we elect. Can a political system
designed to bar tyrants, check power with power, and eliminate the
corrupt and incompetent also produce excellence in government? This
is the practical question which impels the research reported here.

Historically, the answers have stressed law and institutions. Ever
since John Adams and his colleagues set out "from various discords to
create the music of a well-tuned state," Americans have been adjusting
the electoral machinery. The major device, the formally competitive
election, gained new energy and meaning with the growth of two
permanent mass parties, universal suffrage, the secret ballot, and the
direct primary. New sources of talent were opened up, new opportunities for competing were offered. And the conditions for a freer, more
rational choice improved as each man's private vote was counted
equally. Today the remaining legal barriers to full democracy are being
steadily diminished. Constitutionally speaking, the potentialities for
recruiting the best talent for service in government were never better.

To turn these constitutional potentialities into political realities, we
have relied on the spur of ambition. The militant language we use to
describe our politics—our talk of campaigns and strategies and victory
and spoils—perhaps reflects a key assumption: that the desire for public
office is widespread, strong, and deep.

To believe anything else, the insiders tell us, is to be naïve. Thus
Frank Kent, writing for the benefit of the "vast majority of voters"

who "are in a state of ignorance about politics," assured his readers of the twenties that politicians may retire, "but it is never in the least voluntary. I repeat that every man who has held elective office wants to keep it or to get another better one." [1] More recently, Russell Baker of the *New York Times* lampooned the humble protestations of presidential aspirants. He recalls "The Great Decliner," Horatio Seymour, Democratic nominee in 1868, who, "so the story goes, had to be rushed weeping from the convention hall to keep him from refusing the nomination on the twenty-second ballot. 'Pity me, Harvey! Pity me!' he wailed to a friend as the politicians hustled him off the premises." [2] In 1960 Baker found not "a single full-blooded decliner on the horizon."

Yet even at the presidential level the evidence on the depth and strength of candidate motives is uncertain. Was General Eisenhower sincere when, in the winter of 1946–47, he responded to Douglas Southall Freeman's suggestion—"the hand of the Lord is upon you"— with a fervent "God forbid!"? Or were his innermost desires exposed more clearly in his note to General Walter Bedell Smith the following September: "I do not believe that you or I or anyone else has the right to state, categorically, that he will not perform any duty that his country might demand of him." [3] Like St. Peter, Governor Adlai Stevenson is reported to have issued no fewer than three adamant denials in 1951–52.[4] But was his drive for the office really revealed in a slip of the tongue after a conversation with the President later that year? "After refusing comment on the meeting, Stevenson was asked a parting question: 'Tell me, Governor, during the course of your talk at the White House, did the President mention your divorce?' Stevenson answered, 'Yes, he said it wouldn't matter.' " [5]

Behind such speculation is a fundamental problem: to what extent can we rely on *competition* in the struggle for office to produce adequate leadership throughout the governmental system? If such political eagerness is widespread (at least among the better qualified, broadly defined), then perhaps we can put aside a long list of troublesome questions. We need not worry much about matching the person to the office, about the active recruitment of candidates, about the reasons why people choose to run. The system will take care of it. We will have found, in an old American way, an institutional answer for a motivational question.[6] Competition will serve as an invisible hand to guide the supply of candidates to the offices which demand them.

What evidence is there that this is in fact the way our system works?

CAN WE COUNT ON COMPETITION?

Tucked away in the American two-party system are a great many constituencies in which it is unrealistic to talk of *party* competition in any but potential terms.[7] Even allowing for difficulties of definition and measurement,[8] many districts—both inside and outside the South —are perennially safe for one party or the other. Warren Miller provides illustrative statistics:

> In 1955, three out of every four state legislative bodies or congressional delegations were so completely dominated by a single political party that that party controlled more than 66 per cent of the members of the group. Excluding the 15 Border and Southern states, fully half of the remaining 33 state legislatures were controlled by one party holding at least two out of every three seats; in only six states was the controlling margin below 55 per cent. Within the same group of non-Border, non-Southern states, 25 of the 33 congressional delegations were dominated by one party controlling two-thirds or more of the delegation members; only four delegations were so evenly divided as to give the majority party less than 55 per cent of the members . . . over three-fourths of all congressional districts can be classified as relatively safe districts.[9]

The classification of states according to the degree of interparty competition sometimes obscures the presence of many a safe constituency. The scramble for the governorship may be far from typical of state offices generally. For example, Connecticut, as Duane Lockard points out, has been tightly competitive at the gubernatorial level. For more than a quarter-century the winner's vote hovered around 50 per cent.[10] Yet in almost half of the 169 Connecticut towns, one party elected all the state representatives in six consecutive biennial elections after World War II. As Joseph A. Schlesinger concluded after a rigorous examination of competition in the states, there are "enormous discrepancies in voting reaction to different offices" within the same state.[11]

In some areas, of course, competition in the party primary substitutes to a degree for competition in the general election. But in terms of voter participation and attention, such contests tend to be pale reflections of an all-out two-party fight.[12] And the odds against unseating an incumbent in a primary are very high indeed.[13]

What are the effects of competition where it does exist? There are no clear answers on this point. In combination with certain constitutional arrangements, such as legislative malapportionment or direct election of the governor's subordinates, close elections can produce deadlock and confusion.[14] Perhaps two-party competition engenders more effort to meet the needs of the have-nots, but this effect is far from being confirmed.[15] Nor is it clear that competition increases voter turnout.[16]

Considering the general aura of favorable opinion about the effects of competition, it is useful to point out some of its apparently deleterious results. In closely divided constituencies, elections may turn on casual choices by apathetic, ill-informed, "independent" voters. Candidates may be chosen on the basis of their potential appeal to such voters. And even the most scrupulous of nominees, it appears, can be persuaded to base his campaign on Madison Avenue hokum.[17] When competition is too intense, it can "create a gulf between the various portions of the electorate and thereby weaken the viability of any political decision that emerges" and may "have a disintegrative effect on the compromise-oriented groups in the electorate with their 'built-in' predispositions against manipulation." [18] And there is extensive evidence from a large variety of social-psychological studies to the effect that competition, in part because it emphasizes irrelevant differences between contenders, can disrupt group operations.[19]

For these reasons it is clearly wrong to suppose that political competition is either virtually universal or universally virtuous. Close political contests have given us Sam Rayburn—and Joseph R. McCarthy; landslide elections produced Franklin D. Roosevelt—and Warren G. Harding. To rely on competition alone as an automatic device for selecting leaders of high quality is little more than whistling in the dark. Necessary it may be, but there is convincing evidence that it is not sufficient. It is of at least equal importance that parties recruit candidates qualified to fill the offices they contest for. Party reformers should not be satisfied with intense competition among second-raters. As V. O. Key, Jr., wrote:

> Perhaps the most important function that party leadership needs to perform is the development, grooming, and promotion of candidates for statewide office. Although striking exceptions may be cited, it is in its inadequacy in this role that the most

grave shortcoming of party leadership is to be found. To assert that party leadership of many states develops candidates is more an attribution of a duty stated in the textbooks than a description of real activity.[20]

Political leadership selection, then, should be viewed not only as the elimination of certain individuals but also as a process by which candidates are attracted to, recruited for, adapted to, and retained in the public service.

WHO WANTS TO RUN?

There is evidence that party organizations, motivated perhaps by impending competition, often experience difficulty in recruiting competent candidates. The general picture of American political apathy is familiar.[21] To be sure, there are signs of interest among a considerable number of Americans in some forms of political participation. There may be an upward trend in the percentage of eligible voters voting,[22] and in fact our estimates of this proportion may have been unrealistically low.[23] In scattered polls, as many as 22 per cent of the electorate sampled have expressed willingness to do campaign work,[24] and about a third say they are willing to contribute five dollars to their party.[25] Perhaps 28 per cent try to influence others' votes.[26] Government officials (mostly at the federal level) have been rated high in a list of occupations.[27] Such findings show a potential for political action largely unexploited by the parties.

There is a considerable difference, however, between stopping for a moment at the polls, mailing a check to the party, chatting about the campaign, or stuffing envelopes for a few evenings and undertaking to change one's occupation to politics. The very groups which tend to be most active in voting and voluntary group participation—the high-income, college-educated, professional and managerial categories[28]—are those least likely to see politics as a desirable occupation for their sons.[29] Only about 2 per cent of the general population went so far as to belong to a political club or organization in 1952, and there was "very little tendency for upper-income people to join political clubs in greater proportions than those on a lower-income level."[30] Robert Dahl finds that in New Haven political campaigning is much less popular among the "Better-Off" than are other organizational activities,[31] and that college-educated, high-income, high-social-position people are much less likely than others to prefer a job with the city to one with a private firm.[32] William F. Whyte, Jr., has noted that the well-educated organization man takes little interest in politics, partly because he is too geographically mobile to establish the local ties necessary for political advancement.[33] Numerous other researchers have noted a tendency for politics to be relegated to "localists." [34]

Nor have these trends been confined to a business elite. The practice of labor leaders taking appointive or elective government positions appears to have been largely arrested.[35] And while intellectuals are well represented in the Senate, they are typically isolated from and somewhat disdainful of politics in the nether regions.[36]

Furthermore, occupational groups from which political candidates have traditionally been drawn appear to fluctuate markedly in numbers and may be on the decline relative to the rest of the population.[37] From 1940 to 1950, for example, the population of the United States increased 14.5 per cent.[38] Some occupations, such as salaried real estate and insurance men (up 79.9 per cent), increased rapidly, but "lawyers and judges" increased only 1.6 per cent.[39] In median income, lawyers and judges ranked second only to physicians and surgeons. And the purchasing power of the lawyer's income went up 34 per cent from 1939 to 1957.[40] Insofar as these figures indicate increased apolitical demands on, and rewards for, the lawyer, political recruitment may suffer. Perhaps the same could be said for most other categories of self-employment: as time goes on, there is less occupational independence and more affluence. Switching to a political occupation may be becoming less tempting and more difficult.[41]

THE LEGISLATIVE JOB

The shortage of capable citizens with generally favorable predispositions toward politics is only one of the problems confronting the party recruiter. Not the least of his worries is the nature of the product he has to offer, especially in the legislative field.[42] The work involved in a legislative job—if it is conscientiously done—is prodigious and its conditions difficult. The scope, volume, and complexity of legislation have increased tremendously in the last fifty years, but the number of congressmen has remained about the same and the number of state legislators has decreased.[43] State governments are directly responsible for spending more than twenty billion dollars annually.[44] More and more state legislatures meet in annual rather than biennial sessions. Regular sessions have lengthened and special sessions have become more frequent. Several thousand bills may be introduced in the course of a session: the Florida legislature enacted 3,031 bills from April 4 to June 2, 1961.[45] In 1960–61, only three states (California, Florida, and Texas) provided private offices for legislators.[46] The median biennial pay for the thirty-four states using salary plans in 1962 was $3,000–4,000.[47] Very few states can match the luxurious appointments in which California legislators work.[48]

Thus the party recruiter, if he is candid, will probably have to explain the economics of legislative service to the prospective candidate in some such terms as these:

> The typical legislator must rent rooms for his wife and himself at the state capital for the duration of the session. These may be in one of the two or three principal hotels, or in a motor court. During the session he is customarily expected to attend various county, party, and testimonial banquets. Nor is the ordinary legislator unknown at the hotel bar. This is not because he drinks more than other members of the community, but because much of the business of a session is actually accomplished, discussed, or at least pored over in the informal and friendly surroundings of the taproom. The average pay of a legislator, if he is frugal, will usually barely cover the extra expenses of his sojourn in the capital. If the legislator is at all convivial, he cannot live in a hotel for five months for less than $1,000. This appallingly low salary rate accounts in large measure for the quality and character of our state legislators. How many people can afford to drop their regular employment for three to five months every other year? Even if his extra expenses are covered by the salary he receives, he must still meet his running expenses, though he may lose his ordinary income for the duration of the legislative period. This prevents most young or middle-aged business or professional men from entering legislative politics.[49]

Probably few candidates decide to run for these offices on the basis of the salary alone. But probably almost every potential candidate makes calculations as to how much he can expect to lose during the session and how his jaunt into public office will affect the financial security of his family. The greater his achievements in business or the law, the more likely it is that these calculations will work to the disadvantage of legislative recruitment. Already predisposed to believe, as Mr. Dooley did, that "politics ain't beanbags," he may come to share Kin Hubbard's sympathies: "Now an' then an innocent man is sent t' th' legislature."

RETIREMENT FROM THE RACE

Let us suppose that in spite of these difficulties the party recruiter is successful and the candidate is elected to office. The probability is that the same problem will arise two years later. The rate of turnover among state legislators is very high. More than half of the approximately 7,800 members must be replaced every other year.[50] Authorities on state government agree that the failure of the legislatures to accumulate experience weakens their effectiveness drastically.[51] Charles Hyneman's estimate is that three or four sessions are necessary for a legislator to learn enough background to participate effectively. Yet only about 20 per cent of the members and 30 per cent of the committee chairmen had as many as four sessions of past experience in the period 1925–35 in the legislatures Hyneman studied.[52] More recent studies indicate that the problem has persisted.

The reasons why many members retire after a brief sojourn in the legislature are as obscure as their motives for running in the first place, if retirements due to defeat in elections or primaries are excepted. Hyneman found that about 31 per cent of the retirements he studied were attributable to such causes.[53] In Connecticut, the state on which the present study is based, election defeat accounted for less than 26 per cent of retirements from the House in the seven elections between 1946 and 1958. Thus by far the largest proportion of retirements may be classified as pre-election turnover. Paradoxically, when incumbents *do* run for reelection, they are far more likely to win than to lose. Incumbents won 982 times and lost in only 219 cases in Connecticut reelection contests during this period.

In the hope of isolating some of the causes for this pre-election turnover, I arrayed against it a considerable number of characteristics of constituencies: (1) number of elections for representative won by the minority party in the town, 1946–58; (2) 1958 town population; (3) (1) and (2) together; (4) party winning a majority of representative elections—that is, the dominant party in the town; (5) percentage of population change, 1940–50 and 1950–58; (6) distance from the capital city; (7) dwelling units owner-occupied,

1950; (8) urban percentage, 1950; (9) percentage with income of $5,000 or more, 1950; (10) percentage of elections in the county won by Democrats, 1946–58. The results were unclear and irregular.

In addition, trend data were accumulated for the period showing the governor's plurality, the number of Democrats elected, the incumbents reelected, and the incumbents defeated. Again, no clear relationships emerge. Pre-election turnover showed a remarkable stability from election to election in this period: the average number of incumbents not renominated was 96. The highest figure was 111, and the lowest 82.

Yet during these dozen years some remarkable changes took place in the state. The party balance in the House was radically altered when the out-party won a majority for the first time in more than half a century; a governor was elected by an unprecedented margin. A law was passed forbidding the Governor to appoint legislators to other positions during their legislative term. President Truman won unexpectedly, and there were the two Eisenhower landslides. In short, through the years of postwar readjustment, the return of the veterans, the Korean War—times of prosperity and recession, marked population shifts, and strife and reorganization in both political parties—about the same number of legislators disappeared from view before each election. Nor did this regular rate appear to be due to rotational agreements, by which candidacies are passed around from one part of a town to another.[54]

As Hyneman concluded some twenty years ago after an exhaustive study of turnover: "The real task is to find why so many legislators, senators and representatives alike, choose not to run again. Devices and arrangements which reduce the hazards of an election year to a minimum will still not give us a body of lawmakers rich in the experience of their trade. The state legislator must be made more happy in his career . . . The key to rehabilitation of the legislative branch is in the nature of the legislator's job and his attitude toward it."[55]

If governments are to be supplied with high talents, political recruitment should have a high priority on the party agenda. The recruiter must know how to select from the possible candidates those most likely to contribute action and rationality to the governmental process, to attract them to political careers, and to retain them in office once elected. In this task, much depends, it appears, on personal motivations for office-seeking and on satisfactions that individuals derive from holding office.[56] We cannot rely upon a ready supply of excellent candidates presenting themselves for the contest; we cannot be confident that once a man has had a taste of politics his appetite for it will never fade. Those we find participating—at this level, in this institution, at this time—are those who happen to find that this particular political opportunity serves certain needs for them. The nature of these needs and the ways politicians seek to satisfy them can have an important influence on the quality of government.[57]

Matters of Theory

The study of political recruitment and official behavior has been approached in at least three ways. Traditionally, political scientists have attended primarily to the condition of political organizations in a constituency. How does the degree of inter- and intraparty competition affect the channeling of talents into offices? Are substitute organizations or factions available when the parties are weak? What criteria are employed by political leaders in selecting candidates in different political arenas? For example, it is argued that candidates for presidential nominations may be considered unavailable if they are not from large, "doubtful" states,[58] although the criterion of salability by mass media may be superseding such standards.[59]

A more sociological approach often begins with an examination of the background characteristics—education, occupation, class, ethnicity, etc.—of those in leadership positions. Then one observes how these distributions differ from those in the general population. One finds, for example, that lawyers are greatly overrepresented in elective offices.[60] It is probable that being a lawyer facilitates recruitment to these offices. On the other hand, certain other occupational groupings are vastly underrepresented, indicating that their members have few opportunities for attaining office. It follows that each of these occupational groupings (the same holds for class, education, etc.) should be investigated to determine why they are or are not special sources for candidates. It has been suggested, for instance, that the comparative flexibility of the law profession [61] (i.e. the manipulable time schedule, the ease of reentry after an extended absence) and its "broker" character help to explain selection.[62]

A third approach may begin by asking what motivational characteristics distinguish politicians from other people? The question can be answered hypothetically by supposing that the peculiarities of the political role reveal the motives appropriate to that role. Thus power is exercised by political leaders, politicians engage in bargaining, are in the public eye, enjoy a certain prestige, and so forth. The expectation is that people who are most highly motivated in these directions will seek and be selected for public office. Or the exploration may begin by testing empirically the notion that certain needs distinguish politicians. For example, one systematic exploration has found that politically active businessmen, when compared with a matched sample of inactive businessmen, turn out to be higher in "power motivation" and "achievement motivation," but lower in "affiliation motivation." [63]

Each of these rough rubrics covers an immense collection of writing, ranging into almost every discipline concerned with human affairs and backward in time at least to Homer. This is not the place to attempt a comprehensive review.[64] I suggest, rather, some theoretical and methodological considerations that have shaped my own approach—one that combines elements from each of the above-mentioned three perspectives.

What questions would a potential candidate ask himself, as he attempts to decide whether to seek office? At least the following:

(1) Do I want it? (motivation)
(2) Can I do it? (resources)
(3) Do they want me? (opportunity)

The first question concerns choice among competing attractions, not simply a decision to become active. Most people are already active—that is, are already engaged in enterprises they more or less want to pursue. The question is one of the relative desire to move toward this alternative—political candidacy—rather than toward other actual or potential uses of time and energy.[65]

Thus an understanding of political motivation requires some characterization of the motivational object or goal.[66] In part the do-I-want-it question might take the form "Do I want to get involved in politics?" But it seems very likely that answers would vary according to the particular office being considered. There is no reason to expect that the same motives will govern decisions on running for dogcatcher as for governor, for a judgeship as for party chairman. To answer this question, then, we need information on the character of the position. Similarly, the distinctions between *running* for office, *serving* in the office, and *continuing* to serve may be important. A candidacy can be undertaken, as we shall see below, in the full expectation that one will lose the election. And an initial term may be served with the profound intention not to repeat it.

In answering the second question—"Can I do it?"—one surveys his resources for the job. What skills are appropriate for this particular office? The qualifications are not always easy to specify. What does it take to be a county sheriff? A town treasurer? A state legislator? A congressman? The roles in politics are ill-defined and, most significant, a great deal of latitude in behavior is permitted within each role. The idle employee in business can be summarily discharged. The idle legislator will not be eliminated until the next election, if then. One potential candidate may be told, with accuracy, that his oratorical abilities will serve him well in the legislature. Another may be persuaded, with equal accuracy, that his fear of large audiences is no particular handicap. Thus the person's *perception* of the demands of the office on his skill will be an important consideration in his decision.

Another aspect of the can-I-do-it question is the cost involved in terms of time, energy, money, absence from home, etc. Here again it is obvious that offices differ radically, and that the general rubric "politics" is of little use. Membership on a local government board may consume a few evening hours a month; very few governors manage to confine themselves to a forty-hour week. Furthermore, the potential candidate's calculations of cost will be comparative: he will consider political opportunities in the light of his present nonpolitical situation and prospects. To the ambitious clerk, the $20,000 paid to New York State legislators has an appeal which is lacking for the Rockefellers.

The decision to seek or accept political candidacy rests, of course, on the availability of opportunities. The third question, "Do they want me?," takes a variety of forms in different local contexts. The relevant "they" in some constituencies may be a tiny coterie of party leaders; in other communities, where there is no significant political organization, "they" may be the general public, or 51 per cent of them, or a few friends urging a man to run. The criteria by which parties select candidates are not obvious. Even if we were to suppose that every party aims to choose an election winner, the local culture will determine the characteristics this implies. It is doubtful that the same qualities are sought for this purpose in rural Georgia and Harlem, in Los Angeles and Boston, in Chicago and Winnetka, in Harlan County and Bucks County. But even beyond these gross differences, the party may look for qualifications other than election-winning prowess. In a great many cases, there is no question about the election outcome, no matter who is nominated. And occasionally other purposes may override the desire to win.

A candidate may be chosen because he will gain a substantial number of votes ("make a respectable showing"), add prestige to the party, work hard for other candidates, satisfy some important party faction, contribute money to the campaign, offer special skills useful in campaigning, be the best man for the job regardless of his actual chances, accept a nomination as reward for his past sacrifices for the party, take training in this campaign for one he may win later, or be sufficiently innocuous to leave a delicate intraparty balance undisturbed. Calculations along these dimensions will depend a great deal on the peculiarities of the political system within which the candidate is to be selected, including the community's population, stability, party balance, and political values.

Now it is clear that if any one of these three factors—motivation, resources, opportunity—is missing, the potential candidate will not be recruited. What is less obvious is that *no one of these factors can be satisfactorily defined operationally—observed or estimated—without simultaneously considering the other two.* First, motivation. At least two types are relevant.[67] The person may have certain personal needs that might be met by some form of political participation but are not presently linked to politics. The power-hungry person who takes out on his family his need for dominating others is an example. If we were to find that office-holders exhibit more of this need than others do, we could hypothesize that this motive has some effect on recruitment, but we have no way of knowing whether, in the actual decision to run, it outweighed other conditions or motives. For example, it may be that people with high needs for exercising power are most likely to succeed in business or professional life and thus appear to the recruiter as attractive candidates; but the potential candidates themselves may see politics not at all as a chance to exercise power but rather as an escape from the tensions of a power-ridden business life. Here the intermixture of motive with opportunity and resources is evident.

A second type of motive is a general positive predisposition toward politics. For example, a person may appreciate the drama of political contests, or take an interest in the general run of political news. More than his neighbors do, he reads the front page and watches the tele-

vision commentators. But such inclinations are meaningless for political recruitment until they are linked with some specific combination
of resources and opportunity. In any *particular* context, each element
is defined by its relationships with the other two.

Unless these other factors are taken into account in defining
motives, we are likely to make mistakes about the direction of
causality. If political leaders display high need for power, it may be
either because politics recruits such people or because politics creates
such people. To solve this puzzle, we must specify the motives in control of action at the point in time when a particular opportunity is
perceived in the light of particular resources. In other words, in order
to see how the motives are operating, to estimate their intensity and
direction, we need precisely the information that is lacking in a simple
correlation.[68]

The point is clearer yet when we consider the definition of resources.
The necessary skills, finances, time, etc. cannot be specified without
simultaneously specifying the demands of the particular campaign
or office being considered: the opportunity. Nor can the costs be rated
accurately without considering the strength and nature of the motives
involved. In adding up the costs and rewards, the potential candidate
rates them in relation to his motives. Barriers to candidacy which
appear high when viewed from an objective standpoint may seem low
when viewed from his subjective standpoint. It is the cost *in comparison with* his own anticipated reward that is significant. Here, as in the
marketplace, the demand for a product is a function not simply of
prices and income (opportunities and resources) but also of the utility
of the particular product for consumers (motivation).

The existence of a political opportunity for any given individual
depends upon the recruiter's desire or willingness to have him run.
In most cases, the recruiter's actions will depend heavily on his calculations concerning the potential candidate's availability—his possession
of the appropriate resources and motives. When these are in short
supply in a community, the recruiter will have to make do with such
candidates as happen to be available. This scarcity situation brings to
light how opportunities are affected by the distribution within the
constituency of political talents and values. Opportunities are in large
part defined by these factors. We should not be surprised, then, to find
politicians in a community where high talents are rare utilizing criteria
of selection that differ markedly from those employed in more fortunate constituencies. In order simply to understand the meaning of the

opportunities offered, one must know something of how people in the community feel about political participation and what resources they can bring to it.

In theory, then, motivations, resources, and opportunities are the three fundamental elements of political recruitment, providing three different analytical approaches. But from an operational, research perspective, it is impossible to consider each element in isolation. Thus we will be looking not at motivations and then resources and then opportunities, but rather at certain distinctive combinations of these variables, combinations which come to light only in an examination of specific recruitment events.

MATTERS OF METHOD

I have explored such events primarily by asking some state legislators to tell me about them. It has helped, of course, to know a good deal about the character of the constituencies, the nature of the office, and the shape of the intervening party system. Statistics from official records and questionnaire replies have been compiled and interrelated in various ways. These materials provide a background (as it has been observed and recorded by others) and a numerical check of sorts (based, to be sure, on questionable questions). But I have emphasized the long, loosely structured interviews in which the legislators themselves discuss political events in their pasts, presents, and futures.

Specifically, I have utilized three collections of data:

(1) Verbatim transcripts of tape-recorded interviews with twenty-seven first-term members of the lower house of the Connecticut legislature. The interviews were conducted during the 1959 session in a quiet study away from the Capitol; they lasted from forty minutes to about 2½ hours, averaging ninety minutes.

(2) Questionnaire replies from 83 of the 150 first-term members before the session, and 96 replies to a post-session questionnaire. The questionnaire could not be pretested. Comparison of early respondents, late respondents, and nonrespondents indicates that the more active members, in terms of legislative participation, are overrepresented in the returns.

(3) Official election returns, published biographical material, the records of legislative proceedings and committee hearings, newspaper accounts, statistics on constituency characteristics, interviews with former legislators, and professional literature.

The questions asked in the interviews and other methodological details are contained in a separate appendix. I have commented there on some of the particular shortcomings involved in this approach. Suffice it to say that the techniques of data-gathering and analysis used do not permit us to consider the results as more than suggestive hypotheses for further research. I shall not belabor this caution in the chapters to follow, but it should be borne in mind.

The method followed in the interviews is an adaptation of the "focused interview" technique described by Merton, Fiske, and Kendall. The interviewer begins by referring to some event in which the respondent has been or will be involved. The respondent is asked to describe his behavior in this event: what did he actually do? This is followed by questions on his reactions, choices, feelings, and thoughts about this particular event. The method requires the constant moving back and forth between these responses and the specification of the events to which they refer. Ideally, one pursues the matter until the exact connection between event and response has been established: "It is not enough to learn that an interviewee regarded a situation as 'unpleasant' or 'anxiety-provoking' or 'stimulating'—summary judgments which are properly suspect and, moreover, consistent with a variety of interpretations. The aim is to discover more precisely what 'unpleasant' denotes in this context, which concrete feelings were called into play, which personal associations came to mind." [69]

Thus not every facet of his experience is catalogued, not every motive scored, but only those which relate, in this case, to his recruitment and adaptation to official life. And within this collection of responses, we are especially concerned with those thought to have a bearing on his own choices—those responses which reveal factors shaping his behavior when he has some leeway—rather than every political reaction. [70]

Two kinds of evidence emerge from this style of exploration. First we find the respondent consciously linking certain determinants to his recruitment choices. These answers are to be taken seriously. [71] One should not begin by dismissing references to civic duty and the like as mere rationalizations, while accepting references to self-interest as the real thing. Yet at the same time one attempts a second kind of inference, listening for patterns of response other than those the person connects directly and consciously with his political choices. If, for instance, when we ask directly for reasons for candidacy, the "civic duty" theme is expressed briefly, offhandedly, in a flat, unemotional tone of voice, but at other points in the interview a great deal is made of the occupational benefits involved in politics, we have grounds for stressing the latter as probably more significant. The answers and the inferences from them are both kept relevant by the consistent effort to turn attention to the respondent's own specific political experiences.[72]

While it has been convenient so far to discuss these distinctions as they bear on the initial steps of recruitment, they apply equally to reactions and choices throughout a period of service. In a sense, the official continues to be recruited as long as he is in office. He responds to the environment he finds there, employs resources, takes or rejects opportunities, and eventually decides whether or not to try for re-election. A central hypothesis here is that the person moving through this sequence of events displays a consistency and continuity of behavior, indicating the persistent effects of certain characteristic ways of responding to his political environments. Thus I shall be concerned not merely with his first step but with his activity through the first term, and I will attempt to predict the path he will follow in the future.[73]

THE CONNECTICUT LEGISLATORS

The legislators examined here shared several significant characteristics. They were nominated and elected in the Connecticut political culture, with its relatively energetic, clean, responsible, and competitive parties, its peculiar blend of Yankee traditionalism and ethnic ticket-balancing, and its comparatively progressive record of social legislation. They entered a legislature in which party leadership is strong and party unity is the rule.[74] Overcoming one of the worst cases of malapportionment in the nation, Connecticut's Democrats won a majority of the lower house in 1958 for the first time in 82 years. From this historical and political context the legislators drew a set of common attitudes and expectations. As "freshmen" they shared a certain generational spirit. As public officials meeting for five months every two years, they were not yet necessarily won over to political careers, but they had clearly gone beyond strictly amateur participation. In a tentative, transitional stage, involved enough to make a political career a real possibility but still pursuing a regular occupation, they were a particularly interesting group to study from the angle of political recruitment.[75]

But even the briefest perusal of the interviews reveals a rather startling variety among these freshmen members. Each had his special history to tell; each reacted in his own way to his first session; each had a different slant on the future. To generalize broadly about even this select company would obscure more than it would enlighten. In a sense they are all the same; in another sense, each is unique.

Yet between variety and uniformity I found patterns of adaptation, shared styles of political behavior that appear to characterize sub-groupings of members. My typology is based not on mere impressions but on the interaction of two quite definite variables.[76] My hypothesis is that once this pair of factors is known, a good deal about the recruitment and adaptation of these neophyte politicians becomes evident.

Defining Variables: Activity and Willingness to Return

The two variables which define our categories are *activity in the legislature* and *willingness to return for at least three future sessions.* Why might we expect these two factors to outline significant types? If we recall our primary interest in political recruitment and adaptation, the reasons seem evident. Each of the factors has a personal dimension (that is, it reflects to some extent a propensity of the individual) and an institutional dimension (that is, the activity is legislative activity, the willingness is to return to the office). These variables thus may tap key points in the relationships between the individual and the office. We would expect them to divide our respondents into categories that reflect different styles of personal behavior in a special context.

The general dimension of activity-passivity is probably the one most fundamental characteristic of a person's life style. In personality terms such as *ascendance, dominance, initiative, dramatizing, gregariousness, aggressiveness, exhibitionism, striving, achievement, manipulating,* and the like, the significance of the activity element is clear. In terms of group behavior, the fact that in most groups there is a marked distinction between the active minority and a larger number of passive members has been repeatedly verified.[77] From the standpoint of political recruitment some, as we have seen, seek office actively, while others are sought out and recruited. And within the institution itself, as will soon be evident, some members are very active while others are, in terms of legislative work, almost completely quiescent. One of the first and most obvious observations we can make of an individual is his tendency to act much or little.

As a simple measure of activity, I have used an index derived from counts of bills introduced, comments made in committees, and lines spoken on the floor of the Assembly. The details are described in Appendix C.

The second variable, willingness to return, is measured by the legislator's response to the question, asked after his first session, "As of today, how likely is it that you would be willing to serve three or more terms in the Assembly in the future?" The answers were divided dichotomously between those who answered "definitely would" or "probably would" and those who answered "probably would not" or "definitely would not." For the interview subjects, the answers were more detailed, but divided in the same way.

This expression of willingness to return taps, I think, the general attitude the individual has toward his membership in the group. It probably should be taken less as an expression of practical intention than as a current orientation toward the office.[78] Those who give positive answers to this question appear to be saying (and here I judge in part from the interview replies) that on balance, considering all the pros and cons, they find the office attractive, satisfying, an experience they might very well want to repeat several times. Here again we are dealing with a variable of central importance to person-group relations. As Cartwright and Zander put it, a person's "attraction to the group will depend upon two sets of conditions: (a) such properties of the group as its goals, programs, size, type of organization, and position in the community; and (b) the needs of the person for affiliation, recognition, security, and other things which can be mediated by groups." [79]

Those for whom the initial legislative experience is perceived as a transient phase in their lives and those for whom it is seen as attractive enough to be repeated for at least half a dozen more years might be expected to show different patterns of adaptation. Expressed most generally, knowing these two scores only, we have clues to the person's *behavior* in the group and his *attitude* toward the group.

Four Patterns of Adaptation

Our initial common-sense expectation might be that these two variables would be highly correlated. That is, the active legislators would be the ones most willing to return. But the evidence indicates that, on the contrary, the variables operate independently. As is clear from Table 1, almost identical numbers of the more active and less active legislators were willing to return. It is the unexpected deviant cases that are of interest. Why would a "low participant" be willing to return in the future? Perhaps because his legislative experience provides rewards for him other than those involved in taking an active part. Why would a "high participant" be unwilling to return? Perhaps because his relatively intense activity is undertaken for certain limited, transient purposes, which can be achieved in a session or two. In the next two chapters we shall explore these possibilities in more detail.

TABLE 1. *Activity and Willingness to Return, 96 First-Term Representatives.*
Postsession Questionnaire

Willingness to	ACTIVITY		
return three or	*High*	*Low*	*Total*
more times	%	%	%
"Definitely" or "Probably would"	34	31	65
"Definitely" or "Probably would not"	17	18	35
TOTAL	51	49	100
			(N = 96)

When all our data are rearranged according to these variables, the four patterns of adaptation outlined in Table 2 appear. The reasons for their labels will be explained in the central chapters.

TABLE 2. *Four Patterns of Adaptation*

		ACTIVITY	
		High	*Low*
Willingness to Return	*High*	Lawmakers	Spectators
	Low	Advertisers	Reluctants

In each of the four following chapters, I examine in detail three legislators (their identities masked by pseudonyms and other minor changes), who exemplify one of these patterns. Each of these chapters follows the same plan of organization. After a general characterization of the type, a series of statistical profiles, drawn from official records and questionnaire replies, is presented, surveying reports of political activity, ambitions, background, and personal characteristics. Then appear, in each chapter, the following sections:

Nominations: Here the special focus is, first, the community, particularly the social characteristics that shape the nominating process and impose certain criteria of selection on the recruiter, and, second, the candidate's availability, or the interplay among motives, resources, and opportunities that led him to seek or accept a candidacy. Community size and rate of population change turn out to be important variables.[80]

Reactions: When a person enters a new environment, he will be especially struck by certain features of it. He is particularly aware of some objects and seems to be blind to others. Furthermore, he attaches values to the objects he perceives. These sensitivities and blindnesses, likes and dislikes can provide important clues to his personal needs and problems of adjustment. This section identifies these needs and problems by surveying the legislators' reactions to their political experiences. Judging from the evidence available, the types contrast markedly in this regard, yet show within each type considerable consistency of reaction.[81]

Self: Probably the most significant general need everyone experiences is the need for self-approval. Probably the most severe problems of adjustment are those which involve getting along with oneself. In this section, an attempt is made to discover the basic needs and problems that are important in structuring the respondent's political behavior. By what special standards does he judge himself? What is the verdict of this judging? For three of the types, it appears, feelings of personal inadequacy, in each case on a markedly different basis, give shape and organization to their behavior.[82]

Strategies: Most people have developed habitual techniques for pursuing their life goals. Such strategies of adjustment or styles of behavior reflect the person's needs or motives, his abilities or resources, and the support they receive from the environment—that is, the opportunities for satisfaction available. In the political environment they distinguish the rhetorician from the behind-the-scenes conniver, the cautious bureaucrat from the reckless plunger, the creative innovator from the effective implementer. The evidence reviewed here indicates that, far from there being a single political type, there are at least four, and that their contrasting strategies, with perhaps one exception, are unlikely to be much altered by experience.[83]

The legislator and the work of the legislature: Over a very long history, legislatures have developed certain organizational mechanisms for accomplishing their central tasks. The committee system is one example; informal negotiation is another. These mechanisms serve important functions and are very hard to change. The effectiveness of the legislature depends to an important extent on the degree to which the legislators' adjustive strategies are congruent with such task-facilitating practices. If this fit is poor, the legislative process falters or proceeds erratically and irrationally. I find in this regard that the adjustive strategies pursued by many members hamper their effectiveness as legislators. And in fact, a considerable number have little interest in the substantive work of the legislature.[84]

The legislator's political future: No certain prediction on this matter is possible, but in this section some attempt is made to estimate the most likely course for each of the four types.

In the concluding chapter the main findings are summarized and interpreted speculatively. Our purpose is to discover not simply *who* the legislators are, or how they act, or what they say, but, and centrally, *why*.

2. The Spectator

It is probably no mere historical accident that the
word person, in its first meaning, is a mask.

ROBERT E. PARK

Connecticut's capitol building bears some resemblance to a rococo
movie palace. In the Hall of the House of Representatives, the bright
blue rug, the ornate fixtures, and the elaborate stained-glass windows
create a certain theatrical atmosphere. There were times during the
session when the action matched the setting. One thinks of the stately
drama of the inauguration, the lighthearted Saint Patrick's Day celebration, and the sentimental, hatchet-burying ceremony with which
the session closed. Occasionally, debate was dramatic (as in the struggle to reform the state's court system), or pathetic (as in the attempt
to save a local hospital), or comic (as on questions of deer-hunting
with bows and arrows and operation of barber shops on Washington's
birthday). The original verse recited during the session would fill a
small but entertaining volume. For the visiting legislative buff, the
session had its moments.

But they were few and far between. Considered as pure entertainment, the day-to-day operations of the House—the long-drawn-out
committee hearings, the readings of the calendar, the perfunctory
debates on minor bills and irrelevant resolutions—could not sustain
for long the interest of an audience of outsiders. As one who watched a
considerable number of House sessions (often alone in the gallery),
the writer confesses that he often found his attention wandering to
the pigeons conspiring on the windowsills. Most of the time, to the
mere observer, the proceedings are dull.

The members of the House are not, of course, mere observers. Yet
our first group of new legislators, the Spectators, appear to have
reached a different conclusion. Like the other members, they have
"competed" for nomination, "campaigned" for office, and "won"

election, and are now empowered to take an active role in the making of the laws. But once in the legislature, they settle back into the role of members of the audience, attending regularly but participating little or not at all. Unlike other quiet legislators,[1] they place a high value on the legislature as entertainment. "It's just fascinating to sit back and watch," says one; "what more can I say?—there's pageantry, there's entertainment. And you can watch the people—I mean, I like to watch the people. And I'm sitting where I have a pretty good view . . . I mean watching some of these discussions going on . . . and, ah . . . I watch all that. Every moment I'm in that House, I'm watching everything." Another confesses: "I just like being there. I like the idea of coming. I like the capitol building—quite impressive. And just to come in and sit at the desk . . . It's an awfully good diversion. You hate to get in a rut."

Being a legislator, they find, is "a wonderful experience," "tremendously interesting," "an experience that can't be duplicated." "I'm enjoying every minute of it up here, and I wouldn't trade it for anything." In their replies to questionnaires Spectators are the members most likely to choose "listening to debate" as a favorite legislative activity.[a]

Who are the Spectators? What personal needs does their legislative experience serve? What problems do they encounter in adjusting to legislative life, and how do they try to solve them? How do their solutions of these problems affect the work of the legislature?

THE SPECTATOR PROFILES: LOW-PRESSURE AMATEUR

The Spectator category consists of the thirty new-member respondents who were low in activity and high in willingness to return. Three of these members were interviewed at length. All three claimed perfect attendance records at the time of the interview. Yet in the count of "comments in own committees" not one is noted as making any comments; in other committees, they averaged a bare 4.7 comments; and they spoke an average of only ten lines in the Assembly itself.

Looking first at the Spectator Legislative Activity Profile, we see a pattern of general passivity, in comparison with other members.

---

a. Spectators 37%, other new member respondents 21%. They are also most likely to answer that "the excitement involved in some issues" was "helpful, in that it stimulated my interest and attention." Spectators 87% (N = 30), other new member respondents 65% (N = 66).

PROFILE 1: *Spectator Legislative Activity*

	Spectators	Other New Member Respondents	Difference
Originated action to get nomination	17%	52%	—35
Attended many meetings in campaign	23	59	—36
Likes campaigning very much*	33	45	—12
Attributes election to own campaign efforts	7	15	— 8
Often introduced self to others at first of session	70	88	—18
Took an active part in major negotiations	47	71	—24
Was frequently sought for advice	33	52	—19
Achieved leadership or important committe post	12	27	—15
Considers self energetic rather than easy-going	50	67	—17
Considers self more influential than others	50	53	— 3
Self-rating as a legislator: superior or excellent	20	41	— 21

*Indicates presession response and/or change during session: Spectator $N = 27$, Other $N = 56$. All other responses are from postsession questionnaire: Spectator $N = 30$, Other $N = 66$.

The Spectator Political Ambitions Profile indicates that while he is willing to return to the legislature for several more terms, he does not have a strong interest in seeking other political offices. The interviews confirm this pattern: none of the three subjects shows much interest in undertaking more extensive political roles. In his Political Background Profile the Spectator shows relatively few past political connections. The Spectator Personal Data Profile also indicates divergences from the other new legislators in directions that provide hints to factors underlying his political orientation.

The Spectator, then, stands out as a person of modest achievement, limited skills, and restricted ambitions, political and otherwise. He comes from a small town in which political competition is slight. He has lived there for a long time and intends to stay there. His energies have been less than fully engaged by his political activities.

But election to the legislature is one of the biggest things that ever happened to the Spectator. "It's an honor and a privilege," as one of them says.

NOMINATIONS: AVAILABLE VOLUNTEER

Working from these data and the interview records, we can begin to construct a picture of how the Spectators reached the legislature. In very many of the small towns of Connecticut the major problem

PROFILE 2: *Spectator Political Ambitions*

	Spectators	Other New Member Respondents	Difference
Identifies self as a "politician"	33%	44%	—11
Has considered seeking full-time elective office:			
Presession response*	26	52	—26
Postsession response*	30	46	—16
Change during session	+ 4	— 6	
Had considered full-time state appointive office*	23	36	—13
Was interested in district or state party office*	63	77	—14
Was interested in Assembly leadership position*	52	79	—27
Willingness to return for three or more future sessions:			
Presession response*	86	63	+23
Postsession response*	100	55	+45
Change during session	+ 14	— 8	
Ran again for nomination or election to Assembly:			
In 1960	83	79	+ 4
In 1962	57	38	+19
Ran for or served in some government office (including Assembly) after initial session	90	91	— 1

* See note for Profile 1.

PROFILE 3: *Spectator Political Background*

	Spectator	Other New Member Respondents	Difference
Parents interested in politics	54%	71%	—17
Relatives active in politics	57	67	—10
Occupation involves government contacts	30	59	—29
Had held party office*	56	48	+ 8
Had held elective office*	37	48	—11
Had held appointive office*	37	46	— 9
Had long considered running for Assembly	46	61	—15
Reports some competition for nomination*	56	80	—24
Saw election chances as 50–50*	22	25	— 3
Considers legislative activity most important he has engaged in	80	47	+33

* See note for Profile 1.

PROFILE 4: *Spectator Personal Data*

	Spectators	Other New Member Respondents	Difference
Sex: male	60%	86%	—26
Age: over 40	67	35	+32
Occupation: housewife	30	10	+20
Education: above high school*	34	66	—32
Income: over $8,000*	33	46	—13
Town population: over 5,000	40	71	—31
Resident in town: more than ten years	80	65	+15
Expects to remain in town	100	86	+14
Expects more income in ten years	33	71	—38

* See note for Profile 1.

for the local party committee is not resolving factional contests over nominations, but simply finding some minimally acceptable person to allow his name to be put on the ballot. The committee quickly exhausts the short lists of capable business executives, rising young lawyers, and civic leaders—most of whom are already loaded with community responsibilities for charity drives, club offices, church affairs, and the like. A host of part-time, unpaid town offices have to be filled—many towns are still ruled by a miscellaneous collection of boards, commissions, and committees—and these close-to-home offices take precedence over the more distant state representative post. The problem is one of "Who is available?" rather than "Which of these contestants should we favor?"

A considerable number of the first-term legislators were apparently swept into office on a tidal wave of votes for the governor, who carried the election by the largest majority in the state's history. Many of his party's candidates were surprised, to say the least, to find themselves election winners in towns where the party's nominees had been defeated with monotonous regularity. Ticket-filling sessions in these minority-party committees had degenerated, in some cases, to automatic rotation of the same nominees from year to year, or in at least one case, to a sort of political bingo game. Thus one Spectator reports his party's nominating practices as follows: "Came time to nominate candidates for local elections, we would put all the names of the town committee in the hat and draw them out and—'All right, you're going to run for mayor, or first selectman, and this and so forth.' Year after year, the same names running for different offices."

All too often, he says, nominating is a matter of asking, "Do you want it? Do you want it? Who's going to take it?" rather than a struggle for power. In another minority-party case, the committee reached outside the party membership to find a candidate. The invitation "came as a complete surprise," says one legislator; "I think they asked me to run because they couldn't get anybody else." [2]

The situation in the majority party is different, but may involve equally severe recruitment problems. The majority committee has to find a candidate who will not only run but also serve. The committee cannot use the argument that accepting nomination means only a few weeks of minor publicity during a campaign. The five-month legislative session, becoming nearly a full-time job in the last two months at least, requires a candidate who can rearrange his schedule to spend the necessary time and effort away from his regular occupation. The busy executive or lawyer who wants to dabble in politics is likely to prefer some more convenient, more community-serving local board at which he can spend a few evenings a month with a familiar group of his neighbors. For those actively interested in gaining office the dominant party is the obvious channel, and we would expect more competition for office there than in the minority party. But when talents are in short supply the dominant party may have to sell the nomination even more vigorously than the minority does, because the nominee must be persuaded to take on two years, rather than two weeks, of politics.

The representative in office at the time nominations are made is normally in a strong position to gain renomination. The odds are about five to one against defeating an incumbent at an election for representative.[3] To the town committee of the majority party he is likely to be an attractive and hard-to-challenge choice. He has demonstrated his vote-getting power. He has experience. Few are familiar with his record at the distant capital, and in any case his votes were probably "right." His supporters on the committee are loath to desert him if he desires to run again.

When the incumbent decides he has served long enough, his voice is likely to be a powerful one in the selection of his successor. Open opponents of a retiring incumbent typically have an uphill fight in gaining the nomination, and the selection of a replacement whom he considers safe, friendly, and persuasible is a high probability. This was the situation in the selection of the third Spectator interviewed. At the town committee meeting, "They were discussing justices of the peace, for nomination, and the representative was coming up for election and our past representative was there. It never entered my mind that he wouldn't be running again. He's been in several terms so it's one of those habits you get into. And he's an Irish farmer and our town has a lot of Irish farmers. So he represents them—he's kind of a leader, y'know?"

The incumbent decided, however, that he had nothing to gain by staying on as representative and approached the candidate-to-be ("I thought maybe you'd be interested in it"). His approval was decisive in the choice. The Spectator reports: "I called the fellow the next day and he said, 'You'll run?' and I said, 'Yea, I will.' And he said, 'O.K., I'll step down.' "

It is probably true that many a Spectator is chosen for nomination in circumstances like these. If he is short on competence for political leadership, he is long on availability and, as will be apparent below, on caution, tact, and loyalty. The Spectator—rooted in the community, generally apolitical and unambitious, flattered by the honor of the position—provides a quick, easy solution to a series of difficult problems. "Don't worry about it," one was told. "You don't need any background. You learn while you're there."

Reactions: The Search for Approval

In order to understand the personal needs that underlie the Spectator's political style, we must examine his reactions to his political experiences. What pleasures does he derive from political life? What causes him personal discomfort or pain? The Spectator "learns while he's there" in the legislature—learns how to be the kind of politician he eventually becomes. But his learning depends not on what lessons are directed to him but only on those he perceives and incorporates into his own behavior. This process in turn is shaped by the special sensitivities which he bears with him from the past. In the freedom of a long, exploratory interview, these sensitivities crop up repeatedly.

We have seen already in the general characterization of the Spectator a tendency to look to other people for reward; he is entertained, even fascinated, by others. But the interviews indicate that he wants more than a good show from his fellows: his main pleasures in politics seem to come from being appreciated, approved, loved, and respected by others. And his complaints center around situations in which he is left out, rejected, or abused. A closer look at the three Spectators interviewed illustrates this need for approval.

Sam Thompson: "A warm handshake"

The high point of Sam Thompson's day comes when someone appreciates him. Back in his home community, a small industrial town, he occasionally got the satisfaction of a friendly greeting: "And it makes you feel good when you walk through town and somebody comes up to you and says, 'Hiya, Sam, gee whiz, thanks for that favor.' It does make you feel good." But usually, back home, a legislator is "just an ordinary guy": "You get back home and a representative is not appreciated. A representative is just a person, well a $400 a year man. I've noticed it on several occasions—not that I expect a heck of a lot. I don't."

As an example, Sam cites his experience at the Victory Picnic in honor of the winning candidates. He had to buy his own meal. His picture was left out of the paper. "There, again," he says, "that's a little blow to your ego." What he missed were not free food and pictures but the approval due a winner from his party: "There could have been an apology or something." Similarly, he feels that the salary of the legislators should be raised in order "to give the person that certain lift—not just in money matters, but in personal esteem." When he misses out on minor patronage, when the party in the legislature does not hold caucuses, the significant thing for Sam is, as he says, "I feel left out." Material rewards are important as signs of approval.

In contrast to his home-town experience, the legislature provides for Sam "a good feeling," "a warm feeling." "No matter how small it is," he says, "you are still a part" of it. He feels "the same as anybody else" there. "Everybody has a good morning—a friendly good morning, and people will go out of their way to be nice to you. At least that's the way I find it. I look forward to being here. It gives me that certain buildup." Perhaps the clearest example of Sam's reward from legislative service is found in his story of the Governor's Tea. A euphoric tone runs through his account of this event, only to be followed by a sort of ego-crash:

> We were very impressed. I mean you couldn't help but be impressed. It's a beautiful home. The Governor and his wife met us graciously and gave us the full roam of the house—"Go ahead, look at anything you want. Make yourself at home. We'll see you later on." And we wandered around. It's a beautiful home. Everything in it is beautiful. And, ah, then tea was served—so we had coffee (laughs). So we were sitting around, or standing there, and the Governor came by and he talked to everybody, and his wife talked with everybody. So—before that, we drove up in front of the house and a state trooper, there, he opened the car door. The passengers got out. I got out. The state trooper took the car, parked it for me. And, ah . . . so we had tea, and the Governor talked with us. His wife talked with us. And when it came time to leave, we departed. And again, why—a warm handshake. None of this fishy handshake, but a warm handshake. And, ah, they thanked us for coming—whereas normally we should have thanked them for being invited. They thanked us for coming. And we got out there, the state trooper, he opened the car door. And off we go.
>
> Well, as I say, we had a wonderful afternoon there. As I say, we were only there an hour, hour-and-a-half. It was very impressive. You couldn't help but be impressed. And, ah, got back to town, tell different people about it and they got that—"Yeah? That was nice." No comment, you know? I mean your ego is

built up so high, you're impressed here one moment. Then in the [time] it takes to get home, you're right back down on street level again.

This incident was apparently the high point of Sam's legislative experience. The doors opened for him, the gracious greetings and the carefully evaluated handshake, the unexpected "thanks for coming" —perfunctory as they may have been—all strike Sam as signs of approval. Others will go out of their way to show their affection. The callous indifference of his small-town neighbors stands in marked contrast to the warm social environment Sam finds in the legislature.

Sam's few complaints about his life in the legislature are heavily veiled behind the general aura of acceptance and warmth. Jokingly he says that back home, "If they want to call you a so-and-so, they'll call you that, whereas up here they can insult you and do it politely." And in the course of watching others—"how they react to different people" —he notices that "They'll be so friendly to them one time and then another time, maybe a day or so later, they'll walk by and ignore that person. Probably didn't make out too well."

Sam may have had such experiences himself. On the surface, though, he feels personally rewarded by even the most trivial of attentions: being spoken to, being allowed to watch. After the interview, he told the researcher, "What I want to know is your impression of me."

Tom Minora: "Everybody can be a gentleman"

Tom Minora is a quiet, tall, personable fellow from another small town. He is obviously somewhat less dependent on the approval of others than Sam is. In fact, he feels some sense of personal accomplishment as a legislator and takes some pride in having done a legislative job well. But several strands of the same seeking-for-approval pattern run through his conversation and receive special emphasis. Like Sam, he resents the slights he has received in his home town, especially from leaders of the dominant party. "If you're not [an other-party member] there, you're *nothing*," Tom says. "While they're nice, they're not as friendly as they could be."

The legislature is a different world for Tom. In the Assembly "everyone you meet is friendly, no matter who it is—whether it's the Governor or the Secretary of State or all the way down the line, through the legislators, senators and all of them. Very, very nice people." Simply by being a member of the legislature, Tom feels a warm fellowship with the other members. "Once you're a member there," he says, "you're just a part of everybody." On inauguration day he found the most impressive thing "being so close to the Governor, having the Governor speak to you—almost privately, you know?" He derives a glow of approval from such situations, despite the obvious fact that he was one of a vast audience for the Governor's speech and one of a long line of handshakers.

In contrast to the disdainful attitude of the dominant party at home toward him and his party, the legislators treat him with respect. "I have yet to meet anybody that was other than a gentleman there," he says. "Very, very—I don't know if I should call it the best behavior, but . . . I think probably they're there with, and they know they're there with gentlemen and they behave as such. I think everybody can be a gentleman if they want to." Tom can thus feel accepted into a company that was, by and large, closed to him at home.

Personally, Tom is gentlemanly in the extreme—polite, considerate, cooperative. He seeks in the legislature the approval of other gentlemen, as a sort of confirmation of his status. In part this relates to his own estimate of his background, as revealed in the following passage describing his family's reactions to his nomination:

TOM: Well, they liked it very much—my family [he lists them]—they thought I should do it.

INTERVIEWER: Well, why was that?

TOM (small laugh): Well, I don't know what their thinking was but they thought I—there was no one in our family that ever went into politics too much. Maybe . . . (long pause) . . . maybe it's because we have lived in the same town [for a long time] and . . . we weren't wealthy by any means. We had to work hard. . . . Well, ah . . . we never owed anybody any money. We weren't the best dressed in the world, and so on and so forth. We lived on what we made, in other words, you know? And didn't . . . and had come up it the hard way. And ah, maybe it's because we, ah, I thought that the family would be recognized more than we would have if we didn't have it. You know? There's a certain amount of prestige goes with the job anyway. And like I said, none of my family had ever been part or taken part in politics. Thought maybe this would be the break to get someone interested in it, you know?

To be accepted in the gentlemanly world of the legislature, where prestigeful persons treat him as a fellow gentleman, is a pleasant thing for Tom.

May Perkins: "We should speak to everybody"

May Perkins is a plump, well-dressed, highly voluble person, one of the many small-town lady legislators in the Connecticut House.[b] During the interview it was hard to keep her on the subject. She chatted on and on, describing incident after incident in great detail. Almost all the tales have a common theme: they concern her adventures in conversation, her constant social round of speaking to others and being spoken to in return. It is in the course of this continual social interaction that May Perkins seeks the signs of approval that appear to mean so much to her.

Before she came to the legislature, May says, she had "always held it in awe, as something real nice, very—quite an honor to be in and all." But she quickly gets on to her main interest in the legislature: "In fact, I've met a lot of people—I feel, when we're in there, we're all in there for the same reason, we're all in the House or the Senate or something, so we should speak to everybody." She was "real upset" when a member failed to greet her, even after repeated introductions. "He didn't even speak!" she exclaims. "What a snob. What's the matter with him?" Generally, however, she finds the legislature a place where "I don't find any of them now that actually *will not speak*. I haven't noticed anybody that I wanted to speak to. In fact, some of them are more than friendly, you know, make a point of speaking and finding out your name and everything." In a situation she describes as "wonderful," "just so nice," she was spoken to from all directions: "One man called me up to come up and talk to him and another man flagged me before I could leave—'Come over here and see me.' And there were a couple of others I spoke to. So it's real nice."

May is enthusiastic about the "many nice social affairs" connected with the legislature, especially the formal dinners ("fabulous!") and the regular get-togethers with the other female members. Before and after House sessions, she visits continually with those in neighboring seats, pausing to say hello and pass a few words with legislators as they find or leave their seats. May Perkins' happiness is increased when she

---

b. See pp. 233–34 for statistics on women in the legislature.

is surrounded by acquaintances who reward her with attention, recognition, and approval.

May is little interested in the questions the interviewer asks. She has her own tales to tell, stories which almost always point out how others approve her. When others "appreciate anything you do and they recognize—they know you"; when she is told she is "no detriment to society"; when another "listens very carefully now, because maybe my name will be mentioned" on television; when she is told that her group will be honored when others know she is a member—when these things happen, May feels a sense of well-being and, at the same time, demonstrates in the telling of the stories her need for the interviewer's approval.

These three Spectators thus appear to derive considerable personal satisfaction from the approval of others, and to feel hurt or at least uncomfortable when others reject them. This search for approval is perhaps best indicated by Sam's final plea to the interviewer: "What I want to know is your impression of me." The answer he wants is evident: that he is all right, that the other person feels positively toward him. In the legislature he finds, by and large, just the sort of warm, accepting social environment he is looking for.

The Spectator's Rewards

The rewards the Spectator experiences are of three kinds, each stressed by one of our three Spectators.

In the first place, there is the reward of *admission*, of being allowed to become part of the group. All three Spectators show a positive reaction to this aspect of legislative life. They "become a part of everybody" simply by becoming members of the legislative body. For Sam especially, being admitted—having doors opened to him, being allowed the "roam" of the Governor's mansion, being invited to attend the political show—are signs that he is valued by others. Thus the new member becomes an insider, with all the joys of belongingness at his disposal. He has passed through the electoral initiation ceremonies, and is now a full-fledged member of the fraternity. Simply being with others, close to them, seems to show that they value him. For otherwise, would they not send him away? His tendency is to blur over the fact that he holds his seat by right, that he cannot be excluded, and to feel his membership as a privilege accorded to him personally by his fellow members, thus proving that they like him and want him there.

In a second way, illustrated especially in Tom's case, the *prestige* of membership gives pleasure to the Spectator. The others who accept him are worthy as well as friendly. Tom grew up amid hard times in a community where people of his political persuasion were "nothing." Now he is in the company of gentlemen and feels that he can be a gentleman too, if he tries. To have the approval of one's peers is pleasant; to be accepted by one's betters is more so. The person who comes to the legislature from a generally lower status position may be particularly impressed by the fact that he is thrown together with governors and secretaries and chairmen.[c]

Prestige is, of course, a relative thing. The step into the legislature is upward, downward, or horizontal, depending on where one begins.[4] Certainly many a prosperous, highly educated legislator does not feel particularly flattered by his status as a representative. But neither does every lower-status person. Status-mindedness, here in the form of a desire to be approved by those one considers his betters, is in part a personal sensitivity, an inclination to perceive and attend to gradations in rank. The Spectator increases the quantity of affection he receives by thinking of himself as being liked by everybody, by all those other legislators. He increases the quality of the affection he receives by thinking of the others as worthy. To have the admiration of the admirable multiplies the joys of belonging.

Finally, the Spectator is rewarded by approval *expressed directly* to him. In his imagination Tom is able to feel that the Governor's address is aimed at him personally, "almost privately." It would have been even more rewarding if the Governor had paid his respects directly, face-to-face, so that there could be no doubt that they were meant for him. May Perkins, more than either of the other Spectators, is concerned with this problem. She must be spoken *to* in an approving way, and it is very important that her name be mentioned. In her continual participation in ceremonial greetings and small talk she gathers in tokens of affection that have a higher value for being paid in person. Sam's emotional apex ("your ego is built up so high")

c. In their questionnaires, Spectators are the members most likely, after the session, to choose "Generally, the public looks up to a state legislator with respect" rather than "Generally, the public is overly critical of state legislators." Spectators 89% (N = 27), other new member respondents 71% (N = 56).

comes when the Governor greets him personally, and with a "warm handshake" grants him approval from on high.

Expressed most abstractly, then, the Spectator's rewards of approval can be seen in three stages: first, he is allowed near the other; second, the other is worthy; and third, the other expresses approval to him.

SELF: THE IMPOVERISHED EGO

When we find members of the legislature continually turning to others for expressions of esteem and affection, showing marked sensitivity to the opinions and evaluations others express to them, we suspect the presence of some underlying need for this kind of behavior. Undeniably, all of us stand in need of affection from our fellow men. But the Spectator appears to demand this kind of reassurance from his social environment to an unusual degree. Why this continual reaching out for approval?

Apathy?

"Whenever we see glamour in the object of attention," writes David Riesman, "we must suspect a basic apathy in the spectator."[5] Our Spectators, as we have seen, place a good deal of emphasis on the glamorous aspects of the legislative show. And indeed, a close look at their interviews does reveal a basic apathy, a lack of deep feeling about themselves and their world. In a number of passages this emotional impoverishment shows through:

> I hadn't really any complete desire.
>
> I had no feelings one way or another.
>
> If I win, I win; if I lose, I lose.
>
> As far as any special plans or dreams, I have none.
>
> . . . And to me it didn't make a damn bit of difference whether I voted for or against it.
>
> I don't care if I get it or not.

Furthermore, the pleasures he does experience seem peculiarly superficial and temporary—

> I get a big charge out of that.
>
> It's such a nice new experience and we're all getting such a kick out of it.
>
> It gives a person that certain lift.

—or vague and clichéd: "wonderful," "interesting," "new," "nice." The Spectator as an individual, a person with his own special ideas, interests, and wants, does not emerge strongly in the interviews. Even in May Perkins' continual chatter there is a strain of the "weariness, anxiety and diffuse malaise" Riesman found among his "other-directed" subjects. Indeed, Tom Minora illustrates the other-directed type precisely, in this passage: "It's like the old story—when you're in Rome, do as the Romans do, you know? If you're a legislator, act as a legislator. And when you're outside, you act to . . . the environment, I guess." He appears to lack internal guidelines of his own, basing his behavior on a sensitive perception of the demands of the environment.

For such a person, the glamor and occasional excitement of legislative activities lend a much-needed spice to life. Lacking passion, he seeks amusement. So long as he can get a "charge," a "kick," a "lift" out of life, he can perhaps forego the deeper satisfactions. And his own temporary excitement helps to reassure him that he is capable of feeling.[6]

But in the light of psychological research, we must be suspicious of this characterization as well. Surface placidity or indifference may well conceal intense inner turmoil.[7] Riesman's formula can be extended as follows: "Whenever we see a basic apathy, we must suspect conflict within the personality."

Furthermore, "apathy" does not go very far to explain the Spectator's need for approval. Why should the person without feelings of his own ask affection of others? We need to take a careful look at the few occasions on which the Spectator talks about himself and describes the kind of person he is.

Self-Doubt

Sam Thompson gives us an indication when he tries to answer the question, "How would you rate your own performance as a legislator so far?" Sam, hesitating, is encouraged with "That's a hard question."

> No, not necessarily. I think I've done fairly well, to the extent that [long pause] well, gosh, that *is* a hard question. I think I've done fairly well to the extent that . . . I've a feeling of self-consciousness. And since I've come here to Hartford, I don't feel self-conscious any more. I feel as if I can mingle right in with them, and, ah—I first had a fear that, well, all that run

for representatives are probably retired people, well-to-do people, people with financial means, so they could take the time off
from their occupations and spend the day—and that all went
through my mind between the time I was elected and the time
I should go. But as the sessions went on, I feel I'm just as qualified
to present myself to the Assembly as [another legislator]. Sound-
ing a little like an egotist. [laughs] . . . And for that reason,
I feel good. I mean I've overcome—yeah, over . . . came some
of this self-consciousness. Or whether it's self-consciousness, or,
ah—doubt.

Sam classes himself with the "ordinary people" on a legislative committee, in contrast to the witnesses who come before it—people who,
with "their vocabulary, their wordage," are "educated—they know
what they're talking about." He feels he failed as a salesman: "Well,
I'm not aggressive enough."

Similarly, Tom Minora sees himself as "the type of person that's—
I, ah—self-conscious, shall we say?" He would have preferred another
committee than the one he is assigned to, "if I could have handled it."
He feels "like a plain dope" in conversation about politics. "If I'm
anything," Tom says, "I'm too much on the conservative side," by
which he means too unassertive, in contrast to people who "force
themselves on you." And May Perkins had doubts about accepting
the nomination: "I was a little bit scared at the idea of, maybe, what
if I couldn't do it satisfactorily?"

When he rates himself, the Spectator points to "self-consciousness,"
lack of aggressiveness, fear of performing unsatisfactorily. These self-
characterizations are consistent with the idea that the Spectator is
lacking in self-confidence. In fact, however, he seldom rates himself
directly. His main evaluations come in the course of watching others
watch him.

What Others Think

Sam makes a particularly revealing comment in this regard when
he is explaining why he finds the legislative experience "wonderful."
"You get back home, you're just an ordinary guy. You get up here,
it's 'Mister' and 'Sir'—*nobody knows who you are,* your bank account,
the mortgage on your house. And so it's like a tonic to get up here."

Later he repeats this thought: "You're treated with respect because nobody knows who you are." The implication is clear: if the others "knew who he was," they would not respect him. Who would then call him "Mister" and "Sir"? The real Sam Thompson, he seems to be saying, is not worthy of respect.

In Sam's search for approval a great deal depends on maintaining a protective external façade, behind which his supposed inadequacies can be safely hidden. When the front begins to break down, he expects disapproval: "I've seen different members of the committee—not that I'm knocking them personally, but this is just a broad statement— they got holes in their shoes. Their heels are run down. Their ties got spots on them."

When high-class witnesses appear, Sam says, "Sometimes I have my doubts. Sometimes I feel as if there might be some scorn in their eyes or something." His need to keep his inner nature hidden is evident: "I've countered some of my nervousness, so that a person looking at me might have some doubt that I'm nervous. I mean, I know myself that I'm nervous, but the person watching might have some doubts."

Sam can take care of his physical front by dressing neatly and guarding against the outward betrayal of his nervousness. It is when he has to speak to others that the danger of revealing his inadequacies is greatest. No wonder, then, that Sam feels threatened when he anticipates having to address the legislature: "Yeah, when you're in the session there and you have the mike in front of you and the button [for voting] there, that thing can scare you, you know? You have to pick it up and you have to speak into it and there is a tenseness."

Even in informal conversation, he feels a necessity for avoiding the revelation of his own personal preferences: "For myself, I like to play games with people. I like to confuse them. I get a little—I'll say one thing to them, and then in the course of conversation I'll twist my feelings around to the complete opposite. And, ah, I'll look at the people and they'll look at me and wonder what's going on. Words— it's only words."

The outlines of Sam's adaptation to the legislature become clearer in these passages. He judges himself harshly; he has doubts about his worth as a person. For this reason, he avidly seeks the approval of others, the reassurance of their affection. But sensing his own unlovableness, he fears that others will reject him if they find out what kind of person he is. Therefore he hides behind a conventional front, remains silent, and, when he must interact with others, avoids revealing his feelings to them. He thus cuts himself off from the deeper, more abiding affection that comes with mutual understanding. He must make do with the meager rewards of being called "Mister," of perfunctory handshakes and greetings. This is not much but is better than nothing at all. And the alternative—discovery and rejection—is considerably worse.

There is a similar theme in Tom Minora's makeup. One reason he would like to return to the House, he says, is that there he can remain "not too much in the limelight." He avoids political discussions in which he thinks he would perform badly. He tells of an innocent social mistake at the beginning of the session in which he wondered why he was "getting these kind of funny looks, you know?" and concludes, "That was stupid." Tom feels "a little bit squeamish" about speaking and was "very nervous" when he had to once. His retiring habits—"unaggressiveness"—very likely serve protective functions.[8]

In turning to others for self-evaluation, Tom finds a general reaction of friendliness in the House. But on several occasions he expresses doubt that others mean what they say when they praise him. When a town party official asked him to run, he said he thought Tom would be a good man. Reporting this, Tom immediately adds: "You know how they spread it on." His friends congratulated him—but, Tom says, "Of course there's no way of knowing whether they really mean it or not." He finds that witnesses before his committee are "very respectful," but implies that this is only because they are forced to act that way:

> TOM: Very respectful.
> INTERVIEWER: They look up to the committee members?
> TOM: They know we're their judges—they've got to. If they don't know that then they shouldn't be there.

Thus Tom seems to feel it is implausible that others really respect and admire him, freely and willingly. When he is praised, he doubts the sincerity of the praise. Like Sam, Tom also seems to take a somewhat condemnatory view of himself, and to seek approval and reassurance in order to help assuage doubts about his worth. But he cannot quite bring himself to believe in the affection he receives. This suspicion hampers the confident acceptance of direct expressions of approval, and Tom settles for the lesser, indirect rewards of membership, vicarious participation, and withdrawal from the center of attention.

May Perkins appears in the interview as a lady who protests too much. She relates no fewer than eighteen incidents to show that others approve her. If she were confident of her worth, would she go to such lengths to demonstrate it to the interviewer? Why the repeated effort to show that she really is appreciated, to prove in specific detail that others have responded favorably to her? It is a safe conclusion that she herself has doubts about her value and is trying to assuage these feelings by gathering compliments.

May, as we have seen, is excessively sensitive to the impressions that she gives to others and others give to her. Yet there is little in her interview to indicate insight into others' characters or individual variations at any level below the superficial outward aspect. She moves in a world of social surfaces. Her praise is reserved for those who put themselves over by the manipulation of their impressions.

Thus May is enthusiastic about a person who "is so *nice*" as a speaker. "He's got a nice face, to begin with," she says, and "he's so pleasant." "He always speaks and he always passes the time of day." "I guess I just like the Irish," May concludes. "There's something awfully nice—personable about them." The important thing is to give an impression of sincerity, not to be too "cocky" or "aloof," not too "stuck-up" to speak to people. "Did you hear Amos Walker speak?" she asks. "Wasn't he wonderful? He is so good, and he is so darn sincere. And everybody knows that he has nothing to gain by anything he talks on. . . . He's very sincere about it." "The only thing I've found in true experience," May continues, is that "everybody's sincere in his thinking." She then goes on to relate an experience when she was let down by someone who did not fit this rule—who tricked her into a situation in which *she* had to appear insincere. She felt considerable anxiety in this situation because her image was almost compromised.

In another context, May evaluates a party leader: "I think he is trying sincerely to remember everybody. And he's very friendly—he just speaks every time he sees anybody. Maybe he doesn't know who we are from Adam, but at least he speaks, and he acts like he's seen you before." Here the importance of maintaining an impression is most fully revealed: the other is appreciated because he *acts* as though he knows her. A sincere front is the important thing. The reality may be too much to ask.

The differences between May and Sam and Tom in this respect are thus not as wide as casual observation might indicate. May is a talker; Sam and Tom are quieter types. But all three are excessively concerned with presenting a social exterior which they feel will bring them the rewards of approval and protect them from disapproval. The clear implication is that, from the Spectator's point of view, this protective exterior is necessary for approval, because the person behind the mask is unlovable.

The Spectator's need for approval from others, then, appears to spring from his doubts about his own worth. When he appraises himself, he reaches a discomfiting conclusion: he feels inadequate and inferior. Political participation offers opportunities to palliate these feelings. To gain a sense of personal worth by gaining from others signs of approval.[9]

But from the Spectator's own viewpoint, this dependence on others has a threatening aspect, too. The approval he receives is fundamentally spurious; others appreciate him only because they do not know him. His primary problem is a strategic one: he must manipulate his social environment in ways that maximize approval of him and minimize disapproval.

What techniques does the Spectator employ for these purposes?

STRATEGIES: FOLLOWERSHIP AND ITS ALTERNATIVES

When a person confronts the gap between what he is and what he wishes he were, he experiences feelings of tension, feelings that may range from minor dissatisfaction to despair. Certain familiar social strategies are used to cope with such feelings. Without going into the genesis of these strategies,[10] we can summarize them briefly as follows. First, the person may react aggressively. He lashes out at others (either actually or within his own mind) and thereby displaces a good deal of the aggression he feels toward himself. This scapegoating behavior is familiar from studies of intergroup relations. Secondly, he may withdraw into himself. Especially if his inferiority feelings are based on a sense of failure to meet the norms of the groups he is in, he may fall back on internal norms of his own that he *can* satisfy. The superficially self-satisfied person who seems oblivious to his inadequacies is an example. A third technique for assuaging such feelings is achievement. The person recognizes his shortcomings and sets out to do something about them, to achieve self-respect by accomplishing valued ends. Finally, the self-doubting person may react by adopting a follower role. In effect, he seeks to satisfy and placate the demands of those who would reject him by giving in to them. He thus buys a certain amount of self-approval, at the cost of a certain amount of subservience.[11]

Over the course of a lifetime such strategies of adjustment tend to become habitual.[12] It is as if the person makes a decision, adopts one main method of adjustment, and then sticks to it. For each of these patterns pays off with some sort of reward: when the aggressive person finds that he feels better after having hurt someone else; when the withdrawn experiences a comfort in his own mind that he could not obtain from without; when the achiever knows the satisfaction of accomplishment; when the submissive person feels that others approve him for his service—these comforting feelings, if repeated often enough, tend to solidify into a fixed style of adjustment. The person has found a "solution" to his main adjustment problem.[13]

The more severe the internal problems an individual experiences, the more rigid this pattern becomes. At the extreme the psychotic person develops a fixed pattern, which ordinary experience simply cannot alter. Even when his behavior results in disastrous disruptions of his life, he still cleaves rigidly to a pattern that has brought him some reward or relief in the past. Reality no longer has any relevance to his happiness.

As we move from the psychotic extreme toward the "normal" person,[14] the interplay of internal problem and external environment alters. The individual is more and more in touch with reality, more and more able to alter his course according to the rewards and punishments he receives. The fixity of his pattern of adjustment depends, on the one hand, on the intensity of his need for a particular kind of reward, and on the other, on the availability of reward from the environment for the pattern he has adopted. If he feels only an occasional mild twinge of self-doubt, for example, he will probably be able to handle this problem with an occasional mild burst of aggression, withdrawal, achievement, or submission. He need not invest all his efforts in one reward-gaining pattern.

Even if his need for reward is great, however, the fixity of his pattern of adjustment will depend also on the availability in the environment of the particular kind of reward he seeks. The pattern will tend to break down under the impact of repeated punishments for attempts to maintain it—again, assuming that the individual is in touch with reality. The shy, withdrawn person, for example, who finds himself in a group where every member is required to perform publicly and receive criticism of the performance, tends either to leave the group or to change his pattern, perhaps by engaging in some tentative experiments in self-assertion. When the need is great and the environment offers reinforcing rewards, the pattern will tend toward rigidity and permanence. When the need is mild and the environment offers pattern-contradicting rewards and punishments, the pattern will tend toward flexibility and change.

We proceed now to examine the Spectator from this viewpoint. Which set of strategies does he tend to pursue? Given his particular needs, what is involved for him in changing this pattern? Given the legislative environment, what reinforcements does this pattern receive from without? And, therefore, how likely is it that the Spectator will continue to pursue this set of strategies?

Submitting

According to Sam Thompson, the proper role of the freshman legislator can be summed up in a simple formula: "The main function, far as I can see, in my position—I'm a freshman. The main functions of a legislator here are to keep your ears open, your mouth shut, and follow your party leaders." His main complaint against the leadership is that they have not taken a stronger hand:

> SAM: I feel left out. I feel that leadership is doing a poor job.
> INTERVIEWER: How's that?
> SAM: Well, it's a known fact that—I believe there is about 100 new members of the legislature who have to be told what to do and what not to do. Otherwise, I—getting back into known fact —leave a [party group] alone and they'll fight. Right or wrong, they'll fight. And I think they have to be led, have to be steered. . . . The leadership has been too busy or they've taken the attitude that, well, the fellows can operate on their own. And I don't think that's right.

Similarly, Sam takes a "serving" stance toward his constituents. One of the things that has helped him as a legislator, he says, is

> the desire to show the townspeople that they didn't make a mistake, that I can get up there and work for them. Of course, in my campaign I told the people there that my—the limits with

which I could work for them would be limited. Because I'm unfamiliar. I wouldn't know the patterns or the channels that certain things had to go through. Might be limited, but I'd certainly try. And for that reason I feel good.

These passages seem to indicate a searching for opportunities to submit to others, a searching for masters to serve.

Tom Minora agrees with Sam that "freshmen aren't supposed to open their mouths." He says that the party leaders should have done more by way of instruction at the first of the session, "so that you'd know which foot to step on first." "The senior legislators," he says, "don't take you by the hand—at least in my estimation—the way they should, and say, 'Now, look, this is the way you should do it.' " Tom resents the fact that his party has not held many caucuses to familiarize the new members with procedures and the leadership's wishes, "the party thinking." Personally, he does not like to bother the leadership with his problems, but he thinks they could have "done a much better job than they did" in instructing the membership. He seems to welcome the leaders' suggestions, particularly when he has no convictions of his own in regard to a bill.

May Perkins' attitude is somewhat different. She says that some feel her party has "passive leadership" in the House. On an important bill, she wondered "just how to go along" when pulled in one direction by a few of her constituents and in another by the party leadership. Finally she decided she "was safe in going along" with the people in her town. She explains that on "such big issues as that you just wonder if you're doing the right thing, but now I find that I did, because everybody in town has spoken since and they're very glad that I voted as I did. At least I feel that I'm not a party to it if it doesn't materialize properly."

May has a large collection of acquaintances to whom she turns for advice, especially among the older, experienced legislators. And although she says that "I still have to think for myself," her conception of the proper role of the legislator is strongly centered in the representative function: "The main thing is to be voting for the good of the people. We're supposed to be doing things for the people that they cannot do for themselves. We're representing the whole group of the people who couldn't come in here to do it. And we're supposed to think of them at all times, not ourselves personally." Others "know that I'm going to have to go along" with the views of the home-town party. May is in something of a dilemma about whom to go along with, but she, like Sam and Tom, is looking for guidance from others.

The Taboo on Personal Aggression

Expressions of aggression in the Spectator interviews are extremely rare. May is friendly to everybody. "It's all hearts and roses for a while," she says. "You know how—throwing bouquets back and forth. And then we have our first big fight against the sides. He said, 'Well, the honeymoon is over.' [laughs] But on both sides, everyone's very congenial and, ah, nice. Nice harmony throughout." Sam realizes that he is "not the type to go in there and bang people over the head and say you've got to have this for your own good." He is careful to qualify his complaints about others: "not that I'm knocking them personally," "not that I expect a heck of a lot." Tom knows he is "a little reluctant to push myself on to someone—which isn't good, either."

Only two occasions appear in the interviews in which Spectators show fairly open hostility to others. The first is May's reaction to being snubbed. She "just got fed up" with being neglected by another member, and told him directly that she was "sick and tired" of his impoliteness. It is significant that this outburst resulted from a social snub. May can take a good deal from others, but being addressed is too important to her to be allowed to pass. In this case, repeated introductions had failed to gain friendly greetings from the other member. As a last resort, May strikes out at him. "So he doesn't forget me now," she says. The aggression has thus served to force the other to act as if he approved her, whether he does or not. This behavior, then, is entirely consistent with May's approval-seeking behavior.

The second appearance of marked hostility in the interviews comes from Tom. He starts to report the "general opinion" that the lawyers in the House are resented. " 'They have another profession,' members say; 'they shouldn't even be in there.' " Tom then takes a personal stand: "And that is my point, too. I'm quoting myself and I'm thinking that those people that resent them concur with my feelings. I don't believe the lawyers should be allowed in the House." Tom feels the lawyers "tend to make laws to suit themselves," selfishly using the legislature for their own benefit. He seems unusually irritated on this point.

But he immediately pulls back from this aggressive stance. He amends his original statement: "Probably, I shouldn't say that there shouldn't be *any* of them there," he says. He explains that he does not express this feeling in public: "That's my own personal feeling—I haven't discussed this with anybody." And he concludes by reminding the interviewer that his irritation is shared by others: "I have heard several others make the remark about too damn many lawyers being up there." Thus Tom's attack is quickly blunted and hidden among his fellow legislators.

Such aggression as the Spectator feels is far more likely to be expressed indirectly, in the form of complaints about being abused by others. Sam complains that people back home do not appreciate him. Tom tells of a relative who was treated unfairly by opposition-party politicians. May feels she was taken advantage of by a constituent. But none of them goes on to say, "Therefore I am mad at that person" or to show any intention of taking aggressive action toward those who have abused them. The abused feeling remains.[15] The tension is not relieved by attack.

Avoiding Loneliness

Nor do the Spectators appear to choose withdrawal as a pattern of adjustment. On the contrary, they place considerable emphasis on feeling related to others. It is important to Sam, for example, that he finds others in the legislature who are as lowly as he feels he is. At first, he says, "I supposed I might be faced with all these individuals who were financially responsible," but "since I've come up here I've found out I'm not alone." And, he explains, "That helped to build up my ego and helped me to like coming up here, to know that you're not alone in a certain group." May dislikes loneliness: "I couldn't just sit home and do nothing. It isn't my nature. I'm always either doing something for my relatives, baby-sitting, or for my neighbors, or doing something. I—I don't feel it's taxing me too much." Tom is more of a homebody than the other Spectators, but he, too, gains satisfaction from feeling "like any other businessman" and from knowing that he "fits into the middle group" on an issue.

Spectators are not much given to musing about themselves—adding up the past and planning for the future. Rather, they seem to avoid introspection, to restrict their attention to events in the passing environment. Part of the reason the legislature is a grand place is, as Sam says, that "everything is new. You come up here, you don't know what to expect. You don't know what to find on your desk." May sums up her legislative experience by calling it "such a nice, new venture." Her attention seems to be focused on the surfaces that surround her, perhaps *because* this is an alternative to introspection. In the midst of all the "nice social affairs" she has little time for thinking about herself. The "diversion" she finds in such affairs is evident in her description of a party for members of the House:

> MAY: On both sides of the ballroom—you know how long the ballroom is?
> INTERVIEWER: Yes.
> MAY: They had tables set up the full length of both sides, loaded with food. And on one side was a great big basket of flowers—real flowers. A great big floral display. On the other side was an ice-basket, one of those molded ice-baskets? And that had real flowers in it, too. And they had a spotlight on it. Different colors? And it was just a beautiful sight. And then the food was arranged—the turkey and the ham were cut real pretty and laid on trays with pansies and parsley and all kinds of decorations on it. There were molded salads, potato salad and just everything imaginable to eat. And the place was just elegant—and French pastry for dessert—usually you don't get much for dessert at an affair like that.

None of the three Spectators thought long or deeply about accepting the nomination. None has given his political future a thorough personal assessment. Immersed in a world of other people, the Spectator seems to focus little of his concentrated attention on himself. In fact, he apparently needs interesting externalities as a distraction from introspection.

In a sense, the Spectator does withdraw from his environment: he keeps his social relationships superficial, avoids investing his emotions in others, builds a protective shield around his supposedly unlovable qualities. But he does not withdraw *into himself*. His retreat from others stops short of isolated, conscious self-examination. He pauses permanently at the self-other border, with his attention always turned outward.

The Dangers of Success

The fourth pattern of adjustive strategies, personal achievement, is also largely missing in the Spectator's behavior. There are scattered references to legislative success in the Spectator interviews. Sam feels that he "controlled" one executive session of his committee —although his control seems to have consisted of making the first motion to approve a series of bills he knew the committee majority favored. Still, this experience gave him "a shot in the arm." Tom is pleased that he and another member got one bill through—although he feels it was an "insignificant" bill. May says she is "satisfied with what I have done" and that she has "voted very fairly on everything." She, too, has joined in sponsoring a bill, but she says "I don't think it will do any good" because the bill is bound to be defeated. Thus the Spectators see their achievements as minor. They tend to rationalize their lack of participation by claiming that it results from their high standards: "I'm the type of person that I'd never want to speak unless I'm fairly positive about what I'm talking about. And being unfamiliar, I'll keep quiet and listen." Or from the impossibly difficult nature of legislative work: "By being a freshman there and being unfamiliar with all these bills—God, there's over three thousand bills —and I don't think that any individual should be expected to remember all those bills." Nevertheless, the satisfactions of personal achievement are not entirely missing.

When we look at other incidents in which the Spectator might be expected to take pleasure in personal achievement, however, we see what appears to be a strong tendency in the other direction—toward feelings of discomfort and anxiety at personal success. This is especially marked in his report of the election night. For the approval-seeking person, we might suppose that an election victory would bring a glow of satisfaction. He might feel that hundreds or thousands of people had thought enough of him to go to the polls and cast a ballot in his favor. Here is approval on a massive scale.

The Spectator does not react that way. Sam says that while being a candidate "didn't bother me that much," the "big shock" came when he was told, "You're elected." He had worried about arranging the time off from his job: "All the while there was uncertainty—How would I work? My job? Coming up here?" "Oh, well," he thought, "you probably won't get elected anyhow" and "you keep throwing it out of your mind, you know? Back and forth." His feeling when the results were in was one of "responsibility":

> I've got beaten in other elections so it doesn't bother me. And the actual feeling of winning the election—I don't think that would have been such a surprise. Just the feeling of responsibility. Of course, I may have been subconsciously evading the issue beforehand, but the results were in—you can't evade it any longer. That's it.

Sam gives no indication here of personal pleasure at his success. Rather, he feels anxious about the responsibility he has attained almost inadvertently. He has won a victory, but his mind is occupied with thoughts of burdens he can no longer escape. Why does he pass up this chance to pat himself on the back? One gets the impression that he would have felt more comfortable as a loser.

Furthermore, Sam appears to want to excuse himself for any success he might attain. He explains that his nomination was almost accidental: "I'm inclined to believe that it was on the spur of the moment." The town chairman "just happened to see me" at the nominating meeting. If Sam had not attended, someone else would probably have been chosen. Similarly, his election was due not to his efforts or his popularity but to the pulling strength of others on the ballot. "Sam Thompson didn't win the election" in his town; the Governor won the election, and "Sam Thompson was on his ticket."

Sam may be giving a fairly objective report of circumstances in these passages. That he chooses, however, to dwell on the self-deprecating aspects of the situation and neglects to express any self-satisfaction at his election is inconsistent with the pattern of pleasure in personal achievement.

Tom Minora's reaction to his election victory was extreme tension accompanied by sudden illness. "I was very happy I won," he says, "but unfortunately . . . I was deadly sick that night," so sick that he felt he would "rather be dead than alive." He attributes this trouble to "the pressure that apparently had built up inside of me, nervous tension and so on." Asked how he accounts for this tension, Tom says, "Well, you couldn't prove it by me that I was nervous. I didn't know that I was nervous myself. It was just subconsciously, you know?" We cannot, of course, be sure that the election victory brought on this illness, but Tom tells us directly of the extreme pressure, the nervous tension, he felt on that occasion. He does not indicate that the tension was assuaged by news of victory. Whatever the psychosomatic connection, Tom's reaction does not fit the picture of the happy winner.

May Perkins reports that she felt no gratification over her election. "In fact," she says, "I went home that night after election and I wasn't elated one little bit. I felt kind of bad because I didn't win by a terrific margin. . . . I was a little disappointed." May was chagrined that some others thought she had not worked hard enough. "So I just went home after we tallied the votes and that was it, that was the end of my celebration." No pride in success, no glow of approval, no self-congratulation. May, too, conveys a mood of dejection when she talks about her election victory.

Spectators show a consistent tendency to assert themselves or to seek success only in conjunction with others. Sam says that, in his campaigning, "I honestly don't think I've been talking for myself so much as talking for victory. And I consider myself not what you call a real candidate, but talking for the party's victory in the town." Party success, success which can be shared, is legitimate; personal success is questionable as a goal. Tom Minora feels that his success in the legislature "is not earned by myself . . . only in my efforts. The success of us being up here is dependent on so many other people up here who are willing to cooperate." Tom thinks that ambition for any political position above that of representative "would probably be selfish interest," "seeking for prestige." He doesn't have "the desire to be a big politician." May Perkins feels "it would be nice sometime" to hold a higher political office, but she appears to have no well-developed plans on this score. Her actions regarding legislation consist mainly of trying to figure out which side she is "safe in going along with."

Descriptions of political issues in the Spectator interviews tend to be in "we" rather than "I" terms. Furthermore, the Spectators expect initiative to come from others. All three, for example, want to take a receptive stance toward their constituents. Sam dislikes house-to-house campaigning because he sees it as "pleading, begging the people for their vote." He should not have to do that—the others should come to him: "If these people don't have the civic pride or the desire to get out to a town meeting or a caucus or any of these speaking occasions we have, then their interest is pretty small." "I'm sure that there's a lot of legislation that would benefit my town in particular," Tom says, "but yet we are never requested to do this, to put a bill in for it, you know? And I don't feel that we should go in on our own and introduce a bill. As representatives of the people it's O.K. for us to do it, but they should come to us and ask us to do it." May has let her constituents know that she welcomes their phone calls, so that she can "get their general ideas." And the Spectators take a similar attitude toward the party leaders: they should undertake to advise the newcomers.

The Spectator's inability to take pleasure in personal success, his tendency to submerge his achievements in those of the group, and his turning to others for initiatives indicate that the achievement pattern does not play an important role in his legislative adjustment.

The Dynamics of Followership

We are now in a position to attempt an explanation of the Spectator's choice of the follower pattern and his rejection of the other three patterns. We begin with the fundamental psychological problem he experiences: the nagging doubts about his worth as a person. In order to assuage these doubts he seeks signs of approval from others. But this turning to others involves the risk of rejection as well. If the others were to discover what he suspects about himself—that he is unworthy—they would disapprove of him. Therefore he develops a pattern of adjustment that maximizes his chances of gaining approval and minimizes the risk of exposure and rejection. Part of his pattern consists of a set of perceptual habits by which he can interpret events in his environment as indicating approval with minimal risk of exposure: he makes of his *membership* in a prestigeful body a sign of approval. He overinterprets perfunctory greetings as signs of approval. He participates vicariously in the course of watching others perform. He is able to reap these rewards without taking any legislative action whatever except the effort necessary to attend the session.

Beyond this passive reception of impressions, the Spectator attempts to convey impressions to others that will bring approving signs from them. He maintains a front of pleasant, moderate, polite conventionality, to which others are likely to respond with similarly superficial pleasantries. At the same time, the formalism of this front prevents others from penetrating below the surface, leaving his secret self-doubts undisclosed. Conversation is kept on the plane of conventional pleasantries.

On occasions when the Spectator is expected to take some positive position—as, for example, when he must vote on a bill—he seeks to gain approval by submitting to the appropriate authority. His own preferences are generally weak, diffuse, and not very interesting to him. Submitting to the preferences of others (e.g. the party leaders, experienced legislators, constituents, general opinions of the legislature, etc.) fulfills the requirement that he take a position, frees him from lone responsibility (being "in the limelight") for that position, and gives him a sense of belonging with others.[16]

The Spectator's adaptive strategy, then, consists primarily of three techniques: vicarious participation, superficial socializing, and submission to others.[d]

THE PERSISTING PATTERN

The Personal Costs of Change

The costs to the Spectator of switching his behavior to one of the other patterns may be considerable. It is perhaps easiest to see why he does not utilize the aggressive pattern. Aggression directly expressed to someone else would put an end to expressions of approval from that person. The Spectator is already predisposed to anticipate being abused by others—he never quite trusts them; he suspects that aggressive feelings toward him lurk behind *their* fronts. He has staked his self-approval on the approval of others. Even one person who feels hostile toward him confirms his self-doubt. He cannot afford the risk involved in aggressive behavior.

Furthermore, aggressive feelings, even though not expressed, are likely to make him feel uncomfortable: they contradict the "nice" impression he wishes to convey; they make him feel insincere. His pattern of adjustment requires the constant repression of aggressive feelings. They come to the surface, if at all, in the form of complaints at being abused, taken advantage of, or neglected in some way. In this form, such feelings do not challenge his front: he sees himself still as a nice person who suffers at the hands of others.

d. Some Spectator questionnaire replies reflect these themes. They are most likely to answer that "social affairs connected with the legislature were very enjoyable" (Spectators 37%, others 15%). They "made a special effort to memorize the names and faces of other members" at the start of the session (Spectators 80%, others 65%). With a stranger, the Spectator would "reserve my trust until I know him better" rather than "trust him until he lets me down" (Spectators 63%, others 36%). N's = 30, 66. Before the session Spectators answered "the new legislator will very frequently have to rely on the advice of others with more experience or ability" rather than "the new legislator ought to figure most things out for himself, to the best of his ability" (Spectators 74%, others 57%). N's = 27, 56.

The withdrawn pattern is threatening to the Spectator because it turns him back into himself—the very court of judgment from which he habitually seeks escape. Introspection is painful because it reminds him of his inadequacies. Furthermore, being left alone cuts the Spectator off from his most important source of reward—approving signs from other people—and at the same time demonstrates to him that he is not worth the attention of others. He depends on others for guidance; left alone, he feels at sea. He depends on others for stimulation; left alone, he feels bored and dull. Left alone, he might gain a certain respite from anxiety about how others see him, but the risks of despondency are too great.

To a minor degree, the Spectator does utilize the achievement pattern. But there are strong inhibitions operating within him to hamper his productive efforts. Striving for personal success involves for him a direct attack on his feelings of inadequacy. In order to attempt achievement, he must at least temporarily convince himself that he is capable of action, that he is really not so inadequate as he had thought. Since he has based his reward-seeking activities on opposite assumptions this change requires a violent wrenching away from a whole set of adjustive habits. Personal achievement attracts attention to him as an individual. Such individual prominence invites inquiry from others as to who he is, why he wants to gain these goals, or how he has managed to attain them. His strategy of concealment is thus in danger of compromise. He wishes to avoid seeming presumptuous and insincere; others might mistake his honest satisfaction in a task well done for personal conceit.

Two other factors block achievement for the Spectator. In the first place, achievement involves aggression against the external environment. Political achievements—winning an election, getting a favorable committee report on a bill, building a majority for or against a measure—require efforts at persuasion which always include a certain amount of "pushing." Here all the Spectator's taboos against interpersonal aggression come into play, making him hesitate to force himself onto others.

Similar obstructions seem to operate when the Spectator considers asserting himself in ways that involve little interpersonal aggression, such as in drafting legislation, studying bills, and the like. As Horney has pointed out, the very language we use to discuss the mastery of intellectual tasks is saturated with aggressive imagery: we speak of "taking hold" of ideas, "tackling them, grappling with them, wrestling with them, checking them, shaping them, organizing them." [17] The Spectator's inhibition against aggression toward others seems to be reflected in similar inhibitions against these more private forms of self-assertion.

In the second place, personal achievement involves personal initiative, offering proposals to others. But the Spectator's stance toward his social environment is receptive. Others should come to him; he should not have to "beg and plead" for approval. It is as if the Spectator were saying, "Approve me for myself alone, not for what I have done." His preference is for *unearned* affection and support from his environment; praise which has a reason behind it, even if that reason is respect for some achievement, is sullied. One finds many instances in the interviews of expectations of approval as a reward for *being* a kindly, likable, helpful person. Expectations of approval for *doing* worthwhile things are considerably rarer.

This analysis of the inner dynamics by which Spectators adopt and reject patterns of adjustment is necessarily hypothetical. But such tangential evidence as we have supports a view of the Spectator as a person with strong doubts about himself and strong attachments to certain ways of ameliorating those doubts. The intensity of his inner problem tends to rigidify his pattern of adjustment. Viewed from the inside, then, the Spectator pattern does not seem likely to change with time.

Environmental Support

In estimating the rigidity of the Spectator pattern it is necessary to view it also from the outside. To what extent is the political environment supportive or destructive of this pattern? We will consider the three main elements of the pattern, in order: vicarious participation, superficial socializing, and submission.

At no stage of the processes of nomination, campaigning, election, and membership in the legislature is there a formal requirement of verbal participation. One can be nominated by another, remain silent during the campaign period, and sit quietly through committee hearings and floor debates. No member is required to vote on any issue, in committee or on the floor. It is perfectly possible for a legislator to serve an extended series of terms without opening his mouth. Thus at the outer limits, legislative life has a place for the Spectator. The formal environment includes this alternative.

But what of the informal, normative expectations present in the environment? On the one hand, there may be a set of expectations that press the Spectator toward participation. The town committee may require some evidence that he is a bona fide candidate as demonstrated by his active, verbal pursuit of the nomination. His constituents may expect him to speak on their behalf in the legislature. And his fellow committee members and legislators may look to him for an occasional contribution.

On the other hand, other expectations frequently prevail. In some town committees the norm is for the office to seek the man. Candidates are expected to accept only after a decent courtship. In many a small town, audiences for campaign speeches by candidates for the state legislature are simply not available; and where nomination is tantamount to election, community traditions may work against active campaigning.[e] Once in the legislature, the member often receives little attention from his constituents. In fact, he may conceive of his chief business as watching out for bills that may harm his home community, rather than pushing for beneficial measures.

As we have seen, Spectators subscribe to the general opinion within the legislature that freshman members should avoid speaking, should sit back and listen until they have at least one term of experience behind them. As the session wears on through committee hearings and floor debates, many members find more and more of their time taken up with legislative work. They want to get home or back to work at their regular occupations. Every comment, question, and speech lengthens the working day. There are strong taboos against "wasting the committee's time," or "becoming an orator" in floor debate.[18] The Spectator thus can find considerable support in the legislative environment for his stance of interested, though silent, observer.

Furthermore, legislative norms frequently penalize the speaker who is badly prepared. In two passages from the Spectator interviews, members tell how they learned to be cautious about taking an active role. May was persuaded to introduce a bill that "I didn't know very much about." Opposition to the bill in committee led to an unfavorable report. May concludes, "So that was the end of that. And I

e. Cf. Tom Minora's remark: "Down our way there's no campaigning. They just put it on the ballot, or you're nominated and it's publicized through the papers, so on and so forth. You're either elected or you're not elected. You state in the paper what you're going to try to do when you come up here, and that's about it."

thought, 'From hereafter, I will know better when I present a bill—
I'll study it out first, or put By Request on it.' " Sam has learned the
same lesson vicariously.

> Now, ah, I heard several examples of that—where one person
> gets up and makes a favorable statement on a bill and another
> person gets up and he makes a fairly good speech against the
> bill—a spontaneous speech. He just thought of it from a certain
> angle, and it was a good answer. Then the third person got up
> and spoke in rebuttal to the second party, even though both were
> on the same side. The third viewpoint made me stop and think:
> now, that second guy didn't know what he was talking about.
> It was just a good idea at the moment. But it certainly didn't
> carry its weight. And if I'd have been in that position, I'd have
> been embarrassed. Because I don't like to speak for the sake of
> hearing my voice. . . . And had he sat back a little longer, that
> would have been explained. So I'm in the same position, being a
> freshman there, I'm—afraid to stick my neck out because I know
> that what might be a good idea at one moment might be knocked
> down the very next moment.

As time goes on, the Spectator may find more and more environmental
pressure to "sit back a little longer."

Political life offers considerable support for the second Spectator-
adjustive technique: his superficial socializing. There is a strain of
surface camaraderie running through almost all social relationships in
politics. People find themselves together in occasional meetings held
for temporary purposes. Deep friendships may develop out of such
encounters, but often the acquaintanceship remains fixed at the level
of small talk. The constant hand-shaking, first-name-calling, and
exchange of gossip in politics are perhaps more substitutes for friendship than evidences of it.[19] Canvassing for votes, "making the rounds,"
the candidate moves from house to house, visiting lightly with people
he will not meet again until the next election. Such experiences encourage one to develop a sort of genial but noncommittal, pleasant but
somewhat formal, demeanor.

The legislature is also a mannered place, where, as Sam says, "they
can insult you and do it politely." By tradition, legislators refer to
one another in debate in the third person, and committee members
are supposed to be considerate of witnesses and of one another. The

whole affair has a ceremonial aspect, a deferential restraint and formality that fit the Spectator pattern closely. From the viewpoint of his adjustment, the contrast between the back-slapping atmosphere of campaigning and the formality of the legislature is less significant than their similarity: in different ways, both environments offer opportunities for the maintenance of superficial relations with others.

The legislator who has no bills of his own, no political demands to press on the legislature, owes little to his fellow members. His place depends upon the voters back home, not on his legislative colleagues. Thus the politically instrumental value of deep friendships is slight for the member who is not oriented toward personal achievement. Since Spectators present few political demands, this aspect of the environment largely passes them by. They have less reason to cultivate other members than has the ambitious or achievement-oriented member.

Opportunities for superficial socializing are manifold in and around the legislature. The cafeteria, the lobby, the women's lounge, some administrative offices, and numerous neighboring restaurants and bars are available for informal get-togethers. The spectacular Inauguration Ball, committee trips and dinners, and interest-group parties help to fill the social calendar. Members find the House chamber itself a convenient place for socializing before and after the daily session.

At the more formal "outside" social affairs there seems to be a rather mildly enforced stricture against talking shop. Tom refers to this when he says that at committee luncheons and dinners, "I don't think they discuss too much politics there. Just a friendly gathering. You have a couple of drinks and, ah—the topic of the day. And one thing leads to another, you know—it's not strictly politics and that. . . . Everybody has a good time. Let themselves loose." This norm helps the Spectator avoid serious conversation. His superficial socializing pattern is reinforced.

The Spectator finds no shortage of opportunities for submission in his legislative life. Others with clearly defined political aims press him for favorable votes. In the small-town political party such pressures are intensified by the face-to-face character of deliberations. Decisions may be made unanimously by tradition, so that deviance is unexpected and is penalized when it occurs. Loyalty to the party or faction may be highly valued, and may become a criterion for membership. In the legislature, similar pressures tend to develop in the committee phase. The group shares responsibility for a committee report: maverick behavior violates group unity toward the legislature as a whole. The party in the legislature constitutes another group with demands for conformity, as does the total membership on unanimous or near-unanimous decisions. The Spectator is thus surrounded by environmental pressures, which urge him to cooperate, to go along with group demands.

Furthermore, expectations that a member will conform to group demands are widely held. The member wears a party label. He is addressed in formal debate as "the gentleman from . . ." His name, occupation, age, and place of birth are listed in the legislative manual. These labels identify him to other members as belonging to various groups with which he is expected to agree. The Democrat who votes with the Republicans, the rural representative who votes for urban renewal, the retired person who votes against old age pensions—all are looked at askance.

The Dilemmas of Submission

The Spectator's submissive tendencies may get him into painful situations if he is exposed to conflicting demands for submission. For example, submitting to the party leadership might involve risks of irritating his constituents. In such situations we would expect to find the Spectator trying to avoid commitment or, when avoidance is difficult or impossible, expressing himself cautiously and moderately.[20] Both these reactions, as we have seen, typify the Spectator's behavior.

But if his submissive pattern is to be maintained it must not bring down upon him too much tension and grief. If the environment subjected him to continual, severe stress over which group or leader to submit to, the Spectator's general appreciation for and optimism about the legislature would fade. In fact, a number of factors work to reduce the severity of this form of punishment.

In the first place, constituency pressures for legislative action may be nonexistent or mild and diffuse. Legislators frequently comment on their constituents' lack of interest in state affairs. The representative puts an ad in the paper inviting them to let him know their wishes. But no one calls. The town party committeemen, especially in the small town, are primarily interested in local affairs and in the election process. They may lose interest once the party slate is elected. Thus important issues on which the legislator receives demands from constituents and the legislative party may be rare.

This type of conflict is further reduced by the political norm that no legislator should be required to vote against strong demands from his constituents, especially if in response to such demands he has committed himself publicly to a position on the issue. There is a mutual recognition of the requirements of election survival, which tends to legitimate deviation from the party in such circumstances.

But the chances are high that the demands of the member's legislative party and those of his home town supporters will *not* conflict, but will overlap and reinforce one another. Simply because demands reach the legislator from different sources, we cannot assume that they are in conflict. The rural community in Connecticut is likely to send a Republican to the legislature. Demands from his legislative party and those from his rural constituency are far more likely to be mutually supporting than contradictory. The process of nominations and elections tends to select members with complementary group memberships. At the extremes, for example, the elderly, wealthy, Yankee, Protestant, rural Republican and the youthful, poor, Irish, Catholic, urban Democrat may each receive a multitude of demands from his groups. But for the individual, on most issues, all these demands are likely to push him in the same direction.

Even when demands from the member's groups conflict, they are not likely to balance precisely. Yet it is the balance that concerns him. Legislative issues are two-sided: whether to vote yes or no on particular issues. It is highly probable that the demands pressing the member toward one of these alternatives will be predominant. The legislator does not have to decide whether his constituents are wholly right or his party is wholly right. He does not have to resolve all their philosophical differences. He does not have to calculate how their preferences on all legislative issues, taken collectively, can be arranged in a transitive schedule maximizing rewards for both sides. He is faced with a particular bill to vote for or against. Whatever conflicts exist among his groups at the level of justification for a particular vote, he will feel little concern as long as all or most of them fall on one side of the yes–no line. The multiplicity of demands reaching the Spectator from different groups may simply multiply his opportunities for submission. He can "go along" with several of them at the same time.

The sequential nature of the legislative experience also works to reduce conflicts among the demands for submission reaching the Spectator. He moves from one scene to another, in this order: meetings

with the town committee, encounters with the voters, the inauguration and initial legislative session, committee hearings, committee deliberations on bills, and floor debate. At any one time he receives face-
to-face pressures for conformity primarily from only one of these
groups. Particularly because he is a person who attends sensitively to
his immediate environment, the Spectator weighs such face-to-face
demands heavily. Thus he may well find that the demands from his
immediate colleagues acquire a predominance that overwhelms considerations of past commitments and future confrontations. He can
always change his mind, on the ground that he has gained new
evidence. That face-to-face group pressures tend to reach him one at a
time makes it easier to decide which demands to conform to.

Finally, the hierarchical organization in the legislature helps to ease
the pressure of such conflicts. The structure of authority is not entirely
clear—does the county whip outrank the committee chairman?—but
the Spectator can distinguish among those who present demands at
least partly on the basis of the formal positions they hold. Direct pressure from the state party chairman is likely to carry more weight than
pressure from a fellow freshman. The majority and minority leaders,
whips, chairmen, the Speaker, and the Governor and his assistants all
bear official authority superior to that of the ordinary member. Similarly at the local level, official positions within and outside the party
can be used as reference points in resolving conflicting demands.

These elements of the legislative environment can be thrown into
relief if we consider hypothetically the maximum conflict situation.
The Spectator's problem of choosing among demands for submission
is most severe when he perceives (a) equally intense demands, (b)
from persons of equal status, (c) who share group memberships with
him, (d) who express these demands in the presence of him and of
one another, and (e) the demands are equally divided on an important, specific yes or no question. Actual departures from this situation
indicate the extent to which the environment offers escapes from the
discomfort involved in submitting to others. As we have seen, many
such escapes are available. Demands from his face-to-face and reference groups are unlikely to meet in such direct and contradictory
fashion.[21] Usually departures from this model situation will reinforce
one another, pushing the legislator in the same direction. Only occasionally will the Spectator experience severe punishment from his
legislative environment for his submissive behavior.

The Probabilities of Pattern Change

We cannot estimate with any great accuracy the probabilities of change in the Spectator pattern. Events may arise that press him toward new and different styles of behavior. But there are powerful forces working in the other direction, serving to maintain his pattern. Looked at from within, his techniques of adjustment have their roots in a personal history built up over a lifetime. To expect him to make drastic alterations in these techniques at this late stage in life, simply because he finds himself in a somewhat new situation, is unrealistic. There is a continuity about personality that is not easily altered when, in adulthood, one must adapt to new roles. The Spectator has been making similar adaptations for many years—in the family, on the job, in his friendship groups. Such learned processes of adaptation tend to become habitual, altered only at the expense of considerable stress and strain within the personality. Environmental pressures on the Spectator to behave "like a legislator" thus must compete with entrenched pressures to continue behaving like Sam or May or Tom.

Looking at the Spectator pattern from outside, we have seen that the legislature provides significant environmental support for the pattern. Punishments for taking an innocuous, passive role are few and are blunted by the Spectator's perceptual screening: he is seldom faced with pattern-threatening forces that he cannot shunt aside by ignoring or reinterpreting them.

THE SPECTATOR AND THE WORK OF THE LEGISLATURE

What are the effects of the Spectator's pattern of adjustment on the substantive work of the legislature, the process of considering bills and deciding on them? Our prediction must be that Spectators will make few direct contributions to these tasks. They attach their interest, feelings, and energies not to the specifics of issues but to matters peripheral to the main business before the legislature: the social round, the entertaining speeches, the fellowship of the legislature. They are unlikely to develop specialized competence in particular subject-matter areas, in part because they do not derive personal rewards from the kinds of achievement specialization brings. They are thwarted from developing and communicating reasoned opinions about legislative issues by a host of inhibitions.

Nor are they likely to be accurate evaluators of the opinions of others: they listen and watch, but what they attend to are signs of the speaker's manner and status rather than the substance of what is said. Just as in their minds they fail to link their own needs and desires with legislative issues, so they are little able to gauge these connections in other people. Spectators are unlikely to perform effectively as negotiators, who must develop special sensitivities for reading in what others say what they will do, how far they will go, how deeply and intensely they feel about the subject. Furthermore, their inhibitions against aggressiveness and their continual hesitation make it unlikely that they will press others to make prompt decisions. The main business of the legislature, then, is not usually the main business of the Spectators. They occupy positions on the outer edges of the substantive legislative process.[22]

Thus they are unlikely to cause much trouble for those who *are* primarily concerned with action on bills. Their quiet habits and reluctance to "interfere" keep them from making many demands on the leaders, and their submissiveness makes them easy to persuade. Despite their tendency to be swayed emotionally by the rhetoric and audience reactions of the legislature, Spectators are unlikely to vote these emotions. Rather they will choose the safe path, voting with their parties with great regularity.

This throws burdens of responsibility on party leaders that would be more widely shared if Spectators were replaced with more task-oriented types. The leaders and active legislators find themselves saddled with an immense volume of work, relieved only in part by division of labor among a few members of each committee. To cope with these demands, legislatures have developed advisory councils on bill drafting, research, and the like rather than mobilizing the full resources of the membership. These efforts have been partially successful, but largely in the area of technicalities. Insofar as the legislators themselves cannot perform the essential decision-making functions— perceiving and balancing demands, mediating conflicts through compromise, deciding among alternative courses of action—these responsibilities tend to leak away to administrators, constitutional conventions, lobbyists, and other outside forces. Or the legislature may adjourn in a flurry of last-minute bill-passing, leaving behind a legacy of unresolved problems and ill-conceived measures. The Spectator, by filling a seat that might have been occupied by a more capable and energetic member, thus contributes indirectly to legislative irrationality. He does not interfere much; but neither does he help share the main legislative tasks.

Looked at strictly from the point of view of the major tasks of the legislature, the Spectator makes little direct contribution. However, his pattern of adjustment to legislative life has other effects, which support and further the substantive work. In fact, it may be that the policy accomplishments of the legislature depend to a significant degree on the Spectator's presence there.

Role in Reducing Legislative Tensions

The legislator is subjected to considerable strain in attempting to perform his official tasks. The sheer volume and complexity of decisions to be made force him to act continually on the basis of incomplete information. He must live with the feeling that he may be making important mistakes, which could be avoided if he had more time and higher competence. If he is to perform effectively he must find ways to overcome or control this anxiety, to continue to apply his powers of observation and judgment as best he can. If his nerve fails, the legislative process suffers.

But the legislator has more to contend with than the intellectual difficulties of mastering complex subject-matter. His tensions are aggravated by the multitude of external pressures to which he is exposed. His tenure is uncertain, dependent on his ability to satisfy constituents who are unfamiliar with the difficulties of his task and generally disdainful and suspicious of "politicians." His powers are limited; he can almost never be completely satisfied with the results of his work. His efforts at achieving substantive goals risk conflict with others, thus adding to the strains of rational calculation the strains of interpersonal antagonism.

As we have seen, the legislator may react to these tensions by adopting defensive strategies which, in effect, place him outside the mainstream of the legislative process. Only insofar as at least some members are able to cope with these problems of strain and at the same time channel their attention, abilities, and energies into the main policy-making tasks will the legislature operate effectively. Thus the problems of reducing tension and the problems of policy-making are closely related. The pressure for deciding on bills introduces a disturbing element into the legislative community.[23] Successful decision-making depends in no small part on the success of the legislature in resolving these tensions so that active members are freed to concern themselves with major substantive problems.

It is in this tension-reducing task that the Spectators make their main contribution to the work of the legislature. Their orientation as applauding members of the legislative audience helps to maintain an atmosphere of affection, esteem, and respect which is encouraging to those who carry on the main tasks. Their optimism, mild humor, and politeness help to smooth over the interpersonal hostilities introduced by conflicting opinions on bills. And their feelings about the prestige of legislative office, spread among their constituents, work to counteract the more extreme negative attitudes toward politics and politicians.[24]

A legislature composed entirely of Spectators would be a disaster—the work would grind to a halt. But it is perhaps equally true that a legislature without any Spectators would degenerate into an ill-tempered, bickering collection of prima donnas.

The Spectator's Political Future

It is difficult to predict how long the Spectator will last as a legislator. One suspects that despite his present willingness to return, the place would eventually begin to pall on him. The probability is low that he would be diverted to an appointive position, because he neither demands rewards of this kind nor possesses unique talents. Probably the more important determinants of his legislative longevity will be the recruiting practices of the local town committee. If they want to —and can—attract a more capable candidate, the Spectator will be quickly replaced. But if they prefer his pliancy and easy availability he may be in the capital, watching, for many years to come.

3. The Advertiser

> How often have I had it thrown back at me, generally
> by flatterers, that I said to the timid boatman in the
> storm "Have no fear; you bear Caesar." What non-
> sense! I have had no more exemption from the ills of
> life than any other man.
>
> JULIUS CAESAR (via Thornton Wilder,
> *The Ides of March*)

According to the canons of the American Bar Association, it is unpro-
fessional for the lawyer "to solicit professional employment by circu-
lars, advertisements through touters, or by personal communications
or interviews not warranted by personal relations. Indirect advertisements for professional employment, such as furnishing or inspiring
newspaper comments, or procuring his photograph to be published
in connection with causes in which the lawyer has been or is engaged
or concerning the manner of their conduct, the magnitude of the
interest involved, the importance of the lawyer's position, and all like
self-laudation, offend the traditions and lower the tone of our profession and are reprehensible; but the customary use of simple professional
cards is not improper." [1]

Consider the young lawyer beginning a private practice. How is he
to make a start? Living in an increasingly urbanized and fragmented
society, he can no longer rely on the informal processes by which
reputations are spread in the small, homogeneous community. Few of
his potential clients will have followed his career from childhood; few
know of his scholarly achievements. His own home and family life are
likely to be hidden away in suburbia. What can he do to become
known—aside from the casual distribution of "simple professional
cards"—without crossing into the forbidden zone of "self-laudation?"

One way is to become a joiner. Service clubs, veterans organizations,
country clubs, and the like offer opportunities for the display of one's
good sense, pleasant manner, and erudition. Sooner or later, through
such channels as these, the new lawyer is likely to learn of political
opportunities. Even though he may have little interest in pursuing a

full-time political career, participation in political organizations and minor offices provides a chance for him to gain recognition and praise. From there it may be a short step to the state legislature, where publicity and influential contacts are easy to come by. Already interested in the law and its creation, the young lawyer is a natural candidate for legislative office.[2]

Although only half of our second group of freshman legislators, the Advertisers, are lawyers,[3] the others are distributed over various occupations characterized by similar independent and advisory relations with clients or customers. Many of them stress such occupational utilities in explaining why they decided to run for the legislature. They are placed in this category because they show a high rate of activity in their first session together with a lack of long-range commitment to legislative service, as indicated by their unwillingness to return for three or more future sessions. At the level of conscious motivation for office-seeking, their perspective is primarily that of the young man out to let the world know he is alive and available.

Thus one Advertiser sees the legislature as a "golden opportunity" for making "an awful lot of acquaintances," "a chance to get up and get into the limelight and do things." "From a practical standpoint it's been good," he says, "as far as notoriety goes." He explains:

> It's always good for someone practicing law to have something profitable or something like that in the local newspaper—local boy does this or that. And of course even the election itself was —whether or not I was elected—it was beneficial to at least have my name in the paper with a picture shaking hands with senator this, or something like that. Which of course was one of the reasons that I ran in the first place. Because it's—you've got to— you can't go out and advertise or anything like that. And I think a lot of the boys are up here for the same, because of that too.

Another Advertiser relates that his "original intentions were to get something out of this. If I get active enough in the public eye, and politically, maybe I could get myself a ten or fifteen thousand dollar job one of these days." He sees the other legislators as "very good contacts" whom he "should get to know a lot better," so that in the future he would "probably be able to get a few favors for myself."

And perhaps the clearest description of the Advertiser's conscious motivation is in this passage:

But—that's law—a lawyer cannot advertise. The only way that
he can have people know that he is in existence is by going to this
meeting, going to that meeting, joining that club, this club, becoming a member of the legislature—so that people know that
there is such a person alive. And they figure that—"Oh, X, I
heard of him. He's a lawyer. Good. I need a lawyer, I don't know
one. I'll call him." Otherwise you're just in your cubbyhole waiting for someone to come in off the street. And it doesn't happen.

The Advertiser, then, takes a hard-headed, calculating stance toward his legislative office. His primary focus of attention is not on the
softer rewards of good fellowship but on the use he can make of
political office for his own advancement. As we shall see, this surface
attitude of cynical self-advancement conceals beneath it considerations of a different nature. The explanations he offers, which are so
congruent with the popular image of the self-seeking politician, are

PROFILE 1: *Advertiser Legislative Activity*

	Advertisers	Other New Member Respondents	Difference
Originated action to get nomination	56%	38%	+18
Attended many meetings in campaign	38	50	−12
Likes campaigning very much*	8	47	−39
Attributes election to own campaign efforts	19	11	+ 8
Often introduced self to others at first of session	94	80	+14
Took an active part in major negotiations	75	61	+14
Was frequently sought for advice	69	41	+28
Achieved leadership or important committee post	54	26	+28
Considers self energetic rather than easy-going	75	59	+16
Considers self more influential than others	69	49	+20
Self-rating as a legislator: superior or excellent	57	30	+27

* Indicates presession response and/or change during session: Advertiser N = 13, Other N =
70. All other responses are from postsession questionnaire: Advertiser N = 16, Other N = 80.

not to be taken at face value. But before exploring the deeper dimensions of the Advertiser perspective, we need to outline his general characteristics and account for his nomination.

THE ADVERTISER PROFILES: YOUNG MAN ON THE GO

The major dimensions of the Advertiser profile have been mentioned: he is an active legislator who intends to serve only one or two terms in the House. The Advertiser Legislative Activity Profile shows a general pattern of deviation from the responses of others in the

PROFILE 2: *Advertiser Political Ambitions*

	Advertisers	Other New Member Respondents	Difference
Identifies self as a "politician"	44%	43%	+ 1
Has considered seeking full-time elective office:			
Presession response*	31	46	—15
Postsession response*	39	41	— 2
Change during session	+ 8	— 5	
Had considered full-time state appointive office*	25%	33%	— 8
Was interested in district or state party office*	85	70	+15
Was interested in Assembly leadership position*	76	69	+ 7
Willingness to return for three or more future sessions:			
Presession response*	39	76	—37
Postsession response*	0	83	—83
Change during session	—39	+ 7	
Ran again for nomination or election to Assembly			
in 1960	69%	83%	—14
in 1962	31	46	—15
Ran for or served in some government office (including Assembly) after initial session.	81	92	—11

* See note for Profile 1.

PROFILE 3: *Advertiser Political Background*

	Advertisers	Other New Member Respondents	Difference
Parents interested in politics	63%	66%	— 3
Relatives active in politics	50	63	—13
Occupation involves government contacts	75	45	+30
Had held party office*	54	50	+ 4
Had held elective office*	38	46	— 8
Had held appointive office*	62	34	+28
Had long considered running for Assembly	46	56	—10
Reports some competition for nomination*	84	70	+14
Saw election chances as 50–50	46	20	+26
Considers legislative activity most important he has engaged in	38	61	—23

* See note for Profile 1.

direction of more participation, although the differences are not uniformly great.

The Advertiser Political Ambitions Profile reveals little in the way of distinctive striving for political office, other than part-time activity in party councils. This generally average level of interest in future political opportunities is not entirely confirmed in the interviews conducted with Advertisers. One interview subject shows marked interest in becoming a judge. Another has laid plans for the possible eventual achievement of high appointive office, and others indicate similar interests when pressed. Furthermore, there was a shift in the Advertiser's interest in full-time elective office from a deviation of —15 per centage points before the session began to a —2 deviation after the session. Since the interviews were held during the session, these results suggest that some Advertisers began to consider future political possibilities more seriously as their legislative experience developed.

The Advertiser Political Background Profile shows the importance of his occupational life as a link to politics. The Advertiser's Personal Data Profile illuminates his general status as an up-and-coming young man.

The education item here is deceptive; it conceals the fact that Advertisers tend to be either very highly educated (62 per cent have

PROFILE 4: *Advertiser Personal Data*

	Advertisers	Other New Member Respondents	Difference
Sex: male	100%	74%	+26
Age: over 40	25	49	—24
Occupation: attorney	50	15	+35
Education: above high school*	62	54	+ 8
Income: over $8,000*	61	39	+22
Town population: over 5,000	82	46	+36
Resident in town: more than ten years	44	74	—30
Expects to remain in town	94	90	+ 4
Expects more income in ten years	75	56	+19

* See note for Profile 1.

advanced graduate education as compared with 29 per cent for all freshman respondents) or relatively low in education (38 per cent did not go beyond high school as compared with 43 per cent for all freshman respondents). None of them reports ending education in college.

The Advertiser stands out as a young man in the beginning stages of his career, holding hopes of rising in the next decade to an improved economic condition. He is likely to have taken up residence recently in one of the larger towns, where competition for office is fairly keen. His past political experience tends to be closely linked with his occupational life, and he is likely to have held some appointive office in his town. These experiences formed a base for his active pursuit of the legislative nomination. He rather disliked campaigning. Once in the legislature, he gets appointed to an important committee and finds that others seek him out for advice on legislative matters. His political ambitions are uncertain as yet; he is clearly not much impressed with the importance of the legislature.[a]

NOMINATIONS: TALENT AND CONNECTIONS

In the small and stable towns from which most of the Spectators are drawn, competition for legislative office is relatively slight. The party balance is likely to be strongly weighted in the direction of one

a. All of the Advertisers were willing to be interviewed, compared to 80% of the other new member respondents (N's = 13, 70). After the session they were the ones most likely to choose "speaking in the legislature" as a favorite activity (Advertisers 31%, others 8%) and least likely to choose "listening to debate in the legislature." Advertisers 0%, others 31% (N's = 16, 80).

or the other party, most usually the Republican. Nominations in both the minority and majority parties are shaped in important ways by the shortage of candidates. Availability—a noncontroversial record, clean background, and minimal capability—tends to be the overriding consideration.

In many of Connecticut's towns in the postwar period radical population growth has upset the traditional party balance and thus the nominations system. Change brings new and larger issues into the political arena: planning and zoning, school construction, extension of services to new suburban areas, rapidly rising tax rates, and the like become matters of intense public concern and debate. Success in attracting industry brings in masses of new workers and managers with novel political orientations. The old-style friends-and-neighbors politics tends to give way to a politics of organizations competing for political benefits. Almost inevitably, the Old Guard versus the Young Turks dimension is intensified. In the midst of this turmoil of new forces, the political balance becomes progressively more fluid and uncertain. Increasingly, party leaders must take into account the possibility that the next election will be an upset. And they find, more and more, that potential candidates present themselves, uninvited, for consideration. Ways must be found not so much to fill the ticket as to strengthen it. Novel decisions among contenders must be made.[4]

The Advertiser is likely to offer at least three major advantages to his party in this situation. In the first place, he is a "quality" candidate, relatively high in social and economic status, who by achievement or training stands out as a person of special abilities. This makes him especially attractive to the good-government element, the League of Women Voters, and the suburban voter who distrusts the downtown machine. As gossip gives way to the newspaper as a means of spreading reputations, the Advertiser's salable qualities become increasingly significant to the party councils.

Secondly, even though he is a relative newcomer to town, he is likely already to have filled some minor governmental office, probably as a member of a part-time, unpaid board or commission. Thus he is experienced, and his youthfulness and short local history can be overlooked. Such experience can be acquired in appointive office, outside the realm of partisan politics—again, a significant consideration in the appeal to the newcomers. The party chieftains have been able to look him over, to test both his abilities and his cooperativeness. If the Advertiser has managed to build a record of energetic volunteer service, while at the same time avoiding controversy and cooperating with the leadership, his attractiveness as a candidate is enhanced.

A third advantage in obtaining the nomination is likely to be the Advertiser's connections with special groups in his town. As the population increases, formal organizations become more important in the nominating process. Ethnic groups, neighborhood associations, taxpayers' leagues, service clubs, unions, veterans organizations—all make demands on the town government and push for recognition on the party tickets. More frequently, the initiative for including representatives of special groups among the nominees comes from the party itself. Party leaders, even before they reach the stage of systematic ticket-balancing, perceive the advantage of the candidate with a built-in following among his group associates. Advertisers, being of relatively high socioeconomic status, are more likely than others to be officers of such organizations. This factor may be influential in conversations of party leaders.

The Advertiser's youth and newness in the community can be liabilities, although to a certain extent these qualities are perhaps attractive to other newcomers. If he lives in the "new part of town," he may be expected to gather support from his neighbors beyond that which the downtown organization can muster there.[5] From the viewpoint of the party in a competitive situation where the electorate is expanding, the Advertiser may therefore be a highly desirable choice.

The decision as to his availability for the nomination may depend heavily on his ability to arrange for time off from his regular employment and to gain the backing of his special groups. These preliminary hurdles probably screen out more potential Advertiser nominees than are eliminated in the intraparty contest. What kinds of considerations are taken into account in making these pre-entry decisions?

We are probably safe in assuming that the Advertiser cannot lightly lay aside his regular work for a five-month jaunt in the legislature. If he is self-employed, such an interruption at a time when he is not yet fully established in his career may be especially risky. Clients and customers whose loyalties he has begun to cultivate may become irritated at his absence and desert him. By becoming involved in party politics in a closely divided community, he risks alienating nonpartisans and members of the opposite party. His family and employees, dependent on him for regular income, may press him to take no unnecessary chances. If he is a member of a law firm or a junior executive of a corporation, his services are probably not casually dispensed with for an extended legislative tour: others may be unwilling to take on additional burdens to free him for political activities or (and this is perhaps the greater danger) his superiors might discover that nothing much changes after he leaves.

In order for the Advertiser to give serious consideration to seeking a legislative nomination, other arguments must outweigh these anticipated disadvantages, both for the Advertiser himself and for his associates. Unlike the Spectator, who has little to lose by a try at politics, the Advertiser's personal stakes are high. He is likely to risk them only when clear *occupational* rewards are expected that will compensate for the occupational chances he is taking. If he is experiencing grave difficulties in moving ahead at a satisfactory speed; if fears of failure overcome his hopes of success; if he feels discontented with his work or prematurely committed to the wrong profession; if he perceives that he has reached a position beyond which his talents are unlikely to carry him—under such circumstances he is apt to look around for some way to break out of his troubles. If, in addition, his duties can be shifted temporarily to someone else and the enterprise stands to benefit from the publicity he receives, the wider contacts he establishes, and, perhaps, the advancement or protection of its interests through legislation, then his colleagues and dependents may well encourage him to take the step into politics. The decision rests primarily on two factors: the degree to which he is dissatisfied with his progress through regular occupational development and the degree to which rewards for the enterprise are anticipated.

In the earlier stages of population growth, when formal groups are in the process of organizing and recruiting, the Advertiser probably faces few obstacles to group approval for his political aspirations. Such endorsement is likely to be tacit or informal, amounting to little more than acquiescence in his holding public office at the same time he holds some organizational office. Formal endorsement would be opposed on the ground that it would get the group involved in politics at the expense of group unity and acceptance in the community. Later, as the group becomes an established part of the community, its leaders develop contacts with the local party leadership, and share in informal discussions regarding potential candidates. As the size of the group increases, leadership becomes more concentrated. The importance of the group as a channel for political preferment becomes recognized, and the number of would-be nominees seeking group approval tends to increase. Then the leading clique within the group is faced with decisions similar to those the party leaders encounter: which of the contenders should be favored? Such decisions are apt to be made on much the same grounds as those the political party considers: Will the candidate be a credit to the organization? Has he proved himself by active, cooperative, and noncontroversial service to the group? Is he popular among group members? Confronted with a choice between an Advertiser and a Spectator, for example, the leadership is apt to favor the Advertiser.

Drawing together these various aspects of the Advertiser's nomination, two conclusions seem evident:

(1) Given the expanding and politically competitive character of the community, and given the Advertiser's relatively high qualifications, status, and group connections, he is likely to appear to the party leadership as an attractive candidate.

(2) The important determinants of his entry into active pursuit of political office will be his attitudes toward his current occupational progress and his ability to arrange the necessary time off from his regular work.

Thus the Advertiser is perhaps the prime illustration of the ways by which personal events in the nonpolitical round of life bear on government recruiting. To be sure, he may be interested in questions of public policy. He may be impressed with the power and prestige of legislative office. And he may feel a sense of duty to utilize his talents for the common good. But his first consideration—one that overrides the others—is the significance of legislative office for his own career. One Advertiser makes this clear when, after listing a number of reasons why he took the nomination, he says, "But if the one [reason] was missing of the help it might do for me—letting people know that I'm around—I wouldn't have run either. Not at the cost. I couldn't afford it. I couldn't afford it. Not at this cost."

REACTIONS: FRUSTRATIONS FROM WITHOUT

The costs the Advertiser must bear in undertaking legislative service can be expressed partly in monetary terms. The nominal salary and expense allowance, balanced against the immediate risks of losing clients and customer, being bypassed for promotion, and missing out on other developing opportunities in his field, are generally not worth it for the Advertiser in the short run. He is investing his time and energy for long-range benefits. As one Advertiser puts it, "I knew it was going to cost me money, initially, and it has, and I figured, well, I'll chalk that up to the cost—part of the education, part of the practice, just like I went to college to learn law, like an intern. You charge it up to the cost of being an attorney, it's an expense for letting people know that you are alive." The payoff is postponed; the investment is a risk, which causes the Advertiser considerable worry. He may find, as did another young lawyer-politician, Stimson Bullitt, that political participation "makes a man well known but not in his capacity as a lawyer." [6] The real estate and insurance salesman may find that he has alienated more customers than he has gained by identifying himself with a political party, involving himself in politics to the detriment of his image as an impartial, judicious adviser. The junior executive may find that the necessity for making political decisions exposes him to career-threatening cross-pressures on the job.

The Advertiser has made a careful calculation of the financial risks and decided to go ahead, tentatively and experimentally. After a month or so of legislative life, the interviews indicate, he is likely to develop doubts as to the rightness of his decision. The costs, it turns out, are too high, and they are not all financial. In fact, a *generalized* tone of feeling frustrated, blocked, hampered, and pressured by external forces pervades the Advertiser interviews. He is put upon; his powers are confined; his efforts thwarted. If we were to characterize briefly his reactions to the legislature, we might say that he feels frustrated, and believes that this is not his fault. Three interviews illustrate this theme.

Mike Jackson: "No matter what you do you get sliced for it."

Mike Jackson has a somewhat Teutonic look about him: his closely-cropped blonde hair and his corpulent body call to mind the young burgher. His movements are tense and controlled; his mental equipment is mobilized, alert. Mike was extremely cautious and suspicious about being interviewed with a tape recorder. Only after long persuasion and the repeated assurance that his real name would not be used in any published material did he sit down and answer questions. Whenever the interviewer touched on even the public details of his personal history, he turned cryptic or rephrased the question to make a generalized response appropriate. But his feelings and opinions were another matter. Once assured anonymity, Mike poured forth, in vivid emotional language, a sea of complaint against those who make life hard for him.

Asked to report what aspects of the legislative experience he has found enjoyable, Mike says, "I think ultimately that anybody feels that he is in a position, well, a position of power, really—although power that he can't use." The legislature has been "an enjoyable experience, but like everything else, it's been offset with its disadvantage." Political participation, Mike has learned, is "a thankless waste of time"; under present conditions he would never take a second nomination for the legislature. What of other political offices in the future? "The road is too hard," Mike says. "You would starve to death before you got there." Only the man who has inherited wealth or has built up an independent income can manage a political career: "Then you can go ahead and afford to be a public servant." "But if I knew I was going to just go on out, bust my back, wait until I had built myself up here for another five or ten years—well, they can just drop dead."

Mike's wife warned him against accepting the nomination. "Don't do it," she said. "It's a waste of time. It's going to cost you money. How are you going to get your work done? You're going to be away from home and everything else. You're going to spend all that time— and what are you going to get out of it? Nothing. Let somebody else run for it." "And," Mike adds, "she's right, of course." In his home town, in order to get ahead Mike feels that "you've got to join the clubs, you've got to talk to people," even though he detests such activity. He felt forced against his preference to campaign for office. "To go around and shake hands and say, 'My name's Joe Blow. Vote for me.'—if you have to waste your time on that baloney, to me, it's a shame. It's a crock. But you've got to do it, or otherwise somebody else will do it before you get—you don't get their vote."

When Mike is asked how he went about getting acquainted in the House, he replies disconsolately, "Oh, well, you can't help it. You're sitting next to people and in front of people and in back of people, and you're on committees with—you've gotta talk to them."

Taking part in politics is frustrating, Mike feels, "because you've got an opposite party there that's going to criticize no matter what you do. If it's good, they'll find something wrong with it; they'll say it's no good." Unlike the Spectators, Mike found inauguration day a "routine thing that had to be done—the customary malarkey, one of the necessary evils that you have to go through." In his legislative committee hearings, he complains, "you've got to be fair. Even though you disagree with a bill, you've got to listen to the people and listen to their side of the story. If you're in disagreement with a bill—some of the legislators let it out, but they shouldn't. . . . You've got to worry about hurting people's feelings. You've got to."

Throughout Mike's interview he complains of being forced by external circumstances to do things he hates or to abjure doing things he desires. Occasionally he mentions some positive feeling toward legislative life; for example, he likes to work on some of the legislation. But in every case, the advantages are offset by disadvantages: the enjoyment by frustration, the satisfaction by worry. Mike is referring to more than the financial risks involved in legislative service when he concludes: "No matter what you do, you get sliced for it."

Charles Rossini: "You can buck 'em once or twice, but after that . . ."

At 31, Charles Rossini already has the bald head and sports the perpetual cigar of the cartoon politician. Energetic and ambitious, Charles runs a growing real estate business in a suburban town. He feels that his political activities have "invariably helped" in building up his lists. Unlike Mike Jackson, he seems open and easy in conversation, although his difficulties in arranging to be interviewed may reflect some of the same suspicion and caution.

Charles says he has found the legislative experience "very, very good," "a lesson in the administration and the function of the state government that you'd probably have to go to school for many, many years to learn." *What* he has learned gives us some clue to his personal pattern of reactions to legislative life.

Charles reports that during the session, "There was pressure applied —unquestionably—by both parties to keep their members in line." Asked how he felt when this pressure was applied, he replies: "Well, I more or less expected it, and—I accepted it. Of course, I have been in the party for some time, and I have received the same pressure on the local level, so I know what the party machine is. And that they are —no questions about it—they are the power, and you can buck 'em once or twice, but after that you are on the outside looking in."

Charles responds to the question "What have been some of the less enjoyable aspects of the legislative experience?" with a terse phrase: "Party politics." He explains that "there were many issues that, of course, we had to support. If I was allowed to—to—probably vote my own way on the issues, I probably would have voted differently. My own conviction—but ah, that's the machine." "Individually," he says, "I had reasons, probably, of not supporting them. If I was allowed to vote secretly, I would have voted against them, but openly [he chuckles] you had to support them." He was disappointed when some bills he "had done everything for" were shunted aside by the party leadership. Near the end of the session, he says, "everybody seemed to be on edge, a little jumpy about the thing. But it's the pressure again, you know?" And at the end of the interview, he returns to this theme: "Everyone was pressured. They didn't want to admit it, but they were pressured—a guy walking out of there with two broken legs [laughs]."

Charles's special sensitivities show up when he describes the methods party leaders use. "I got the feeling," he says, "that they didn't have to say it to you directly—'Either you get in line or else.' They didn't threaten you in the exact words, but they let it be known. So I mean, I think that's where a lot of the [chuckles] 'harmony' came along. . . . It would be phrased diplomatically, but you knew what it meant: 'Get in line or else!' " [b]

Charles does not display in these passages the curdled bitterness Mike Jackson shows. But in his repetitious references to pressure politics he, too, seems to feel blocked and forced by external circumstances. He expected pressure; he found pressure; he had to give in to it, against his personal preferences. He sees the threat behind what party leaders say. The picture is not as clear as in Mike's case, but there is a common theme: one's wishes and wants are bound to be blocked by powerful external forces.

Bob Muldoon: "It makes you feel resentful sometimes . . ."

A junior executive in a large manufacturing company, Bob Muldoon represents a "town" of some 50,000 in the Connecticut legislature. Bob took his time in answering the questions, especially those which concerned his political background. "I'm glad this is confiden-

---

b. In their questionnaires, Advertisers stand out in agreement with the statement "Many legislators experienced a great deal of pressure from their party leaders during the session." Advertisers 88%, others 63% (N's = 16, 80). They are the ones least likely to choose this alternative: "Most legislators, on most bills, will need to take the word of the appropriate committee or caucus" (Advertisers 8%, others 30%), and least likely to agree that "the new legislator will very frequently have to take the advice of those with more experience or ability." Advertisers 46%, others 66% (N's = 13, 70).

tial," he says as he begins a long and complicated account of his nomination. Asked to describe some of the less enjoyable aspects of the legislature, he can think of nothing, despite repeated probing. In general, Bob seems to have a lower energy level than the other two Advertisers, and he has less to complain about. But he does not sound wholly enthusiastic when he says, in a flat monotone: "Less enjoyable parts? I don't think I've had any yet. I've really enjoyed it, truthfully and honestly. I've enjoyed every moment of it. There's no hardship on me at all. I enjoy it."

Bob thinks he will probably run once more for the legislature, but after that he will let someone else have the job. "As far as public interest is concerned, public life, I don't especially enjoy it that much that I would want to make it a long, lifelong career of it—to be 'Dean of the House' one of these days, or something like that. No interest that way at all." Even so, he would like one more chance. When he was nominated, he reports, a party leader gave him explicit instructions, saying, Bob reports, "If we do nominate you, naturally you will be elected. There are very few things we want you to do for us, and unless you're morally opposed to some of these things that we ask you to do, we expect you to go along with them. You should certainly put that in your mind now, rather than say after you're nominated, 'Well, the hell with you, I'm going out on my own hook.' " Bob explains that "Of course the thing they can do is not renominate me for the next session if they so desire. And there wouldn't be much I could do about it."

During the session, an issue did arise on which Bob's personal preferences were strong (although not "morally" so) in one direction and the party chieftains much preferred the alternative. Bob gave in, although "deep inside it hurts." He feels that "if you do go against them, there's plenty of things they can do—if you were looking forward to staying, keeping alive for a while, that's one good way of stopping you. You know, if you're bucking the party every time on everything that comes up." Bob had heard that the legislative party leader "didn't care one way or the other on it, but I know darn well he does."

The tone of being confined by party pressures seems apparent here, although not as strongly as in Charles's case. It is in another set of relationships—with his constituents—that Bob's sense of frustration and powerlessness reveals itself more clearly.

Bob begins one of his answers in an analytical and somewhat didactic fashion: "Of course, the difference between a small-town legislator and a big-town legislator is completely different." In the small town, he explains, "you're the big boy. Actually there aren't many people that have more to say than you do. You go out there and make their laws and they have to depend on you." There the state representative "has a hand in everything," "they're *in* on everything." By contrast, the

> big-town legislator like myself—we don't get involved in these things. Perhaps it's because Boss Clayton is so closely connected and the problems of the town would go through him. . . . In a big town you can't be in on everything. You act on a district level, you know things about your own district, maybe the town committee, but that's as far as it goes. You get the rest from the newspapers and your friends. You've never actually had an active part in everything—and unless you've had an active part in everything, you can't actually come down and say that you know this and you know that, these things are being done this way, and the way it should be done. Actually it makes you feel resentful sometimes of the fact that you don't come from a small town.

In these passages, Bob is reacting against blocks to the assertion of his influence. He, too, would like to be one of the "big boys" in his town, but in fact he is enmeshed in a complicated network of organization politics that leaves him little room for independent maneuvering. He expresses a similar feeling when he complains that in committee work, "Something should be done to give everybody an active voice— but that's politics." Not sure yet just what it is that he wants to say, he resents being denied the opportunity to say something.

The Advertiser's Costs

As will become clearer when we discuss the Advertiser's view of himself, members of this category do not find the legislature a particularly pleasant place to be. Their reactions are marked by feelings of frustration, by resentment over the imperious demands of outside circumstances. The costs are personal, not just financial. In several ways, the Advertiser feels uncomfortable about being forced.

In Mike's case it is clear that he is irritated at being *forced to do things* he does not want to do. He complains of a long list of activities which he has to engage in as the price of being a legislator. He *must* shake the voter's hand, join clubs, socialize with boring people, act fairly to committee witnesses. He feels imposed upon by politics; its evils are necessary ones, but evil nonetheless. He is unable to accept these costs in time and effort as fair exchange for legislative office, because he sees the office itself as a burden, not a prize, a means to self-advancement, not an end in itself. He pays and pays, and gets nothing—at least not yet.

A second source of frustration is external compulsion to *give up one's preferences,* to act contrary to one's personal beliefs and desires. Charles has little objection to spending time on politics, but it bothers him to vote different from the way he would if the vote were secret. Bob feels put upon when he must conform to the wishes of the leadership—he does it, but he does not like it. For the person used to speaking his mind freely and openly, the responsibilities of public office may weigh heavily. His political opinions now have consequences. The Advertiser comes to resent the limitations on his freedom of opinion inherent in official roles.

Third, the Advertiser feels forced to *surrender his rightful powers* over others. Like Bob, he feels that his official authority should entitle him to considerable political influence; he has a right to be a "big boy." But he finds that he is only one among literally hundreds of legislators. There are alternative channels to power that bypass him. Desiring to take an active, leading part, he finds that the Speaker will not recognize him, the home-town boss feels no need to bother with him, the committee chairman runs his own show. "Politics"—other politicians— block his assertions of power. No one need really be dependent on the Advertiser himself.

The Advertiser, then, would like to say "Leave me alone" to those who demand that he perform politically. He would like to say "I have a right to my opinion" to those who press him to act against his preferences. He would like to say "Listen to me!" to those who are unimpressed with his authority. But he feels he cannot. He conforms, and he suffers.

SELF: THE PERILS OF AMBITION

The feelings of frustration and impatience that we find in the Advertiser interviews fit well with our image of him as a person in a hurry, seeking, partly through politics, to reach a position of power and security. His attention is occupied by calculations of his place on the ladder of success. When he looks down, as Mike Jackson does at one point, he experiences a fear of falling: "I'll go on welfare. My secretary will quit. My landlord will throw me out. My auto and my house will be repossessed. And I'm losing clients." When he looks around at those on other ladders, he compares his progress with theirs, as witness Charles Rossini's concern about others who are "gaining a little bit of prominence," his desire to be "in the upper group, where we could get something out of it," his satisfaction that others were "looking up to us for different things."

When the Advertiser looks up the ladder, in the direction of the goal of his life, his vision is uncertain. Mike Jackson's thoughts about the future are particularly revealing. "Others may not have the hopes that I have," he says. He would like to be a judge some day, "where you have tenure." "A judgeship is something any—it's like a philosopher, a professor. He's not a multimillionaire, he doesn't make a million dollars. He loves his work. He studies, he has time for research. He loves to do his work—at least I think so, that's my impression." A judge "lives comfortably, he makes ten or fifteen thousand dollars a year, has enough to feed his family, his kids. Has enough to retire on—what else do you want out of life?" In these sentences Mike focuses on the security, the safety, the calm and comfortable aspects of the judge's life. He seems to be looking forward to the day when the struggle will be over and he can relax. But having paused in this imagined Elysium, he moves on:

> Judgeship—I'm in the law, I like the law—I can make the reputation. I can be known as a good judge. Not only that, but if I'm good, if I work at it, if I spend my time, you can become a higher judge, and a higher judge, and go up to the State Supreme Court —you can go up to *the* Supreme Court. And then also, if the person is any type of an individual, he wants to, if he can, become a great judge.

At the end of Mike's ladder there is no resting place, only the beginning of another ladder. He must go on and on.

Ambition poses a heavy burden for the Advertiser. When he begins to doubt that he is moving fast enough, that he is on the right occupational ladder, that others are not surpassing him, that the goal is possible of attainment—he feels anxious. But he also bears other doubts which generate, at a deeper level, considerable personal stress. Is he, he wonders, doing right as he searches for advancement? What means are legitimate for attaining his goals? Will he come out on top at last only to find that he has so sullied his character in the process that he can no longer respect himself? Perhaps we should not be too surprised to find that the Advertiser is much concerned about ends and means, is consciously grappling with his conscience as he struggles upward. Not all the barriers are outside; not all the frustrations come from others. Underlying the Advertiser's sense of being hampered there is considerable evidence of an inner moral concern.

The Dilemmas of Might and Right

In the course of our conversation about campaigning, Mike Jackson grew philosophical: "Once again, you go back to your human nature," he says,

> and that's all politics is—human nature. The individual—likes to—be known for having accomplished something good, for having accomplished something in life. For I, I wish I could think of the term—people don't want to be a nobody. If a person, or an artist, for instance, creates a beautiful work of art, he has something that will live after he dies: "This is something that Hans Schmidt made. I have accomplished something—here is a thing of beauty that will live on."

Mike, too, wants the feeling that he has accomplished something good. But as Mike continues in this passage, his tone turns from admiration to reproach: "Now, a representative—'I'm now a representative'—he's accomplished something in life. he's something." In campaigning, "all of a sudden he's a center of attraction. His name is in the paper. He's on the bulletin board. You're going to vote for him. People are going to take the time out to—recognition, that's it. 'I'm running for the House of Representatives.' [And they say] 'Oh!' —you know—he figures that people swoon. He figures that 'I'm an important individual.' " The handshaking candidate is easy to understand, Mike feels: "There goes the ego again. Why? They're not getting money for it. They're going out and saying, 'Look, look at me— ain't I wonderful? Look—me, me, me, me, me, me!' What is it? Nothing else but that."

Mike illustrates here what seems, from a careful scrutiny of the transcripts, to be a central personal problem for the Advertiser. He sets for himself a high standard of achievement; he wants to be great, to accomplish something immortal. But in the course of pursuing his goals he finds himself in morally ambiguous circumstances, threatening to his integrity. The desire to achieve good things is blemished by the necessity of using questionable means. The Advertiser feels anxious about his life strategies; he also seems to feel guilty about his tactics.[7]

It is clear from the interview that Mike feels his standards of performance are high ones. "If you feel that you are right," he says, "you stick by your principles and don't get discouraged." "Once I've undertaken any job," Mike says, "I don't care what it is, I've got to do it *right* or I don't feel right." He likes the committee executive sessions, where "you can express your honest opinion, as you and your good conscience feel, for or against the bill. Whether it's popular or whether it's not popular—or whether you think in a certain way—you would express yourself."

When he compares these standards with his own performance, Mike has "some mixed feelings." He feels "as though I'm letting down people who had faith in me." He illustrates his conflicting feelings exactly when he says, "There are good contacts to be made—influential people come up and see me. And not only that—even if they didn't come up here, I want to do a good job." "Most of the legislators," he complains, "don't have any guts," but even those who do must compromise themselves to survive: "It's a matter of self-preservation." In another passage he says, "Once again, I'm an egotist, like you and everyone else. You like to be in the public eye, you're a big shot—that has its advantage. Because you're accomplishing something. You—even if you don't feel you are, as long as somebody else does—it's recognition." The ambiguity puzzles him, and he changes the subject: "I ah, ah— it's a sense of—I mean, the human element, to me, the human psychology, ah—of the individual is so important in determining why these people are up there . . ." But the nagging question keeps after him: Is he a man of principle, a "decent, self-respecting lawyer," seeking to contribute his talents to the general welfare? Or is he an "egotist," out to get his, while the getting is good? When he began as a legislator, Mike said to himself, " 'Oh, boy—this is nice.' I mean, you know, 'I'm going to do a good job.' Because it—everybody wants to do a good job. At least I do. Because if I do a bum job of it, I'm going to be known as a bum." But, he adds, "It's a matter of ego, a matter of self-satisfaction." [8] The struggle between idealism and cynicism is evident in Mike's case. He seems to find it hard to believe in his own beliefs.

Charles Rossini echoes Mike's theme when he says that "every legis-lator wants to do a good job." "I support a measure because I think it's good." He would like one more term as a legislator, because "I think I could do a better job the second time, a much better job than I am doing the first time." As a legislator, Charles says, "You're up here to do a job, and what's best for the state, do it." Partisanship should not interfere with consideration of bills on their merits: "All of them ought to get a fair shake."

Charles, we recall, objects to party politics in the legislature; he feels that pressures by "the machine" account for many of the faults of the legislative process. Yet he sees himself as a politician, seasoned in the local battles over place and prominence. He presents a long and detailed account of his past maneuvers, which show a preoccupation with which faction to join, when to make his play, whom to cultivate. He speaks admiringly of a local leader who "is a real politician. He was really good, you know? And he could doubletalk—a good politi-cian can doubletalk. I mean, he can satisfy the answer to the question, but actually, if you go back and analyze his answer you'll find it mean-ingless—it could mean two or three things, altogether." Similarly, he thinks the Governor made "a very good speech" on inauguration day: "You can't pin him down on too many items."

In the course of the interview, Charles alternates between a stance as an independent, impartial, high-motived maker of the laws, judging each issue on its merits, and a stance as the party politician, who keeps the local party registration low, manipulates the legislative machinery, and trades votes for votes. At the same time he feels frustrated by party pressures, he admires the diplomatic finesse the party leaders use, and he sympathizes with their efforts to handle problems "that we have on the local level, too."

These competing identifications appear to have contributed to Charles's feeling that he has not measured up as a legislator. "Person-ally," he says, "I think, I'm not—at all satisfied with the type of job I'm doing up here. I mean, I think I could have done better." When he is outmaneuvered on a bill, he says, "it leaves me with a funny feeling, that, I mean, that you're not doing a good job, or actually what the public reaction would be." In fact there was little public reaction, but he cannot quite decide whether or not that makes his failure all right. Here again, the conflict between standards of might and right is evident.

Bob Muldoon, the third Advertiser, takes a similarly moralistic stance toward his legislative work when he suggests: "Let us think of whether it's right or wrong, whether it's good or bad, you know, on a general basis." The technicalities can be left to the lawyers (who "mix up everyone with their legal language.") The layman like Bob should ask himself "things like, will it do someone any good, or hurt anyone, and so on." Straight party voting, which helped him get elected, is a "bad thing"; the legislative procedures are different from what he thought they would be—"not that there's anything wrong with them." Throughout the interview, Bob refers to a vaguely defined moral dimension.

On the other hand, Bob resembles Charles in his acceptance of the code of the politician. Like Charles, he has experienced the ins and outs of local politics and has an extremely complicated long-range plan for maneuvering for higher office. More explicitly, when he describes an incident which "some wouldn't think was the right thing to do," he concludes that "I think this was a political move, and a good one, too. It certainly—if you're going to play politics, and live politics, you certainly should do it the right way. And I don't think there's any other way to do it." Yet he continues to feel ambivalent about such techniques Of another incident, he explains:

> Morally speaking it probably wasn't a good thing, but politically it was a big break for us, because we've got one guy that's going to work like the devil for us for the next ten years, because of what we did for him. And—so—it's politics—of the worst sort. Some of these deals are—dirty, are—certainly, probably, shouldn't be done. But they're done every day by everybody else, and you get to thinking, "Gee, why don't we try and do it too?" And, ah, it's just a bad circle, that's all. At the very beginning I was completely opposed to even getting rid of a parking ticket, but thousands of others have been getting rid of them these days, so why shouldn't we get rid of one? So—I still am quite opposed to it, but if you're going to let everybody else do it—you can't stop it. You're fighting something that's bigger than all of us. The human mind, I guess—I don't know what it is.[c]

c. In questionnaire replies, Advertisers are more likely than others to choose "It is impossible for a legislature to work effectively without a good deal of horse-trading or vote-swapping" rather than an alternative condemning such practices as "morally wrong." Advertisers 77%, others 47% (N's = 13, 70).

Is Bob "quite opposed to" political dealing, or does he feel "if you're going to play politics, you certainly should do it the right way"—that is, without bothering too much about your scruples? Bob is not sure. He, too, ends in confusion: "I don't know what it is."

Conflicting Standards

Like the Spectator, the Advertiser is much concerned about how others see him, preoccupied with manipulating his public image in order to maximize approval and minimize disapproval. But the similarity is a superficial one. The Advertiser judges himself in relation to two sets of standards. In the first place, he measures his distance from and rate of approach to certain goals of achievement, primarily occupational success. He rates his behavior as speeding or slowing his march toward higher positions. This is the root of Charles's concern about "what the public reaction would be" to his moves, of Mike's anxiety about "making the reputation," of Bob's worry over what "some would think." They are looking less for signs of love as such, more for practical support and help. The important angle here, and one carefully calculated by the Advertiser, is to make people see him as worthy of advancement. When he fails to meet these standards, the Advertiser feels anxiety, not guilt.

But he refers also to a second set of standards, those which command him to behave in ways acceptable to his own conscience, whatever others may think. He must "do it *right*," stick to his principles, consider the good and bad of political situations. Failure to meet these internal moral standards makes him feel guilty.[9] When he succeeds in carrying off a maneuver for gaining support from others, he tends to feel that he has dirtied himself somehow, that he buys his reputation at the price of his integrity.

The Advertiser feels trapped and hampered not only by the external forces discussed above, but in a deeper and broader dimension—he is trapped within himself, held in a tension between his ambitions and his ethics. His ambitions demand that he make speeches and shake hands; his conscience damns him as a phony egotist. He wants to be a decent, self-respecting person, but he cannot see how to keep clean and move ahead at the same time—human nature being what it is.

These are not uncommon feelings in a restless society. But the Advertiser, to an unusual degree, seems unable to resolve these conflicts in any satisfactory way. Rather he shifts from one set of standards to the other, talking now like an indignant Puritan, now like a scheming Machiavelli, without reaching any compromise acceptable to himself. Again and again in the interviews, one sees the sequence from an idealistic, highly moral statement to a cynical, "inside-dopester" explanation, to a confused trailing off into an irrelevant topic. The tensions remain; failing to resolve them directly, the Advertiser seeks other, indirect ways to reduce them.

Strategies: Paths of Aggression

From the viewpoint of the struggle for gaining personal satisfactions, the Advertiser appears to have three fundamental problems. They vary in emphasis and intensity from individual to individual in this category, and the rigidity of the adaptive patterns of each individual depends largely on the severity of his difficulty. Nevertheless, these difficulties seem to be shared by most members of this category of high activity and low commitment.

His first problem, and the one most often present in his consciousness, is *anxiety* over personal advancement, a nagging fear of failing in his occupation, or falling behind others of his age and training. He has not yet either failed or succeeded; the uncertainty adds to his tension. Success—unique, outstanding success—can be intensely important to him; the strong value he places on high goals adds more tension.

His second problem is *guilt*. His moral standards are perfectionist, driving him to call into question his methods for achieving success. The inner battle between idealism and cynicism creates tensions of considerable severity for the Advertiser.

His third problem is *frustration,* allied to the other two but with the added dimension of being blocked from without. His feeling that his integrity is threatened and his progress hampered by external forces adds further to his store of anxiety.

These tensions harry the Advertiser long after he has reached adulthood. He has not yet brought them out into the open, faced them, and discovered satisfactory ways to resolve them. They continue to hamper his adjustment and to shape his patterns of adapting to his environment.

The most general characteristic of the Advertiser's pattern of adjustment is activity. His techniques are positive ones, striving, working, manipulating, moving against his environment. He strikes outward, energetically fighting against the forces that threaten him. His response is aggressive.[10] But rarely is it *directly* aggressive. Realizing as he must that overt aggressive behavior is dangerous to his reputation (on which so much depends) and in conflict with his own personal standards (which demand so much), he channels his aggression into safer, tangential lines of activity.

For example, in the interview situation Advertisers were more likely than other legislators to resist answering questions (particularly personal ones), to reject the interviewer's summaries of their opinions, and, on a few occasions, to act in mildly threatening or denigrating ways. They were not overly unpleasant but appeared somewhat irritated and resistant to the interview experience.[d] The attack was there, but it was muted, controlled, often obscure. The Advertiser cannot be discovered by identifying the fist-shakers, the insulters, the loud aggressors among the members. How then does he go about dealing with these special tensions?

Perceiving Others: the Weak, the Selfish, the Powerful

Advertisers share with other people the tendency to distort perceptions of others in need-satisfying ways. Asked to categorize fellow legislators, they frequently referred to various forms of personal weakness as typical of the members in general, or some group within the legislature. Charles, for instance, complains that

> There's more women. Now there's a subject, the woman subject. I just—I don't think women should be allowed in the legislature.
>
> INTERVIEWER: Why is that?
>
> CHARLES: Ah—it's funny, their views on different bills are so different from a man's. I mean their—I heard one girl say, "Gee, I wouldn't support that bill, there, I just didn't like the looks of the fellow that discussed it." You know? And, gee, I don't know —it was very, very poor. . . . I couldn't put my confidence in them. I mean, even the party itself, as far as the vote on different measures, they were definitely the weak spot.

Bob Muldoon has similar feelings about "the farmer type of guy," "the guy that seems to never know anything about anything." [11]

d. Or perhaps they were irritated at its content. Advertisers, in their questionnaire responses, were least likely to report having taken "much interest in the psychology of other legislators." Advertisers 19%, others 51% (N's = 16, 80).

They just make fools of themselves. I think if I were going to make a fool of myself I'd just as soon keep my mouth shut. . . . Now, I say, I don't damn anybody for the way he speaks, or his language or his grammar, but it's just that if he can be understood, fine and dandy. But if he can't even be understood—certainly they must understand that after he's through and everybody, a few people are snickering and laughing, start making "Awwrg, haa," sounds like that. And they should realize that after a while. . . . There's no need for that element.

When Mike was asked to categorize the members, he responded immediately: "I told you—a herd of cows." The retired people in the legislature are "real turkeys." Others are "like sheep—too stupid to come in out of the rain or to exercise their own judgment." He mentions the "factory workers, housewives, and retired people that spend all their lives and get nowhere, have accomplished nothing," who "have an inferiority complex." He speaks of those who "don't have guts enough" to stand up to their critics, of "the mediocres," "the ones that want to live off the fat of the land, that are too damn lazy to work."

Mike (who says, "These extreme things I don't like. Moderation is the best thing") is more extreme in these opinions than the other two Advertisers. But not once does an Advertiser, in categorizing other members, refer in clearly and exclusively positive terms to a group of which he is not a member. Not once does he comment on special strengths he does not share. Many of his colleagues are failures, he feels, people who through laziness or incompetence cannot measure up to his standards of achievement.

Nor do the others meet his standards of moral excellence. Their motives are essentially selfish, directed at grabbing whatever they can get. The weak, lazy, and incompetent are selfish in the sense of refusing to improve their behavior or to contribute effort; they "want to live off the fat of the land." But as the Advertiser directs his attention to categories of "stronger" legislators, he finds an increasing incidence of self-seeking behavior. Competence and selfishness are correlated in his perceptions.

"Everybody is an egotist," says Mike, "I don't care who it is"; the "basic thing about human beings" is that "they're egotistical." Certain ones "have plenty of power, but they're only human beings, and they become greedy, avaricious, they become little dictators. They let the power go to their head and then they become dictators!" The "structure of Connecticut is as rotten as it could be," "rotten as a decayed tree—the whole core of the government." "There are thieves that are doctors, thieves that are lawyers, thieves that are engineers, and thieves that are assistant professors—human beings." The only way to eliminate thievery in politics, Mike feels, is "when you kill off all the human beings." Human nature has two fundamental elements: "ego and jealousy."

Everyone, Mike says, wants to be "a big shot"; "everybody wants to be Governor, everybody wants to be President." Those who would deny this are "full of prunes." At social affairs, "each one is trying to out-bull the other—that's all they live for," "they want to tell everybody how much more wonderful they are than the next person." And coming closer to home, he says, "The only reason why most of the lawyers, in my opinion—as a matter of fact, all of them, are there" is "because of the advertisement that they get through the publicity."

To leave the government to people who "tossed in their names with the expectation and the hope that they wouldn't get elected"—"people *like that*"—is a "sad commentary," Mike feels, although this is not far from his description previously of his own attitudes toward the nomination.

Charles shares Mike's estimate of the lawyer's motivations. All the lawyers want to speak on every controversial bill; "I don't know what the hell they were getting—we all knew they were there." "Maybe to get a little publicity—I think most of them were speaking for a little publicity on each act or bill." Furthermore, the lawyers "get technical" and "they have a tendency, because they know law and that, to belittle the layman." And in a different context Charles says that, now that he is on the inside of the party organization, he tries to keep the "fence-jumpers" out, although he has done his share of fence-jumping in the past.

Bob Muldoon thinks that "most of the people in there are just envious of the fact that lawyers make a heck of a lot more money than the average professional." He notices "people that are always trying to make trouble, they're always looking for an argument—make a name for themselves, perhaps." Lobbyists "respect us, to the extent that they can get away with something now—that's the general opinion." Few legislators are in politics for a hobby: "I think most of us are eventually looking forward for something," such as an appointive job. The honest man in politics, Bob feels, is "fighting something that's bigger than all of us—the human mind, I guess."

Egotism, greed, envy, inordinate ambition, publicity seeking, disdain for others, insincerity, hunger for power—these are the qualities the Advertiser perceives in the social world around him, especially among his more capable colleagues.[e] One looks in vain for compliments of others unmarred by derogatory comment. Those who seem affectionate or conscientious or sincerely interested in issues only seem to; in reality, to the Advertiser, they are either weak or sly.

A pattern that might be expected to exist among Advertisers, namely direct identification with powerful persons in the immediate environment, is largely lacking in the interview material. Charles expresses some muted admiration for the *techniques* legislative leaders use and Bob seems to come around to adherence to some of their *norms* (although ambiguously). In neither case was their apparent identification with specific leaders as persons. Mike refuses to accord exceptional qualities to the leaders, despite numerous opportunities in the interview. The legislators themselves, he says, are incapable of fulfilling their role, and thus "it amounts to [everything depends on] the Governor that you have and the legislative leaders that he has under him," but repeated probing elicited no general admiration:

> INTERVIEWER: They're the ones that are really running the show?
>
> MIKE: Well, they've got to run the show—who else? The legislators can't do it. . . . So the Governor has to take the time— and you've got a good Governor, but he's getting paid for it— he's got prestige, got power. . . .
>
> INTERVIEWER: That's where your leadership—
>
> MIKE: Well, that's all you've *got*. . . .
>
> INTERVIEWER: Sure, well, you've got to have leadership—
>
> MIKE: Sure—well, not only you have to have the leadership, because individuals don't have the time to do it. And they're not qualified to do it. That's why we've got to rely on the leaders. It isn't because the leader is such a genius. He may or may not be.

e. More than other new members, Advertisers reveal in their questionnaires a preference for the statement "Most career politicians are mainly interested in what is in it for them," rather than "Most career politicians are trying to do a good job for the public." Advertisers 31%, others 10% (N's = 13, 70).

This is hardly to be classified as worship of the powerful. Mike seems rather to be resisting strongly any implication that there are those around him who are more capable or powerful than he is.[12]

There is little here of blind admiration for strong and clever leaders, little of the Spectator's emotional response to the "good speakers." None of the three Advertisers interviewed was much impressed by the Governor on inauguration day. Charles comments that the Governor "made a very good speech, being a middle-of-the-roader. He's quite—you don't pin him down on too many items" and calls him sarcastically "the best Democratic Republican we have." Bob notes noncommittally that "the people voted overwhelmingly for the Governor; they must think he's a good man." Their attitudes toward other leaders are similarly low key. Committee chairmen are "a little bit lax" (Charles); "not on their toes" (Bob); the party floor leader is nervous—"He's got to have his notes ready" (Mike). Party leaders are to blame for "commanding things" (Bob), are "bending over backwards to please the other party" (Mike); "I don't think he's that strong of a person that they make him up to be," says Charles of a party leader. By and large, then, the Advertiser's orientation toward specific leaders is unmarked by any strong appreciation of their charisma. The Advertiser is not a protofascist, ready for mobilization behind a strong man.

As will be clear later, Bob may be shifting his position somewhat in this regard. Mike Jackson's attitude toward leadership is probably more typical of the Advertiser pattern. In a revealing passage, Mike illustrates the dangers of submission. Referring to another legislator who is "real stupid, typical of his kind," Mike adds:

> That's the type of guy that made me shudder when I was in the service—to think that I would have to follow a guy's orders like his. Made me want to shoot myself. Because he had the stripes and you didn't—it made me shudder to think that I would have to get into combat conditions and follow that type of leadership. Real bigoted. . . . Wants to have people do what he says, even though he's wrong.

These comments indicate that the submissive pattern is unlikely to be an attractive one for the Advertiser. Leaders are seen in some cases as less than fully effective, in others as devious and dangerous.[f]

f. In their questionnaires, Advertisers are most likely to agree that "I influence others more than others influence me." Advertisers 69%, others 49%.

Fighting and Working

Not all the Advertiser's aggressive channels are internal and perceptual. There are abundant opportunities for overt expression of
aggression in the course of campaigning, negotiating, and debating.[g]
But Advertisers report only a few such occasions: Bob fought hard
in a hotly contested race (for another candidate); Charles "got into
a little hassle" near the first of the session and, in the rush near the
end, felt sufficiently "antagonistic" to "get involved in a couple of
arguments myself." More nearly typical was Mike's behavior in a
debate during the campaign. "I spoke my mind," he begins; "I made
some enemies. I told them exactly what I felt." But, he continues, "I
told them—indirectly. I either told them directly or indirectly. Because you have to be candid in some respects. . . . I let them know
I was in favor of it—in an indirect way. I didn't say it—it might
have gone over their heads, but . . ." Here and in other Advertiser
reports of actual aggression the attack is indirect, hidden behind
questions or stands on issues. Charles is "not afraid to ask questions";
Mike reports having shown some witnesses at a hearing that he knew
his material—"I was giving them the needle." But much as in the
interview situation described above, there is little bombastic crusad-
ing, open challenging, direct opposition in the actual Advertiser
pattern.[13]

The tone of the Advertiser responses shifts considerably when we
move from reports of actual behavior to anticipated or fantasied situations. This is especially clear only in Mike's case, although Bob reports he plans to back a bill and "fight for it myself" in floor debate.
Mike anticipates that if and when the party leadership pressures him,
"if it's for a special interest bill or just because one group wants it,
then that'll be the day they talk to me—they can go to hell." A
"greedy" pressure group "is going to cut its own throat eventually";
its members will "rile up the people" so much that it will be put down;
they should be "punched in the nose and thrown out of there." When
legislators refuse to go along with good legislation, Mike says, the party
leaders "should use all the pressure, they should bang them on the
head, and they should kick them in the teeth and threaten them and
everything else. . . . If they don't have brains enough to know that

g. In questionnaires, Advertisers are more likely than others to see legislative politics as
"a battle." Advertisers 31%, others 13% (N's = 16, 80).

it's good, that it's about time it happened, they should be kicked in the teeth." Thus the Advertiser—at least in Mike's case—can gain some release of pent-up anger by imagining situations yet to come in which he will fight or his enemies will receive their due punishment.[14] These thoughts probably serve to reduce tension even though they are never acted upon.

Attacking the work load is another way of working off aggression. Judging from their reports, Advertisers pour a great deal of energy into their work. Charles campaigned as much as fifty hours a week in the last four weeks before the election. Bob says that "in the six or eight weeks prior to the election I worked every night from approximately six to eleven o'clock at night—canvassing, getting things straightened out in the district." Mike has worked regularly far into the night to keep up with his practice while attending the legislature.

Reports of intense work effort appear in a number of contexts in the interviews that help to illuminate the functions work serves. Charles, for example, says that near the end of the session "the dam broke! Boy, you never had a minute after that! Had something to do all day long." Bob's hard work at the district level was really unnecessary to his own nomination and election, but, he says, "there's so much other work to do that you can bring yourself down to the district level and forget about yourself." The emphasis here seems to be on keeping occupied, on the go, taken up with a host of jobs to be done.

Mike adds another dimension: work as escape from talk. Of social affairs he says: "I just can't stand them—they talk about nothing. It's too—I was going to say, stupid. But it's a waste of time. Each one is trying to out-phony the other. I mean, if they were talking about something sensible—but just to sit there and talk and talk about nothing! I can't und— I just can't stomach it. I'd rather mow my lawn and build something or fix my basement, or read a book." Mike returns to this theme several times in the course of the interview, comparing the uselessness of idle chatter with "real" accomplishments such as waxing his car, weeding his garden.[15]

To what extent does the Advertiser's intense and energetic effort indicate his selection of the achievement pattern as a strategy for maximizing satisfactions?[16] Does he invest his energies in specific pursuits, achieve success, and take pleasure in the accomplishment? With a very few exceptions the evidence is strongly in the other direction. Charles does report that when he won the election he was "very, very—I don't know—it's like you had reached the pinnacle, probably. Kind of hard to believe that you'd won it." But he goes on to say that he had known he would win from the first, and that he would have been more elated on another occasion if he had won instead of lost. Bob describes in detail the steps to his nomination and says "I'm bragging about myself" when he relates that no other candidate was seriously considered. But he "didn't feel any particular elation over myself [his election] because I didn't even worry about it."

These are the only two occasions in the Advertiser interviews when specific completed accomplishments, important to the individual, are described and accepted as pleasant. Mike was not even particularly pleased at his own election: "To me it didn't make any difference whether I got elected or not."

It is especially clear that Advertisers do not link their personal interests or emotions with specific legislative accomplishments. References to particular political issues are almost entirely missing from their stories. Charles and Bob present long, detailed accounts of their nominations and campaigns, but with almost no mention of their interest in issues. Mike's account includes one brief reference to an issue but he has forgotten its specific content.

Each of the Advertisers introduced several bills at the beginning of the session but apparently had little interest in their passage. Bob says yes, he introduced some bills, but "not of my own doing, all by request. Those bills that I introduced, they're all by request. And like I say, there were only four or five on which I knew hardly anything about. If they were to appear to committee hearings, someone else would speak on them."

Pressed for details about these bills, Bob shows a remarkable lack of interest. One he expects to succeed—"It's just an ordinary bill." The others, he expects, will fail, but he is indifferent: "I didn't have any convictions about the bill"; and "I was going to appear, just to say I introduced the bill. . . . There was very little concern with it there. I just didn't do that [appear for the bill.]." Bob is similarly indifferent. He "didn't know anything about" the number one bill of the session. He "could read that platform a hundred times and still not know what they were talking about." He will go along with the leadership on the main issues. "As far as other bills, you may receive, oh, a hundred letters about a bill. That's justification enough to give you a little indication of how you should vote. Along with your own sound thinking—if you have any thoughts about the idea. There are bills that come in there that you don't even care about. [On these] I will go along with some literature I've got or something."

Charles "had several measures that I wanted introduced," but "I didn't know how to go about it. I introduced only four bills." On one of them ("I was interested in that!") there was no discussion and Charles apparently made no effort to get any. He seems less than fully interested in its details: "I forget the percentage off-hand." He recalls the occasion of his first controversy on the committee, remembers with whom he argued, but "Geez, I can't remember even what the bill was or anything like that." Charles mentions no bill in his discussion of committee work, and his few passing references to legislation are almost always in terms of hypothetical situations ("If I thought the X bill was good—"), supporting others on something he had little interest in ("I did everything for the fellows from—"), or criticizing the techniques or timing of others' legislative tactics.

Mike feels a kind of satisfaction. "Look, I'm making laws. Out of the several odd million people I'm one of the few that help make the laws. I vote for or against. There's that satisfaction." But his feeling that "politics is a thankless waste of time" has apparently carried over into legislative politics:

> INTERVIEWER: Have you introduced bills?
> MIKE: Yeah.
> INTERVIEWER: What do you think their prospects are, for getting through this time?
> MIKE: I haven't even considered it. Not much interested in it. I think it was about fifteen bills I introduced. Some of them I was in accord with. There are two bills, three bills that I am really interested in, on X, Y, and Z. The others I don't care.

But not even the two or three important ones are described any place else in Mike's interview. He will vote on the main legislation of the session but gives no indication that he has or will do anything beyond voting.[h]

These passages are explored at some length because they illustrate

h. Advertisers contrast with other new members in agreeing with the questionnaire statement, "Once a bill was passed or defeated, I tended to lose interest in the subject." Advertisers 50%, others 19%. They agree that "the ability to get along with people is more important than expert knowledge for success in the legislature." Advertisers 81%, others 54%. They agree that "every piece of legislation is a gamble—it doesn't make sense to hold back until you are completely certain you are right." Advertisers 44%, others 19% (N's = 16, 80).

the important difference between activity as such and what might be called *engaged activity*.[17] The Advertiser's pattern of adjustment includes a considerable amount of the former, much less of the latter. He is placed in this category, it will be remembered, in part because the records of the session show that he ranked above the median in participation indices: he made numerous comments in committee and on the floor and introduced a fairly large number of bills. It is only when we look behind the raw indices at the Advertiser's sentiments toward his own activity that his adjustive style becomes clear: he expends energy, but he does not fasten on legislative opportunities for achieving success.

Suffering and Believing

Two minor themes in the Advertiser interviews illustrate techniques of adaptation available to at least some members of this category— aggression against the self, and the holding of certain social ideals. On the first score the evidence is scattered. When the Advertiser complains that he is being maltreated, he seems in part to be communicating his perception of himself as a sufferer: one who worries, toils, and grapples with life, with only partial success. Expression of these themes may serve a need for aggression against the self. This view is best supported by various of Mike's observations:

> You can suffer. You'll suffer plenty.
>
> My attitude was, well, I'll suffer through it.
>
> So we'll go hungry for a while, we won't get the things we want.
>
> This is one of the bad things about life, one of the bitter things about life that you've got to go through.
>
> So, do it. Get it over with, suffer with it, and that's that. That's the way I feel about it.
>
> The group that's suffering . . . like I have done.
>
> I'd work my head off, I'd break my back.
>
> So what the hell am I going to do, shoot myself?

Mike seems to turn his election victory into an occasion for self-flagellation in the following passage:

> Now here's one thing: Here's—you want to know the true feeling. During the election day, I wanted to get elected badly. I regretted the fact that I didn't go house to house, and I regretted

the fact that I didn't campaign more. Why? It's a matter of saving face. Nobody likes to be a loser. It hurts your ego. You don't want to lose in a fight. Everybody feels bad when they lose.

Now, so I wanted to win. After I won . . . I'm glad at least I didn't lose face. But now the work starts. Now my headaches begin. Now—not work, but headaches. And there's no sense of achievement or anything else. To me it was something I undertook, and I knew it was going to hurt.

In another passage Mike refers to a mental suffering: "I mean, I may be, I may almost have a paranoiac tendency in this respect. I mean, not paranoiac in a real sense but that characteristic when you think everybody is picking on you, or everybody is saying bad things about you. I mean in that respect—I'm sure I'm not paranoiac." And he indicates a connection between his suffering and the need for self-punishment when he remarks, "But I am not going to suffer—*even if I wanted to suffer*—I'm not going to let my wife suffer and my children suffer." [18] These themes are rarely so explicit in the Advertiser interviews.[19] But all of them show persons who communicate a sense of uneasiness, a certain flavor of martyrdom, an impression of self-hurt.[i]

The Advertiser's *social* ideals, as contrasted with his personal ones, do not emerge strongly from the interviews. He does not spend much time talking about his utopia. But a few common threads seem to unite the social values of these members. They prefer situations marked by moderation, order, security, harmony. Bob thinks legislative rules should be changed ("I don't think it's fair . . .") to put an end to conditions that "give a lot of confusion all the time." He was mildly interested in a bill to curb juvenile delinquency. He sees that "dissension" in an organization "can hurt any one person" and concludes that "there should be strong organization."

Mike agrees that "naturally, you've got to have an organization, a group of leaders. Because if you don't organize you get nothing. It's like an army: if you don't have an organized—each one becomes his own general and you get chaos, you get nothing." He rejects those who "go haywire, go to extremes." He believes in "moderation"; he believes he is considered a "good guy—you know, inoffensive." In a modern complex society, he stresses, "We've got to have rules of play, of living—whatever will help make things easier for all of us, or, if not

i. Advertisers appear to lack an important source of solace; of the new member respondents, they are least likely to agree with the statement "I am a deeply religious person." Advertisers 31%, others 49% (N's = 16, 80).

easier, not quite as bad." [20] Charles is concerned with the importance of running the local party "harmoniously": "There's an awful lot of people that you have to pacify." After any controversy "we try to come out harmoniously." He sees himself as an organization man, not a maverick.

These few hints point to a conception of the good society as one in which aggressions are subdued and harmony established, within a framework of just rules. The Advertiser's resentment at being coerced by the environment does not carry over into an anarchistic creed.[21] Insofar as he thinks at all about utopia, it is a quiet, orderly place.

The Functioning of the Aggressive Pattern

We now hypothesize the functions served for the Advertiser by the adaptive patterns just described. In what ways do these mechanisms help him to allay his anxieties about getting ahead, soften his guilt over using "bad" methods, and provide some releases from the frustrations he experiences?

The Advertiser's main conscious anxiety concerns his rate of advance up the ladder toward vaguely defined goals of success, prestige, power, and security. By perceiving others as weak and incompetent, he feels less threatened by their competition. Uncertain of his progress, he looks outward for comparative evidence that he really is capable and therefore that he is more likely to succeed than others are. His Darwinian view of the world makes a competitive, comparative frame of reference especially appropriate; he can succeed only insofar as others fall behind. Attending to the weaknesses in others serves the function of reassuring him that he is one of those marked for a preferred place.

Anxiety is further allayed by activity. Besides contributing to his progress, intense activity distracts him from his troubles, fills up his hours with practical work. He escapes from introspection and from the kind of idle conversation that may turn to general comparative assessments of one's accomplishments. The Spectator finds this sort of distraction in the social round; the Advertiser turns to work. Effort must lead to success; since he is expending a great deal of energy, guarding against wasting his time, resisting idle recreation, he can expect with reason (and demand with justice) that he will be rewarded.

The Advertiser's aggressive feelings add to his anxieties about moving ahead. He has a public-relations orientation. He stakes a great deal on his ability to maintain a front of respectability and sincerity, an image of the "good guy—you know, inoffensive." By keeping tight control over his aggressive impulses, releasing them mainly through socially acceptable channels such as asking questions, voting his convictions, and grappling with the work at hand, he avoids the threat that he will be rejected as an aggressor.

The Advertiser's social ideals help, in a minor way, to combat his anxieties. His vision of the good society is blurred, but he seems to contrast the jungle world he perceives with a world of harmony and order he believes in. Contemplating such values may, in itself, serve the function of reducing his tensions over the uncertainties, the chaos, of the competitive society in which he lives.

Guilt poses a second important problem for the Advertiser. His high moral standards come into conflict with what he sees as his duplicity. He is playing a part, pretending to be interested in what he is doing but primarily concerned only about where it is getting him. Two perceptual habits help him to deal with these feelings. By seeing others as essentially egotistical, he can feel that he is not a lone pariah among innocents. Others share his faults and, in fact, surpass him in their selfishness. The system that forces him to pretend is their creation, their responsibility. Self-seeking is not only widespread, it is the universal, fundamental moving force in human behavior. Surely he cannot justly be required to be the sole exception. The Advertiser's everybody's-doing-it attitude enables him to quiet an insistent conscience.

His perception of himself may also serve to reduce his feeling of guilt. He pays a good deal of attention to his own troubles. His stories reflect considerable interest in the various ways he is suffering, being disappointed, worrying. If he is a scoundrel, at least he is miserable. This stance of suffering enables him to attribute his troubles to others and at the same time to feel that he is being sufficiently punished for whatever blame he himself may bear.

The Advertiser's frustrations are ventilated in fairly direct fashion occasionally, despite his general caution. He "needles them" at committee hearings, gets into a "hassle" now and then. But it is interesting to see how aggression anticipated and imagined can also serve the function of relieving frustrations. The time dimension is highly significant for the Advertiser. He sees himself not only as acting but as getting ready to act; his present is an unhappy phase of a movement into the future. At the conscious level he is willing to sacrifice now in order to gain later. He is perhaps less fully aware that his anticipations help make the present bearable in deeper ways. Holding back his aggressions is a little easier because he believes he will soon express them. This passing, temporary nature of the Advertiser's conscious frustrations softens their force. When the sense of frustration is severe, as in Mike's case, he may turn to imagined situations, in which the wicked are punished and he has a hand in it.

Finally, the Advertiser's fundamental indifference to political issues —his personal disengagement from the bills he has introduced and from the major legislation of the session—cuts down his risk of failure. He escapes the pains of responsibility. He maintains his opinion that party politics in the legislature is beneath him. He remains the sophisticate, above the naïve enthusiasm of other freshman legislators.

Unlike the Spectator, the Advertiser is actively involved in the work of the legislature. But like the Spectator, his heart is not in it. Both avoid important (although very different) risks by refusing to invest their conscious attention in the specific practical details of making laws.

STABILITY AND CHANGE IN THE ADVERTISER PATTERN

Of the four main patterns of adjustment we have posited,[22] the aggressive pattern best characterizes the Advertiser's behavior. To what extent is his selection of this pattern a final choice? As for the Spectator, the answer depends primarily on two factors. The rigidity of the pattern increases with the intensity of an individual's need for a particular type of reward, on the one hand, and the availability of these rewards from the environment, on the other. We will examine these factors in order, first exploring the severity of the Advertiser's demands for aggressive release and then considering the environmental supply of rewards for this pattern of behavior.

Alternatives

To what extent has the Advertiser invested his adaptive energies in the aggressive pattern to the exclusion of the other ones? The withdrawal pattern appears on first examination to be attractive to him. On the surface, he would seem to have little reason for involving himself with his fellow man, whom he perceives as a pretty undesirable character. On one occasion Mike follows this pattern, when he says of those he meets in the legislature, "I've got enough of my own headaches without worrying about them." But when he does withdraw in this fashion, he comes face to face with his own worries.[j] Like the Spectator he experiences discomfort when he contemplates himself. His damning conscience waits for him just this side of the self-other border. He needs to attend to others not only as distractions from his own worries but also as targets toward whom he can direct his aggressive impulses, thus pushing them away from himself. Like the prurient moralist who cannot resist reading about the latest Hollywood scandal, like the racist who follows closely the affairs of those he detests, the Advertiser finds it difficult to move away from the objects of his aggression.

Perhaps a more important reason for his resistance to withdrawal techniques exists at the conscious level. He has concluded that his personal advancement depends heavily on his public reputation. If others do not "know that he is alive," he cannot expect them to prefer him, promote him, come to him as clients. The risk of isolation is greater than the risk of exposure. He has learned that others will not come trooping to his door; he must seek them out, impress them, make them aware of his competence and sincerity. Considering the high significance he attaches to occupational success, it is likely to be the Advertiser's main reason for avoiding the withdrawal pattern.

This is not to say that the Advertiser enters into intimate relationships with others, that he has a strong empathic sense. He sees others stereotypically; he is far from being acutely and sensitively aware of individual variations in motives or behavior. Anyone who can reduce human nature to "ego and jealousy" is less than fully perceptive of the nuances of the species. He needs others intensely—as "contacts," as targets for denigration and hostility—and this need distorts his vision of them as individuals.

Advertisers utilize the achievement pattern to a minor extent in the legislature itself and somewhat more in their home-town election campaigns. But the main flavor of their interviews is one of a fundamental indifference to the specific, the particular smaller-scale tasks that would eventually fit together to build a sense of accomplishment. The Advertiser's lack of interest in particular political issues and bills has been mentioned above. What would be involved for him in investing energy and attention in such matters? First, he would have to slow

j. In their questionnaire replies, Advertisers are most likely to agree that "in my leisure time, I would rather be with people than alone." Advertisers 75%, others 59% (N's = 16, 80).

down. His customary impatience with himself and with the pace of activity around him would have to give way to calmer habits, habits of study and reflection, deliberation and debate. Second, he would have to withdraw a certain amount of his attention from contemplation of his long-range and somewhat grandiose plans for success. Third, he would have to cooperate closely with others, linking his chances of accomplishment to their abilities and good intentions. Each of these steps would involve for the Advertiser some rather marked shifts in behavior. Judging from the materials we have reviewed in previous sections, such changes seem unlikely.

The Advertiser's indifference to specific achievements reflects other elements in his make-up as well. He is temperamentally something of a gambler, looking for a sudden big killing rather than a series of little ones. He has no long-range commitment to legislative life that might encourage steadier efforts at building a reputation within the chamber. His cynicism makes it difficult for him to view legislation or specific issues as important in themselves rather than simply as weapons in a struggle for survival. And, to a lesser degree, his tendency to be contemptuous of the intangible (clear only in Mike's case) may discourage him from taking part in legislative word-mongering.

The picture is considerably cloudier as regards the submissive pattern. From one point of view it seems the set of techniques least likely to attract the Advertiser. Submitting to others is dangerous to his adjustment in at least two ways: he would have to put himself on the same level as the followers, the placid "sheep" who are "too stupid to think for themselves," and he would have to accept the leadership of persons who can be trusted to consider his welfare only insofar as it coincides with their own. This would involve an admission of inadequacy and the surrender of certain targets of aggression. The Advertiser seeks domination—why would he accept its opposite?

Yet in one case scattered bits of evidence seem to show the beginnings of such a shift. Bob Muldoon, at several points, relates experiences more nearly typical of the Spectators. Of one political leader he says, "He always impressed me as being a very good speaker. I always enjoyed listening to him." He reports that when he had a hand in putting over another candidate, "I think that was the greatest joy that we had, I had." And, looking to the future, he says, "I'd just as soon go through the election with someone else, you know, supporting someone; hoping for an outcome that favors yourself, or your friends."

His characterization of another as an impressive speaker and his report that his "greatest joy" came from another's success clash with the Advertiser pattern.

The aggressive pattern itself involves severe tension, some risk, and not a little suffering. Bob may be indicating in these passages that he has found it too hard a fight, too much of a continual struggle to maintain an independent stance toward all others. Despite the costs involved, he may be tempted to recede from the limelight a little and accept the leadership of someone who can eventually do him some good. To generalize this possibility, it may be that over the years tired Advertisers will be recruited to the Spectator ranks.

But much will depend on the complex relations between his needs and the environment within which he seeks to satisfy them.

Environmental Support

The member of the legislature encounters there only a few minimum formal *requirements* that he take certain actions. On the other hand, he finds many formal *opportunities* for a wide variety of activities. These factors provide the basic outlines or boundaries within which legislative customs and practices, norms and expectations, play important roles in encouraging or discouraging certain activity patterns. Much of this informal environment is ill-defined, contradictory, uncertain, seldom explicitly stated. Even after years of experience, seasoned legislators disagree about what the normal rules of the game include. For the freshman legislator these uncertainties are a source of considerable strain and anxiety. For the freshman Advertiser the problems are even more severe than they are for the Spectator, for while the Spectator sits back and watches, the Advertiser seeks to take an active role. More so than other members, he feels confused and frustrated by the uncertainties of legislative life.

But with time the formal and informal influences within the legislature register with him, and his habitual adaptive strategies are rewarded or punished. It is convenient in considering these relationships to divide the Advertiser strategies into two categories: those which involve some overt, visible behavior and those which are primarily internal practices of perception and belief.

The legislature as a formal system provides many chances for the Advertiser to speak, to act aggressively toward others, and to work on bills and reports. The role of legislator includes the expectation that he will do something, although this expectation is not translated into a formal requirement. The norm against oratory by freshman members, however, operates in the other direction. And it includes a provision of particular importance to the Advertiser's pattern: the stricture against wasting valuable legislative time on matters of little importance. Most of the Advertiser's efforts concern matters that he himself considers of minor importance; other members are likely to share his opinion in this regard. When he introduces a bill only to drop it later; when he makes a speech on a subject already covered in detail; when he prolongs committee hearings with questions aimed at needling the witness—these practices are likely to bring him considerable animosity. Judging from comments by Advertisers themselves and by other legislators, his front is not entirely successful. Others see, as he does, that he cares less about what he is saying than that he is saying it. Since his public reputation is highly significant to him, the Advertiser is thereby penalized.

Legislatures institutionalize conflict. There is an expectation of, and an organization for, the expression of contradictory viewpoints. There is little debate in everyday conversation, few opportunities for one to force others to listen to him, few situations in which one person is required to answer the questions another poses. The legislature formalizes such practices. It furnishes numerous chances for the Advertiser to blow off steam.

But the very formalization of these opportunities takes away some of their attractiveness for the Advertiser as aggressor. Aggression within the rules is somehow less completely satisfying than aggression outside the rules. Legislative combat is in this respect more like a prize fight than a street fight, more like a ballet than a battle. Mike's complaint that in committee hearings "you've got to be fair" illustrates this point. The Advertiser's aggressive style is cramped to a certain extent by the gentility and form of legislative conflict.

There are plenty of opportunities (and no requirements) for attacking the legislative work load. But of what does the work consist? Primarily of reading and talking: reading bills and reports and negotiating with others about them. The Advertiser may gain some aggressive release through grappling with the text of a bill, but he brings to the task little of the necessary patience and interest that would enable him to master the subject. He may keep busy dashing from committee to committee, but his temperament is ill-suited for the work of friendly, man-to-man negotiation. The nature of legislative work, particularly its intangibility and its requirement of social contacts, fits unevenly the Advertiser's pattern of adjustment.

The legislature is composed largely of part-time political amateurs, underpaid and overworked. For many of them the tasks they encounter in the legislature are far more complex than those they meet in business or in household management. In any particular legislative session nearly half of them are likely to be newcomers. They make mistakes. Their errors are publicized by the newspaper reporter who suspects he could do considerably better. And the Advertiser's habit of perceiving his colleagues as incompetents is thus lent support.

His view of the abler members as motivated primarily by self-interest gains support from another popular opinion—that characterizing the politician as an ambitious schemer. Most people have little interest in politics. They do their jobs, enjoy their families, cultivate their gardens. The candidate for legislative office stands out against this background as someone who wants to undertake an extra occupation, a "moonlighter" in public affairs. The natural tendency is for his fellow citizens, supported by an old myth, to feel that he hopes to gain something for his efforts, probably something material—that being the easiest motive to understand. Widespread feelings of disdain for the "mere politician" provide environmental support for the Advertiser's perceptions of the more active and able politicians as self-centered dealers.

These common themes probably serve, in general, to unify the legislature. Members joke among themselves about being "politicians," about their innocent mistakes. The club spirit is probably enhanced by the realization that outsiders, who cannot possibly appreciate the problems they face, condemn them unjustly. But the insider who shares these negative opinions threatens the solidarity of the group. He sides with the critics against his colleagues. He becomes known as one of the "negative thinkers" that Tom Minora, the Spectator, refers to. The Advertiser thus finds support for his attitudes toward others, but it is primarily support from outside the legislature.[23]

The Advertiser's tendency to see himself as a sufferer may have a very real basis: the chances are that his regular work does suffer, and nearly everyone in the legislature finds the work there difficult and demanding. Especially among other new legislators he is likely to find many who agree that the job is "impossible." If he becomes a nagging complainer, injecting into every conversation his sour view of the world and himself, others tire of his presence and avoid him. This may simply confirm his viewpoint—their rejection constitutes one more of his burdens. But it seems more likely he would prefer to have their sympathy (else why does he *express* such complaints?) and that we must add the general norm of optimism to the environmental factors that conflict with the Advertiser's pattern.

Finally, the environment *as he perceives it* provides little support for the Advertiser's minor hope for, or belief in, an orderly and harmonious social life. He tends to see the legislature as a scrambling herd of lions and lambs. While others share his values in this respect—harmony, peace, stability—they find more evidence that such qualities already exist to some extent in the legislature. The peaceable aspects of legislative life are not apt to make much impression on the Advertiser.

The Attraction of Other Arenas

In a number of significant respects, then, the strategies of the Advertiser come into conflict with the formal and informal prescriptions of the legislature. These conflicts help to explain the shift in Bob's style of adjustment, for example. When, as in his case, the investment in the aggressive pattern is not yet complete, these environmental forces will push the Advertiser to modify his behavior. For the Advertiser whose attachment to aggressive techniques is more deeply rooted, the costs of such modifications may be too great. The likely alternative for him is to seek other arenas where the environment offers better satisfactions. The most probable choice of the Advertiser is a return to intense effort in his regular occupation, which is the central dimension of his life.

But if he remains at all in politics, it is more likely to be at the home-town level than in the state legislature. In comparison with the legislature, the home-town situation involves fewer uncertainties. Fewer formalities constrain him. Less effort is required to make a bigger splash at home than he can make in the Assembly, and his potential clients and customers are more immediately made aware of his achievements. The accomplishments of local governments are tangible ones: a new school, a road paved, a fire house—real things, in contrast to the abstractions of the legislature. In the politically competitive towns from which Advertisers tend to be recruited he finds many opportunities for campaign aggression; and while the intimacy of intraparty relationships may gall him, he is more likely there than in the legislature to know what is happening, to be involved with the major political powers. He will find plenty of people there (perhaps more than in the legislature) whom he can characterize as fools and knaves.

The Advertiser has his problems in the home town, to be sure; but they come to seem less troublesome when he compares them with his legislative experience.

THE ADVERTISER AND THE WORK OF THE LEGISLATURE

It is clear that the Advertiser, unlike the Spectator, contributes little to the morale of the legislature. His complaining attitude, his denigration of others, his general disdain for the legislature and its work, and his fundamental cynicism regarding himself and his fellow men all operate to depress the level of happiness in the chamber. It is not hard to imagine conversations between Spectator and Advertiser in which the latter takes delight in puncturing the sentimental optimism of the former, scoffing at his silliness, and leaving him depressed and bewildered. The Advertiser seems to share little of the team spirit of his party or of the legislature as a whole. He is a limelighter, not a team man; achievement for him is sullied by being shared. No man who sees his equals as competitors, his superiors as tyrants, and his inferiors as animals can be expected to play the role of booster.

The Advertiser, aware of his feelings, tends to justify his existence in the legislature on other grounds. He is unhappy, yes, but sees himself at the same time as a worker, an achiever, a producer. He demands respect, not affection. His life is hard but earnest, full of energetic effort. To what extent does his high level of activity contribute to the work of the legislature despite his air of discouragement? Certainly he is no social relations specialist, but how does he do in the area of fulfilling tasks?

The effectiveness of a legislature depends heavily on at least three work habits that Advertisers find problematical. Legislative work is difficult: it demands attentive concentration to the task at hand. Legislative work is incremental, in the sense that its results are piecemeal, incomplete, partial steps toward the solution of continuing problems. This requires patience of the member, an ability to accumulate skills and understanding, to settle for less than perfection and yet keep going. Legislative work is complicated: it can be accomplished well only on the basis of extensive specialization, organization, and compromise.

In all three of these respects the Advertiser falls short of the ideal by a wide margin. In the first place, he lacks the active commitment to his work that makes concentration possible. His participation is too tentative, too oriented toward his own ambitions. His attention is focused not on the policies, the bills, the specifics of legislation, but on himself and his audience. Advertisers refer to legislation offhandedly, as if the business of the Assembly were someone else's business.

Secondly, the Advertiser lacks the patience necessary to master the legislative arts or to put up with the halting pace of progress. His reaction to slowness in others is not to demand a speed-up but to reject the process itself, to disengage himself from a progressive, developing set of moves toward common goals. His impatience with himself and his progress toward his personal goals is reflected in his impatience with others in the legislature. But the Advertiser's time perspective is peculiar: he seems to forge events in his personal career—past, present, and future—into a sequential chain leading to high success. Here his calculations are dominated by considerations of time. He is concerned with his rate of advance, with proper timing of his moves, with the ways by which one step leads to the next. But his view of society is unusually static. He takes little interest in the *process* by which the world he perceives (marked by injustice, conflict, selfishness, and weakness) might be altered progressively in the direction of the world he desires (marked by harmony, ease, peace, and justice) by means of cooperative action in the present. This inability makes life in the legislature difficult for him and at the same time makes much of his effort irrelevant to the continuing development of policies.

Thirdly, the Advertiser finds it difficult to take his place in the legislative organization. He is more interested, for example, in the *rank* of a committee on a scale of status and power than in its specialized contribution to the work of the House. Specialization requires that members agree to play particular roles which are narrower than that of the general legislator. Organization requires the acceptance of a position lower than the top party or committee offices. Coordination requires entering into computations about imperfect solutions. The Advertiser tends to dislike each of these aspects of the process; his needs to break out of a narrow, low, imperfect place conflict strongly with the needs of the legislature to get its work done systematically.

The Advertiser and the Rationality of Legislative Conflict

A legislature composed entirely of Spectators, we have said, would grind to a dead halt. Is it the Advertiser, then, who infuses the system with action and controversy? Surely a certain amount of aggressive conflict is useful in a deliberative body—useful for purposes other than the entertainment of the Spectator.

Political scientists tend to be suspicious, I think, of a governmental group in which there is no, or very little, conflict. If the issues dealt with are important ones, and the decision-makers are in reality answerable to their constituents or clients, then one expects arguments. Unanimity (except perhaps in the final roll call) probably indicates abdication of the group's proper functions, or the presence of an irresponsible elite, or both. To normatively neutral expectations or predictions of conflict many would add a value or functional dimension: conflict is seen as serving certain important needs of the organization. It arouses interest and attention. It forces the contenders to rationalize their positions, to communicate their reasons to one another, to answer one another's questions. Conflict stimulates invention, helping to ensure that key factors are not overlooked and provoking the imagination to discover workable compromises. It puts pressure on the contenders to seek allies, thus broadening the range of participation and distributing rewards more widely.[24]

The degree to which conflict actually produces these advantages is not known with certainty. It could be argued, for instance, that conflict is an aid to rationality in decision-making only in those situations where the best practical solution is unknown. This would seem to take in most governmental policy problems, but there are also a number of important ones on which there is widespread and well-informed agreement, at a given time and place, on the broad outlines of desirable actions. Yet it is a rare piece of important legislation that requires debate on neither generalities nor details. Conflict in legislative debate becomes obstructive, irrational, or dysfunctional when (a) it is out of proportion to the importance of the issue, (b) it "gets into personalities," or (c) it "misses the point." Legislators complain frequently and with justice that much debate falls in one or more of these categories. Perhaps the most usual complaint is that members repeat arguments previously heard in order to go on the record as having reasons for their votes. The pressure of time makes such interruptions irritating.

Advertisers are apt to contribute substantially to these negative aspects of legislative debate. Given their desire to impress their constituents, they are particularly tempted to make "go on record" speeches, playing for a paragraph in the local paper. More fundamentally, the Advertiser, being basically uninterested in the substance of the issues, is unlikely to apply any very stringent criteria of relevance to his remarks. The important thing, to him, is that *he* is speaking, not that the issue is being clarified. Equipped with enough intelligence to see many implications for any one issue, the Advertiser lacks concern with the problem of allocating available time in the most efficient way, a concern that might induce him to leave some things unspoken.[25]

Furthermore, the Advertiser's participation in legislative debate is likely to be *ad hominem* in several directions. He decides when and how to speak on the basis of essentially personal criteria (Will his comments impress the other members and the press? Will he appear on the winning side?) rather than criteria of relevance, clarification, and decision. And given his aggressive posture toward others, he finds it difficult to keep his animosities from flavoring his argument. The ability to separate the debate about issues from the conflict of personalities is a highly useful one in legislative decision-making. Judging from the evidence we have, the Advertiser is unlikely to exhibit this capability to any significant extent.

These characteristics of the Advertiser as debater should not be exaggerated. He does contribute in some ways to the rationality of debate. He rarely makes stupid mistakes of argument or rhetoric; his intelligence takes care of that. His cynicism operates to some degree as an antidote to the maudlin sentimentality of the Spectators. But it is cynicism he purveys, not realism. And his intellectual powers are harnessed to his ambitions, not to his legislative judgment. Nor can we say with conviction that his expectation of conflict works to legitimatize conflict in the legislature. He does not value controversy for its decision-making utility; in fact his ideal excludes controversy. Slightly below the surface, the Advertiser gains rewards from conflict situations that allow him to express hostility. But at the conscious level he wants to win, not fight.

The Advertiser's Political Future

All things considered, it seems unlikely that the Advertiser will stay very long in the legislature. His original intention is to serve a short hitch and move on. Remaining at any one level of government for an extended period would be discouraging for him. Furthermore he tends to find the experience a frustrating one and the role less influential than he anticipated. On the other hand, two forces appear to attract the Advertiser back to the legislature—or on to other kinds of political participation.

In the first place, he may be able to rise within the legislature—to become a committee chairman, perhaps—and thus be rewarded by the exercise of power and the enjoyment of status. Secondly, politics may get into his blood, into his emotions. Politics is still a field where conflict is expected. The terminology of battle used to describe political life reflects a partial truth. For the Advertiser the political world has elements that confirm his general outlook on life as essentially a struggle for place and power, and provide institutionalized outlets for his aggressive feelings. These psychic utilities may come to have such importance for him that he will seek nomination again and again. It is more likely, however, that the Advertiser will pass on the mantle of office to someone else—after giving him the inside story of what politics is *really* all about.

4. The Reluctant

Only he who can say "In spite of all!" has the calling
for politics.

MAX WEBER

If the Advertiser had entered politics around the turn of the century
he would have found ample confirmation for his view of the political
world. As writers like Lincoln Steffens, David Graham Phillips, and
Ray Stannard Baker raked into the muck of political corruption, it
began to look as if American government—municipal, state, and national—was in fact controlled by a few powerful operators with the
right connections and the wrong morals. State legislatures were prime
examples. Thus E. L. Godkin of the New York *Nation* wrote in 1898:
"If I said, for instance, that the legislature at Albany was a school of
vice, a fountain of political debauchery, and that few of the younger
men come back from it without having learned to mock at political
purity and public spirit, I should seem to be using unduly strong
language, and yet I could fill nearly a volume with illustrations in
support of my charges." [1]

Undoubtedly some reacted with despair; but others felt the revela-
tions of the muckrakers as a challenge to the forces of decency. Something had to be done. When Elihu Root spoke to the students of Yale
University in 1907, the rolling rhetoric of his peroration must have
brought them to their feet:

> The selfish men who have special interests to subserve are going
> to take part; the bitter and malevolent and prejudiced men whose
> hearts are filled with hatred are going to take part; the corrupt
> men who want to make something out of government are going
> to take part; the demagogues who wish to attain place and power
> through pandering to the prejudices of their fellows are going to
> take part. The forces of unselfishness, of self-control, of justice,
> of public spirit, public honesty, love of country, are set over
> against them; and these forces need every possible contribution

of personality and power among men or they will go down in the irrepressible conflict. The scheme of popular government upon which so much depends cannot be worked successfully unless the great body of such men as are now in this room do their share; and no one of us can fail to do his share without forfeiting something of his title to self-respect.[2]

If to the modern ear these sentiments sound overdrawn, this should not blind us to the fact that Root was expressing something more than mere inspiration. His call to action had a philosophical basis, one long a part of American tradition. The process by which men learn to govern themselves, Root said, "is long and laborious; for it is not merely a matter of intellectual appreciation, but chiefly of development of character." He then went on to describe the specific elements of character upon which democracy rests:

> At the base of all popular government lies individual self-control; and that requires both intelligence, so that the true relation of things may be perceived, and also the moral qualities which make possible patience, kindly consideration for others, a willingness to do justice, a sense of honorable obligation, and capacity for loyalty to certain ideals. Men must be willing to sacrifice something of their own apparent individual interests for the larger interests of city, State, country; and without that willingness successful popular government is impossible.

A man retiring at the age of sixty-five in the year 1958 was fourteen years old when these words were spoken. It is likely that similar ideas found their way into his consciousness sometime between the beginning of his schooling and his first vote. Such ideas appear to have played a critical part in the political lives of our third category of legislators, the Reluctants. In this chapter we shall explore how character—in the old-fashioned sense—helps bring some members to the House, how it poses special problems of adjustment for them, and how they work these problems out in the course of adapting to legislative life.

These members are called Reluctants because they appear to be serving under protest, as indicated by their responses to questions about their nominations and future plans. Reading over the interview transcripts, one sometimes wonders how members of the group overcame their own arguments against accepting nomination. When a party leader first suggested to one Reluctant that he run, the prospective candidate "dismissed it as quickly as possible, and we made lighter conversation." Much later, when he was asked again, his reaction was quizzical: "What the hell makes them think that I could?" He continues: "I mean I truthfully didn't seek the nomination. . . . I did *not* seek the nomination at any time. I never dropped any hints. I never said anything to anyone that would make them believe that I would want to come to Hartford." Now that he is a legislator, he has "no political ambitions for the future" and "wouldn't want to come back here under conditions as they now are."

When the second Reluctant had been approached, several years previously, he had said, "No, nothing doing," because he had other things he wanted to do. "And I said, 'I don't want to get into that.' And I said that I thought there were plenty of others who would be more used to . . . that type of job than I have been. But anyway, they kept talking about it. And when we had our [party nominating] caucus, I practically told them I wouldn't do it. And they kept urging me, and I finally said, 'Well, it's up to you,' I said, 'I am not seeking a job.' " Despite repeated probes by the interviewer, he sticks to his intention to quit the legislature after one session.

A third Reluctant member "had no idea of going to the legislature any more than you have." Learning that others planned to nominate him at a meeting, he said, "No, you're not. I'm not going—I don't want to be bothered with it," and he went to the meeting "to stop it." After a number of adamant refusals he finally accepted: "I was drafted, you might say." As for the future, "this is first, last and always. I'm not looking—I told you before—I wasn't looking for anything and I'm not looking for anything more." He simply is "not going to be bothered" with further political work.

THE RELUCTANT PROFILES: RURAL AND RETIRED

The Reluctant category consists of the seventeen new member respondents who were low in activity and thought they probably would not return to the legislature for three or more future terms. Their profiles, indicating the extent of their differences from other first-term legislators, provide a preliminary outline of their legislative adaptation.

With the exception of the item on liking campaigning (perhaps because there was little of it) the Reluctant Legislative Activity Profile shows a relatively low level of participation in all phases of current political life. Judging from the interviews, a few Reluctants did campaign fairly energetically, at least in comparison with their general rate of activity. But the broad picture remains one of relative inactivity.

PROFILE 1. *Reluctant Legislative Activity*

	Reluctants	Other New Member Respondents	Difference
Originated action to get nomination	29%	43%	—14
Attended many meetings in campaign	35	51	—16
Likes campaigning very much*	58	38	+20
Attributes election to own campaign efforts	12	13	— 1
Often introduced self to others at first of session	76	84	— 8
Took an active part in major negotiations	47	67	—20
Was frequently sought for advice	24	51	—27
Achieved leadership or important committee post	0	35	—35
Considers self energetic rather than easy-going	59	62	— 3
Considers self more influential than others	35	56	—21
Self-rating as a legislator: superior or excellent	24	37	—13

* Indicates presession response and/or change during session: Reluctant N = 12, Other N = 71. All other responses are from postsession questionnaire: Reluctant N = 17, Other N = 79.

The Reluctant Political Ambitions Profile indicates a general lack of interest in political advancement. The possibility of accepting an appointive office was mentioned in a few of the interviews, generally as a less demanding alternative to running for election. It is interesting to note the two items for which we have pre- and postsession answers: in both cases the desire for further election activity declines. The Reluctant, then, appears relatively uninterested in a political career.

The Reluctant Political Background Profile is a mixed and interesting one. The Reluctant is likely to come from a community where there is little competition at election time. His family has taken some

PROFILE 2. *Reluctant Political Ambitions*

	Reluctants	Other New Member Respondents	Difference
Identifies self as a "politician"	35%	44%	— 9
Has considered seeking full-time elective office:			
Presession response*	41	44	— 3
Postsession response*	17	45	—28
Change during session	—24	+ 1	
Had considered full-time state appointive office*	33%	31%	+ 2
Was interested in district or state party office*	53	75	—22
Was interested in Assembly leadership position*	41	75	—34
Willingness to return for three or more future sessions:			
Presession response*	41	75	—34
Postsession response*	0	82	—82
Change during session	—41	+ 7	
Ran again for nomination or election to Assembly:			
In 1960	77%	81%	— 4
In 1962	41	44	— 3
Ran for or served in some government office (including Assembly) after initial session	94	90	+ 4

* See note for Profile 1.

interest in politics and he has held some minor elective office among the many boards and commissions so chosen in the typical rural town. He is not particularly impressed with the legislature as compared with the government work he has done at home where partisan politics is unusual.

Some items in the Reluctant Personal Data Profile require explanation. The age difference indicated is probably conservative; if the break in the data is made at age 50 rather than 40, the proportion of older Reluctants is 24 percentage points greater than that for other

PROFILE 3. *Reluctant Political Background*

	Reluctants	Other New Member Respondents	Difference
Parents interested in politics	76%	63%	+13
Relatives active in politics	77	61	+16
Occupation involves government contacts	41	52	—11
Had held party office*	50	51	— 1
Had held elective office*	67	41	+26
Had held appointive office*	33	39	— 6
Had long considered running for Assembly	59	56	+ 3
Reports some competition for nomination*	75	72	+ 3
Saw election chances as 50–50*	0	28	—28
Considers legislative activity most important has engaged in	53	58	— 5

* See note for Profile 1.

new members. Furthermore, every one of the six Reluctants interviewed had experienced some severe physical ailment, usually within
the past few years. And several of those who list their occupations as
other than retired are devoting considerably less than full time to
regular work. Thus the questionnaires probably underplay the characteristics of the Reluctant as elderly, or at least old before his time.

PROFILE 4. *Reluctant Personal Data*

	Reluctants	Other New Member Respondents	Difference
Sex: male	82%	77%	+ 5
Age: over 40	59	42	+17
Occupation: retired	24	9	+15
Education: above high school*	50	56	— 6
Income: over $8,000*	24	45	—21
Town population: over 5,000	24	70	—46
Resident in town: more than ten years	83	67	+16
Expects to remain in town	76	94	—18
Expects more income in ten years	53	61	— 8

* See note for Profile 1.

The two items about the future—expectations of "living in the same town ten years from now" and "making more income ten years from now"—are probably deceptive in a similar way. The negative differences, judging from marginal questionnaire comments and the interviews, reflect in some cases the respondent's doubt that he can expect to be among the living a decade hence, rather than any general expectation of poverty or lack of commitment to his community.

NOMINATIONS: THE WOOING OF THE ELDERS

The typical New England town has become progressively less typical in recent years in Connecticut. The village green, guarded by ancient elms and oaks, is benched and fenced and paved out of existence. Quiet country lanes are converted to parkways; stone walls are bulldozed under to make way for housing developments; the country store is replaced by the shopping center, the community hall by the drive-in movie. Perhaps the crowning blow is struck when the cemetery is removed from the center to the outskirts of town.

More significant than the physical changes have been the shifts in composition of population. First came the waves of European immigrants who had to be assimilated into a predominantly Yankee culture. Recently the invasion by the new suburbanites has upset a number of traditional balances, ranging from the school budget to the more delicate equilibria among ladies' clubs. These shocks have been felt in politics as well, affecting patterns of recruitment profoundly.[3]

But such developments have been far from uniform in the state. Some small towns remain much as they were fifty or even a hundred years ago. Others have managed to incorporate substantial numbers of newcomers without much alteration in their traditional ways. It is from these small rural towns, relatively undisturbed by the forces of modernity, that the Reluctant is likely to be recruited.

The system for nominating candidates in these towns tends to merge with the general social system. There is a continuity about village life that extends backward in time and outward in social space, wrapping the whole political process in a bundle of traditions, personal and family relationships, and community beliefs. Small-town political life reflects to an unusual degree the culture and society in which it takes place. The multitude of interconnections is too large to be dealt with in all its complexity here, but a few main relationships, of special importance to legislative nominations, need to be considered.

Community Social Life: Confined, Continuous, Integrated

Three social characteristics of the small, rural Connecticut town stand out as especially significant for politics: the narrowness of social contacts, their continuity in time, and the extensive overlapping of social roles.

The small-town citizen has fewer opportunities to choose his friends than the urbanite has. One is friendly with his neighbors or with no one. The significance of this narrowness is perhaps less in the stultifying effects it may have on deviant individuals (a phenomenon noted by many a novelist) than in the pressure it places on each friendship. People must derive the rewards of social intercourse from the available supply, without much choice in the matter. Unless one prefers solitude, he cannot afford to alienate those he meets again and again, at church, in the store, at social gatherings.

The continuity of social life over the years adds to the importance of maintaining interpersonal harmony and makes the problem more difficult in some ways. The small-town citizen is apt to have known most of his neighbors most of his life. Each encounter takes place within a context of memories—of promises kept and broken, school adventures, performance in prosperity and adversity. To these memories is added the expectation that the relationship will continue to exist far into the future. One is committed to his friends in a permanent way, unlike the more casual commitment to temporary acquaintances. Both of these time dimensions—the awareness of a common past and the anticipation of a common future—operate to make social behavior important and intense, dangerous and promising.[4]

When an individual deals with the same people in a large number of social roles, distinctiveness of any one role fades. The demarcation between role and personality is blurred. Both the role-player and his audience tend to see the *person*, the full collection of roles as integrated in the character and standing of the man, rather than any one particular side of him. "In a town," says one Reluctant, "you have to weigh the individual." The grocer, for example, may also be a churchman, Elk, creditor, PTA-er, volunteer fireman, father, part-time town assessor, gardener, and neighbor. His public character is compromised when he fails to act responsibly and consistently as he moves from one role to the next. He can no more separate his political activities from his other roles than he can divorce his business clientele from his church congregation, his family from the neighborhood. If the Advertiser's problem is one of bridging the gaps in a fragmented life—for example, by connecting politics and profession—the Reluctant's problems spring in part from his inability to untangle any one role from the others.

The Threats and Demands of Democracy

Small town social relations, then, are marked by an unusual degree of role integration, in contrast to the role fragmentation of the suburbanite. Yet even in the small town some persons must be singled out for governmental office, and the process of selection must be at least formally democratic. To be democratic the selection process must include at least formal conflict—the opposition of names on the ballot. Every two years, on schedule, democracy demands a fight. But precisely because of the nature of social relations in the small community, political conflict is threatening: threatening to the cohesion of the community, risky for the candidate. In larger communities campaigning may be more intense, but the conflict is softened by the anonymity of the candidate-voter relationship, by the temporary character of their encounter, and by the compartmentalization of "politics" as an arena separate from the main concerns of life. Lacking these conditions the small community must find other ways to satisfy the formal requirements of democracy without disrupting the system of social relations.

One of the Reluctants interviewed gives a fairly clear picture of some mechanisms for accomplishing this:

> Well, I don't think politically the town is very—takes such a serious part politically as a lot of the other towns and a lot of the larger places. Because in our town government we pick the man that's best suited for the job, and has the time and is willing to take it. And whether he's a Republican or a Democrat, why, we put him in there. And all our different organizations—the school board, and the library, and all those various organizations, why, we try to divide up the chairmanships, you know, on the committee, among both parties. And there's been no, ah, feuding [laughs] among the two parties at all. They're very amicable in our town. It's a small town.

Here we see in operation the following suppressors of conflict:

(1) Politics is not serious. There is no really important basis for controversy, and therefore it is to be treated lightly.

(2) The electoral decision is between individuals, not party groups. The scope of the contest is confined, does not involve competition between the wider-ranging party memberships. Thus such competition as exists affects only a relatively few personalities, leaving the community at large in peace.

(3) There are prizes enough for everyone—plenty of chairmanships and memberships, so that each party always wins something. The potential general conflict is reduced to a series of individual conflicts, with results that tend to cancel one another out. Neither political group risks complete defeat.

The main effects of these techniques are to restrict the scope and reduce the stakes of the election. But it is still necessary to make choices among the individuals who "have the time and are willing to take it." Our respondent posits a single criterion to be applied in such cases: the man "best suited for the job" is to be preferred. If this principle of selection could be applied definitely and automatically to each choice, the community would have found another way to bypass controversy. But neither the requirements of the job nor the personal qualities needed are clear. Elective offices consist mainly of boards and commissions to oversee the routine housekeeping functions of the town. Technical matters are the province of employees and expert consultants, such as the superintendent of schools and the town attorney. The citizen board is supposed to handle matters of policy, but, because the community is stable, big issues are few and far between. Similarly, at the state legislature level technical prerequisites and policy implications are seen only vaguely by small-town residents. Thus not many contenders are eliminated by the particular requirements of the job.

In the absence of such definite criteria the choice might turn on considerations of personal character—sound judgment, honesty, reliability. But these standards are difficult to apply *publicly* to the available candidates. How can the town stay amicable if the argument comes down to who is more honest? Small-town politicians appear to take pride in the contrast between their ways and those of the big city where the candidates blacken one another's characters with impunity.

Even the implication that one's opponent is a charlatan is to be avoided. Other standards, public ones, must be found that will detour the necessity for comparisons of personal virtue.

The easiest way out of these difficulties is probably the one most often followed by the rural community: avoid conflict by reelecting the incumbent. He tends to acquire a right to the job; the burden of proof is on those who would depose him, and they find it hard to say why he should step down. When he retires from office, the incumbent may be accorded the right to pick his successor, thus postponing the problem indefinitely. This system of inheritance,[5] like the rotation system in some larger constituencies, represents a compromise with democracy, one that serves important nonpolitical functions.

Surveying these techniques for avoiding conflict, one begins to see how rarely the rural community experiences a true contest among individuals, much less a full-scale, all-out, town-wide political fracas. But occasionally the incumbent, in good impartial style, refuses to choose among his friends; and the out-party, in most cases, does go through the motions of nominating an opposition candidate. In these circumstances the question of choice can no longer be completely avoided. What criteria are the town committees and the electorate likely to use?

The Reluctant's Availability

Judging from the interviews, the qualities sought in political leadership are precisely those that will help guard against the threats to community social relations posed by the requirements of democracy. The standards of selection fit closely the major social characteristics described above. It is almost as if the community recognizes that the dangers elections present can be averted only by using the election process to counteract them.

The Reluctant legislators who were interviewed have wide circles of friends in their communities: "And the reason I got elected from the town was because, I think, everybody knew me." Most of them have had occupations involving widespread and frequent contacts with their neighbors. Being enmeshed in the close network of personal friendships, these candidates will hesitate to bring up issues that would divide the community. Moderation comes naturally to the man with friends on all sides of all fences. Thus one Reluctant explains why he does not like a political scrap at home: "I'm not too keen on it—I don't know. Most of the people in town, as I say, I've known all my life, and most of the [other party] I know—a good many of them are close personal friends, and if any of them had run I definitely would not have run. Because I would not have wanted to get into a campaign with them. I mean, that's the way I feel. . . . In fact I had so many close [other party] friends that so many of them were accused of deserting their party and voting for me—which I didn't like either, because I didn't ask them to do it."

Most of the Reluctants have lived in their towns for a lifetime or the greater part of it, and expect to end their days in the same town. (One considers himself a newcomer after nearly a decade of residence.) Many of them are from old families in the community, a further evidence of their commitment to the past and future of the town.[6] Thus they lack the flexibility of the temporary resident. "As long as I live," one says, "I have to face them out there." This tends to make the candidate unusually conscious of the long-run implications of his acts, reinforcing his moderate tendencies and protecting the community from sudden disruptions. Here again, candidates are selected on the basis of criteria which dampen conflict.

Finally, Reluctants tend to be people involved in many social roles, with overlapping group connections. Our hypothesis is that this overlapping makes personal character especially important in the selection of candidates, because the stability of social relations depends on the continuity of individual performances as the person moves from role to role. As will be clear when we examine the interviews more closely, the criterion of personal character plays a highly significant role in the selection and attraction of Reluctants to office, although character is rarely a factor in the public debate.

Thus the Reluctant's style in social relations, his time perspective, and his personal character fit well with the needs of the community in which he lives.[7] The threatening aspects of politics are softened by choosing candidates who will resist the pressures toward conflict, innovation, and the emergence of distinctively political roles that are implicit in the democratic election process.

But candidate recruitment is a two-sided affair. The party leaders decide on the basis of certain criteria that certain individuals are available. Then the problem becomes one of persuading the potential candidate to run. As we have seen,[8] Reluctants require a good deal of persuasion. Part of this may be ceremonial—the courtship between party man and potential candidate follows a mannerly course from first flirtation to a marriage of purpose.[9] But the marriage does not always come off. Why has the recruitment effort succeeded in attracting these particular candidates to political effort? In a later section [10] we shall look more systematically into the reasons the Reluctant himself gives—his explanation at the deeper levels of personal motivation. Here we are concerned with factors in his social situation that contribute to his political availability.

Not all the Reluctants interviewed are old men, but most of them do share certain problems of adjustment typically encountered by the elderly. Several of the younger Reluctants, as has been mentioned, have been forced into early retirement or part-time work because of severe physical disabilities. Like the elderly, they must adjust to certain "insults to the self" which accompany retirement. Robert Havighurst has described a number of these changes, some of special relevance to political recruitment.[11] Old age brings loss of physical attractiveness, fear of bodily failure and helplessness, declining ability to perform a hard day's work. Seeking confirmation that he is still as good as younger men, the elderly person may look for opportunities to use his body even more intensively than previously. He overcultivates a garden patch, builds an addition to his house, takes up tennis, or travels to the point of exhaustion. Political activity can involve a good deal of physical stress and strain, including door-to-door canvassing, meetings late into the night, and, for the legislator, a long drive to and from the capitol every legislative day, not to mention the strain of sitting still and paying attention for hours on end. The Reluctant complains about these burdens, but they can serve important functions for him: showing that he can still take it, that he can outlast the youngsters, that his physical strength has not deserted him.

Retirement at 65 or so means that the old man suddenly finds himself unemployed, in a culture that places a high value on productive work, and bereft of the status and income accorded him in his middle age. "There is left the custom of respecting older people for what they once were, not for what they are. A few specific roles of older people become available, and have some value, such as those of grandparent, world traveler, village sage. But these are usually poor substitutes for the roles we have lost." [12] So a basic problem for the elderly person is to find assurance that he still counts for something. Service in a part-time government job offers a chance to demonstrate that one is still important. And the extra income is helpful—not only for maintaining one's standard of living but also in avoiding dependence on the children or on a degrading government dole.[13]

Recruitment to politics may be easier because the elderly man fears or dislikes loneliness. Havighurst refers to the "loss of supporting persons": "advancing years . . . rob us of the people who could best reassure us that we are still attractive people, worthy to be loved." [14] The death of lifelong friends, one's wife, or close relatives is disturbing; one may soon be left alone. The elderly may find it hard to strike up new friendships, especially with younger people whose pace and style of life are so different.

But political activity can be especially helpful with these problems. Small-town politics tends to be monopolized by the old-timers, and there is a sizable contingent of them at the state legislature. The small-town Reluctant can find in politics a ready-made group of his contemporaries to share his problems.

Reluctant legislators were asked how family and friends felt about the Reluctant's running for the House. In most cases they encouraged it. The family may find it particularly difficult to arrange routines and emotions to accommodate a somewhat irritable old fellow at home for most of the day. More important, they want him to be content, and they realize that he needs a meaningful extra activity. We can see this need in the description one Reluctant gives of his retirement: "If I wanted to get up at eight o'clock in the morning, I got up. If I wanted to get up at six, I got up. In other words—but of course around a place like that there's no one to take care of it and there's lots of loose ends. If I want to work an hour or so, I could straighten out this, I could straighten out that, you know. I kept busy around the place. And I told my wife when I came in, 'I've been busy all day but I don't know what I've done.' " Another notes that his wife "wanted me to run. And that had to do with my physical disability, too. She thought that I was settling down too much, getting too close to home. I mean, she thought that I had slowed myself down too much. She thought it would do me good to get out and stay in contact with people the way I always had."

These are some of the reasons why the party recruiter may have good luck in persuading retired or partially disabled men to take a nomination. Politics offers a chance to do meaningful work, some independence, and companionship with contemporaries.

REACTIONS: THE STRANGENESS OF THE PLACE

> INTERVIEWER: What have been some of the enjoyable aspects of the legislative experience?
>
> RELUCTANT: Well, it's work.

The Reluctant finds plenty of work to be done when he arrives at the state capital to begin his first session. Later on, he complains a little about fatigue in traveling and sitting through long committee hearings, but generally he seems to enjoy putting his energies to some use and getting acquainted with other old-timers in the legislature. His report of initial reactions emphasizes the strangeness of the place: "Well, it's all been new to me, as far as that's concerned. I—of course I've heard of the legislature all my life, but I was never in there. And I'm just commencing to realize some of the workings of it. It's all new to me."

This respondent is not being entirely accurate when he says everything is new to him in the House. He has held an elective office back home; he knows something already about committee work, voting procedures, budget-making, and the like. His community activities in a variety of civic organizations have given him some experience in negotiation, agenda planning, and the preparation of resolutions. Compared to the Spectator, the Reluctant arrives in Hartford with a good deal of general political savvy in his possession. He does not have to overcome a total unfamiliarity with law-making, but rather faces some large and specific differences in degree between the home-town traditions, which have become second nature to him, and the new legislative situation. A close look at the reactions of three Reluctants to their experiences in the House brings out the features they find most disturbingly new there.

Jim Pickens: "It's a League of Nations"

Jim Pickens and I had a long, leisurely conversation on a wintry New England day. He felt he had had so many interesting new experiences in the past six months that "If I knew how to do it, I could write a book or a darned good story" about them. An elderly, rail-thin Yankee, he had retired from the grocery business several years before being persuaded to run for the legislature. His job background, he said, had "been a help—to meet people. And all kinds of people, because there's good, bad, and indifferent, I don't care where you go."

His church work and other civic activities helped too: "It all builds up to help you meet the situation" in the legislature. Campaigning in his small town, Jim had canvassed house to house and "learned a lot about my town that I didn't know." "I found a lot of nice young people in town," he says, "and I found some things that weren't so pleasant—there are some people living in some places that I don't want to live." Even though he "got a fine reception all over" and "didn't get any doors slammed in my face," he did not enjoy campaigning much: "I don't like it anyway. It just was one of those things that I knew I had to do and I went and did it." He disliked it mainly because, he explains, "I hate to ask anybody for anything." On the other hand, he was pleased and surprised to find people who remembered some of the good things he had done for them in the past: "I never realized when I did the things that I did, that I was helping myself for the future."

Jim had "seen pictures of the legislature before" but had never visited a session. On inauguration day he "just wondered what's ahead of me"—and, he adds, "You know, I'm still wondering what's ahead of me."

> You've got to keep your mind on what you're doing—and you don't know—well, it's so different to me. You take fellows have been in there four or five years, they enjoy working the bills through, something like that, getting a bill through. But of course, that—to me, I wouldn't know how to start—I'd have to go and ask you or somebody else. See what I mean? I've got to depend on somebody else to do it for me. I wouldn't know how to—well, I think I could commence now and start and perhaps work a bill through.

> And that's the question: "What to do?" Because there's bigger things back of some of these things than a greenhorn can grasp. You know? Some of these things there's something in back of them that you don't know.

If he had had a college education, he could "grasp things quicker"; as it is, he has to "learn the hard way."

As might be expected, Jim gets tired in committee meetings, feels the strain of the long daily drive to Hartford, finds the procedural intricacies somewhat confusing. But these problems have not bothered him excessively: "I don't know that I've had anything that I'd want to complain a great deal about."

One of the major adjustment tasks for any new member is learning to get along with the people in the House. Jim has experienced this problem—"I don't get acquainted too well"—although he is generally a tolerant and open person. His conscious attitude toward others is an accepting one. Even so, he illustrates nicely a difficulty that seems to be of special importance to the Reluctants: adjusting to people who are not only strangers but also a fundamentally different sort of folk.

Discussing enjoyable aspects of the legislature, Jim says, "You meet nice people, you meet all kinds of people—but you meet some people who you'd like to see again. There's all kinds in there." What are some of the kinds that stand out in Jim's mind? Asked how he would categorize them, he replies tersely: "It's a League of Nations."

> INTERVIEWER: League of Nations? How's that?
> JIM: There's all nationalities in there.
> INTERVIEWER: You mean, for instance, the Italian and Irish—
> JIM: Italians, Irish, Scots, Jews, Germans, French, Negroes—they're all in there. This is a typical, what I would call a typical American meeting. You know, the United States is made up of the whole world. There's people in there from—born in most any country you want to mention in the world. America is the boiling pot of the world, isn't it? You've got a fair picture.
>
> The Irish had their St. Patrick's day celebration in there, and the Jews were passing around those unleavened crackers or something the other day for you to eat. 'Cause it's Passover. Sure. True, you might say—I don't know how you'd want to mention—there's all kinds. Italians . . . Norwegians, Swedes, Austrians, Russians. You haven't got one of those books, have you?[a] One of those books that tells all the names and tells where they're born?

Jim's special sensitivity to nationalities is evident. At no time does he indicate any active dislike for foreigners or ethnic minorities, but his selection of this type of categorization indicates its salience for him. This theme is clarified when, later in the interview, Jim describes his own origins. He grew up among

a. The "book" indicates the name, party, age, occupation, town, vote, past legislative tenure, and seat position, as well as place of birth for each member.

the *old stock*. The old New Englanders, now, I'm talking about.

INTERVIEWER: Is that right?

JIM: The old New Englanders, I'm talking about. The old names without the "skis" on them. And that's—those were the people of the town: Turner, Wells, Adams. Blake. Gates. Knox . . . Come right down to the house. [He is naming his childhood neighbors.] Right down below there was, right aside me was Clinton. Booth. Peel. Brewster. Pickett. Tyler. Wren. No "skis" on those names. Those were the neighbors I was born into, you might say.[15]

It would be a mistake, I think, to interpret these remarks of Jim's as antiforeign, anti-ethnic, or anti anything else. It is the suddenness of contact, the difficulties of communicating with people of strange background, that make this dimension of his social environment salient and somewhat bewildering. The effect is heightened by the contrast with the ethnic homogeneity of his boyhood environment.

Another contrast, however, does bring out a certain aggressiveness. Jim himself has vivid memories of his hard struggle for a living in his home town. He got through the depression of the thirties by intense work and austere habits. In the legislature he meets people who seem to him to be seeking a different way out of their troubles.

INTERVIEWER: Are there any of those groups that you'd just as soon weren't there or that don't contribute as much as others?

JIM: Why, I think I can see a group working there that I don't like.

INTERVIEWER: What's that?

JIM: There's too many, what-you-call labor fellows, I think. . . . I'm not opposed to labor. But I think labor in some places has gone too far. There's got to be a reckoning some day, the way I look at it. . . . If it hadn't been for unions, labor would have been in mud up to here. You've got to have them, there's no question about it, but they don't use—*I don't give a continental!* —you aren't hiring me unless you're going to make some money on it. And you got a right to. Because you've got to produce what you produce so that it can be sold in competition, haven't you? Or else you're not in business.

Here again, Jim's attitudes, developed over a lifetime, conflict with those he meets in the House. The aggressiveness is under easy control—

he is no fanatic. But he finds it hard to get acquainted with those whose values and backgrounds are apparently so different. To the delegates from the provinces the League of Nations must have seemed a strange place indeed.

Paul Kincaid: "People that are stampeded—it's dangerous"

Paul Kincaid is a husky, bald, straight-backed, middle-aged farmer. Because, several years ago, he suffered a severe injury to his right arm which still gives him considerable pain, he has had to slow down. His nomination was "just one of those things—you happen to be in the place they wanted you at the time they wanted you." The campaign was a low-pressure one, but Paul sometimes "got madder than hell" when his supposed friends circulated malicious rumors about him to the effect that "because you were running for the House, you're just too god-damned ambitious." He was "very embarrassed about going up to a door and rapping on it" at first, but finally conquered these feelings and came to enjoy it.

When he first arrived in the House chamber, Paul felt awe-struck by the place:

> Well, of course it looked like a—as many things do—it looked like you would never be able to become a part of it, if you know what I mean. Here's all these people, all these seats, all this bigness, and how could you ever break in and become part of it? I stood there just wondering if I had done what was right, if I would be able to hold up my end of the bargain, if the folks back home would want me to come if they knew how I felt at that moment, you know what I mean? It was a little bit, ah— it caused some concern.

But he had been associated with some "very, very high caliber people, very sharp thinkers" in the past, and thus "soon lost my fear of the people over here."

Paul's more heartfelt reactions to legislative work and his role in it emerge when he is asked to rate himself as a legislator:

> PAUL: Well, I might say this—that I feel rather inadequate.
> INTERVIEWER: What are some of the reasons for that?
> PAUL: I just don't think that I have knowledge enough of what's going on.

Asked what personal characteristics of his have helped him as a legislator, Paul replies, "Golly, sir, I don't know." He finds the work complicated, tiring, and—most significantly—too fast for him. Paul Kincaid illustrates clearly how the pace of legislative life tends to conflict with the Reluctant's slower habits.

"If you have ever tried to rush most of the farmers—" Paul breaks off and then continues, "You see, they're good people, and they do things in a little slower way than a lot of business people do. And as soon as you try to rush them, a percentage of them became suspicious. So the only thing to do is just let them stew a couple of minutes. When they're cooked, they'll tell you."

Paul sees himself in the same category: "I don't like to give opinions and make decisions when you don't have time to weigh them a little more." He feels that "tincture of time" is a great remedy, that "time takes care of most of the untruths," and that "anything that is good is good tomorrow as well as today." Paul uses these standards to judge the legislature and develops a metaphorical explanation:

> I didn't think that we could stampede anybody in a responsible position. I didn't think that people could be stampeded quite so easily. I know there are many times in our life that we have to make quick decisions and snap decisions, but they usually don't involve something that has been studied and thrashed and mauled as well as we did maul.
>
> We all know that in a—in something like a football game, for instance, decisions have to be made quickly and plans have to be changed. You have such a short time to do these things in. And maybe it was boxing—might decide on one strategy and change his mind when he gets a punch in the nose. But people like to compare our activities sometimes to a football game—we have to shift and move rather quickly—I suppose there are times. But not when things have been thrashed out pretty well.
>
> INTERVIEWER: A somewhat different picture from a football game?
>
> PAUL: It certainly is. A quarterback's fine, a captain's fine. I've played a little baseball, and many times I've changed my mind soon after the activity started. But it can't be compared to a session of the legislature. Some people like to use it as an argument, but I don't think it stands up.

The image of the legislative "stampede" crops up again and again in Paul's interview: "I'm not too happy about some people being stampeded at times"; "And the stampede, even though it stampeded to my way of thinking, I still don't like to be connected with people that are stampeded—it's dangerous." "Who the hell stampeded who? Who did what to who? If you ever find out let me know"; "to be stampeded is a lot of nonsense."

Paul has done much hard physical work all his life and, like Jim Pickens, he feels a certain antagonism toward those with "socialistic views." "I guess socialism would be a wonderful thing if you could make it work, but I don't know where anybody's ever made it work." He admires a man who "didn't have too many socialistic views—kind of an old-fashioned man." He draws the analogy between the management of a household and that of a government: neither should spend more than it takes in. These familiar themes show again the contrast between the Reluctant's past, in which an unbalanced budget in household or local government was a sign of failure, and the strange economic ideas many legislators seem to have today.

Paul did not grow up in the town he represents, although he has lived there for many years. At first he "figured that you could never become a native—either you had to be born there or you'd be an outsider forever." Judging from his interview, he has managed to adapt quite well to the town's mores, however, and perhaps his newcomer status works to make him especially sensitive to questions of pace and timing in the legislature. In any event, Paul finds it somewhat difficult and threatening to ride along with the political stampede, a movement headed in directions he would just as soon not follow.

Dan Thomas: "I feel kind of lost still"

Dan Thomas looks like a senator—a big, genial man with a florid face and thick, white hair. He used to be a miller before he retired six years ago; he knew most of his rural neighbors quite well. Dan was an active community "organization man" when he was prevailed upon to run for the legislature: "I enjoy meeting people, and I always have." There were those in his party who wanted to sling a little mud during the campaign, but Dan wouldn't hear of it; he said to them, "I'll tell you right now, if you're putting out anything like that you can count me out right now. I've lived here all my life and I've got friends in both parties and people who are not in either party—

independents and everything. And if I can't run on my own reputation without doing that, I don't want it." The campaign was decorous even by small-town standards.

Dan's first impressions of the legislature are familiar ones: "Oh, golly—it's all new. And when we first went in there, I hardly knew anybody and knew nothing of the routine or anything." He is "gradually getting acquainted" with the people, but the routines still puzzle him. On the day Dan was interviewed, an important question was scheduled to come before the House. Dan understands that "both leaders want to suspend the rules, but there are others who want it to take its regular course. And, ah . . . that's another question—that's something for me to—you see, I don't know any of these things." Dan found that "a lot of the work is done outside [the chamber]. It's been discussed and more or less planned and found out what the sentiment was on the different bills before they're brought into the House, and more or less planned out a plan of action on them, because otherwise it would be—would have to be more or less like that. But I haven't heard too much about that, myself."

Dan's reactions to the strangeness of the legislature seem to collect around the political procedures, the formalities, the routines of the place. He thus provides an example of still another set of Reluctant difficulties: the confusion felt by the small-town member when he confronts a system of decision-making which is highly structured and complicated, in contrast to the more direct, man-to-man relationships he is used to at home. That Dan has felt this problem rather intensely is clear when he says: "And of course with this job, I do my best to find out all the various angles of it, to do my best while I'm here at it. I doubt very much if I would consider keeping up with it—in fact, I know I wouldn't. I'm getting too old, for one thing." His sense of confusion is shown when he describes how he organizes his day:

> Because lots of times you get up there and you want to look over the bills that are coming up, and, for hearing on the committee, at home, but lots of times you get out there and find out there are a lot of things you didn't know till you got out there and, or you looked at your legislative bulletin for the day and you find out there are things you didn't even know were coming up the day before, or maybe they're coming up for the next day, and you want to get the ones from the last day, so as to look them up for the next day, so—

Dan has done his best to take notes in committee, has "tried to analyze" the bills, has worked hard "to get the routine." But he still feels that "it's pretty hard to know what's what" in the House. He concludes that he is "kind of lost still, I mean, on some of these things—especially when they're talking about the different political, ah, angles of it, you know? I don't know too much about that." Thinking it over, he decides he would "rather be, as they say, a big toad in a small puddle than a small toad in the ocean, or something like that."

Dan echoes Jim Pickens when he is asked to categorize the members:

> Well, goodness, in looking over the history and all that, and meeting the people, there's quite a variety. There are all types, to lawyers, to farmers, and businessmen and laborers—there are all types. And all nationalities, too. X—I think he was born in Yugoslavia, wasn't he? I think so. And Y was born in Holland. Goodness—in looking over that—I've forgotten, I counted up how many people were born in countries outside the United States and where they were born. They might have been born there and still have been United States citizens, but they just tell where they were born. And from all over the United States, and from all types of work, too.[16]

It is interesting that one of Dan's first techniques for getting oriented in the House was to count up how many were born where. As in Jim's case, there seems to be little if any animosity behind this categorization —just a feeling of strangeness, of being in a situation that is alien in several senses.[17]

The Reluctant's Discomforts

Reluctants experience neither the Spectators' relatively intense pleasure nor the Advertisers' relatively intense pain in the legislature. They are perhaps best described as being uncomfortable there. Their discomforts arise primarily from the adjustive burdens they must try to cope with at an age when personal change comes hard. And the changes that the legislative environment seems to demand are larger ones for the Reluctant than for others, because his past is in such sharp contrast with his present. To review some of these contrasts and the problems they pose:

First, the Reluctant is struck by the *exotic people* in the legislature, people whose strangeness reaches back to their birthplaces and their fundamental values. His home-town social relations have been relatively intimate ones; the Reluctant tends to view people as either close friends or outlanders. He finds it difficult to establish and maintain an intermediate type of relation, an acquaintanceship. The task is made harder when the others seem to speak a different language.[b]

Second, the Reluctant is impressed by the *headlong pace* of legislative decision-making. His life-style is attuned to the seasons, not the eight-hour day. Back home there was no hurry; tomorrow would do as well for almost any important personal or governmental decision. A sense of legitimacy, whether for a person or a policy, was acquired through years of responsible behavior, months of discussion. In the legislature, the Reluctant feels rushed and therefore suspicious that something is being put over on him. The scenes change too swiftly for him to follow the plot.[c]

Third, Reluctants tend to be baffled by the *intricate processes* of lawmaking. Sometimes in the home town the issues themselves had seemed complex—there are a lot of angles to the question which road to pave next—but the *process* was definite, simple, and familiar. There was little necessity for paperwork, little need for procedural folderol. The Reluctant is used to a personal frame of reference in decision-making: once one understands the main characters involved in any civic drama, one can predict the outcome. But in the legislature one encounters group coalitions, broader political relationships, multiple committees and caucuses, and an unfamiliar leadership structure. The task is divided into so many parts that fit together in so many complex and changing patterns that the Reluctant feels a sense of disorientation. Or, the strangeness of the legislature may be reflected in the contrast between certain puritanical ideas and big city ways, as illustrated in the attitudes of these three Reluctants on alcohol:

> JIM: You've got to be a good mixer and sometimes I wonder if you can be a good mixer if you don't use liquor, but I don't. I tell you, I think a lot of people think liquor helps—they think

b. In the questionnaires, Reluctants were least likely to find "social affairs connected with the legislature" "very enjoyable." Reluctants 6%, others 25% (N's = 17, 79). And they are most likely to choose the statement "Legislative work may be socially unpleasant, but the opportunity to accomplish something worthwhile makes up for this" rather than an alternative stressing enjoyment of the "opportunity to get to know many new and interesting people." Reluctants 50%, others 16% (N's = 12, 71). Cf. Earl R. Carlson, "Motivation and Set in Acquiring Information about Persons," *Journal of Personality*, 29 (1961), 285–93.

c. More Reluctants than other members report: "On roll call votes, I often made up my mind at the last minute." Reluctants 47%, others 17% (N's = 17, 79).

it helps them, but in the overall picture, I don't think it does.

PAUL: I'd like to devote more time to it, and I don't mean to go down to the City Bar and sit around drinking cocktails.

DAN: At some social affairs, they just get there and have a good time and probably drink and things like that.

Another Reluctant says, "I'm not terribly social minded. I am not a social lion and—I am not opposed to alcohol, but on the other hand, I don't care for it. I certainly don't feel like going and spending a lot of money on cocktails that I don't like (laughs). After other people have had two or three cocktails, I don't enjoy them any more. So that's one part of politics that I'm not terribly interested in."

SELF: THE CALL OF DUTY

The Advertisers in the legislature are apt to characterize the members we have called Reluctants as "retired bums" or "political hobbyists." If in fact the Reluctants were in Hartford for an extended vacation with pay, they would feel little concern about the difficulties of adjusting to legislative life. Why would they bother to get to know the strange people there, to keep up with the pace of work, to master the complex procedures? The general answer is a simple one: they feel that they should. More than most other members, the Reluctants are strong on doing their duty. Being the kind of people they are, they can no more relax and enjoy the legislative show than the Advertiser can—but for very different reasons.

The Advertiser's moral sense focuses primarily on two main facets of his self-image: his rate of progress toward certain individual achievement goals and his personal integrity. Reluctants, on the other hand, tend to stress, first, the debts they owe to others, living and dead, and, secondly, the personal virtues that make social relations pleasant and peaceable. They feel a strong sense of obligation—not guilt; they feel socially restrained—not ashamed of themselves. Generally they seem to be somewhat happier, more easygoing people than either the Advertisers or the Spectators, and thus are best described in terms of attitudes rather than inner drives and conflicts.[d] But these attitudes are not less significant because they are shallower; they help considerably in understanding why the Reluctant is to be found in

d. Reluctants are least likely to agree with the questionnaire statement "I have sometimes wished I were another person." Reluctants 18%, others 37% (N's = 17, 79).

the legislature in the first place, and why he behaves as he does when he gets there.

The Duty to Serve

When Jim Pickens is asked why he allowed himself to be dragooned into accepting the nomination, he reaches far back into the past for an explanation:

> Well, of course, my father lived in this town all his life, and the town has been good to him and, well, he's been good to the town. And I thought to myself—of course, father's dead and all that— but I said to myself, Dad would say, "You've got the time, you ought to do it." So that's about the way I felt, that I was doing what was really set out for me to do, that I should do. I felt a, well, I felt duty bound to it, that's all. It wasn't a great hankering that I had. . . . I thought I owed it to, to the years back, not— I know Dad would have told me to have done it, said, "You go ahead and do it," Dad would say, "Well, I'll get you by anyway." And he got me by, but I come by, thank the Lord, I got by myself.

"When you say what's helped you," Jim says, "at my age it's what I had in back of me—it ain't what's up front, as they tell in the cigarettes." Jim returns to his parents again when he is asked to describe the qualities of a good legislator:

> Well, I don't know, of course, a good legislator—you've got to go back. If you weren't any good as a man in the first place, you wouldn't be any good as a legislator. You go way back to your mother and father, the way they brought you up. They give you —if they give you ideals, that you was always looking down at your feet instead of looking up—see what I mean? I did the things that I have accomplished the way that my mother and father instilled into me the principles that I should look to— bigger than I am all the time. Of course, if I was satisfied all the time there would be nobody that was—I'd be one of those fellows that if you could buy them for what they're worth and sell them for what they think they're worth, you'd make money.

The Reluctant interviews are dotted with references to the duty to serve. Jim complains some about the stresses and strains of legislating, but adds, "I don't call them unpleasant—they're doing a duty." He must prefer the town's interests to his own; "the other way would be selfish." Paul Kincaid feels that "responsibility itself tends to make life worth living." He accepted the nomination in part because "the world is full of people who complained but never did anything about it." He doubts very much that he will come back to the legislature, but in the home town "if I can be of any help I most certainly want to be."

Dan Thomas takes a great deal of pride in his home town: "People come in there—we have all types of people—they come right in there and they just enter right into the spirit of the town and take hold. Both of us [he and his wife], all our lives, have been in things—public-spirited things—and I don't know as we've accomplished much, but I think we've helped out some." And "anything you can do in the town to help out—that's what I've always wanted to do." Dan reports occasion after occasion when he took some community role "just to help them out." This desire to be helpful was evident for some of the Reluctants in the interview situation. They would interrupt to say such things as: "Well, I hope my answers are going to help you."

The emphasis in these passages is clear: the Reluctant sees himself as duty bound to be of service to others, particularly his small-town constituents. This need to serve comes from the inside, grows out of a deeply ingrained sense of civic duty. There is little here of the Spectator's somewhat maudlin worship of leaders, or the Advertiser's somewhat compulsive demand that he do things *right* or not at all. The Reluctant's press is toward playing some useful, helping part in whatever tasks the situation offers. He wants to "enter into the spirit of" things, not vicariously but actively, not apparently but really.

Are the Reluctants content with their performance? Are they the self-satisfied old fakers they are often made out to be? Not if we take seriously their own statements. Thus Jim hesitates to give himself a rating—"I don't ever like to talk about myself"—and then goes on to confess that "I don't feel that I'm the equal of a lot of others" in the House. He has "worried probably all my life" about his shortcomings. He explains "I don't like to be satisfied. I like to think that there's something bigger than I'm doing, see what I mean? The fellow that's satisfied, I don't like that. If I was satisfied, there's a lot of things that I never would have accomplished." Paul strikes a similar note when he says, "I have never rated myself very high in anything—I've always felt there was always so much room for improvement." We recall Dan's repeated feelings of incompetence.[18] Even in old age the Reluctant continues to feel a certain tension between his ideals and his performance. His conscience is very much alive and its force is probably increased by his feelings of being a somewhat unnecessary old person at home. Another Reluctant, asked if the legislative experience has been an enjoyable one so far, illustrates this theme clearly: "No, I wouldn't say it has been enjoyable. But that I think is a matter of your own personal makeup. I am not—I'm not easily amused. I think that I'm more serious, and perhaps even a solemn sort of character. And I'm not there for the purpose of finding any enjoyment. The enjoyment that I could have found would have been in accomplishments, would have been in seeing that things are done well, efficiently, and purposefully. And I'm not able to find that type of enjoyment."

The Duty to Keep Peace

A lesser theme in the Reluctant's self-image deserves mention. He seems to have incorporated, as a result of training in home and community, a set of social values that cluster around the idea of preventing conflict. He admires workers, but not fighters. Clearly negative references to others are quite rare in the Reluctant interviews, but the few that occur are aimed at disturbers of the peace. Dan mentions a person at home who "is interested in the town" and "I like him ever so much," but "he doesn't get out and mix with people," "antagonizes people," "gets off on the wrong foot with everything and gets the people against him." Paul refers to a "back-biting little bastard" whose "thought is always 'Who can I push aside, or step on, or cut down, or double-cross to accomplish what I want?'" Jim makes no such references but mentions a situation as undesirable when, "if we're talking on opposite points, we'll soon have an argument perhaps on our hands."

Dan sums up this value nicely when he says, "I try to get along with everybody—I don't want any enemies at all," and "I'd rather do most anything—I mean, if I think I'm right on something and I think someone else is wrong, I'm not going to let them put over on me. But outside of that, you know, I can sort of detour around a lot of things and still get your point without, lots of times, trying to force it." When we recall Jim's conscious tolerance of the outlanders he meets in the legislature, Paul's concern that he not be considered too ambitious, and Dan's general air of easy geniality, the Reluctant's peaceable qualities seem evident. The point here is that these qualities appear as a positively valued part of the Reluctant's self-image, as something more than protective strategies for avoiding involvement in controversies.

Duty, Desire, Disability

Let us attempt to draw together the threads of the description so far in preparation for an examination of the Reluctant's adjustive strategies. We have a picture of the man's social situation at home and the ways in which that helps to account for his presence in the legislature. We have taken a close look at his reactions to political life, and isolated certain features of it that are problematical for him. And we have tried to account for his need to seek satisfactory solutions for these problems by studying how he sees himself. These steps parallel those we have taken with the Spectator and the Advertiser, moving from the external situation to the internal one. The approach is the same but the results in each case are contrasting ones.

The main features of the Reluctant's adjustment as developed so far are clear. His major difficulties in adjusting to legislative life are due to the jarring contrast between his habitual way of life, nurtured over a lifetime in the small-town environment, and certain factors in the legislative environment. The people, the pace, and the procedures he finds here seem strange to him. His advanced age, educational limitations, and lack of social skills make flexible adaptation to the strangenesses difficult, yet he feels a duty and a desire to overcome them in order to be of service. The alternative—relaxing, loafing through the session, playing the casual political dabbler—comes unnaturally to him after long years of hard work. If the Reluctant's physical disabilities sap his energies, his moral inability to let his constituents down makes him try to assert such powers as he has.[e]

These factors, then, help to account for the pressures he feels to adapt himself to life in the legislature. We turn now to an examination of some of the strategies he uses in pursuit of that goal.

e. Reluctants, in their questionnaires, agree more than others that "Far too many legislators do not take the work seriously enough." Reluctants 59%, others 44% (N's = 17, 79). They choose the statement "Political deals, 'horse-trading,' and vote-swapping are morally wrong and have no place in a state legislature" over an alternative characterizing these practices as necessary. Reluctants 58%, others 35% (N's = 12, 71). And they are more likely to bring to bear "my own personal moral convictions" on legislation, rather than "general American ideals of liberty and justice for all." Reluctants 82%, others 39% (N's = 17, 79).

STRATEGIES: RETREAT BY STAGES

The Reluctant's conscience pushes him toward participation; his feelings of incompetence to cope with the strange legislative environment tend to pull him back into himself. In the midst of this pulling and hauling, he attempts to work out a series of partial adaptations that will satisfy both these tendencies at once. If he cannot become a full-fledged legislator, he tries to take at least some part. If this proves too much for him, he begins to withdraw his interest and attention from legislative work. And if, at last, he finds he cannot make any headway as a member, he leaves. Of our four types of legislators, the Reluctant comes closest to fitting the pattern of withdrawal. But it is a strategic retreat by stages he practices, not a headlong flight from the scene of battle. And this process is a reversible one; in certain circumstances he may enter the fray again.

The Retreat from Politics

Each of our three Reluctants takes care to differentiate himself from the stereotype of the politician. Asked the standard question, "How did you get interested in politics?", Jim replies, "I was never interested in politics—never had time for politics." He had been on a local board where "you're elected when you're nominated," but "Oh, I was never a politician." He "never gave politicians a great deal of thought," "never expected to have anything in connection with it." And he recalls that "My father used to say, 'Politics makes funny bedfellows,' and I still think he knew what he was talking about." The man he beat in the election was "a politician all the way through," who "lived on politics all his life."

Paul Kincaid connects politics with the rapid, shifty decisions he dislikes, "these decisions where people all rush into one little office and beat each other over the head and come up with an answer." He separates himself from the politicians: "You know, there are people who are trained politicians, and I'm afraid I'm at their mercy, because I don't know anything about campaigning, I don't know anything about how to create discontent and what have you." He "didn't have any great knowledge of politics or how they work" and, in fact, "never knew whether I was a Republican or Democrat, to tell the truth." He found some right on both sides, so never felt that he was "strictly a party man."

Dan makes perhaps the cleanest separation from the politicians when he is asked what he thinks of the party leaders:

> Well, of course, politicians are in a class by themselves, I think. It's a profession for them, I think. Just like a lawyer with his job, it's a profession for him. And it's a different attitude, I think, than for a person who is just a—they're party men, and a man who's just going up to represent a town or a city, they're probably just as interested in a way, but it's just the different way of getting at the different things. No question about that they know what they're doing. And with a politician, I think it's really party first and, ah, maybe other things afterwards.

Dan sees legislative social affairs as primarily for the "what-you-call politicians" who are trying to "keep in with the powers" in hopes of getting jobs. "And that's one of the reasons why I don't care too much about going to them."

Like his feelings of separateness from the "foreigners" in the House, the Reluctant's feeling of separation from politicians is not marked by aggressive sentiments. Dan ties these two feelings together when he says that "In politics, there's always a lot of Irish, anyways, and you have a lot of Italians," but he rejects neither category. The political leaders in the Assembly are admired for their competence, receive sympathy for the cares they must bear, and are accorded respect for their interest in legislative matters by the Reluctants.[f] But the politician is perceived as inhabiting a different world, performing strange arts. By contrast, as Dan says, "There is no politics in it at all in our town."

Now it is never quite clear in the Reluctant interviews just what they mean by "politics." The ambiguities of the word make it available as a convenient residual category: whatever the Reluctant finds discomforting, strange, conflictful about the process of nominations, elections, or legislating, he can characterize as "politics" and thus push it away from himself. Scanning the interview transcripts, we find a great many situations and individuals placed in this category by one or another of the Reluctants. Persons long in public office or ambitious for it, enthusiastic partisans, people with extensive experience in party work, legislative party leaders—all are "politicians." Situations characterized as political include most conflict situations at home or in the

---

f. All the Reluctants, in their questionnaires, choose "Most career politicians are trying to do a good job for the public" over "Most career politicians are mainly interested in what is in it for them." Reluctants 100% others 83% (N's = 12, 71).

legislature, as well as the whole range of informal negotiations in the lobby and at social affairs. The boundaries of the "political" are blurred and flexible; the Reluctant can exile a good many troublesome problems to this foreign territory.[19]

Three other adaptive strategies help the Reluctant to justify his inability to participate fully in legislative life. Two of them—the tendency to see legislative debate as essentially meaningless, and the habit of focusing attention on the harmonious aspects of the legislature—are similar to techniques used by Spectators and Advertisers, but have a few twists peculiar to the Reluctant. There are minor complaints about the time consumed in unnecessary debate, the failure of talk to persuade anybody, and Paul's mild disdain for those who "talk with their brain in neutral and their tongue engaged." In addition, the Reluctant explains that he can stay silent because others say what he would say; so long as the idea is expressed, it is unimportant that someone else expressed it. Thus Paul mentions that there have been "several times when I fully intended to have something to say, and as the committee hearing progressed, or in the House, someone has expressed my thoughts, so it wasn't necessary." And Jim says, "I don't want to talk —there's plenty of talk in there. They'll all talk and express my opinion." The Reluctant hears the legislative talk in the context of the task to be done. While he shows some trepidation about speechmaking, he is less concerned than the Spectator on this account. Unlike the Advertiser, he is content that others express his thoughts, so long as they get expressed somehow.

Reluctants report talking more easily in committee executive sessions, where the atmosphere is, perhaps, quite like that of the home-town boards they are familiar with. But the Reluctant may be somewhat inhibited even in small-scale informal conversations: his style in these situations has been learned in home-town gossip sessions, where one must be careful not to go too far. Thus Paul wants to avoid "gossip —a man wouldn't say too much, but say just enough to sort of create suspicion." He admires a man "who minds his own business," and believes that "you can't accuse a man of doing wrong if he shuts up when he might do himself harm." Paul adds another reason for remaining silent—the idea that the facts should speak for themselves.

> We have some very staunch [party people], as they call themselves, in the town, who won't let a dead horse stay dead. They still want to beat at this [local issue] situation, and point out the

mistakes that the [other party] made in that. Well, dammit, to straight-thinking people, you're not going to have to point out those mistakes. If they've made mistakes the people will see them. We must show more respect for our voters. I mean, let them make their own decisions. If you're constantly trying to cram something down their throats, they get a little bit weary. And I don't think that any party can go on indefinitely fooling the public. It almost seems that way at times, but there's always a day of reckoning.

Jim says, "I don't ever like to talk about myself," and "I didn't dare open my mouth" once when he lacked information. He instructs his grandchildren carefully in the need for thinking before speaking. We recall Dan's practice of "detouring around" unpleasantries in conversation. Insofar as he realizes that his contacts with others in the legislature are superficial and temporary, the Reluctant can relax these inhibitions. But by the time he reaches grandfatherhood, his caution has become too ingrained to be given up lightly.

Perceiving harmony is a second minor technique Reluctants use to put aside politics. At home, Dan says, "They're all nice—there isn't a one of them we don't enjoy. I'm getting away from politics, but that's the kind of a town we have," a town where there is "no haggling about whether they're Republican, Democrat, Socialist, or what they are." He finds that in the legislature "everybody seems to be amiable and sociable and happy and contented. But what might happen to change that, I don't know." He has been "surprised that there's been so much harmony" there. Paul likes "to listen to two friends on opposing parties agree so often." And Jim says he is on a "friendly committee": "I haven't seen any of that, what-you-call political play. I haven't seen that." Politics is connected with conflict; the Reluctant can avoid both by keeping his eyes on the brighter side, looking the other way when controversy comes along.[20]

When conflict does intrude itself on the Reluctant's attention, he tends to dismiss it as unimportant. Thus Dan says that legislative fights are confined mostly to the leadership on both sides and indicate no significant antagonism: "It's all in a day's work for them," just "quips back and forth, arguments, back and forth." He explains: "Of course, you know, it's like a couple of lawyers, the two leaders are going to get up and have controversies on things that are probably not important—I mean the matters are not important. They're going to have a test of strength on certain things. . . . Call for a roll call on things that don't really amount to anything—would be just a test of strength of the party." The Reluctant denies the existence of conflict, confines it to the leadership, or reduces it to triviality.

Reluctants, to a man, see their first legislative duty as watching out for home-town interests. This orientation is widely shared in the House, of course, but may have a special importance for the Reluctants. Coming as they do from some of the smallest towns in the state, they seldom encounter issues in the legislature that have any clear and direct bearing on the home community.[21] If they take the stance of guarding against change, preserving the status quo back home, they are likely to find few occasions for taking any positive actions. Like most state legislatures, Connecticut's is apportioned heavily toward the rural side, so that any one Reluctant has many allies to help watch out for his interests. Thus his personal legislative agenda is a brief one: most of the politicking can be left safely in the hands of others.

The Reluctant, then, has a number of methods for sidestepping political controversy. He differentiates himself from the "politicians," a category that is almost infinitely expandable, with room enough for virtually any unpleasantness. His habitual caution in conversation tends to remove him from informal negotiations. By focusing his attention on harmony, he misses whatever discord there might be in the House. And he can spend much of this time in watchful waiting for some issue salient to his home town to arise.[g]

The Retreat to Ritual

If the Reluctant tends to withdraw *from* politics, what does he withdraw *to*? What takes up his attention? As in the case of the Spectator, we must suspect that interest and emotion withdrawn from one aspect of the environment are likely to be fastened onto other aspects,

g. Certain questionnaire responses bear on these themes. Reluctants are least likely to report that "party labels made more difference in the campaign" than in the legislature. Reluctants 18%, others 42%. They are most likely to "go to someone I know and like" for advice rather than an expert. Reluctants 53%, others 35%. More of them agree that "seeing my name or picture in the paper made me feel a little uneasy." Reluctants 24%, others 9%. Fewer of them agree that "I influence others more than others influence me." Reluctants 35%, others 56% (N's = 17, 79). They tend to agree that "the legislator ought to vote the way he feels, regardless of party considerations." Reluctants 58%, others 30% (N's = 12, 71).

or directed inwardly, toward the self. One always *pays attention*, although the things attended to may shift rapidly and radically. The Spectators, as we saw, devote considerable attention to the dramatic and rhetorical features of the legislature, desiring as they do to avoid both involvement and introspection.

The Reluctant tends to retreat to those aspects of the decision-making process that he feels he can learn to handle most easily: the formal procedures, the routines of the place. As we have seen,[22] he has trouble enough with these matters. Our interest here is in the fact that he tends to turn his attention away from politics and toward the intellectual task of mastering the formal rules and routinizing his own efforts. We have seen this especially in Dan Thomas' case; he is to be found most of the time quietly studying the "regular rules," systematically taking notes in committee, reading over the printed bills and schedules. He is a little irritated that the lobby is too crowded with conversational groups for him to get much studying done there. Jim Pickens begins his interview with a long and detailed account of the route of a bill through both houses of the legislature, referring frequently to various manuals and calendars. Paul appears as somewhat less a scholar, but he, too, reports reading bills and he would like to have more time for study:

> PAUL: I think truthfully that any man who is here as a legislator should have a good four hours a day to himself.
> INTERVIEWER: You mean, to his own business?
> PAUL: I mean, no, to do his reading, his research—opinions—it's surprising how much good information you can get out of newspapers, magazines—even statistics. There are so many times that I just wish I had more time.

In these activities we see the Reluctant still involved in the substantive tasks of the legislature, but concentrating on parts of the task that are relatively unthreatening to him. He attempts to impose order on a chaotic environment by focusing on its orderly aspects: the formal processes, the formal organization. Or he spends his time in intellectual work which involves little mixing in the political hurly-burly. The legislative machine produces too many and too great a variety of issues for him to keep up with, so he turns from the product to the machinery itself. These tasks seem more tangible than debating or negotiating, involve fewer risks, and demand a smaller expenditure of energy. Given his way, the Reluctant would like to make a specialty of understanding these things.

The Reluctant's efforts in this direction may go a long way to satisfy his need to take an active part in the House. If his retreat from politics stops at this point, he may develop considerable skill as a parliamentarian or become quite familiar with some particular topic of legislation.

But this can be at best a partial and somewhat unstable form of adaptation for the Reluctant. The formal processes are too entangled with the informal, "political" ones to be understandable by themselves. The rules of the game are themselves stakes in the larger contest: politicians manipulate and use them for ends beyond maintaining order. The Reluctant is in for some rude shocks if he thinks he can take an important part in the legislative process solely on the basis of careful study of the rule book. Furthermore, this task alone can be an endless one; as we have seen, the Reluctants seem to have considerable difficulty with it. For these reasons they may find this ritualist position an insecure one and retreat yet farther away.

The Retreat to Character—and Beyond

When a person experiences failure or discomfort in dealing with his environment, he may turn his attention inward, retreating to a safer or more comfortable place within himself. When the Reluctant tries this, he usually encounters a conscience which pushes him outward again, toward serving others in some useful way. In this situation he employs three rather subtle adjustive techniques, permitting him to get along more easily with his feelings of duty. In the first place, he may reduce his level of aspiration somewhat. Paul says, "I guess if we're happy 25 per cent of the time, we're fortunate, in a deal like this." And Dan mentions that, as a legislator, "so far I haven't had much chance to be one thing or another." Here the Reluctants seem to be reminding themselves that they do not have to set the world on fire in order to be of some assistance to their colleagues and constituents. The impact of conscience is softened by a realistic appraisal of the available opportunities for success. The Reluctant's conscience does not require big successes; it asks only that he take *some useful part*.

Secondly, the Reluctant may stress to himself those commands of conscience that he can obey most readily: the injunction to be a good person, to practice the traditional moral virtues. Jim's equation, "A good man is a good legislator" illustrates this technique. Reluctants emphasize a morality of means rather than of ends. The good man is honest—"His word's his bond"—kindly and patiently tolerant; the bad man is "a liar," "a back-biting little bastard," one who "antagonizes peoples." In neither set of criteria do we find much reference to accomplishment. The main requirements are formal ones (to be active and virtuous) rather than substantive ones (to achieve certain valued goals). These moral standards the Reluctant can meet fairly well. In any comparison with the Spectator he can feel he tries harder; in comparisons with the Advertiser, he can feel he is a little straighter inside. Such feelings probably give him some personal comfort when the stresses and strains of legislative life seem too much for him.

In the last analysis, of course, the Reluctant can leave the legislature altogether. This is the final retreat: an adamant refusal to return for a second session. But even before he leaves physically he may escape psychologically, thinking of a better time long ago or of better times yet to come. Jim Pickens returns to his childhood again and again during the interview. His typical response to a general question is, "Well, you've got to go back . . . ," back to his parents—"Nobody ever had a better father and mother than I had," back to his boyhood—"Any man's help is started back when he's a youngster." When we recall Jim's tendency to shift into conversation with his father [23] and to describe for the interviewer not his present neighbors but those he grew up with, we can understand better his reminder that "you're talking to a man that's gone by." The past is still very much alive in Jim's mind. Withdrawing inward, he slips easily into pleasant reminiscences.

The mere anticipation of leaving the legislature may serve similar purposes, making the present more bearable because relief is coming in the near future. Dan can look forward to getting on with some very different tasks back home: "I'll have plenty to keep me busy, with my own place there. And we love to work out in the—we live right out in the country, you know. We love to work around the place. I've got vines and gardens, and then we've got work to be done around the house." Paul, who would "rather go sit on the bank of a fishing stream, just to keep busy doing nothing" than waste his time in unimportant tasks, remarks that "the end of the session will soon be here" and that "if all goes well, why within three months I will have forgotten the disagreeable aspects of being here. I hope so anyway." To a certain extent the Reluctant can dismiss from his mind the adjustive problems he faces in the legislature by confining them to a temporary present, a stressful interlude in a long story.

The Temptation to Withdraw

The Reluctant's tendencies to withdraw in stages from legislative life can perhaps best be understood as a series of tempting alternatives to full participation. The development of his political adaptation will depend to a marked degree on his success in resisting these temptations. Given his relatively modest abilities and his flagging energies, the most fundamental temptation he encounters—not only in politics but in his life in general—is the longing for peace, the desire not to be bothered, the temptation to quit trying to perform like a youngster. When this desire becomes intense and general, senility begins, first with an overall slowdown and then with a flickering out of interest and activity in one sphere after another of his life.

Compared with most people in their age group, Reluctant legislators probably are better able to resist these temptations. They are unusual oldsters in some important respects: they are habituated to hard work and social intercourse, and they have consciences that place a special emphasis on being useful and sociable. We find them, in the interviews, far short of senility. If they feel exhausted when they have too much to do, they also feel uneasy with nothing to do. The Reluctant's problem, then, is not so much whether to participate as it is how to find a role short of full participation, in which he can nevertheless make some meaningful contribution. It is in the lines he draws, the distinctions he makes in the process of determining his role, that we find him grappling with subtler temptations.

How does the Reluctant typically deal with unpleasant aspects of his environment? He often begins perceptually, by narrowing the boundaries around the threatening situation as much as possible. This is especially clear in the way he handles conflict in his environment: it is progressively confined—to a few leaders, to trivial issues, to rare events. Having isolated the situation, he attempts to increase his distance from it, to push it away by dwelling on the contrasts between it and himself. For example, he sees "politicians" not only as a group with special characteristics but also as especially and markedly different from his own group. The last step in this adaptive sequence is rationalization: the contrast is moralized, the distance turned into a measure of virtue. It is in this final step that the Reluctant is most dangerously tempted, because it is here that he begins to see his adaptive problems not as difficulties to be overcome but as evidences of his finer qualities.

We have seen a few examples of this moralizing in the interviews: Paul's justifications for his slower pace, Dan's antipolitical values, Jim's moralistic reduction of the good legislator to the good man. In other cases distinctions are drawn without being moralized: Jim finds the people in the legislature strange but not bad—his conscious attitude is that it is a fine thing to have such variety there. Dan complains of the difficult procedures but does not pat himself on the back for being above mere detail. In each of these situations the key question is the extent to which the Reluctant sees his retreat as a temporary step backward in preparation for moving forward again, or as the taking up of a position to be defended with moral entrenchments. Given his limitations, it is reasonable for him to restrict his efforts in some way, so that he can develop slowly and carefully a fuller repertory of legislative skills. But if he is to be the helpful person he wants to be, he needs to keep his pattern flexible and tentative, to avoid transforming adaptive devices into a protective moral armor.

THE POTENTIALITIES OF THE RELUCTANT PATTERN

The Reluctant's pattern of adjustment to political life can thus be seen as a sliding scale or continuum along which the member takes up certain positions. We have hypothesized that the rigidity of a person's pattern of adjustment will depend primarily on two factors: the intensity of the personal needs it tends to satisfy and the support the pattern receives from the environment. We turn now to estimating these tendencies, beginning with environmental support. Our question here, it should be remembered, is not the degree to which the Reluctant techniques contribute to legislative decision-making, but rather whether they are encouraged or discouraged by the external environment.

Environmental Support

To take the simplest case first, the legislature obviously offers considerable support for the Reluctant's concentration on ritual and bill-studying. The rules seem excessively complicated to most new members and the person who can master them will be sought for advice. There is an overwhelming supply of reports, schedules, bulletins, manuals, publicity materials, and so forth available to be studied.

The Reluctant can keep busy for the entire session working through this pile of words. Although the noisy chamber sometimes makes a poor reading room, it is usually not too difficult to shut out the surrounding clamor. The Reluctant's scholarly efforts, then, are likely to be rewarded.

So is the stress he places on personal honesty and, to a smaller degree, his general emphasis on the moral virtues. Honesty is highly valued among politicians. They operate in situations where responsibility is ill-defined, yet opinions count. Far more than most other occupations, politics is a verbal—or better, an *oral*—business in which one must often depend on the spoken commitments of allies and enemies. Lying arouses not only indignation but uncertainty, disorientation, incalculability. Politicians complain among themselves less of those who take the wrong stand or even ambiguous ones than of the quick switcher and the fellow who says one thing and does the other. In the back room and in the legislature, as well as in affairs of state, *pacta sunt servanda* is a strongly supported value. Members appreciate the man whose "word is his bond."

As we have seen in the discussion of Spectators and Advertisers, several minor aspects of the Reluctant's pattern are also supported from without: his caution in conversation, his emphasis on harmony, his normal geniality. But there are at least two features of his pattern that other legislators probably dislike and thus penalize him for: his apolitical stance and his predilection for escapist reverie. Few legislators consider themselves rabid party men, but most of them identify much more strongly with their parties than the Reluctants do. The chamber has no middle section for independents; wherever the Reluctant sits, he is surrounded by partisans, who expect him to display the same loyalties they hold, to react as they do to the party's call. Even though the Reluctant is likely to be immune to the harder forms of party pressure,[24] he can suffer many a stony stare should he go so far as to vote with the other side. He is in the game; he is expected to back the team.

Similarly, the Reluctant's nonpolitician stance is penalized. In a less extreme way than the Advertiser, the Reluctant, who separates himself from the politicians, sides with the critics against his colleagues. As amateur, part-time politicians, legislators are often amused and sometimes a little hurt by allegations in the press and by other outsiders that they are minor-league Tweeds, Hagues, and Crumps, out for whatever pelf and patronage they can get. They see their honest compromises characterized as "deals," their crusades as "demagoguery," their plans for progress as "ambitious scheming," their tedious labor as "hack work." As a result they develop a camaraderie of the damned. The Reluctant risks rejection when he sides with those doing the damning. Nor does his intention to quit the legislature after one term endear him to his fellow legislators, who may treat him as an overnight guest in a resident hotel.

When the old-timer lapses into quiet reveries about his childhood, tells long tales of his past, or dwells overlong on the unique virtues of his home town, other members may tire of his company. The House is a highly social place, a talk-shop where one is expected to visit easily with those in neighboring seats. The Reluctant may find other oldsters to commune with in committee meetings and in the House chamber, but most of the members are not of his generation. And of all the members the Reluctants are probably least likely to be *au courant* with the going gossip, the political inside dope. Others may consider him somewhat odd or quaint if he lets his mind wander. On the other hand, his thoughts on legislation are likely to be listened to, provided he has studied carefully.

Thus in a number of ways the Reluctant's environment tends to pull him out of himself, to encourage his studious efforts, but to penalize the more withdrawn aspects of his pattern. He has help from without in resisting the temptations to escape from a responsible, participating role.

Changes in the Long Run

Despite his intention to the contrary, the Reluctant is likely to return to the legislature for several more sessions. His dutiful feelings persist, and when nominating time comes around again, the home folks will make the most of them, thus avoiding once more a disturbing controversy. Perhaps Jim Pickens is the most adamant of the Reluctants in insisting that he did not want the job in the first place and will not take it again. Yet at one point in the interview his resolve falters and we see an opening for the party recruiter: "I appreciate the town sending me, and the confidence they got in me. And I've always felt obligated to do what I could. . . . Perhaps—I say I don't want it. Perhaps if they came to me and—but then I don't know. It's too darn much work." We are fairly safe in predicting that they will come to him again, and that after suitable demurrers he will give in and accept. Judging from the statistics on tenure of rural legislators, this is a recurring phenomenon in Connecticut. Thus we need to estimate the Reluctant's tendencies over a period of years. To what extent, and at what costs, is he likely to shift in the direction of a different pattern of adjustment?

Generally, it is likely that if he changes he will change slowly, building a more active role on the basis of his growing familiarity with procedures and issue topics. With time and talk the other legislators will seem less strange to him. As he becomes more familiar with the procedures, the pace of legislative life will seem to slow down to a manageable speed. With increasing knowledge he may acquire the confidence necessary to speak up now and then. At his age, he will never become a socialite, a facile expert, or an orator; eventually his mind and his body will really begin to fail him and he will withdraw in earnest. But in the interim we can expect some Reluctants to emerge gradually as valued members, although not as legislative stars.

For his personal investment in the more extreme forms of withdrawal is incomplete, and the pattern itself unsatisfying in many respects. The pattern involves several important contradictions: he cannot really do useful work and stay out of politics, help others and yet keep them at a distance, contemplate his virtues and yet not exercise them. It exposes him to a certain amount of enmity and contempt from other legislators. Most important to him, this kind of behavior leaves him feeling guilty that he is not doing his bit for the home-town folks, not meeting his responsibilities as their representative.

The Reluctant, then, is pressed from within and without toward attempting achievement in the House. The other two patterns—submission and aggression—are likely to be considerably less attractive to him. In a few passages in the interviews, the Reluctant seems to be veering in the submissive direction, but the emphasis is almost always on what he can do for the other person, not what the other should do to him. Thus Jim says, "There's men bigger than I am and I like to look up to them," and "I've been working with the big boys lots of times. But if they wanted a speech made, they didn't ask me to do it. But I was in back of them, doing the work." There is nothing here of the Spectator's demand for being directed, being led and instructed. The stress is on the practical things Jim can do, given his limitations as a speaker. He has worked *with* the "big boys," not under them.

Dan Thomas has a positive attitude toward government leaders— "I do sympathize with those people who—like you have the President or the Governor or any of those people, they certainly are under some handicaps trying to do a good job. Whether they want to or not, it's pretty hard." But this is sympathy for the burdens they bear, not blind admiration for their glamor. While he is "not what you'd call a party man, I'm afraid," Dan "will go along with the party in just about everything unless I feel that it's really bad, because that's the only way you can get anything accomplished." This thought contradicts Dan's generally nonpartisan stance, but even here his reasons for going along are different from those of the Spectator: he conforms in order to get something accomplished, not to escape personal responsibility or lose himself in the crowd.

Reluctants value independence too much to take a strictly passive role. "I don't think that a legislator should sit back and let other people make decisions for him," Paul says. We recall their feelings about people who make no effort, who want things done for them.[25] These sentiments probably reflect to some extent the Reluctant's personal fears of becoming a dependent old man who must rely on his children or the government for support. One retired Reluctant, in the midst of talking about government fiscal policy, mused: "Our whole attitude toward society [is] that society owes me something, society owes me a living. I have reasonably few and small obligations toward anybody, but I have a right to be here, and here I am, and somebody's got to take care of me. But I can't take care of myself. I think that that is a situation which exists at the present time." More broadly, the Reluctant differs from the Spectator in that he has been one of the shakers and movers back home, not a quiet watcher. Both habit and conscience make him react against being someone else's man.

Similar sentiments are likely to prevent the Reluctant from developing far in the aggressive direction. If he refuses to be put upon, he also tries not to force people. We notice in his perceptions of others a mellowness that contrasts radically with the Advertiser's curdled indignation. Shifting to aggression would mean altering the adaptive habits of a lifetime that have enabled him to get along so well at home. As we have seen, these peaceable practices have become a central part of his value scheme; he has internalized this feature of his culture.[26] He is no longer interested in personal advancement, and so feels little need to push others out of the way. His needs are to feel useful, not dominant; he wants to help accomplish something, but not at the price of a fight.

Generally, the Reluctant is in the legislature to satisfy needs that differ fundamentally from those of the Spectators and Advertisers, and thus feels little pressure to adopt their patterns. He feels somewhat inadequate to his office but lacks the Spectator's suspicion that he is basically unlovable. Consequently, the Reluctant seeks confirmation that he is capable, rather than evidence that others feel affection for him. The Advertiser's worry about the progress of his career is similarly foreign to the Reluctant; by his age, he knows fairly well where he stands in the general scheme of status and power. Consequently, he is not driven to undertake the kind of self-assertive personal politicking on which the Advertiser thinks his future depends.

THE RELUCTANT AND THE WORK OF THE LEGISLATURE

If the Reluctant succeeds in resisting the temptation to withdraw, he may in time make a significant contribution to the work of the legislature. Much will depend on his ability to build on minor achievements: to branch out slowly from a few friends to a broader acquaintanceship, to use his growing understanding of the rules and routines as an instrument for working on substantive legislation. These potentialities are there, but we should be careful not to exaggerate them. Throughout his legislative experience the Reluctant will continue to be hampered by his provincial background, his limited education, his declining energies. With long tenure, a few Reluctants may develop into the wise old men to be found in every legislature, the elder oracles to whom every newcomer is advised to attend. But for the most part, the Reluctant can hope to contribute only modestly to the immediate task of making laws.

The Reluctant and the Rules of the Game

The Reluctant has certain broad characteristics that facilitate the legislative process in less direct ways. More than most other members, he helps to ensure that the legislative rules of the game will be followed. If we try to imagine the House minus Reluctants, this contribution becomes especially clear.

Political scientists have not reached a consensus on exactly what constitute the rules of the game, but most agree that such rules are important to lawmaking.[27] The phrase is taken here to mean informal understandings among members as to proper legislative behavior. They concern what is legitimate, not simply what is expected; they are norms in the sense of standards that the good member feels called upon to respect and meet. These rules probably include as a minimum two major themes. Members believe that they should be especially careful to keep their commitments, and they stress the importance of holding conflict at the level of issues, not personalities.

It is fairly easy to understand why these norms have developed and been maintained in lawmaking bodies. The political opinions of most people on most specific issues, most of the time, have few important consequences. Americans take their politics casually; only extremists are penalized for their opinions. If the average citizen feels like changing his mind about the gasoline tax or home rule or highway bonding, no one has much reason to object. But these offhand attitudes can be disastrous in a legislature. For there the member speaks for his constituents, to colleagues who must depend on him, about important issues which they will decide collectively. It is crucial, then, that he make his opinions fit his responsibilities, learn to give his word on political matters only when he means to keep it. In a culture where opposite expectations prevail, that can be a lot for a man to learn. Consequently, there is a need for a strong norm, for driving this lesson home to newcomers.[28]

Reluctants help to enforce and maintain this norm when they express their sentiments to others. Cautious in committing themselves, they attribute a good deal of importance to honesty. Jim reiterates his admiration for "a man they can depend on—depend on his word. A square shooter, I call them. And the Speaker is one of them. . . . His word's his bond. That's what my father used to say: 'If you give your word, stand by it.' " They take their opinions seriously and their attitude toward liars is especially severe. As we have seen, Spectators and Advertisers feel considerably less committed to their opinions, the Spectator because he has few opinions of his own and feels that his ideas are not worth much, and the Advertiser because he sees his opinions as strategic devices and feels little constraint in using ideas to advance his own personal position. In a House without the Reluctants, the interplay between Advertiser oratory and Spectator pliancy might well result in wavering, ill-considered policies.

A second important norm concerns the impersonality of conflict.

Again, there is a marked contrast between the legislative situation and normal behavior in the general culture, so that special rules are needed to make the legislature work. The average citizen very rarely finds himself involved in any sort of formalized controversy in a situation where antagonists confront one another, debate, and decide. And when he does get into an argument, the personal dimension is likely to be closely entwined with the issue under discussion. Entering into rational debate requires an artificial wrenching apart of the substance of what is being said from who is saying it, a pretending, a denial of one aspect of the real situation. The common tendencies are those we have seen in the Spectators and Advertisers: one is either so taken up with avoiding rejection that he lacks the courage to state a clear position or so concerned with impressing and manipulating the other that he loses track of the merits of the issue. Perhaps the highest ability in debate is to be able to deal consciously with the substance of an issue while at the same time keeping in mind the parallel personal relationships. But this is a subtle skill; most members will find it too difficult, especially when the audience is a large one. Debate thus always verges on fighting, always risks hurt feelings and blind anger. Legislators need standards of impersonality to counteract these tendencies if they are to decide by reasoning.

Reluctants, during their first session at least, are probably too hesitant to speak up. But over the long run, as some of them begin to take a somewhat more active part, they may help considerably in keeping debate on an even keel. Their belief in peaceable social relations fits fairly well with the legislative norms which mute personal antagonisms. And insofar as they can continue to perceive interpersonal differences without moralizing them, they help to keep the debate on the level of issues.

If the Reluctant reminds the Spectator that his opinions are important and the Advertiser that his temper is controllable, he also acts to restrain those who are in a hurry to get things done. The task-oriented members of the House, the ones whose attention is taken up with action on bills, may find the formal and informal rules obstructive. Form and substance never quite fit in legislating: bills can be lost in the maze of procedures, even the measures most members favor. The more intense the member's interest in getting a bill passed, the more alluring the idea of making an exception in this one case. Yet in the long run, too many exceptions may destroy rules that are generally functional for rational deliberation. As Reluctants master the rules, they tend to insist on them, thus slowing down the process. They want an explanation of important issues and will not be content with repetitious, meaningless verbiage. They resist "those decisions where people all rush into one little office and beat each other over the head and come up with an answer." These brakes can be applied too hard, too frequently: if the regular rules were never suspended, very little would get done. But there are times when the Reluctant, as guardian of the rules, serves a useful purpose in reminding the bill-pusher that they are more than mere proprieties.

The Reluctant's Political Future

In the Reluctant, we meet "a man gone by," as Jim describes himself. His legislative experience is neither the greatest thing that ever happened to him nor the first step on a ladder to success. His pace is slow: it will take more than one session for his legislative style to develop fully. Despite his retrospective orientation, the Reluctant probably has at least one or two terms to look forward to, since the folks back home are even less likely now to take no for an answer. If he gives in to the temptation to withdraw, we should expect to find him several years hence ruminating quietly at his desk in the legislature. But if he resists and learns, we may discover him surrounded by his juniors, who, though impatient for action, want to check first with the sage of the House.

5. The Lawmaker

> May we not even say, that that form of government
> is the best, which provides the most effectually for a
> pure selection of these natural aristoi into the offices
> of government?
>
> JEFFERSON

How does the legislature manage to get anything done? Peopled as it is with those who come to be entertained, to advertise themselves, or to perform a vaguely defined civic duty, the legislature appears more like a clinic than a machine for the production of laws.

Yet it did produce. During the five months of the 1959 session, members of the legislature passed more than 1,450 measures, authorizing the spending of nearly 700 million dollars. They approved nine proposed amendments to the state constitution. They reorganized the state's entire minor court system, replacing a maze of local courts with a State Circuit Court. They abolished county government in Connecticut—a system in effect for nearly three centuries—and distributed its functions among various state agencies. They became the fourth state legislature to enact a uniform commercial code, covering virtually all commercial transactions. They made major changes in the executive branch, creating new departments of Consumer Protection and Conservation. They authorized the issuance of $345 million in bonds for an immense highway program.

Not all their actions were of such far-reaching significance: they also took time to define the word "stop," to specify the height of junkyard fences, and to establish the Irish Heritage Association. But both critical and enthusiastic commentators agreed that the record of the 1959 legislature was "remarkable" and "historic."

The session was unusual in another respect: the close division between the two major parties. The margin was so thin that on key roll calls every vote counted. Thus each freshman representative very often played a crucial part, simply by being there and voting. Beyond voting, however, there were marked differences in the quality and quantity of participation by new members. The actions of most of them, most of the time, were peripheral to the main bill-formulating and negotiating efforts—at least as regards major legislation—and only occasionally did they take a leading role in some particular enterprise. As we have seen in examining the Spectators, Advertisers, and Reluctants, these peripheral members affect the legislative process in important helpful and harmful ways. But we should not be surprised to learn that in the House, as in most organizations, a relatively small minority carry the main burdens of the business.

Legislators in our fourth category are called Lawmakers because, in comparison with other new members, they appear to devote an unusual amount of attention and energy to the formulation and production of legislation. The category consists of the thirty-three respondents who were high in both activity and willingness to return for three or more future terms. On both sides of the aisle, these were the new members who came to grips with the substantive problems of the legislature and contributed considerably more than their share, proportionately, to the final results.

Most of the interview questions were posed in general terms, asking broadly for reactions to the legislative experience. Yet the Lawmakers continually turned the discussion in the direction of specific pieces of legislation. Long descriptions of the particulars of this or that issue were typical; one of the most frequent nouns encountered in the Lawmaker transcripts is "bill." A few examples, taken from three different interviews, illustrate this tendency toward concern with substantive issues:

> INTERVIEWER: My first general question is, what sort of an experience has this been for you so far—just from your own personal viewpoint?
> LAWMAKER: Well, actually, I have found it very fascinating, really. I mean all aspects of it—the hustle and bustle, the confusion—I think perhaps some of the excitement that goes with it, too. I mean, as you know, we've got a big day coming up tomorrow: the X bill, that does Y and Z. Little things like that I have found actually exciting.

> INTERVIEWER: How do you think you've done so far? How would you rate yourself?
> LAWMAKER: Well, I think I've done pretty well. For this

reason, that I supported several issues. I served on two important committees, and I supported many main issues—when I say supported, I mean not only voted, but took an actual part in promoting and speaking for them. Appeared before many committees on subjects that were important to my constituents and to the projects that I mention. So I was successful in getting bills that our town needed, and also other bills.

INTERVIEWER: How do you feel that you have done so far in meeting your goals?

LAWMAKER: Well, I feel that I've done a big thing in being able to vote on the X bill. I think that was simply tremendous. And of course there are other bills in which I'm *very* interested. I introduced the bill for Y. And then the bill for Z will be heard tomorrow morning. That would be a step forward.

These relatively active, committed members were there, plainly, to make the laws.

THE LAWMAKER PROFILES: BUDDING POLITICIAN

The Lawmaker Legislative Activity Profile reveals a picture similar to that of the active Advertisers, but with some interesting differences. Compared with other new member respondents, the Lawmakers appear generally more active, having sought the nomination, campaigned hard, and found important roles to play in the House. Of special interest are certain contrasts with the Advertisers.[a] Lawmakers are considerably more likely to have attended many meetings in the campaign (Advertisers: 38%) and to have liked campaigning very much (Advertisers: 8%). They are less likely to choose speaking in the legislature as a preferred activity (Lawmakers: 12%, Advertisers: 31%). Otherwise, Lawmaker reports of legislative activity differ little from those of Advertisers, indicating that the two groups share a generally high level of activity.

In the Political Ambitions Profile, some more marked contrasts appear. Lawmakers clearly emerge as the freshmen most strongly interested in pursuing some political future, especially in elective office and leadership within the legislative body. Again, certain comparisons with the Advertisers are evident. Lawmakers are far more likely to have considered full-time elective office (Advertisers: presession, 31%;

a. For the full Advertiser profiles, see above, pp. 70–72.

PROFILE 1. *Lawmaker Legislative Activity*

	Lawmakers	Other New Member Respondents	Difference
Originated action to get nomination	61%	30%	+31
Attended many meetings in campaign	82	30	+52
Likes campaigning very much*	55	33	+22
Attributes election to own campaign efforts	15	11	+ 4
Often introduced self to others at first of session	91	78	+13
Took an active part in major negotiations	82	51	+31
Was frequently sought for advice	58	40	+18
Achieved leadership or important committee post	48	19	+29
Considers self energetic rather than easy-going	66	59	+ 7
Considers self more influential than others	55	51	+ 4
Self-rating as a legislator: superior or excellent	42	30	+12

* Indicates presession response and/or change during session: Lawmaker N = 31, Other N = 52. All other responses are from the postsession questionnaire: Lawmaker N = 33, Other N = 63.

postsession, 39%), to be sure they will run again in the next election (Advertisers: presession, 15%; postsession, 15%), to take an interest in being a House leader (Advertisers: 76%), and to have considered full-time state appointive office (Advertisers: 25%). They are more likely to consider themselves "politicians" (Advertisers: 44%), although this contrast is less marked. Broadly, Lawmakers rank well above the other members in political ambition, and the contrast is especially marked in comparisons with Advertisers.

Few of the scores in the Lawmaker Political Background Profile show marked differences between Lawmakers and other members in general, although they fall mostly on the positive side. Looking again at Lawmaker-Advertiser differences, we find Lawmakers more likely to have had parents interested in politics (Advertisers: 63%), relatives active in politics (Advertisers: 50%), and to have held some elective office (Advertisers: 38%). On the other hand, more Advertisers report occupational contact with government (Advertisers: 75%), are much more likely to have held appointive office (Advertisers: 62%), and slightly more likely to have held some party office (Advertisers: 54%). It is interesting to note that more Advertisers report they saw their election chances as being "50-50" at nomination time (Advertisers: 46%), thus indicating that they come from more competitive towns. Lawmakers are more likely to have been considering a run for the House for some time (Advertisers: 46%) and to evaluate legislative work as their most important activity (Advertisers: 38%).

Generally, then, Lawmakers appear to have a more deeply rooted

PROFILE 2. *Lawmaker Political Ambitions*

	Lawmakers	Other New Member Respondents	Difference
Identifies self as a "politician"	55%	37%	+18
Has considered seeking full-time elective office:			
Presession response*	64	29	+35
Postsession response*	61	29	+32
Change during session	— 3	0	
Had considered full-time state appointive office*	42	25	+17
Was interested in district or state party office*	80	67	+13
Was interested in Assembly leadership position*	93	56	+37
Willingness to return for three or more future sessions:			
Presession response*	81	64	+17
Postsession response*	100	52	+48
Change during session	+ 19	—12	
Ran again for nomination or election to Assembly:			
In 1960	85	78	+ 7
In 1962	39	46	— 7
Ran for or served in some government office (including Assembly) after initial session	94	89	+ 5

* See note for Profile 1.

PROFILE 3. *Lawmaker Political Background*

	Lawmakers	Other New Member Respondents	Difference
Parents interested in politics	73%	62%	+11
Relatives active in politics	70	60	+10
Occupation involves government contacts	60	44	+16
Had held party office*	45	54	— 9
Had held elective office*	45	44	+ 1
Had held appointive office*	32	42	—10
Had long considered running for Assembly	63	52	+11
Reports some competition for nomination*	80	67	+13
Saw election chances as 50–50*	26	23	+ 3
Considers legislative activity most important he has engaged in	48	62	—14

* See note for Profile 1.

interest in elective politics—stemming from family participation—than the Advertisers do, while Advertisers tend to have come up through appointive ranks and to stress more recent, occupational ties to politics.

In their personal characteristics, Lawmakers, compared to other freshman respondents, are young, well-educated, upward-mobile people, similar in all these respects to the Advertisers. But there are again some differences: Lawmakers include more women (Advertisers:

PROFILE 4. *Lawmaker Personal Data*

	Lawmakers	Other New Member Respondents	Difference
Sex: Male	82%	76%	+ 6
Age: over 40	27	54	—27
Occupation: Attorney	30	16	+14
Education: above high school*	73	44	+29
Income: over $8,000*	48	38	+10
Town population: over 5,000	90	46	+44
Resident in town: more than ten years	66	71	— 5
Expects to remain in town	88	92	— 4
Expects more income in ten years	78	49	+29

* See note for Profile 1.

(100% male), fewer lawyers (Advertisers: 50%), fewer of the well-to-do (Advertisers: 61% over $8,000). They are somewhat more likely to have lived in their town for a decade or more (Advertisers: 44%). In all other respects, Lawmakers and Advertisers are quite similar in political background.

These profile comparisons stress the Lawmaker-Advertiser dimensions because the few contrasts which stand out between these categories may be important clues to the marked differences in legislative style which the two groupings of active legislators display. Most significant is the fact that Lawmakers have, in their pasts and in their perceptions of their futures, considerably closer links to elective political processes. And it is perhaps equally important that these links appear to be cemented by something other than occupational benefits. The Lawmaker, it seems, needs politics, but not for his bread and butter.

NOMINATIONS: THE POLITICS OF ISSUES

In preceding chapters we have related some typical community situations to the types of political representatives most likely to emerge from them. The personal histories of the Spectators illustrate how the scarcity of potential candidates in small communities may lead to the nomination of persons whose primary qualifications for office are willingness to serve and an antiseptic, if innocuous, public record. In the case of the Reluctants, recruited from the smallest rural towns, we described how the threats to community peace and order that the election process poses tend to be met by nominating individuals who embody certain primary community values and characteristics, persons who are strongly committed in various ways to the home-town system as it is. We connected the nomination of Advertisers to change in the community, especially rapid growth and increasing inter-party competition, which presses the party leaders to recruit blue ribbon candidates who can be marketed in the newspapers as qualified, experienced, and active.

There comes a time in these expanding communities when something more than high personal qualifications is demanded. When both parties nominate apparently well-qualified candidates, the party leader must seek other ways in which to boost his man. It is in such circumstances that issue considerations tend to come to the fore, and the Lawmaker is differentiated from the Advertiser.

How Stupid Are the Voters?

Much evidence has been gathered on the degree to which American voters are informed about and interested in political issues. Invariably, the findings have been interpreted as showing how little people know or care about such matters; and indeed, quotations from interviews with voters reveal seemingly appalling gaps in their political understanding.[1] Such interpretations, however, need qualifications: rating the general level of knowledge and interest high or low depends on the expectations (and, to some extent, the values) that the analyst brings to the material. Historical comparisons must await the accumulation over time of systematic studies, but it is highly probable that rising levels of education, increasing social organization, and the expanding role of government are working to intensify interest in and responsiveness to political issues by the general population. Voting participation has been rising gradually throughout the country. And in a number of key areas new types of political organizations, based primarily on issues, have been burgeoning and enduring beyond initial enthusiasms.[2]

Perhaps it is even more significant that a great many people *think* they know something about political issues, regardless of how accurate their knowledge may be. A large-scale study of voting behavior by the University of Michigan Survey Research Center shows that between 70 and 90 per cent of a national sample interviewed in 1956 had some opinion on items in a list of sixteen foreign and domestic policy issues, despite the fact that "The presentation of each policy item was prefaced with the direct suggestion that it was quite proper for the person to respond by telling us that he (or she) did not happen to have an opinion on the question."[3] About two thirds of the sample, on the average, not only held an opinion on the issue but also claimed some knowledge of what the government was doing about it. More than a fourth of those interviewed not only met these conditions but perceived some differences between the two parties on the issues.[4] Nineteen out of twenty respondents reported some exposure to the campaign through mass media, and more than one out of four reported trying to show others "why they should vote for one of the parties or candidates."[5] It is possible to interpret these findings in two ways: to many journalists, educators, public relations experts, and campaign managers they can be cause for despair. But from a different point of view, the same figures show a considerable potential for issue-oriented politics, and give some indication of the pressures party leaders may feel to choose candidates who can handle the issues.

The state of Connecticut ranks quite high in voting turnout compared with other states: about three fourths of the civilians of voting age cast ballots in 1956. However, there are marked variations from town to town in political activity. In a good many communities, some 90 per cent of the adult population is registered, and about 90 per cent of those registered actually vote in presidential years. More than 60 per cent of the students graduating from high school in thirty-four towns in 1962 planned to go to college. It is from such communities as these—politically involved, highly educated—that Lawmakers tend to be recruited.

The presence of large numbers of active and sophisticated citizens in a community poses special problems for the party leader. Such people are unlikely to be particularly impressed by a candidate who has higher education. In their circles such things are taken for granted. Nor are they easily swayed by broad rhetorical appeals, torchlight parades, or beer-and-oyster rallies. These are the people who attend the League of Women Voters' candidate meetings, follow political affairs in the press and magazines, and consider it *de rigueur* to have something interesting to say at social gatherings about government policies. Thus the party leader needs to find some candidate who can handle not only the supermarket handshaking tour but also the neighborhood political tea party. When the electorate is both active and educated, the "good government seal of approval" [6] goes to the candidate who can talk issues.

The New Politicians

In recent years many a party leader has been surprised to find voters of this type knocking on the door of the party clubhouse. The thrust of reform politics in the United States seems to be changing: people who once would have confined their activities either to nonpartisan civic organizations or to movements to emasculate parties through election reform now show increasing tendencies to accept the parties and to work from within. Nor are they satisfied with a seat at the back of the room. Increasingly, issue-oriented participants demand recognition within the party in the form of real influence over nominations, platforms, and campaign strategies. Ultimately they may insist on the candidacy of one of their own.

Through such channels as these the active, issue-conscious Lawmakers have been brought forth for legislative nominations. The party leadership, in most cases, has recognized the usefulness of a candidate who is at once clean and capable, participating and policy oriented.

The Lawmaker's Availability

The Lawmaker tends to view his nomination as a natural extension of his work in civic organizations and his party at home. The transition to candidacy is smoother than with the other types. In numerous passages, Lawmakers make this link between their recent activities and the nomination:

> I have had considerable experience in speaking before small groups, large groups, meeting with all kinds of people. And that, of course, made it easier for me to participate in school affairs and church affairs in my own town. So all those things were not things that I worried about when I got involved in campaigning.

> It's not such a new experience for me as it might be for some, because I've not only worked with people, but—in situations like this, where there are people from all over the state or all over the country coming together, and so I've had opportunities like that.

> I don't think I've missed over half a dozen town meetings. I have always taken an active part in them. In the debate on the issues—I just kept falling into motion then, taking an active part in everything and, well, here I am today.

The reasons Lawmakers offer for taking the nomination are too varied and numerous for extensive quotation. The Lawmaker undertakes the job in the context of considerably broader and deeper political interests than the Advertiser does. This means that he relies much less on a single motivating force, such as occupational ambition, and thus is open to rewards from many different directions when he gets to the legislature. The Advertiser is a gambler in this regard: he stakes all on the professional payoffs; and when these fail to develop he feels a deep disappointment. But the Lawmaker can see many different and complementary reasons for participating: to get action on issues, to boost his party's chances at home, to satisfy his natural curiosity about politics, to work off excess mental energy.

In most cases, Lawmakers made themselves available for nominations despite their knowledge that their occupational life would suffer. They were aware of the demands of the job, but asked for it anyway. Thus they have already crossed, in the nominating process, a bridge which lies ahead of the Advertiser when he arrives at the capital: the conscious decision, in full awareness of the costs, to undertake a part-time political career.

At the time of his nomination, the typical Lawmaker could find in his personal background precedents for political action, particularly the precedent of family participation. While there is little evidence on this point, it seems likely that a positive attitude toward taking part in politics tends to be inherited, like party identification. Put another way, Lawmakers need not rely entirely on their interest in issues to move them into politics. Such participation seems natural and legitimate to one raised in a home where politics was not only a topic for discussion but also a matter for action. This background counteracts tendencies to disparage politicians, to see politics as merely entertainment, or to focus mainly on self-serving participation. Politicians, it seems likely, explain their political activities to their children in morally positive terms, stressing the accomplishments, the real contributions one can make by joining in party affairs. The young lawyer whose father was a politician can thus seek a nomination without experiencing either much guilt or much anxiety: politics is familiar to him, in the root sense of the word.

Furthermore, the Lawmaker's background in elective politics casts a different light on his nomination. More than many other candidates for the legislature, he is used to a political environment in which participants are expected to take sides on issues—to agitate and debate and vote on matters ranging from who should be party leader to what should be the party's stand on local issues. The candidate who comes up from appointive office, particularly the young lawyer who has been town counsel, is more likely to have been trained to take a neutral, technical role in decision-making. He is supposed to confine his advice to questions of the legality or efficiency of means, not the desirability of ends. Lawmakers have been to a different school, one which teaches that politics is a way of implementing principles, not a violation of them.

Lawmakers thus appear in the interviews as people who are at the same time more involved in politics and less dependent on any one particular aspect of political life for rewards than are other legislators.

Party leaders choose them in part for their personal talents, in part for their appeal to a wider range of the electorate.

REACTIONS: THE DRIVE FOR DECISIONS

From the time he arrives in the legislature, the Lawmaker's attention is taken up mostly with bills. As indicated above, the interviews are replete with detailed accounts of the pros and cons involved in a multitude of issue choices. Yet it would be misleading to characterize the Lawmaker as a completely rational, supremely efficient human computer, concerned only with cranking out correct answers to specific questions. Like the other members the Lawmaker experiences pains and pleasures in the House, reacts with positive and negative emotions to the environments he perceives there. Like others, he selects certain elements of the situation to pay special attention to and neglects other elements. These reactions reveal some of the special problems of adjustment that the issue-oriented member encounters in the legislature.

Lawmakers are so categorized in part because they have indicated a willingness to return to the legislature. Thus it is not surprising that they share with the Spectators a generally favorable set of reactions. One Lawmaker begins his interview with Spectator-like enthusiasm: "Well, so far I love it—I think it's terrific, to me—I think it's just wonderful." Yet the interviews also show numerous dissatisfactions: one says simply of campaigning, "I hate it," and another has sometimes "really found things depressing to the point where you weren't quite sure what you should do or could do about it." The emotional peaks and troughs are there, and they are not irrelevant to the Lawmaker's adjustment. Three interviews show some of the main sources of these feelings.

Don Bennis: "Not merely participation . . ."

Don Bennis is an articulate young attorney whose Harvard background is expressed in precision of thought as well as pipe and glasses. Don has found the first part of the legislative session "a very stimulating, very rewarding experience." "The reason," he continues, "is that the individual member has an opportunity to express himself and to produce concrete legislative results, actually, to a much greater extent than in previous sessions," because of the closeness of the party balance in the House. Don believes that "we're going to come out of this session with some tremendously fine legislation," and much of his interview is taken up with specific features of the important bills. He has taken an active part in preparing, considering, negotiating, and speaking for several of these matters. But he is not satisfied simply by having the opportunity to be heard:

> INTERVIEWER: Then I take it that a chance to participate and be active is an important thing for you?
>
> DON: Well, participation, as I say, not merely participation, but participation with a possibility of effectuating a concrete legislative result. Now I don't know if I would have been active [if that chance were lacking]. I might have gotten a big kick out of getting on my feet and talking, but I think the possibility is that after about a week, after I'd seen the votes going overwhelmingly one way, I probably would lose a good deal of interest in doing it. Because it wouldn't be any more effective than getting up on a soapbox on the corner of Fourth and Main. Of course, a number of people, I'd imagine, a good number of my colleagues, like to speak for the sake of speaking, but it doesn't particularly satisfy me, unless you get some result, which I participate in.

Don repeats this theme several times in the interview: he shows a pressure for production, for completion. He is openly disappointed when bills he favors are defeated, and pleased when they go through. Thus pleasure in participation depends, for Don, on (a) his taking part, (b) the matter coming to a resolution, and (c) the decision being in the direction he desires. When any one of these elements is missing, Don is less than fully satisfied as a legislator.

A second set of rewards for Don centers in the opportunities he finds for rational persuasion in the House. He complains that the party leadership "thinks in terms of numbers, in terms of voting strengths, in terms of attendance—they don't think in terms of persuasion." Don feels that an important measure "could have been put over if every member had taken it upon himself to talk to one opponent, let's say. I did it myself, I spoke to several of them." "If you're able even to persuade five or six or seven people, then you have an opportunity to be effective in a concrete sort of way," he says. Because the House is so closely divided and so many members are new, "these new members are relying heavily on the people who are familiar with the problems," and "this small minority of people who have abil-

ity and are concerned with problems have a strength disproportionate
to their numbers."

In these passages, Don adds another dimension to his sentiments
about legislative action: positive results attained by simply corralling
the necessary votes are less desirable than those which flow from conscious deliberation and persuasion of members. A coerced result is
somehow incomplete.

Don's reactions to the other members of the House illustrates a
third aspect of his rewards. None of these responses appear to be
marked by strong feeling, either positive or negative, but rather by
a calm acceptance of others based on an unusually sensitive empathic
ability. For example, Don would like to see more participation in
debate by capable members. He feels that "there is a tremendous
waste in manpower in that House, in this respect; there are an awful
lot of people there who can contribute, are in a position to contribute,
but they feel inadequate to the situation. They don't want to talk,
and their ideas would be very helpful." Such people "are afraid that
they may be laughed at."

> But there are very many bright ones. The tragedy is that asses
> are the ones that do most of the talking. You see, the ones that
> have some sense are the quiet ones. They're the ones that should
> occasionally express themselves, but don't, either because they feel
> that they'll make an ass of themselves or because they are afraid
> that they may say something that won't be in accord with the
> party position.

Don shows here considerable understanding of the emotions felt by
members who are unlike himself. Similarly, he notices that many new
members find the session "an upsetting experience," are "disturbed by
the fact that they don't know what is going on" or "by the hardships,
the fact that their time is being consumed." In contrast, Don sees
himself "in a fairly good position" on an important committee "where
I know most of what's going on." And despite the fact that his practice has suffered, he has made a conscious decision to devote the necessary time to legislating: "Actually the time demand is only a variable,
in that you don't have to put in the time. As I say, you have to
choose, actually. The individual lawyer has to choose between whether
he's going to emphasize his practice or whether he's going to emphasize his job here. He can't do both equally well, see what I mean? The

choice in my case happened to be this, because I find it a good deal more interesting."

In these passages, Don is describing others who have characteristics different from his own and is putting himself in their shoes. He has not made a special study of legislators' adjustive problems; yet he refers fairly clearly to matters described in previous chapters: to silence stemming from feelings of inadequacy (Spectators), to cognitive disorientation (Reluctants), and to occupational problems due to the pressure of time (Advertisers).

Don's interview indicates three general reactions to the legislative experience. He derives pleasure from producing; he enjoys persuading others; and he accepts other members on the basis of an understanding of their personal problems as legislators.

Ben Yerby: "It isn't all just a waste of time and confusion"

Ben Yerby is a mustachioed ex-newspaperman from a growing suburban town. He got interested in politics through activity in his home-town PTA, which he began to attend at the unanimous urging of his seven children. Ben's occupational background is reflected in the enjoyment he finds in collecting and organizing information: "There's a certain amount of preparation that goes into it, and perhaps trying to get together some of the thoughts you had on it in the past, or comments that you've heard in the corridors." But he has been somewhat disappointed, "perhaps because I was expecting too much." He had "felt that perhaps where some of the more humane issues were concerned, there would be more consideration and more decisions arrived at as a result of the merit of the legislation, rather than the political aspects of it."

Like Don, Ben Yerby is interested in results. He has "thoroughly enjoyed being a part of it." Ben explains: "I mean, to see these things develop, and to see a lot of them work out, and of course, if it's something that you're particularly interested in and the goal is reached, and you actually see the bill or the proposal ultimately become law or public act—well, it's very gratifying to know that you were a part of it. . . . I think there's a great deal of personal satisfaction in the feeling that anyway you're accomplishing something. It isn't all just a waste of time and confusion." On election night, Ben reports, "I felt good, because all my previous effort in the campaign wasn't down the drain. You felt that all that mad scramble that you went through was worth the effort, because, well, here were tangible results that it paid off." In discussing voting, Ben says, "I know there are lots of times when you have the feeling as though you're picking the lesser of two evils—but even that has to be done, even that has to be done." Ben feels pressed to decide, and experiences pleasure when he can take an effective part in bringing about a good decision.

Ben objects to decisions being made "with no questions asked." He finds committee executive sessions "more fun than the hearings," because "you have a better opportunity to participate, to start hammering away at it." "Everybody sounds off and says his piece and we kick it back and forth a few times, and then hope that if you take a vote it'll indicate something." Here Ben shows an inclination to take part in persuasion; he is also concerned that the deliberative process work rationally, as this complaint indicates:

> There always seem to be one or two that keep raising side issues— perhaps that's the sort of thing I objected to, found myself getting perhaps a little irritated with, when too much time was devoted to discussing things that weren't exactly pertinent to the bill that's being discussed. They were worrying too much about something that had little or no effect on something we were trying to decide on. It's very easy to do when you get 15 or 20 people together—they get rambling.

Ben shows two significant reactions in these passages: he takes pleasure in group deliberations, but is displeased when they trail off into irrelevancies.

Ben resists categorizing the other members. He says he "thinks of certain individuals" but hesitates "to lump them together." In discussing individual party leaders, senior legislators, other new members, etc., he shows a good deal of insight into their problems, in passages which cannot be quoted here. He gives a summary view of his feelings toward the members when asked for his first impressions of the House.

> INTERVIEWER: At these first brief sessions, did you have any impressions of the other people there, the other members?
>
> BEN: No, except that I think there was a certain feeling of fellowship that you feel with the others, even though most of them are strangers. Perhaps it might be something similar to something you might feel in a fraternal group. In other words,

you have the feeling as though we're all in the same boat, and we're going to have to work these things out together. I think you have the feeling that you certainly have something in common with all these other strangers about.

In contrast to the Reluctants, Ben here stresses the feelings he shares with strangers in the legislature, rather than the difference between him and them. And his reaction to others is a clearly positive one.

Katherine Howell: "Constructive group action . . ."

A social worker whose spontaneity belies the stereotype, Katherine Howell has been active in youth work for years. Talking of her first impressions, she says "the shine has not quite worn off yet," and "I have really enjoyed it and find it stimulating." With a smile she says she has "an overdeveloped conscience," which requires her to make a special effort "to keep track of what's going on" and to "follow through" on legislation. Katherine has found herself involved in some basic issues which "I find very interesting," especially because they concern "the constant problem of defining how far society's responsibility goes—and I think it's a critical question before our whole society today." Her interview shows considerable attention to specific measures for implementing her ideals.

Katherine has been somewhat disappointed in her committees—"executive sessions bore me terribly"—because "these committees don't really function as a group," owing to poor scheduling and multiple assignments. She wants a committee which can "produce constructive group action," "work together as a team," "a real committee that defines its purposes so that they will know what they're doing, and really try to talk things through and then come up with a group decision." At the more personal level, she has been worried about the "problem of making the right decisions" in situations where the right and wrong are not entirely clear. "It would be so nice if you just knew you had done the right thing, and yet there's always the feeling of really tremendous responsibility—you have to make a decision, and there's always the possibility that this may have been the wrong decision." Katherine feels some disdain for people who are unwilling to "go to a meeting and commit themselves" on issues; she herself often finds this difficult to do, but she does it.

These passages stress the negative side of Katherine's reactions; they need to be read in the context of her generally positive sentiments toward the legislative experience. Despite committee inefficiencies, for example, they do "report out the bills." And despite her difficulties in deciding, she is "not a person to worry about it once it's done. I mean, that's that—you can't really change it [laughs], so you might as well go on to the next thing." The point here is that Katherine, like Don and Ben, is especially concerned with producing, acting constructively, making decisions. Her eye is on the legislature as a policy-making body. She has had "a modest experience in working on committees and in making decisions," and would like to carry over such habits into the Assembly.

Katherine shows a similar interest in the possibilities of rational persuasion. Her experience and perceptions in the campaign illustrate this theme. She "wasn't a very great campaigner," she says, because "I just hate selling—and it is selling." She "tried to campaign on an educational level, which was something that the party didn't support me in, which made me mad as the devil." She explains that "My approach from the beginning, and I tried to carry it out as best I could, was that the way to campaign was to inform the people on the issues which were important. . . . To go and talk about the different things that were in the news. . . . I said all the time that there is no need to be destructive, that you can campaign in a constructive way. . . . I insisted on debating on the issues." Some of the personal attacks in the campaign were "vicious," but Katherine consistently attempted to keep the contest on a policy plane. In the legislature, she is similarly concerned that reasoned persuasion precede decision: she dislikes the situation where "you're under such pressure to do something—report out this bill, or do something—without really having a chance to talk it through."

Katherine's attitudes toward other members are shaped by perceptual habits developed in her regular work: "I've always worked with people, and so I have a way of sort of standing back and observing these different types that are elected. That's not such a new experience for me as it might be for others." She is struck by "the thought of all these people gathered together for one purpose." In categorizing the other members, Katherine sees distinctions, appreciates variety, and stresses shared goals:

> Some of them are very cultured people in educational background, and others have a very limited educational background.

Some of them, I'm sure, have great social standing, whereas others are working people who work with their hands. Some are very intelligent and shrewd people, and others—I'm not sure how they got here. I think some of them have limited abilities along that line. And I'm sure that from the point of view of their basic motivations there would be a great variety there, too. I just don't think I've ever seen a group of people, collected together for one common purpose, who are so representative—which, of course, is what they're supposed to be. And that is a good thing, maybe.

In spite of the final "maybe," this set of categories, culminating in a reaffirmation of common purposes, is unusual in its emphasis on abilities and characteristics relevant to the major functions of the legislature: to deliberate and to represent. Katherine thus shows appreciation for the capable, but also understanding of the need for variety.

The Lawmaker's Satisfactions

Legislative office is perceived and evaluated in different ways by each of the four categories of members we have described. In each case, holding office is instrumental to some need beyond itself. The satisfactions that Lawmakers derive from being in the House show an emphasis on the prescribed tasks of the body as a source of reward, rather than the prestige, power, or worthiness of the office. Furthermore, their satisfactions come from the active manipulation of the process, rather than passive reception of benefits. In other words, Lawmakers more than other members stress adaptation to the role, rather than the status, of legislator. They invest intellectual and emotional energy in coping with the elements of the environment most relevant to the tasks which define this role.

In the first place, Lawmakers achieve satisfaction from *producing desired legislation*. Lawmakers show a pressure for completion, for following through and finishing legislative tasks. Activity for its own sake, or for the sake of some extraneous purpose, is of little interest to them. They are especially pleased when they themselves take some effective part in a successful action. They recognize the difficulties of making decisions, but accept these difficulties as necessary.

Secondly, Lawmakers are concerned that the *decision process be rational*, especially in the sense that deliberations are well-organized, long enough, and germane to the issue at hand. They derive pleasure from participating in persuasion "on the merits," not bullying or emo-

tional propaganda or calls to duty. If the method is coercive—even if
the Lawmaker gets his way—he is less than fully satisfied.

Thirdly, the Lawmaker's attitude toward others is one of *acceptance
based on insight*. Part of this insight consists of a consciousness of
shared goals (Katherine's "common purpose") being sought in a
shared situation (Ben's "we're all in the same boat"). In addition,
Lawmakers seem to have unusual empathic abilities (as illustrated
especially in Don's comments), which make it easier for them to
accept others who are perceived as different or even inferior. Thus
the satisfactions they derive from others are less dependent on warped
perceptions; they find it easy to like others, because they understand
how others feel.

The Lawmaker's satisfactions, then, frequently contrast significantly with those of the other legislator types. Others are less important to him than to the Spectator, less threatening than to the
Advertiser, less alien than to the Reluctant. Yet he is not indifferent
to them. In part because he places overriding importance on the work
to be done, the Lawmaker is pressed to understand and like his fellow
workers.[b]

SELF: IDENTITY AND GROWTH

The Lawmaker's reactions provide several useful clues to the view
he takes of himself and his political environment, as well as to the
underlying needs which his participation serves. The first thing one
notices in the interviews is his apparent immersion in the major legislative tasks. This interest seems to have at least two significant roots:
one in his past—an interest in matters political stemming from childhood and community participation; and another more deeply grounded
in his personality—a tendency to concentrate his attention on *whatever* task he confronts at a given time. In other words, he displays a
generalized ability to pay heed to the work at hand, whether it be
politics or something very different. For example, in the interview
situation, Lawmakers appeared unusually interested and cooperative,
attentive to the questions, thoughtful in reply. In their reports of

b. In their questionnaires, Lawmakers are most likely to have taken "much interest in the
psychology of other legislators." Lawmakers 61%, others 38%. They are least likely to feel
that "far too many legislators do not take the work seriously enough." Lawmakers 36%,
others 52%. They are the ones most inclined to seek advice from "the best expert on the
bill regardless of whether I know or like him." Lawmakers 70%, others 50% (N's = 33, 63).

activities at home, they refer repeatedly to problems and situations they have approached in a similarly active and committed way.

Probably no other capacity is more important than this one for the Lawmaker's adjustment. Spectators and Advertisers are, perhaps, equally attentive to certain other aspects of the legislative environment (to the rhetorical nuances that speakers display, for example), but not to the practical details of legislation. It is the Lawmakers who, more than any of the others in our categories, have broken through to the issues. Thus there is a rare harmony between the Lawmaker's main interests, on the one hand, and the major purposes of the legislature, on the other.

Furthermore, the Lawmaker's perceptions appear to be unusually objective. He is much less prone to distort reality for defensive or need-fulfilling purposes. He is something of an ideologue, but lacks the fanatical devotion to narrow principle that would hamper his effectiveness. Don illustrates this nicely when he responds to the question, "Do you worry much about what goes on here?" "Well, I don't know whether—I've been fortunate so far, in that the particular legislation that I've wanted has gone through. It's not so much that I'm worried about it. I'm probably concerned about the work I'm doing, and I'm conscientious about it. I don't think I'd be particularly upset if certain things didn't go through as I've wanted them to because they're not personally that important to me. But I do take a more than average interest in anything I'm doing."

Thus, despite his interest in legislation, the Lawmaker maintains a certain distance, a certain coolness toward his work, which prevents his emotions from getting in the way of his objectivity. Similarly, as we have seen, he perceives other people in the legislature with insight, and this is possible in part because he seems to need them less, either as objects of worship or as targets for aggression. The Lawmaker's interest and emotion appear to be at the same time more intensely committed and freer; perhaps he is best described as one who chooses, rationally and voluntarily, to invest himself in his work.

These sentiments find support in the Lawmaker's relatively high intellectual abilities and relatively high energy, but they also reflect certain practices of self-perception and need management at deeper levels of his personality. Advertisers have intelligence and vitality, but their adjustive efforts are hampered by strong inner conflicts. Spectators have a positive attitude toward legislative membership, but their need for affection interferes with their adaptation.[7] Law-makers are able to handle these problems because they can draw on sources of inner strength that other members find lacking. Successful adaptation to legislative life, in other words, depends not on the absence of adjustive problems but on the capacity to deal with them effectively.[8]

The Recognition of Self

Lawmakers are unusual in the degree to which they recognize the relevance of their personal values to the task of self-evaluation. Many members, it appears, turn elsewhere for such evaluative criteria—to others in the present or past—and thus present a rather diffuse and fluctuating picture of themselves as individuals. The Lawmaker, however, shows continually an awareness of himself and his values. Asked for a self-rating, Lawmakers respond primarily in terms of practical accomplishments, but they sum up in personal terms. Don answers, "Let me say this: I haven't done anything that I would be ashamed of as far as I, subjectively, am concerned." Ben says, "I don't feel that I have let *myself* down." And Katherine, after admitting that she has been fairly successful, adds, "Well, of course that's what I call success: I'm only saying that I've satisfied my own standards." They refer repeatedly to their own thoughts and feelings about legislation—to "certain things I felt strongly about" (Ben); to the feeling "that I should indicate that I felt it was a good change" (Don); to the "feeling of really tremendous responsibility in making a decision" (Katherine). They comment in passing on their own more general characteristics and interests: Katherine recognizes her special sensitivity to criticism, Don his penchant for the subtleties of politics, Ben his tendencies toward occasional depression. Thus in a number of ways the Lawmaker emerges from the interviews as a self-conscious person, not in the sense of timidity but as an individual aware of his own special concerns.

As will become clearer when we discuss the Lawmaker's adjustive strategies, he devotes a good deal of attention to self-examination, to defining who he is and how he can relate himself effectively to legislative roles. His need for rational mastery extends beyond grappling with the environment to include the need to master himself by means of conscious self-analysis. While not given to brooding, the Lawmaker practices introspection when faced with hard personal decisions: Katherine reports that on such an occasion she "sat down and talked to myself for a long time" and Ben says that often "you get a grip on yourself and straighten yourself out" by thinking over your purposes. Don is less prone to generalize about himself (he reports "twinges of conscience" occasionally), but relates in detail specific situations when he has tried to figure out what he is doing and why. Much as he appreciates others because he can empathize with them, the Lawmaker can appreciate himself through conscious attempts to understand his own problems. He does not retreat into reverie but rather pauses in the midst of the game to examine his position and his goals.[c]

Lawmakers rate themselves carefully, but the outcome is in every case a positive one. None of them considers himself wholly successful; yet they are clear in the conclusion that given their resources, they have done well. Don expresses what most Lawmakers seem to be saying: "Personally, it's been tremendously enjoyable. Of course, I had an idea when I ran for it I would be adaptable for it, and I would enjoy it. My expectations were more than rewarded." Katherine discusses various achievements and shortcomings and concludes that "when it's all over, no matter how critical some people may be of it, I will be satisfied that I've done all that I could have done. I don't feel that I've slighted it in any way." She adds, "I'm not inclined to give my time to something I thought somebody else could do as well or better. I try to do things I have a certain aptitude for, or training, [so] that I think that perhaps I'm the one that should be doing that job at that time." And Ben says, "I feel that I have been able to keep abreast of things, I mean as far as taking part in what I have been able to take part in, anyway." These expressions of satisfaction with one's own performance are perhaps more impressive for being in a low key: the Lawmaker is not overly impressed with himself, yet he maintains a solid core of self-respecting confidence.

This confidence shows through especially in the Lawmaker's ability to laugh at himself and his own mistakes. His sense of humor helps him to keep his worries in perspective, to forgive himself for being

c. Two questionnaire items seem to bear on this theme. Lawmakers are the new members most often agreeing that "I am a deeply religious person." Lawmakers 55%, others 41%. They are least likely to agree with: "In my leisure time, I would rather be with people than alone." Lawmakers 42%, others 71% (N's = 33, 63).

less than perfect, and to check tendencies toward narcissistic self-inflation. This is clear from the interviews; each of the statements below is followed by the notation " (laughs) ":

I was very embarrassed. (Katherine)

I have perhaps more than some people an overdeveloped conscience. (Katherine)

This disturbs me. (Katherine)

But that shows how naive I am, I'm sure. (Katherine)

But I never blame myself for that. (Katherine)

I martyred myself. (Katherine)

I was just scared of the responsibility I would have. (Katherine)

I'm sure they don't know I exist. (Katherine)

I don't know how much it will take to disillusion me. (Katherine)

You're not sure. (Ben)

You've been thrown into a situation—everything is really green. (Ben)

I knew that if I was there, I perhaps might become inspired emotionally to open my big fat mouth. (Ben)

There wasn't anything they had against me—I hadn't done anything. (Ben)

You begin to wonder, "Well, gosh—I hope they don't expect me to decide on that." Certainly not alone anyway. (Ben)

I don't think [my decision] marked the death knell of the republic, you know? (Don)

I personally didn't feel as though I were violating any principle, as far as I was concerned. (Don)

[The idea of being a judge] doesn't occupy all my waking hours. (Don)

It may not put me in the best possible light. (Don)

Taken out of context, these statements have a serious, anxious ring to them. But when we know that they appear with laughter, they indicate a light touch, an easy acceptance of the amusing side of one's struggles. They also show the Lawmaker as a person who can afford to laugh at his errors and doubts, in part because he has a capital of self-confidence in reserve.[9]

The Self as Developing

The Lawmaker, then, knows and likes himself, but this does not mean that he basks in self-satisfaction. He not only is active himself but feels that everyone should take an active part.[10] He sees himself as one striving, working, manipulating the environment, exerting effort to accomplish valued ends.

But inevitably and continually these efforts fail, as they do for anyone who involves himself in tasks which are never fully comprehended, never performed perfectly, never really finished. Legislative work is probably more frustrating in this regard than are many other kinds of endeavor. The legislator must make many decisions for which he has no special training or experience; he must accept the necessity for compromise with a large number of others; his decisions initiate but cannot fully complete social policies. Consequently, if he is to be effective, he must learn to live with failure, to take some satisfaction in imperfect accomplishments. The alternative is the kind of diffuse despair we have encountered so frequently in the foregoing chapters: intensification of feelings of inadequacy, discouragement, and resort to protective strategies that hamper achievement.

Lawmakers manage to sustain both self-confidence and interest in legislative tasks in large part because of a special attitude they take toward themselves: a sense of the self as developing. This means that in adjusting to new situations the Lawmaker allows himself time and leeway for learning. He approaches new roles experimentally, expecting to grow and change in the course of adapting to them. This practice enables him to shuck off much of the guilt and anxiety that burden those with more rigid self-views. Ben Yerby illustrates this attitude clearly:

> INTERVIEWER: What are some of the things that have helped you to make a success of this?
>
> BEN: I'm thinking now in terms of goals that may be set by an individual. Certainly there is the sort of thing that you hope and dream about as an ultimate goal, but as a newcomer and a freshman legislator I perhaps try to be more practical, and at least try to realize that those goals, for a newcomer, anyway,

were beyond my reach. So I think in the first term, anyway, I set rather simple goals for myself. And I think perhaps some of those have been achieved. I would have been happier—and will be happier—if I can extend beyond those simple goals and perhaps come within reach of something a little bit higher.

INTERVIEWER: That's very interesting.

BEN: But not—it all depends on what you have in mind in the way of goals. Are these simple goals that you set, knowing that if you work hard and give it an honest effort, that we can reach? Or are these perhaps, well, perhaps the sort of things that we dream about? I mean, like, well, you may have a couple of pieces of legislation that you have in mind that perhaps are quite progressive, or might involve a considerable amount of reform in our state government, in some way or another. And if you are—not ideally dreaming, but perhaps hoping and praying that something like that will be realized—well, no, I've fallen far short of something like that. Because one of the bills would have been X. But I realized when I agreed to introduce it that this was something that was going to perhaps align me with some advanced thinkers, and that it might take more than one session—it might take two or three sessions before you could get the other members of the legislature or your committee to come around to your thinking. Now if that had been a goal for this session, I'd be miserably disappointed. That was a hope, but it wasn't a simple goal. . . . But simple goals: being able to fulfill a responsibility as a representative from my town, keeping alert and aware of what is going on, and knowing what is going on, and making a point of being there when perhaps your vote or your presence may have some significance. Things of that sort. These are simple goals. These I feel I have been able in the most part to achieve. But if, as you say, if speaking of ideals or perhaps more distant goals—no, I've failed miserably.

Here Ben places himself in a context of goals arranged in a temporal series, increasing in importance and difficulty. The ultimate goals are postponed, not surrendered. The proximate goals are seen as responsibilities to be accepted in the present; they are not discarded as essentially trivial or worthless because they are of lesser importance. These preliminary accomplishments are seen as accumulating over time, building a basis for approaching the ideal. Yet they also have value in and of themselves: thus the Lawmaker can garner satisfactions as he goes along.[11]

The Lawmaker's sense of time and his place in it appears to be one of his most powerful personal resources, enabling him to maintain the self-confidence necessary for action. In contrast, the Advertiser's disappointment and impatience represent an inability to tolerate the distance between his present situation and his ultimate goals. His attention is so occupied with speeding his rate of ascent toward very high goals that he finds little to please him in the present. The Lawmaker, on the other hand, can wait for perfection, taking satisfaction in steady progress. Unlike the Advertiser, he can accept his past as preparation for present and future development. The Reluctant tends to retreat backward in time in order to escape the discomforts of the present; he is tempted to reject his contemporary self and find solace in a glorified view of the way he was in the old days. For the Lawmaker, however, the past is always incomplete, always moving into the present and future. His history is relevant mainly because its lessons can be applied here and now. He does not reject himself-as-he-is-today in favor of himself-as-he-was-yesterday because he recognizes a developing self which includes both these phases of growth.

The Spectator's time sense tends to be extremely short-run; his consciousness is dominated by the immediate situation. He rates himself primarily according to his current success in gathering esteem and affection. This perspective makes him continually wary, subject to depression and anxiety when he receives some momentary slight. In a sense, the Spectator stakes his whole value on each day's experience. The Lawmaker's self-evaluation remains a tentative, experimental one; he rates himself not by what he is at any given moment but by what he is in the process of becoming. This view of the present as an extension of the past and a beginning of the future enables the Lawmaker to experience temporary reverses with awareness but without despair.[12]

This sense of the self as developing is illustrated throughout the Lawmaker interviews. In numerous passages, the Lawmaker (a) recognizes that he has fallen short of his goals, (b) places such shortcomings in the broader context of his general ongoing development, and (c) accepts himself finally as justified by continued effort to do right. Looking toward the future, he links it to his present.

This is clear, for example, when Don, Katherine, and Ben discuss their political prospects. Don says he has not given serious thought to running for Congress and would wait "until my practice was sufficiently established at home before I would think about it." He continues: "I would probably give it considerable thought. I'd make sure I was ready for it in terms of having put in the necessary time here, in handling bills, and so forth. But the possibility has occurred to me, but it's not an immediate prospect." Katherine reports that when she was nominated, "I said I didn't care too much about the future," but adds: "I said this before but I care more now than I did, because I have enjoyed it so much and I can see how it really would be a disappointment not to be reelected. . . . I really don't have any great political ambitions but it appeals to me a great deal, so if some way opened up, you know, to stay up for another term or to do something else that was related, I would be tempted to do it." And Ben, asked about the possibility of running for Congress, says that "at the moment I don't consider myself qualified. Because I've got so much more to learn about state government, local government, right here." In each case the Lawmaker makes connections between his current legislative activities and future political possibilities.

Personal and Social Time

One other aspect of the Lawmaker's time perspective contrasts significantly with that of the Advertiser.[13] The Advertiser's *personal* time perspective—his perception of his own future course—appears to be considerably longer than the Lawmaker's. Advertisers are apt to have long-range plans for achieving occupational success. Lawmakers concentrate more on the middle-range future; their personal plans concern the next few years. But the Advertiser's *social* time perspective—his view of society as it will develop in the future—is considerably shorter than the Lawmaker's. Advertisers are little concerned with the way the world will look a decade or so hence; rather they tend to talk about immutable human nature in a way that suggests an essentially static society. Lawmakers refer on numerous occasions to their interest in legislative programs extending far into the future and, at times, to even more general social developments. In each case the member shows a comparatively longer view in the direction of his major interest: for the Advertiser, his own ambitions; for the Lawmaker, the social policies he is involved with.

Perhaps the major themes in the Lawmaker's personality can best be understood on two levels—the first, the level of his interaction with the environment, and the second, a set of internal interactions. His most important characteristic at the first level is an ability to perceive the environment realistically without becoming fundamentally discouraged. At the second, deeper, level the Lawmaker shows a capacity for maintaining a strong sense of personal identity without freezing that identity into a rigid structure. Both of these capacities draw strength from his awareness of personal growth, his cognizance of himself as a developing human being in touch with a developing situation.

STRATEGIES: STEPS TO ACHIEVEMENT

The Lawmaker considers his main task in the House to be decision-making on bills. He spends most of his time thinking, studying, talking about legislative issues. His satisfactions come from successful personal action on these matters. In other words, more than other legislators, he adopts the achievement pattern of adjustment. In the course of this effort he tends to become aware of several new, important, and recurring choices regarding his roles [14] as a politician and legislator—choices that need to be made if he is to participate effectively. For example, as we have seen in Ben's case,[15] the Lawmaker who makes a conscious decision about feasible goals in his first session can then move on more freely to attack the practical work at hand without being distracted by nagging feelings of inadequacy. Don's deliberate choice to devote the necessary time to legislative work removes a very common cause of anxiety for the legislator. Such preliminary general decisions about his basic responsibilities reduce the tension involved in making a large number of subsequent more specific choices; he does not have to re-examine his whole philosophy every time a new issue arises. Role-definition is the counterpart, on the level of managing his official tasks, of the Lawmaker's self-definition—his awareness of himself as a certain kind of person.[16]

The roles attached to the office of legislator are nowhere officially prescribed, and there is little agreement among members on exactly what behavior is expected of a legislator as such.[17] One might suppose, for example, that every legislator in order to operate effectively would have to block out some particular policy topic as his specialty. But as we have seen in the case of the Spectator, there are members who show little personal interest in operating effectively; and, as the Advertiser illustrates, there are those whose inner problems prevent them from taking on the little jobs that might accumulate to build achievements. Defining the task roles that accompany legislative office is a matter of intense concern only for those members who try to come to grips with the main work the office entails. Judging from the interviews, many more take office than take these roles.

From the point of view of the individual, then, role-definition is a problem of adjustment, a question that arises when he experiences some conflict regarding the task. For the Lawmaker, with his emphasis on rational mastery, these conflicts appear most often in the form of some tension that threatens to interfere with his use of reason in legislative work. One such tension develops when he perceives that the volume and complexity of legislative issues are too great for any one person to manage. If he were to resolve this tension by giving up —by voting randomly, or as a leader instructs, or not at all—this decision would cut him off from further reasoning about issues. Instead he decides to concentrate mainly on the most important bills [d] and those his committees are responsible for. This strategy increases his opportunities for using his mind on issues, as well as furthering his chances for success.

In the two following sections we look first at the process Lawmakers tend to use in making such decisions, and then at the solutions they have developed in defining their roles as public figures, as campaigners, and as political compromisers.[18]

The Planning of Roles

Postponing for the moment the description of the Lawmaker's solutions to these problems, how does he go about solving them? There is, of course, no single method applied by every Lawmaker in every case, but a review of their role-defining comments does show a pattern, a set of intellectual strategies. The steps are seldom exactly in order; some of them may be omitted. The Lawmakers we encounter during their first session, although they have not yet worked these matters out completely, have made enough of a beginning to permit a general characterization of the process. In planning his legislative roles the Lawmaker tends to use the following techniques:

(1) *He shows a personal awareness of the problem.*

d. A majority of Lawmakers interviewed distinguished between "trivial" and "important" bills.

(2) *He delineates the boundaries within which choice is possible.*
(3) *He hypothesizes various alternatives within the boundaries.*
(4) *He evaluates alternatives according to their social and personal implications.*
(5) *He makes a tentative choice of role characteristics to be emphasized.*

A good illustration of these techniques at work is Katherine's discussion of her role as a representative of her constituents. Lawmakers are especially aware of the incongruities between their own reasoning about issues and their responsibilities to constituents who may disagree. Katherine develops this problem as she thinks out loud in the following passages, which are keyed to the numbers in the listing above:

Another—I know we're perhaps a little off the subject, but I've given a lot of thought to the problem but haven't arrived at any very intelligent conclusion;	(1) Shows personal awareness
that is, to what extent are you supposed to be up here as a representative of your town, promoting their special interests and representing the people as they want to be represented?	(3) Poses alternatives (4) Evaluates: relevant others
And to what extent are you supposed to be using your own best judgment, because they have elected you as having confidence in you and you're studying it, and you're better informed than most of them.	(4) Evaluates: own values
This has always concerned me with elected officials,	(1) Shows personal awareness
because I'm sure you can't deny that responsibility to the people who elected you. Because you're their voice. On the other hand, you can't just come to the point of feeling that they should just be able to dictate to you.	(2) Delineates boundaries

Like some of the representatives —they have a town meeting, say "We've got to oppose this or that," and then there is the representative—what is the responsibility? This concerns me,	(4) Evaluates: relevant others (1) Shows personal awareness
because I'm probably. . . . I'm so afraid of these descriptive terms, but—more liberal than the majority of the people in the town I represent. This is the crux of it, that I'm really quite liberal in social attitudes and I'm sure there are many people in town that think differently.	(4) Evaluates: own values, relevant others

.   .   .

I don't think I have really got it completely, but I was thinking of a way that I would put it down, one, two, three. I think the first thing is to do your best to figure out	(5) Decides: priority
what is to be right and best for for the whole state	(4) Evaluates: own values
and your second one is to interpret and represent	(5) Decides: priority
the interests and needs of your own constituency. This goes back to the problem I said before [laughs], I wasn't sure	(4) Evaluates: relevant others
whether that came first; I don't think that it does.	(5) Decides: priority, tentative decision

.   .   .

There seems to be quite a feeling, a lot of times that you choose somebody to go up there and fight for your town, that that's their job, to go up there and get some new roads for you or a stop light—this, that, or the other thing.	(4) Evaluates: relevant others

And I didn't think this came first.	(5) Decides: priority
I think that you choose somebody that can be part of a group that considers the overall good of the state. Because the time is long past when any little town can sit there and just think of itself —we're all so interdependent.	(4) Evaluates: relevant others

This style of thinking contrasts in many significant ways with that of the other legislator types. The Spectator tends to avoid such problems altogether, or to jump to the conclusion that they are unsolvable. The Advertiser finds it particularly difficult to accept the necessary limits, to entertain and consider seriously alternatives that challenge his own choice, or to admit the relevance of others' opinions on the matter. The Reluctant is likely to find the question too complicated to figure out; he may lack the imagination necessary to hypothesize what he might do in various future circumstances.

On this same subject of one's own ideas versus those of constituents, Ben and Don use techniques much like Katherine's. Ben says that in considering the problem, "you find yourself in mixed emotions," "you find yourself torn," and "that's when you have to come to grips with yourself and figure out, well, whom am I serving here? Which role do I play here?"

> In other words, you're thinking in terms of a pending piece of legislation—how is it going to affect my town? Now this may be detrimental to your town in one way or another. But in the overall picture it's good for the state. So now—you as the representative of that town—do you fight it? Oppose it? Or do you consent to go along with the majority and favor it? Even though you know your town is going to lose by it—either financially or in some other way?

He is concerned with where to draw the line. He considers how "a good many members of the House were thinking" about this problem, and what "the thinking in your town very easily could be." "You hear some of their feelings about it and you begin to think, well, maybe they're right." He decides that ultimately his town will receive benefits from legislation for the good of the whole state, and concludes: "I would prefer to think in terms of my own town."

Don has found that his constituents do not demand much of him on issues, although he gets some pressure on matters that concern individuals. He works out the problem in this manner:

> I think an individual who is up here can pretty well operate on his own. To a certain extent he's got to satisfy local pressures. But I haven't yet on any—I think people appreciate an exercise of independent judgment on most matters. I think a lot of the things are over their heads. And they only become emotionally involved in emotional issues, which most of these are not. There are important issues here, but they are not highly charged issues. Now, when you get to a civil rights or capital punishment situation, you get that emotionalism. It makes it a lot more difficult to operate; you feel the pressures much greater. But I think that it's fairly easy to be your own boss, actually.

The Lawmaker, then, uses his reason not only to analyze particular pieces of legislation but also to work out general guidelines for legislating. He feels these problems more intensely and personally than other members do. His analyses of them usually include a conscious determination of the scope of choice, a posing of alternatives, and an evaluation in terms of his own values and needs and those of others with relevant opinions. At the end of the process is a choice which may be amended tomorrow but is to be acted upon today.

Some Strategic Role Choices

We should not be surprised to find certain minor themes among the Lawmakers that reflect the other types. Don Bennis, as a young lawyer, might be expected to show some Advertiser-like qualities. And indeed, at one point he does refer to his purpose, "from a purely practical standpoint, to make professional and political contacts on the state level." The Spectators include an unusually large proportion of women; Katherine shares with them appreciation of the legislature as a "stimulating" place to be. "It really does make you feel important, in a way," she says; "it's exciting for that reason, too." Ben is not an old man, but certain Reluctant themes appear in his interview, as when he says that "perhaps curiosity more than anything else got me into it [i.e. the nomination], but still at the same time I had the feeling—the same feeling in regard to this that I had in regard to a willingness to serve in the church or in the PTA or in the town. In other words, this was an opportunity to play a part in something that I believed in." Occasionally he has found the legislature "very, very confusing," and sometimes felt "that I just wasn't capable of coping with the whole thing. But then," he continues, "I figured, well, others have in the past, so [laughs] maybe we can see it through."

Thus each Lawmaker shows some evidence of inclination toward one of the other styles of adjustment. Especially for this reason it is interesting to see how Lawmakers overcome certain obstacles to political effectiveness that are apt to divert other members into less productive channels. We have seen something of the Lawmaker's general technique for defining his roles—what kinds of tentative solutions does he develop by applying this technique?

At least three role problems, besides the one illustrated already, confront the Lawmaker as he moves into political activity. He becomes a *public figure* and thus is fair game for public criticism. As Stimson Bullitt writes, "The danger line is crossed when a man starts to appear in the papers," [19] but as a political candidate the Lawmaker finds himself faced with an organized opposition expected to be critical. Not only his political opinions but also his fitness for office, his personal capacities, even his integrity may be called into question. For many Lawmakers this is a novel experience, one for which they need to work out some reasoned reaction.

A second role that needs attention is that of the *campaigner*, especially as this involves calculated rhetoric in campaigning. As we have seen, Lawmakers favor reasoned persuasion on the merits in the legislature; they tend to prefer high-level issue debate in the campaign also, but often find voters more interested in their personalities or in entertaining conversation than in heavier questions of state. The Lawmaker thus faces a choice: shall he entertain, educate, or do a little of both?

A third role choice involves the legislator's stance as a political *compromiser*. This set of problems becomes especially relevant when he reaches the legislature and finds that the bills he favors are being packaged with other less desirable bills—and with numerous strings attached. His decision-making on such occasions is facilitated if he develops some preliminary orientation, some tentative position on the limits and possibilities of political trading.[20]

How do the Lawmakers, each with his tendencies toward another type, approach these problems? All their solutions are not yet fully developed, but some beginnings are evident.

Public Figure

The Spectator is apt to find the public figure role a particularly un-comfortable one. He feels exposed and hurt when others censure him and is thus tempted to conceal his opinions and play some supporting part. Katherine Howell says that "I'm very sensitive to criticism, I hate to be criticized." The campaign was "just vicious," marred by attacks she could not help feeling were personal ones. The opposition "dragged up all sorts of things that weren't true." But she resolves the issue by taking note of the reactions of others and her own values:

> In fact, probably another reason I won was because they were so vicious in their attack on me personally. I'm so susceptible to that kind of attack, and the people that knew me knew that this was just pure politics and ridiculous, and really reacted against them, if you know what I mean.
>
> Actually, it didn't bother me as much as people had thought it would bother me—apparently it was so ridiculous that it really didn't. . . . And so I insisted on debating on the issues, while all my supporters thought I was crazy. And I don't know if it paid off or not, but at least I can respect myself afterwards for it.

Katherine shows that she feels the sting of criticism much as a Spectator would, but she moves beyond this feeling to determine where she stands and why.

Advertisers tend to react aggressively to criticism, either by striking back or by thinking dark thoughts. Don Bennis, a young lawyer in much the same position as the Advertiser Mike Jackson, sketches out the alternatives in this passage:

> I wouldn't call myself an aggressive politician. I don't go out looking for a battle. I don't think that people welcome political warfare as such. I enjoy the subtleties of political competition. . . . It's normal in politics to do a certain amount of infighting. And whether you do it by blasting people from the floor of a convention, or whether you do it by indirection, without neces-sarily sacrificing principle, and without being unnecessarily vin-dictive. But I think it's the same type of thing. But the competition isn't necessarily damaging. There's something—this competitiveness is something that you respect in politics.

Don himself has not been subjected to personal attacks but he entertains the hypothetical possibility with no difficulty: "Well, I would
probably be rather sensitive. I don't know how I would react to that.
Of course, the best politicians, the most effective ones are probably
the ones who are least sensitive or are least quick to anger. . . . You
can be sensitive and still respond without aggression. But the outward
aggression is something that is a handicap in politics." Sensitivity
without aggression appears as Don's tentative solution to the public-
figure role. In defining this role, he utilizes a number of the steps
described in the general process outlined above.

The Reluctant is unlikely to receive any very personal criticism in
public, although he may find himself a new topic for private gossip at
home. His peaceable propensities make it likely that he would react to
criticism not by withdrawal but by intensified effort to patch up
differences, to soft-pedal controversial matters. Ben Yerby gives us
some hint of his strategy for meeting such problems in this report:
"No, I didn't get involved in any name-calling or anything like that.
I felt I had no reason to. There were certain things that I felt strongly
about, that I believed in, and I felt that if they agreed with me on
those things, well, that was fine. But I wasn't going to give in to any
name-calling, either on the part of individuals or the party as such."
It should be noted that the strong beliefs Ben is referring to here are
not general principles, but specific legislative programs to which he
shows a continuing commitment as a legislator. Peace, for him, is not
to be bought at the price of softening these stands.

Thus in three slightly different ways Lawmakers counteract inclinations toward ineffective strategies by adopting ones which provide
for continuing activity on substantive issues. Perhaps Don's sentence
best summarizes the Lawmaker solution: "You can be sensitive and
still respond without aggression."

Campaigner

The role of the campaigner is an uncomfortable one for the Spectator. He risks being put in the limelight, being asked embarrassing
questions on unfamiliar topics. He feels much more at home in the
audience than on the speaker's platform. Insofar as the Spectator does
campaign, he tends to keep the whole affair on a plane of light conversation. Generally his strategies here are concealment and superficial
socializing. Katherine, the Lawmaker, shared some of these feelings

during her campaign: "I hate campaigning. And I hate going from door to door asking people for support." At first she refused to do this but then changed her mind: "I said I would not go from door to door. I told them this from the beginning. But sometimes in the campaign I had to do it because it was only fair to them to get out and work because they were working so hard."

Finding house-to-house canvassing distressing, Katherine shifted the emphasis to small meetings in homes. This technique was not very successful, "but we persisted in this approach," continuing to "campaign on an educational level," to "inform people on the issues which were important." The choice here is clear: Katherine adjusts her campaigning methods to her personal predispositions, finding alternatives through which she can maintain an issue-based campaign. The coffee parties are not allowed to degenerate into merely social affairs. Thus Katherine persists, where many a Spectator would retreat.

Some Advertisers are active campaigners, but they express considerable cynicism about the role. The voter appears in their interviews primarily as a pawn to be used; the Advertiser finds it hard not to feel contempt for him. Issues are important mainly as rhetorical devices. He experiences little pleasure in campaign work, in part because he feels he is doing something fundamentally dishonest. Lawmaker Don Bennis reports that he found at most "one or two or perhaps three meetings at which issues were discussed and in which I had an opportunity to discuss issues." While "my stand on those particular issues might have impressed some of the people that were at those meetings," Don feels that "they had nothing to do with my being elected." With few exceptions, state-level issues are "pretty far removed from most people" and "it's pretty difficult to relate to people with issues." House-to-house canvassing, Don finds, is "strictly a personal approach—it's sort of a brainwashing sort of thing; they saw you and they didn't see the other guy."

Don says he enjoyed campaigning although "I had some twinges of conscience about it because it was a mechanical approach." He resolves the problem in this way:

> Well, I rationalize it, in the sense that it's a necessary part of campaigning. And in a small town it's almost entirely a matter of personality, of liking you, see, for yourself, not for your stand on issues. It's not that important—just liking you personally. And

having that personal contact. Now, it may be a phony, mechanical way of doing it, but I think that my views on issues meant something as far as my serving [is concerned], rather than my campaigning. I don't feel as if I fooled the voters; I think all the voters wanted to know is who I am. It's a matter of identification, that's all.

Don's decision reserves issue discussions for meetings and other similar occasions, rather than insisting on doorstep speechmaking. He maintains a personal interest in issues in the midst of a personality-oriented canvass. In contrast to the Advertiser, Don shows little guilt about this approach and no contempt for the voter. His role-definition makes it possible for him to campaign actively and effectively without becoming an issueless hack—and to enjoy the process.

Reluctants tend not to bother much with campaigning, to run on their reputations and let it go at that. Out of a sense of duty they may occasionally sally forth to visit their neighbors. Not much discussion of political issues is to be expected in these encounters. Ben Yerby, the Lawmaker, "found that I enjoyed it" although "it wasn't the sort of thing that you looked forward to with bated breath or enthusiastically or anything—you felt that it was something that you should be doing and really had to do if this thing was going to be successful." The campaign, Ben reports, was mainly "a certain amount of social activity, from the standpoint of meeting people and being with people and doing things with people." Ben liked this, but a close look at his report shows that he enjoyed especially occasions when issues came up:

> I found that once I got doing it, I enjoyed it. In a good many cases people asked some intelligent questions, or in many instances giving me some very interesting information. I just enjoyed meeting them and talking with them, and in some cases they wouldn't say much, and you'd wish them well and be on your way. And in other cases you'd actually get into a very pleasant conversation or discussion about some particular situation they were interested in, either on the local or state level, and enjoy discussing it.

In the course of the campaign Ben participated in a number of informal meetings in homes where "the candidates who were involved in the campaign would be available for questions and discussions." Such meetings were quite informal, with conversation ranging from children to the weather, but including "in a good many cases, politics— that's what we ended up with."

In these passages Ben recognizes the necessity for active campaigning, accepts and enjoys its social side, and finds a place in it for the discussion of issues. Put in another way, he defines a role for himself in which personal satisfactions and necessary work are combined.

Compromiser

Defining his role as a political compromiser is not apt to be much of a problem for the Spectator, for at least two reasons. He lacks the strong personal beliefs and commitments which might give rise to indignation at illegitimate trading, and he finds it difficult to criticize anyone in a leadership position, such as the party leaders who are the central figures in negotiations. Katherine, on the other hand, takes a different slant. "This concept many people have of the 'politician' interests me," she says, "to see how the people over here fit that pattern." Asked what the pattern is and how well it fits, Katherine explains:

> I don't think it fits too many of them, although I'm afraid it fits more closely those who have real influence over here. This [laughs] disturbs me. I sometimes wonder how really effective in the long run those of us are who consider ourselves not real politicians, you know. I'm sure there's something of ego in it too. There certainly are all types of people over there, there's no doubt about that—I suppose that's good. And I haven't met too many people that would fit what most people consider to be the "politician," that's always making a deal under the table: "You vote for this, I'll vote for that." But there's more of it than I like to see. And I'm sure that I'm not aware of most of it.

Katherine thus shows that she is mildly disturbed by the dealing she finds in the legislature, but she places it within the larger context: there is not too much of it. She will suspend judgment until she knows more of what is going on. Of committee politicking she says there is "not enough of it to distract the committee from functioning." She has not yet become an enthusiastic fan of the party leaders; she discusses them dispassionately as individuals, saying of the top leader, "I'm still waiting to see." And she feels that another leader "is doing a fairly good job as party leader, but I haven't known enough about what the role of the party leader would be to really form an opinion yet." The criterion she applies throughout is contribution to the task —committee "functioning," the "role" of the party leader. There is little here of the Spectator's blind admiration.

Advertisers are sensitive to the problem of political compromise but tend to exaggerate it: the system is seen as fundamentally corrupt and therefore there is no effective limit on deal-making. The Advertiser shrugs his shoulders—that's the way the game is played. In contrast, Don spends a good deal of intellectual effort on defining the limits and functions of political compromise. He begins with the problem as it appears in minor legislation:

> I was aware of the negative aspects of this business—the bargaining and trading, you know, with bills and so forth. It's present, I'm aware of it, and haven't been particularly shocked by it. I found that a good deal of it I don't feel is too bad because a lot of the bargaining and trading is with matters that are not of substance, matters of local interest, which don't particularly involve any tremendous issues, you see. And it may be morally reprehensible, but politically, I mean from a governmental standpoint, doesn't have any particular bad result. I'm speaking of these private bills, which are strictly pork barrel types of things. But I don't think they're bad in the sense that—in fact, they're good because it's a form of, you might say, welfare. It's an aspect of welfare work at the state level, except it's on an individual basis.

Having decided that minor-bill compromise is relatively harmless and partially useful, Don turns to the major issues: "It's particularly distasteful to me when bills that I think are of importance are traded back and forth. You see what I mean? And bills which have no rational relationship to each other." He develops this point with an example, objecting to "putting things together in a bill which have no reasonable relationship, in order to trap the other side." This sort of action he finds especially "distasteful" if "used to promote a bad result," somewhat less so if the result is good.

Don's distinctions in these passages result in a sliding scale of "reprehensibility," ranging from bad major bills packaged together despite unrelated substance to questionable minor pork barrel or individual welfare bills. He carves out a set of criteria that he can subsequently apply to the large and small issues of the session. The limits

Don defines are general ones, but he has moved beyond either condemnation of all trading or cynical acceptance of any deal.

Reluctants, as we have seen, are tempted to divorce themselves from "politics" and, more generally, to stress the importance of character over political criteria. Ben Yerby expresses somewhat similar sentiments about political compromise but comes to some rather different conclusions. He thinks that "if you had a larger majority of dedicated people" on a committee "they could do an awful lot of good and cover an awful lot of ground." He then proceeds to illustrate clearly the Lawmaker way of defining this role. He would like to see more

> people that were not resigned to party platforms, or campaign promises, or something like that. I realize that you're bound to have a certain amount of that. And to some extent the party position has to be respected and certainly has to be considered. But—I don't know, maybe if the individuals were, if I can use the term, more dedicated, and there were more of them, a lot of what might be considered good legislation could be forced on the administration or the party. I just feel a lot more ground would be covered. And I feel very, very strongly as far as politics is concerned, if you find a policy or a program that you believe to be right, while there may not be a survey to indicate how many people are for or against it, but you feel from all standpoints—legally, morally—that this particular program is good and that the state would benefit by it, and that it was economically possible, regardless of what the political expedient was at the time—if you have these convictions that what you are doing or are trying to do is right, then in the long run, regardless of which way the political wind is blowing, you are going to be proven right.

In this long last sentence Ben reminds one of Elihu Root,[21] but the general tenor of his remarks is clear: political considerations have their legitimate place, but a greater emphasis is needed on objective consideration of policies and programs. Ben shows that he values character primarily for its effects on the legislative process—more ground would be covered, more good legislation produced if there were more "dedicated" members. In later passages he makes it clear that he has had a good deal to do with negotiations with the party leaders on particular issues and decisions. They neither shock him nor scare him; his relations with them have been close and amicable—and productive.

In no two cases do the Lawmakers come to exactly the same conclusions as they work to define their political roles. Nor has any one of them reached a final solution to these problems. What they seem to share is a consciousness that these preliminary decisions, if faced up to and tentatively resolved, can help to guide them through the complexities and dilemmas involved in many more particular decisions. Effective use of this strategy requires them to overcome certain unproductive tendencies, certain distractions that threaten to divert them from the work at hand.[e]

THE BALANCE OF THE LAWMAKER PATTERN

The Lawmaker's main strategy—rational mastery through role definition—appears to be not a temporary expedient but rather an habitual style of action utilized in many phases of his life other than the political. The particular solutions he works out by means of this method may change considerably as he accumulates political experience, but the method itself, the practice of consciously organizing his approach to his roles, is probably sufficiently ingrained in his personality to outlast many a disappointment. Furthermore, this strategy is *more likely than any of the others* to be effective in bringing him the kind of reward he is most interested in—practical success on legislation. We reserve for the moment the question whether the successes are likely to be sufficiently numerous and important to sustain the Lawmaker's interest in legislating, raising here only the question of the probability that he will switch to one of the alternative patterns we have discussed. Our answer is that the achievement pattern, by and large, has tangible payoffs that contrast markedly with the minor satisfactions the other patterns bring.

The Contradictions of the Other Patterns

Beyond their ineffectiveness, the other patterns involve additional personal costs to the Lawmaker. A switch to the submissive set of strategies would be especially expensive; it would require a fundamental modification of the Lawmaker's strong sense of personal identity, a surrendering of individuality. To be sure, he may make a

e. Lawmakers, in their questionnaires, are most likely to have "found the fact that much of the legislative work is open to the press and public" "not at all distracting." Lawmakers 79%, others 59%. They most frequently report that the "excitement involved in some issues" "had little or no effect on me." Lawmakers 33%, others 19%. But they most often agreed that "I made a special effort to get my views on legislation before the public." Lawmakers 73%, others 52% (N's = 33, 63).

conscious decision to follow the lead of persons he trusts on certain
specific matters. For example, he may learn that he can rely on the
judgment of a particular committee chairman on a topic he is unfamiliar with. But as a general strategy the Spectator's continual other-
directed search for guidance as an escape from personal responsibility
will seem an unnecessary and an unreasonable abdication to the Lawmaker. He would have to forego an important source of reward: the
feeling of subjective satisfaction he gains when he has met his own
standards of behavior. Spectator-like submission makes such personal
values largely irrelevant and the accompanying rewards unattainable.
The Lawmaker is unlikely to be much interested in the minor joys of
dependency.

If the submissive pattern looks unnecessary and unappealing to the
Lawmaker, the aggressive pattern, as practiced by the Advertisers,
probably seems somewhat threatening to him, in that it involves the
risk of a descent to irrationality. Rational mastery requires an ability
to maintain a certain emotional distance from others, a certain tenta-
tiveness in one's commitments to goals, a certain objectivity toward
oneself. The kind of aggressiveness that the Advertiser uses to gain
some release from his anxiety, guilt, and frustration represents a
weakening of each of these abilities. Accuracy of observation suffers;
one's perceptual apparatus is put at the service of intense emotional
demands. The general effect is one of gross oversimplification; complex
individuals become stereotypes, unrealistic goals are given an all-or-
nothing significance, and the self becomes all-absorbing. The Lawmaker is likely to recognize the self-defeating character of these
strategies and to resist them successfully.[22]

In periods of defeat and discouragement the Lawmaker may feel
some of the Reluctant's temptation to withdraw, to reduce his aspirations and contemplate his virtues. But he has a strong resource against
this tendency: his sense of personal development. His orientation is
primarily toward the future; fleeing to the past would involve an
abrupt reversal, a fairly fundamental redefinition of his approach to
life. The Lawmaker is always in the midst of some work yet to be
completed, and he knows from his past accomplishments that satisfaction can be won with diligence and intelligence. In his scheme of
values character is not enough. While he shares the Reluctant's dislike
for coercion and needless antagonism, he retains an interest in active,
rational persuasion. Nothing is to be achieved without a certain

amount of self-assertion; Lawmakers cannot rest easy with rusting talents.

Environmental Support

The Lawmaker asks more of his legislative environment than a chance to be active. Successful action, the completion of desired projects, is required for his satisfaction. Since he is not a fanatic, he demands not that every one of his ideas be translated into law but rather that his record show at least some important positive achievements. In legislative terms this means that the Lawmaker is generally found pressing for new action, for innovations that will move society in directions he desires. By and large, this places the Lawmaker in the liberal camp, in that he is likely to be more interested in creating and completing programs for progress than in maintaining the status quo or returning to some simpler past. The Lawmakers interviewed—in both parties—tend to confirm this picture.

As already noted, the particular legislative session (1959) during which the interviews were held was unusual in the scope and volume of legislation passed; Lawmakers could gain particular satisfaction from the impressive list of reforms enacted, many of which had long been on the agendas of good government groups in Connecticut. In 1961 the major questions concerned how to pay for the programs that had been put into effect; the legislature returned to normal. The predominant issue was the budget and most of the session was taken up with a prolonged, acrimonious deadlock. The 1963 session was even less productive. The Lawmakers among the members must have found it a frustrating experience.

If there can be such a thing as a typical American state legislative session, it probably resembles 1961 or 1963 in Connecticut more than 1959. The path of a bill through the system is dotted with stop signs. Proposals must meet a number of technical requirements of form and timing before they can even begin the journey. Bills can be placed at the bottom of many a pile of papers, assigned to an unfavorable or inappropriate committee, laid to rest by committee action or inaction, delayed in the process of formal hearings and readings, allowed too brief an appearance in debate, lost in the shuffle of frantic action as the session closes, made a matter for perpetual study and restudy, amended out of existence, and/or voted down on the floor. Once passed by the House, the bill faces another long series of hurdles: the

Senate, which is based on a different system of apportionment; the Governor, who is responsible to still another constituency; the administration, headed by independently elected directors and responsive to special clienteles. At times the system seems less an instrument of the majority than a series of veto points, each under the control of some smaller group or coalition of groups. Perhaps the system allows access to almost every important interest in the society, but this is small comfort if access means only the power to stop the government from acting. Such a system is in no way the equivalent of majority rule, because it is so constructed that even a majority of the minorities can be rendered powerless, since only one veto somewhere in the sequence is necessary to end action.

In a more nearly typical session, then, Lawmakers will be disappointed more frequently than they were in 1959. The environment will be punishing for the member whose sense of satisfaction is suspended until his policies actually go into effect. What is likely to be the Lawmaker's reaction to such failures? More specifically, what effects will they have in the long run on his pattern of adjustment?

Reactions to Institutional Failure

As we have seen,[23] the Lawmaker's scheme of things has a place for failure so long as it is not complete and final. His view of himself and of his place in the process of social development allows him to pick up and move on after temporary political reverses. His habitual reaction to frustration is exertion, especially in the form of intellectual analysis of the situation. If the legislative process continually blocks action on bills he considers important, he is likely to ask why, to break the problem down into its components and causes, and to explore possible alternative courses of action to overcome it. He may drop his concern with particular bills temporarily and direct his attention to reforms in the system itself. Thus many ideas for improving the Assembly's procedures are found in the Lawmaker interviews, ideas for the more effective use of time and talents and for bringing about the conscious resolution of questions. Or the Lawmaker may focus on the need for better qualified legislators as a key to the problem and work in his party to recruit more able members. This is a special concern of Ben's —the necessity for getting "more dedicated people"—and he has taken an active part in efforts to attract such people and use their abilities in his home town. Another alternative is education of the electorate: if the issues were more widely understood, perhaps they would be more intensely supported. Katherine's persistent effort to organize meetings of her constituents to discuss the major issues is an example. As they gain experience, Lawmakers may move into publicity and platform activities on a higher level. The final payoff remains the enacted bill, but the Lawmaker who finds himself hamstrung in getting that has a number of alternative angles from which to attack the problem.

At the margins of the Lawmaker category some members will give up and go home after a session or two. But the Lawmaker's personal strengths, his long-time political interest, and his abilities to think and to act help guard him against defeat and despair. And an occasional session like that of 1959 will do much to lift his spirits.[24]

THE LAWMAKER AND THE WORK OF THE LEGISLATURE

We turn now to look at the Lawmaker–legislature relationship from the opposite viewpoint: to what extent does his pattern of adjustment contribute to effective legislative decision-making? Broadly, it is clear that his presence is likely to facilitate work on the major tasks, primarily because he brings a clear head and an intense interest directly to bear on legislation. This is more than a matter of intellectual competence and energy; equally important is the fact that the Lawmaker has decided to invest these talents in *political* issues, in defining his *legislative* roles, in coming to grips with specific problems of *legislation*. The politically significant result of the Lawmaker style is the infusion of reason and energy into an all too often irrational and sluggish system.

There is an analogy between the way an institution organizes itself to operate effectively and the way an individual organizes himself for productive action.[25] The Lawmaker's adjustive strategies reflect in many ways the practices that legislatures have developed to handle their tasks. Specialization, for example, comes naturally to the Lawmaker—it is one of his primary techniques, as illustrated in his role-defining efforts. The sequential steps of the legislative process and the incremental nature of most legislation parallel his sense of his own development. Legislative debate at its best is much like the debates he carries on with himself: problems are defined, limits explored, alternatives posed and evaluated, and a concrete decision completed. Lawmakers find it easy perhaps, to accept the necessity for hierarchical organization in the legislature to the extent that they are used to setting priorities among their own goals and wants. In these and many other ways the Lawmaker's personal style resonates with the demands of legislative work.

Possible Shortcomings

Concentration on the major distinguishing features of the Lawmaker style may create an impression of perfection. Yet, as we have seen, he shares certain unproductive tendencies with the other members.[26] His special qualities stand out in marked relief against the background of Spectators, Advertisers, and Reluctants, but he is no paragon. And when his special strengths are exaggerated, they can themselves have negative effects on the legislative process. This is especially true when the Lawmaker overemphasizes the virtues of rationality and production. Lawmakers sometimes sound as if they want the legislature to deliberate like Plato's Academy and then take action like Caesar's army. Neither practice may be appropriate for a representative assembly whose decisions must be acceptable to the masses as well as to the elite.

The Lawmaker may become so enthralled with reason that he forgets the necessity for inspiration. Ready himself to act on the basis of rationally derived conclusions, he may neglect the fact that others, particularly the great majority of people who lack the time or interest to follow his chain of logic and evidence, need to be spurred into action by the invocation of patriotic symbols, by crusades, by sentiment and myth. If the legislature were composed entirely of Lawmakers, they might well come quickly to common understandings about such matters and spend their time in working out the technical methods for implementing their values. Potential in the Lawmaker pattern is the tendency to neglect the rhetorical necessities involved in public decision-making. To some extent the Spectators help him counteract the tendency. Spectators ask for and appreciate the kind of speechmaking that the population at large likes. This is not a happy conclusion, but it is probably realistic.

A second kind of destructive exaggeration potential in the Lawmaker pattern is a tendency to press on to a decision, once the merits have been debated, without due consideration for the proprieties of form. The set pattern of the legislative process is a safeguard against hasty, ill-conceived legislation, but it must be followed even when the bill results from years of study and is desired by nearly every informed person, and when the ultimate outcome is certain from the start. The

Lawmaker may become impatient with delay, may want to rush the bill through committee, sidestep a public hearing, push it to the top of the agenda—essentially, to make an exception in this or that case. But the accumulation of such occasions can be particularly harmful in the long run; doors once opened for special exceptions may be hard to close later on. And the public may become suspicious of a legislature which too frequently bypasses the sometimes tedious regular procedures. Reluctants, with their attachment to the rules of the game, help to check such tendencies by reminding the Lawmaker that the House's traditions deserve respect even in the case of urgent, important, highly desirable bills.

The Lawmaker's Political Future

As long as major decisions with broad social consequences are made through the political order, the Lawmaker will find his talents needed—and will be attracted to participate—in the larger debate. Circumstances may intervene to preclude political activity temporarily, but the best prediction is that they will be overcome more often than not. Probably the main force operating to draw him away from political service will be competing demands for his talents, especially in his own occupation. He is likely to be accorded ever-increasing responsibilities in his regular work that will become harder and harder to interrupt and then return to.

Another set of circumstances detracts from the appeal of public office for the Lawmaker. If he observes, at first or second hand, that the governmental system has gone lame, that the legislature fiddles with trivialities while massive social problems accumulate, that progressive programs invariably disappear in a tangle of checks and balances, then he may decide to turn his back on the whole affair.

But barring such unfortunate developments, Lawmakers will be drawn back to the House by powerful forces. Having become involved in certain programmatic fields, they will want to see things through. Some may go on to other policy-making offices, even to Congress, but few will be satisfied with lesser administrative posts. All things considered, the most probable sequel to the Lawmaker's initial legislative experience is a lifetime of political involvement, in or out of the General Assembly. Perhaps this, rather than any particular piece of legislation, is the one most promising outcome of the Lawmaker's first session.

6. The Development of Political Personalities

> Whether a man become a king or a beggar, there will
> always be the same eye, dark or grey, the same mouth,
> prudent or rash, the same hand; between this persist-
> ence of nature in each of us, and the endless variations
> of circumstance, our history passes as it were through
> the rollers of a printing press, continually receiving
> the two-fold impression.
>
> ALAIN

Politicians, being human, are not just competitors, decision-makers, wily grafters, or idealistic public servants. Like the rest of us they have their hopes and fears, their doubts and convictions, their pleasures and pains. Like the rest of us, they vary in the ways they work out their destinies. The stresses and strains of a prodigious task affect them in different ways; their responses reflect old habits, continuing needs, and, in the last analysis, the fundamentals of personality—the kinds of people they are and think they are and wish they were. A legislator's political style is only a segment—currently, for him, a significant segment—of his personal style.

An Overview of the Findings

In the pages above I have drawn attention to certain aspects of political behavior that result from the interplay of personal motives, resources, and opportunities, as illustrated in the recruitment and adaptation of some state legislators. The relationships are, of course, exceedingly complex, varying from person to person and from situation to situation. But they appear to be reducible, in their main features, to a limited set of patterns, which emerge when we take into account only two variables: the person's level of activity and his commitment to the office, the latter being indicated by his willingness to return to the legislature for an extended period of service. The activity variable separates those whose satisfactions are met primarily by acting on the environment from those whose satisfactions depend primarily on being acted upon by environmental forces. The willing-ness-to-return variable separates those for whom the legislature is currently perceived as meeting certain temporary or peripheral needs from those who perceive it as a source of continuing, deeper satis-factions.

The resulting fourfold division of the data reveals a number of significant regularities or patterns of interaction between the member and the institution. I have approached this material with a guiding assumption—that the individual's political behavior represents a col-lection of adjustive techniques or strategies by which he attempts to maximize the satisfaction of his needs. The particular strategies an individual employs depend on the special needs he brings to his political experience and the availability in that environment of satis-factions for these needs. If the needs are intense and the environment includes important sources of satisfaction, the pattern of adjustment will be modified or surrendered only in exceptional cases. To the extent that either of these factors is weak or absent, the pattern will tend toward flexibility and change. In turn, these patterns will have important effects on the legislative process insofar as they support or interfere with certain central functions that the legislature is called upon to perform.

The word "environment" has a special meaning here—the subjective environment. Although an individual will not be totally unaware of the most obvious facets of the world around him, or perceive objects which are in reality totally absent, he does pay special heed to some things and neglects others. Furthermore, he tends to react emotionally to objects he encounters, attaching positive and negative signs to things. The particular selective and value-attaching practices a person employs amount to his reactions to the environment. Insofar as most of the real environment is common to all members of an institution, it is likely that differences in reactions are attributable to differences in the needs an individual brings to his new experience.

When we look closely at these reactions, the patterned nature of a person's adjustment begins to emerge. We appear to be dealing not with scattered relationships between this particular perception and that particular strategic device but rather with sets of these factors, sets that fit together functionally, complementing and supporting one another. This patterning leads us to suspect the presence of some underlying factor by which the perceptions and strategies are integrated. The data support the hypothesis that this integrating can be understood most clearly as a product of deeper personal needs revealed in a person's conception of himself.

The self-concept is marked by selectivity and affectivity in ways similar to perceptions of environmental objects. The individual sees himself as a certain kind of person and he reacts evaluatively to what he sees. Both these aspects of the self-concept seem to have had much to do in shaping our legislators' political behavior. For three types—the Spectators, Advertisers, and Reluctants—much of this behavior represents compensation. For three quite different reasons these individuals seek in politics opportunities for enhancing and protecting a sense of self-approval, employing strategies symptomatic of relatively low self-esteem. The Lawmakers, on the other hand, tend to evaluate themselves rather more highly and thus to be much less concerned with bolstering their egos.

Each type bases its self-estimates on different major criteria. The Spectators are concerned mainly with their unloveableness, the Advertisers with their impotence, the Reluctants with their uselessness, and the Lawmakers with their achievements. In each case the self-concept shapes and organizes the legislator's political activities.

In the following list the central characteristics of each of the four types are summarized, following the approach utilized in the main chapters but omitting many details.

SUMMARY OF LEGISLATOR TYPES

THE SPECTATOR

Defining characteristics: Low in activity, high in willingness to return.

General legislative style: Watching, being entertained.

Background and expectations: Typically a middle-aged, lower status housewife of modest achievements, limited skills, and restricted ambitions.

Nominations: Recruited in noncompetitive small-town candidate shortage. Offers negative virtues.

Reactions: Enjoys the drama and color but specially sensitive to approval and disapproval. Rewarded by admission to a prestigious, intimate group.

Self: Little sense of individuality; other-directed. Pervasive sense of personal inadequacy and unattractiveness.

Strategies: Vicarious participation, superficial socializing, submission to others.

Pattern persistence and change: Pattern meets strong needs, is supported by environment. Alternatives risky.

Legislative work: Little involvement in substantive work. Blocked by conflicting strategies. Contributes some to tension reduction.

Political future: Uncertain, depends on candidate supply at home.

THE ADVERTISER

Defining characteristics: High in activity, low in willingness to return.

General legislative style: Exhibiting self, seeking occupationally beneficial contacts.

Background and expectations: Typically a young, upward-mobile lawyer experiencing occupational difficulties. Linked to politics mainly through occupation.

Nomination: Seeks nomination in growing, politically uncertain, larger constituency. Offers apparent skills; availability dependent on arranging time from work.

Reactions: Frustrated by environmental restrictions. Feels forced, exploited, powerless.

Self: Dominated by conflict between intense ambition and strict conscience. Anxiety, suffering. A sense of impotence.

Strategies: Indirect aggression, projection, displacement; competing and working; dwelling on own suffering; contemplating utopia.

Pattern persistence and change: Pattern meets strong needs but is punished by the environment. Leaving legislature more likely than pattern change.

Legislative work: Intense activity masks indifference to substantive work. Lowers morale, cannot accept a beginner's place in the system.

Political future: Short unless opportunities to express aggression engage strong needs.

THE RELUCTANT

Defining characteristics: Low in activity, low in willingness to return.

General legislative style: Doing a civic duty under protest.

Background and expectations: Typically an elderly, infirm, retired person, of moderate achievements. A lifelong home-town reliable, with many friends.

Nominations: Recruited from traditional, small, rural noncompetitive town. Embodiment of community values. Helps avoid conflict.

Reactions: Bewildered by the strange cosmopolitan environment, particularly the exotic people, headlong pace, and intricate decision-making process.

Self: Strong moral sense of social responsibility, especially for preserving harmony. Feels inadequate to legislative tasks. A sense of uselessness.

Strategies: Tempted to retreat from politics, perceive harmony, withdraw to reverie or ritualism.

Pattern persistence and change: Withdrawal pattern palliates temporary anxieties, but gradual learning and minor achievement probable in the long run.

Legislative work: Hampered by provincial background, limited education, declining energies, but helps maintain important legislative norms.

Political future: Long, depending on health and constituency stability.

THE LAWMAKER

Defining characteristics: High in activity, high in willingness to return.

General legislative style: Attention to substantive tasks.

Background and expectations: Like Advertisers, young and mobile, but with deeper and more varied political roots and much more interest in full-time elective office.

Nominations: Seeks nomination in larger, moderately competitive, highly educated constituency. Offers interest and competence in issues.

Reactions: Concentrates on bills, decisions. Pleased at opportunity to produce desired legislation, participate in rational process, work cooperatively with others.

Self: Strong sense of individuality, personal standards. Stresses rationality; sense of the self as developing maintains and enhances self-approval.

Strategies: Conscious definition of central political roles.

Pattern persistence and change: Pattern meets strong needs for rational mastery, but environmental support varies. May turn to other arenas.

Legislative work: Makes most significant contributions, aided by congruence between personal strategies and legislative task-organization. But may neglect need for inspiration, get impatient with formal proprieties.

Political future: Long, depending on competing demands for his talents and availability of productive political institutions.

In Chapter 1 three broad dimensions of political recruitment and adaptation were described: motivations, resources, and opportunities. The initial steps into public office and the style of political behavior practiced in office result from particular combinations of the needs the person brings to the situation, the skills and other resources he has available to him, and the opportunities the situation offers for meeting needs and utilizing resources. In the speculations below I begin by exploring certain aspects of these three elements, separated for analytical purposes, as they bear on the general problems of political recruitment. But I have argued [1] that in any *specific* recruitment event these factors are intertwined so as to be discussable only in combination. The succeeding section takes up recruitment to a specific office, emphasizing the special features of it which contrast with competing alternatives. Then I turn to official behavior in this particular legislative context, with emphasis on the process of coping with its stresses.

As will soon be apparent, the presence of the three less effective legislator types poses special problems of interpretation. Much of our concern in what follows will be an attempt to account for the recruitment of Spectators, Advertisers, and Reluctants. But in the final section we return to the practical problem with which we began—the recruitment of high talents to public office—and thus focus especially on the Lawmaker.

MOTIVATIONS: SELF-ESTEEM, IDENTIFICATION, AND POLITICS

Long before a person faces a decision whether to undertake a particular candidacy, he may have developed certain motivational potentialities inclining him to office-seeking. I have suggested that these potentialities can be usefully classed as, first, personal needs of a general character, such as the need for power or display, which might be met in politics but are not so engaged at present; and, second, predispositions toward politics specifically, such as an interest in following political events in the press.

When we consider the first potentiality, we are immediately confronted with a contradiction. Many studies of political participation [2] indicate that there is a close correlation between high self-esteem and such activities as voting, discussing politics, and interest in elections and political news. Yet the Spectators, Advertisers, and Reluctants appear in the interviews as people with rather severe deficiencies in self-esteem. Furthermore, their low self-estimates seem to be linked in significant ways with their political participation. These legislators resemble more closely the political figures Harold Lasswell describes as suffering from marked feelings of personal inadequacy or inferiority, who seek out political opportunities for compensating for these feelings.[3] How is this disparity to be explained?

"The More, the More" Hypothesis

A hypothesis which would deny the validity of this last set of findings might be called "the more, the more": the more healthy, efficacious, and confident a person is, the more he participates in politics. The evidence for the validity of this hypothesis as regards a considerable collection of activities *short* of office-holding is impressive. By a process of extension one would expect that officials would show even more self-confidence than the politically active citizenry.

Yet the hypothesis is, it seems to me, based on certain assumptions that need examination. If it is to apply to the whole spectrum of political participation, from voting to holding high public office, it must posit a scale or continuum encompassing the full range. Individuals would then be ranked along this scale and these rankings compared with their scores on tests of self-esteem. How might such a scale be constructed? The most logical method would be to list the various forms of participation, score individuals on each of them, and then combine the scores into an overall index of participation. In this last step it would of course be necessary to weight each kind of participation (for example, discussing politics, or serving in the Senate) according to the amount of political activity involved. The emphasis in this measurement process is necessarily on the *quantity* of activity, whether indicated by frequencies of certain acts or by some other continuous (interval) measure.[4]

If we include public office-holding in this array, it is necessary to take great care in placing offices in a hierarchy of participation. There is no a priori reason for rating a judgeship, for example, higher or lower than a party chairmanship, the president of the local chamber of commerce or municipal union higher or lower than the state legislator. We know that within any collegial governmental body there is a wide range of participation, from virtually complete lethargy to the most intense activity. If possible, one would want to observe or measure directly the individual's activity rather than deduce it from the fact of office-holding. And it would be most desirable for this purpose to be able to distinguish his political acts from nonpolitical acts. Is the lobbyist acting politically when he addresses a legislative committee but nonpolitically when he addresses the members of his organization? And finally, since we are interested not simply in finding out who the socially active people are in the population, we should be specially concerned to locate individuals who spend an abnormal proportion of their social energies on politics.

Let us suppose that these difficulties could be overcome, perhaps through a series of approximations, and that we wind up with a positive correlation between self-esteem and political participation, official and nonofficial. Certain implications for the recruitment process are evident. It would be reasonable to expect that the incumbents of the highest-participation positions would be recruited from those most active at the next level, and so on down the line. From the finding on self-esteem we would similarly suppose that the topmost participants would be recruited from those at the next level who were most self-confident. These two flows of personnel would culminate at the top in a collection of very active persons who were very sure of themselves. In effect, the promotion from one level to another would depend on one's having high self-esteem.

If such findings could be accumulated, they would suggest that the evidence indicating low self-esteem among public officials is faulty or its interpretation in error. Our Lawmakers would find a place in the picture, but the Spectators, Advertisers, and Reluctants would be considered very doubtful cases.

The Specialization Hypothesis

An alternative way of looking at this contradiction would make room for both sets of actual findings. This approach emphasizes variations in the *nature* of participation as well as in its quantity or intensity. Questioning the utility of the general rubric "politics," it focuses on the specialized nature of various political activities. More specifically, it hypothesizes a marked discontinuity between minor forms of political participation, on the one hand, and running for or holding public office, on the other. The former represent a collection of relatively widespread, general activities, while the latter are restricted to a small, specialized segment of the population. There are reasons for believing that at the level of citizen politics, self-esteem and participation are strongly related, while at the official level the picture is mixed. But an explanation of this point requires a brief detour.

Normal and Abnormal Politics

An individual's self-esteem probably both reflects and enhances his general adaptation to the culture in which he lives. Persons who, from childhood on, behave in accordance with cultural norms are rewarded for such behavior and thus come to value themselves more highly than those who are continually out of step with their environment. Conversely, high self-esteem increases the individual's ability to adapt successfully to his culture.

Now the cultural norms with which we are concerned are of two kinds: general and specific. General cultural norms consist of widely shared values regarding what everyone or nearly everyone should do. Being "straightforward" and "friendly" are American examples. Specific cultural norms consist of widely shared values about the characteristics and skills appropriate for particular specialized roles in the society. For example, a banker should possess above-average "number" skills, a doctor should not be squeamish about the sight of blood, etc. Such norms insist not that everyone should be a banker or doctor but only that those who undertake these occupations have the appropriate characteristics.[5]

How do the general and special norms apply to politics? It is clear that minor participation of the citizen in politics receives strong support from the general American value system. From an early age the American citizen is taught—in the family, at school, from the pulpit, through his organizations, over the mass media—that it is a good thing to vote and take an interest in his community, nation, and world.[6] Indeed, the "ideal citizen" is, in our culture, practically indistinguishable from the "ideal man." Consistently those who are more "successful" in terms of social status show higher rates of voting, discussing politics, and the like. Minor political participation is seen as a natural complement or extension of one's other activities; the good father is a better one if he takes time to vote in school board elections, the good neighbor becomes more so when he attends a zoning hearing. These activities, it appears, are valued in large part for their own sake. That is, one is taught to "participate," "vote," "take an interest," without any specification of the particular goals to be sought by these activities. The conflict and uncertainty inherent in the purposes of such activities are masked by consensus on the worthiness of participation as such.

The formality of the norm is evident in the fact that a majority of those who say they have little interest in a particular political campaign, "don't care at all" which party wins a specific election, or think their vote will make little or no difference nevertheless turn out and vote.[7] In Erie County, Ohio, no fewer than 83 per cent of the men who said they had no interest in the 1940 election voted, as did nearly three-fourths of those in a national sample who thought the outcome of the 1952 election of no importance to the country.[8] By contrast, only a small fraction (13 per cent in 1956) of American voters who lack a "sense of citizen duty" bother to vote.[9] The general picture is clear: Americans invest little of their emotional energies in the tensions and conflicts of political issues (although they may hold opinions on them), but nevertheless troop to the polls in impressive numbers. The explanation appears to lie less in the fleeting appeals of various candidates and programs than in a broad tradition of participation as valuable in its own right.[10]

The citizen participant, then, need make no special explanations for these civic activities; he gets a pat on the back for doing his part. The barriers to such participation are low, requiring only a modicum of skill and motivation to overcome them. We would expect, therefore, that individuals who are generally best adapted to their culture would also be best adapted to this aspect of it. And since such people will usually possess higher self-esteem than others have, there will be a positive correlation between participation and self-esteem.[11]

This argument can be reduced to the following proposition:

1. High self-esteem is associated with successful adaptation to general cultural norms.

2. These norms include a widespread positive evaluation of minor political participation.

3. Therefore high self-esteem and such participation are associated.

The dividing line between citizen politics and public office-holding is clear despite some uncertain middle-ground cases such as membership on a small-town government board—an office not much different, in terms of time and effort, from service on a Lion's Club committee. The distinction is most evident when we consider the degree to which the person's daily routine is disrupted. Even service in a state legislature requires a marked readjustment in one's round of life, alterations of a significantly different order from those required for attending an evening meeting every few weeks. In contrast to the act of voting— limited by law in some places to one minute—the legislature requires months of full-time work. It requires, during this period, a shift to another place, where one associates with a different set of people. In other words, it represents a change or disruption of one's normal role in job, home, and community, rather than a minor complement to this role.

For higher offices the contrasts are even greater. A senator or governor is not just doing more than the citizen who writes him letters. He is devoting his major daily efforts to a specialized political office while his scrivening constituent continues in his regular occupation.

Nor does office-holding enjoy a clearly positive popular evaluation. Obviously, running for political office is not the "normal" thing to do in the sense that voting is normal—that is, expected of and valued for everyone. The general value question regarding voting is, it seems evident, whether one should do it or not—and the answer is unambiguous. The question regarding a political career is very different: whether one should be a public official or pursue some other occupation.

One general attitude is relevant, however. While minor forms of participating such as voting, discussing politics, reading the news, and the like are seen as unquestionably "good," running for office has both a good and a bad dimension. It is true that the public accords remarkably high ranks to certain public offices as such [12] and that public officials are invariably overrepresented in poll choices of "most important" or "greatest" men. But at the same time there is in the public mind a dirty side to political candidacy, getting on the public payroll, taking part in political deals. No one has to explain why he votes. But every candidate probably has to explain to those who know him why he is getting mixed up in politics. The aura of risk, danger, temptation, and doubt that surrounds this kind of participation contrasts markedly with the clean-cut flavor of citizen politics.[13]

The move into political candidacy, then, in contrast to participation in citizen politics, does not receive unambiguous normative support in the general culture. Nor is it guided and justified by unambiguous *specialized* cultural norms. No clear image of what the office demands or what criteria the public thinks should be used in selecting candidates is evident. Take, for example, the apex of attention, the Presidency. The criteria applied in the 1952 selection of General Eisenhower were concerned in large measure with the pros and cons of his previous military experience.[14] The reelection of President Eisenhower turned much more on his personal qualities—his honesty, sincerity, and general likeableness versus his age and health. For some reason Governor Stevenson's divorce was of more concern to the voters in 1956 than in 1952; on both occasions the people were also concerned with his articulate or, as some thought, "highfalutin" speechmaking. Television viewers responded to the 1960 Kennedy-Nixon debates primarily in terms of which candidate agreed with their views and seemed better informed, more sincere, and more specific.[15] And there is good evidence that Mr. Kennedy's religion was considered a highly salient matter in 1960 by a great many voters.[16] There appears to be little consensus on the qualities the Presidency demands—although perhaps if voters were asked directly for a list of such qualities a consensus would emerge.[17] Yet the public probably has a much clearer idea of the Presidency than of any other public office. The specific norms applicable to legislators, sheriffs, governors, and the like are even more amorphous. It would be interesting to know what personal qualities the public thinks are necessary for one to be a good legislator. We would be safe in predicting considerable variety in the response.

The translation from citizen to politician, then, is not facilitated by definite cultural cues as to who has the appropriate qualifications. Nor is either the time of entry or the office to which entry is appropriate defined clearly.

One becomes a member of the electorate at a certain definite age. One becomes a lawyer, normally, upon graduation from law school. But politics as a career is a "late-entry, late-leaving" occupation.[18] No birthday or graduation ceremony automatically ushers one into an official role. The element of uncertainty and choice is considerably greater. Furthermore, if there is a typical course it is to move from an occupational role one has held for years over into a political role. Unlike the relatively uncommitted new graduate in law or business, the new politician enters late upon a political career by breaking off (or severely bending) his connections with a regular, recognized occupational role and status. This decision represents an interruption or diversion from a relatively long-standing *personal* identity which the individual has established in his work. In a sense his candidacy is a public admission that there was something incomplete or unsatisfactory about the course he was pursuing.[19]

The appropriate level or office of entry and the proper progression from office to office are also ill-defined.[20] One does not necessarily move through an apprenticeship as a party worker to some minor office at the local level, and on up the ladder to state and national office. A great many national officials have held no previous local or state office.[21] A number of governors have had little or no experience in other offices.[22] Probably a majority of state legislators enter that office without even having worked in their political parties.[23] And it is not at all unusual to find local candidates whose first political activity is their own campaign.[24] The starting points are as various as the starting time is indefinite.

Political candidacy is best seen not as a simple extension of citizen politics but as a shift into a different frame of reference, one involving a rearrangement of one's regular, normal commitments and, from a personal viewpoint, considerable uncertainty. Insofar as such a step depends on deeper motives, it is most likely to be taken by two kinds of people: those who have such *high* self-esteem that they can manage relatively easily the threats and strains and anxieties involved in this change; and those who have such *low* self-esteem that they are ready to do this extraordinary thing to raise it.

In the Lawmaker we have a person who can call upon exceptionally strong personal resources—particularly a deep sense of personal identity and self-acceptance—which enable him to handle this shift with a minimum of personal stress. Like Riesman's autonomous man, Lawmakers are freed to deviate from the common path precisely because they are in possession of powerful techniques for dealing directly with accompanying strains.[25] From among the ranks of the politically active in a community these persons are likely to select themselves for candidacy. They overcome with relative ease barriers that are much more difficult for others to surmount.

Those whose self-esteem is very low, crippingly low, are unlikely to be available for political candidacy except in very unusual circumstances. But among the availables in and out of active community participation there are those whose self-doubt, while obvious, is not disabling. Our three less effective types of legislators, each in a different way, experience such doubts. Often they appear to have undertaken political office despite themselves; often they recognize their own lack of any preparation or special aptitude for the job. Our hypothesis must be that they are attracted to politics by forces strong enough to overpower all the objections they are aware of. Politics must offer them personal rewards that offset the strains involved in switching, often at an advanced age, from the regular, normal round of family, job, and community life to something as off-beat as running for the legislature.

On the motivational side, such deep-reaching appeals are very likely to be linked to the self system, to the fundamental need such people feel for getting or confirming a higher self-esteem. As we have seen, political office-holding can offer some strong and specific rewards to the damaged self, bolstering up an ego here, offering an extra chance there, conferring a moral blessing in another place. These rewards may compensate for much of the embarrassment, frustration, and confusion the unconfident person experiences in stepping out into politics. From among the politically available such attractions may entice candidates who are not socially active or whose social activities are inadequate compensation for their needs.

Political candidacy appears, then, as a form of deviant behavior, drawing toward it exceptional people—exceptional either in their high abilities or in their strong needs. Our tentative estimate regarding self-esteem must be that elected public officials possess either rather high or rather low levels of self-esteem compared with other persons who have the same social characteristics. In statistical terms, their dispersion around the mean on a scale of self-esteem will be greater.[26]

Translated into propositional form, this argument states:

1. Initial political candidacy represents a marked shift in the continuity of the person's regular life at work, in the home and community, a shift not clearly evaluated by general cultural norms nor clearly guided by special norms.

2. The changes involved in this shift pose strains for the individual that are of a different (higher) order of intensity compared to shifts involved in low-level political participation.

3. In order for a person to take a candidacy, he must be able either to manage these strains directly or find substitute, compensating need-satisfactions that make up for them. Exceptionally high (but realistic) self-esteem may be an important resource in dealing directly with these strains; exceptionally low self-esteem may be the basis for a compensatory pattern.

4. Therefore the candidate population is likely to exhibit more variation in self-esteem than will be found among a matched group of noncandidates.

An Illustration from Another Game

These abstractions can perhaps be clarified by drawing a concrete hypothetical example from a completely different realm—the world of sports. Consider the following three baseball players. Mr. A played some sandlot baseball as an adolescent and made the college team in his junior year. After graduation he settled down to work and family, but retained a good deal of interest in baseball. He follows the sport in the newspapers, attends games occasionally, and refuses to be distracted by family complaints during World Series time. Many of A's friends share this interest and enjoy discussing it with him, particularly since he is unusually well-informed on batting averages, prominent players, the rules of the game, current controversies about managers, and stadium characteristics. A's wife encourages him in this hobby because she feels it helps him forget his cares and the perils of middle age. At last report A was attempting to organize a softball league among the office staff, to the delight of the company president, who believes that everyone should participate in some form of physical exercise. Secretly, *A* hopes to play pitcher and can be found practicing in his back yard most weekends.

Mr. *B* graduated from the state university a few years ago. He was captain of the varsity baseball team. *B* is an exceptional physical specimen, strong of arm and steady of nerve, wide awake and well-coordinated. After college he took a job with a sporting-goods company, continued to follow baseball in the press and television, and played with local teams from time to time. *B* likes his work but misses the intense effort and challenge of regular team play with others of comparable ability. Recently he approached an old friend of his, a big-league team manager, and asked to try out for the team. The manager, anxious about his prospects in the coming season and aware of *B's* collegiate record, jumped at the chance. *B's* employer is also enthusiastic; he is confident that *B* will do well and be a credit to the company.

Mr. *C's* intense interest in baseball dates back only to last year. *C* was a rather sickly child; he admired and envied school sports stars, but it seemed that every time he was drafted into a game he got hurt. At college *C* was known as a quiet, scholarly fellow, with little interest in sports. After graduation he found employment as an assistant librarian. Last spring the library's softball team lost its third baseman, and *C*, being the only male nonplayer on the staff, was asked to fill in for a season. *C* accepted. Since then he has become the most ardent baseballer in the building. He attends every practice session and insists on pitching, which he does very badly. His exertions leave him too physically exhausted to do his library work correctly and his supervisor continually reprimands him. At home *C* talks about nothing but baseball, to the dismay of his wife and friends. He continually nags his young son, whose interests run more to reading, to go out for the Little League team. Recently he announced his plan to quit library work and seek a position as pitcher for a minor-league team.

If we substitute political for baseball terms in these imaginary cases we can see the significance of thresholds for the selection of public officials. Mr. *A* is analogous to the interested, active political participant. In another context he would be found voting regularly, discussing politics, taking part in minor organizational activities. These activities, like *A's* baseball hobby, are supported by strong cultural norms. They dovetail nicely with middle-class job and family interests, supplementing and complementing these main concerns. For this kind of activity in this kind of culture the barriers to participation are low, and we would expect that those whose general life adjustment is good will be the ones who will most likely take part.

Mr. *A* was content with an occasional softball game; *B* and *C*, on the other hand, undertook to become professional players. In this culture big-league baseball players are generally admired. Similarly, although one supposes for different reasons, public officials are admired. But there is a great deal of difference between admiring someone and actually attempting to follow in his footsteps. This helps to account for the ambiguous finding that despite their admiration for public officials, few Americans want their sons to go into politics.

In the case of our hypothetical Mr. *B* we see a man who easily surmounts a threshold which is extremely high for most people, because *B* has special resources appropriate for the job. Similarly, the Lawmakers move into legislative candidacy and officeholding much more easily than do persons who lack the appropriate skills or are inhibited by deep-seated doubts. Lawmaker types select political alternatives freely, on the basis of their special characteristics and strengths appropriate for the position.

In the somewhat exaggerated case of *C*, the late-blooming baseball fanatic, we are at once led to suspect some special, obscure reason for his mysterious behavior. How can we explain it? In a culture that would encourage, perhaps, some slight part-time baseball activity on his part, there is certainly no support for his intense and inappropriate ambition. Not only does he lack the necessary skills but he also receives continual punishment in the course of participating. Nevertheless he chooses to seek even more of the same. The explanation is not evident, but it seems clear that some aspect of baseball playing has tapped some deep-seated personal need, providing rewards important enough to overcome the concomitant costs.

Latent Links to Politics

One kind of predisposition for political candidacy, then, may develop out of certain features of the person's basic self-image. These characteristics are, in some cases, linked to politics only at the time the opportunity for nomination presents itself. But in other cases the potential candidate has also developed, parallel with his self-image, an image of the political world that facilitates his recruitment. Whether or not he participates in any active way, he may take an observer's interest in certain facets of politics. The media continually bombard him with messages about even the most remote political events. While we would expect the Lawmaker to attend generally to these messages, it is probable that the other types perceive them in highly selective ways, focusing closely on some aspects and ignoring others. Such perceptions may accumulate, over a lifetime, to form latent links or bonds with politics that are activated at the time of recruitment. In deciding to run, the person calls upon his stored-up impressions of the political world; he "remembers" what politics is about and applies these memories in making his choice.

For the Lawmaker these impressions are quite consciously held and are linked with his own direct experience and participation. The other three patterns are more obscure in this regard. How might such latent links to politics develop in the person whose self-esteem is low?

When we speak of the person as having a low self-estimate, we refer to relations between two aspects of his self-concept.[27] Part of this is his ideal self, his image of what he should be like. This ideal self is largely the product of experience in the family leading the child to incorporate into his own personality a conception of himself as he ought to be. An important influence in this process of ideal-self development is identification: the person seeks to model his behavior after that of some other person. His ideal self appears originally in the form of perceived others "who seem to be more successful in gratifying their needs" [28] than he is.

The other part of the individual's self-concept is his perception of himself-as-he-is. This perception is heavily dependent on the person's experience in interacting with his environment. He learns who he is by the reactions he elicits from others. An important determinant of his perception of himself-as-he-is will thus consist of the rewards and punishments he experiences.

A low self-estimate, then, consists of an awareness (sometimes only partly conscious) of a disparity between ideal self and perceived self. Persons who are not completely overwhelmed by such feelings, yet experience them as painful, will seek to reduce this tension. In order for this seeking to gain significance for political participation, the person's problem must be translated in some sense into political terms. The individual must come to link up his ideal and/or perceived self with political objects and/or experiences. Much of this linkage process may be latent in the pre-recruitment phase. That is, persons with low self-estimates may collect, at the periphery of attention, perceptions of politics that ready them to seek or accept candidacy when the chance arises.

Such predispositions may develop through identification with political figures.[29] One way for the person to close the gap between ideal and perceived selves is to imitate or get close to the ideal self, which is the product of an original process of identification. Links to politics may thus be established by the operation of a desire to approach (in the psychological sense) public figures who display the most important characteristics of the person's ideal self.

The legislators we have examined differ markedly in the particular bases for their low self-estimates. We would expect that the Advertiser, whose low self-estimate stems from the feeling that he should be powerful (perhaps as a result of early identification with a powerful father),[30] will be especially sensitive to political leaders who are strong and forceful. Consciousness of such leaders will be painful insofar as it highlights his own impotence, but one way of reducing this tension is to identify with them, attempt to be like them, try to find ways to share their power. Leaders who show lovable characteristics—kindness, sincerity, benevolence—are likely to attract the attention and imitation of persons like our Spectators, whose low self-estimates are based in part on an ideal self with these characteristics. The Reluctants, who see their failure as an inability to meet high standards of duty, service, and right moral conduct will be attracted to leaders who display these qualities.

The political scene can supply important objects for such identifications. Of all the nonfictional personalities pictured in the mass media, top political leaders probably appear more frequently than any other single category. The political context is especially important because, in contrast to sports and entertainment figures, political leaders act in the real world in benevolent, powerful, and righteous ways. They are in a position, and are expected, to display a wide range of nurturant behavior, caring for the needs of large numbers of people.[31] They control the machinery for making and executing laws; their power is real, has widespread effects, and involves coercion. They are linked with the whole mythology of patriotism, public service, and the performance of a high duty. In all these respects, other available objects for identification tend to be at a disadvantage. One need only make a mental comparison between the President and the movie star, or the industrialist, or the great scientist, or the television personality, in regard to their roles in distributing general indulgences, exercising authoritative power, and manipulating the symbols of national duty, in order to see the possibilities for such linkages developing. Political leaders provide objects for identification in ways of special relevance for the person with a low self-estimate, according to the particular form that this problem takes for him. Other persons, less concerned with problems of self-esteem, are less likely to develop these particular links with politics. On the contrary, they tend to see political leaders instrumentally rather than as compensators.

Perhaps for some people politics is attractive precisely because it is a "dirty," forbidden thing to do. Erik Erikson notes that a person may form "a *negative identity*—meaning an identity which he has been warned *not* to become, which he can become only with a divided heart, but which he nevertheless finds himself compelled to become, protesting his wholeheartedness." [32] There are no doubt cases in which rebellious feelings that one cannot express directly toward his moral mentors break out indirectly in the form of political gang-joining and hell-raising. There appears to be a touch of this theme in the sentiments expressed by two of our Advertisers, Charles Rossini and Bob Muldoon,[33] although we have no information on its origin. But Robert Lane presents convincing evidence and argument that rebelliousness is dampened in the American family (even when the father is a drunken tyrant) and is unlikely in any case to be channeled into politics.[34] In the main, the personal identifications of recruits to candidacy are likely to be positive ones.

But a second set of latent predispositions toward politics may develop out of experience in being punished or deprived by various political forces. Low self-estimates tend to be rooted not only in high ideals but also in a personal history of being rejected, dominated, or accused.[35] Such experiences teach the person that his "real" self is far below the ideal and, equally significant, instruct him as to the particular character of his shortcomings.[36] He develops special sensitivities to certain forms of deprivation, responding to those aspects of the situation that threaten him in familiar ways. Probably the most usual response to such threats is avoidance: the person attempts to keep himself out of situations in which the threat is intensified. But such avoidance may be extremely difficult to arrange. If the sense of failure is deeply ingrained in the personality—or, put another way, if the threatening forces have been internalized—the individual will experience attack and deprivation in many encounters that others do not interpret in this way. This predisposition to be hurt tends to turn every social situation into a punishing experience regardless of its objective character. In addition, avoidance is hampered when the person is actually in a position where escape is impossible or very difficult, either because the environments available to him are pervaded with threat ("no place to turn") or because the threat is concentrated in some central, indispensable environment that he can leave only at great cost. Under such conditions the person may attempt to alleviate his discomfort by approach rather than avoidance, by working on or through the source of threat itself, trying to correct or remove it. He attends to the depriving aspects of the situation and watches for ways to turn them to his own purposes.

Punishing experiences can be connected with politics in a variety of ways. In the small community especially, the political order tends to be mixed in with the general community system of status and prestige. Persons of ethnic or religious minority groups or of low economic status are discriminated against in most social organizations, including the political parties. Thus the Spectator may become aware of politics as one dimension of a general status system which accords him a low place, excludes him from the inner circles, and leaves him feeling rejected. The dominant party represents the social upper-crust, which also dominates church life, the service clubs, the PTA, etc. In a sense the person who is especially sensitive to social rejection may find himself surrounded by it. But in comparison with other alternatives politics may offer better opportunities to palliate the consequent anxieties through participation in party affairs, particularly since the parties cannot publicly set many restrictions on participation.[37] Social rejection, then, may predispose a person to political action.

The Advertiser appears to encounter politics primarily through the central dimension of his life—his occupation. Here the power aspect is the most significant one. The lawyer, the real estate operator, the insurance man all operate within a framework of extensive legal regulation. The rules are imposed on them from without; when the rules change, they must change their practices accordingly. Almost inevitably, the power-oriented person in such a situation becomes aware that politicians have a great deal to say about how he must go about his business. Thus in a way different from that of the Spectator, the Advertiser experiences a special political frustration in a central dimension of his life. Here again, however, politics offers a way out— the Advertiser can join those he cannot lick. The other major source of frustration in his life—a powerlessness to attract clients or customers and thus succeed in his occupation—has a less definite, more diffuse configuration, which offers no readily apparent target. His predisposition to participate in politics is intensified because he is dominated by politics, because he can clearly identify the dominators, and because he has ways of becoming one of them.

The Reluctant's milder self-denigration seems to be based on a consciousness of moral shortcomings. Politics probably entered his consciousness in a double form: inspirational sermons about heroic national leaders, and tales of political corruption told by the muckrakers of his day.[38] Politics for the Reluctant, then, seems both very clean and very dirty. If the ideal side is likely to be linked with his need to identify with virtuous leaders, how does the corrupt side connect with his tendency to accuse himself? Primarily, I suggest, through his strong commitment to his community. Corruption in high places, communicated to him by the mass media, offends him as an American. But more immediately, corruption at home introduces a disturbing sense of guiltiness, which is made all the more severe by his feeling that he is somehow responsible for what goes on in his community. Judging from accounts of small-town politics in the interviews and other sources,[39] politics is a pervasive topic of conversation there, discussed in predominantly personalistic and moralistic terms. The "corruption" is likely to be insignificant by big-city standards but not by the standards of the village street corner. Reluctants, brought up in straitlaced families and strongly identified with the community, probably feel a certain sense of threat when they hear of shady dealings at home.

These themes can be generalized: politics offers, for many, a second chance. If things have gone poorly in one's occupational life (and judging from the occupational-choice literature disappointment is very likely),[40] or in the search for approval or respect, one may seek some extra way, some special departure from the ordinary, in order to break out of a wrong assignment. If politics is linked in some way with his troubles yet offers relatively better chances for improvement, the person may find his interests and inclinations drifting toward political opportunities.[41]

RESOURCES: THE EBB AND FLOW OF AVAILABLES

If political recruitment were merely a matter of motivation, the story could end at this point. Of course it is not; the step into office requires certain resources not possessed by every wishful politician. At the moment of initial recruitment the actual resources demanded by the office are obscure to the potential candidate, but his immediate circumstances are clearer. In deciding whether he can afford to take an extended absence from his current round of activities, he will tend to survey them carefully.

The *availability* of candidates depends to a large extent on their ability to arrange their affairs to accommodate an extended sojourn in a distant place. This tends to limit candidacies to (1) those who can give up what they are doing without financial sacrifice, (2) those in flexible occupations who can postpone or temporarily pass on to others their current duties, and (3) those whose superiors are willing to release them for candidacy and office-holding.[42]

The Female and the Elderly

The first category consists mainly of housewives and the retired, for whom legislative service means added income rather than financial sacrifice. The supply of women available for political activities is increasing; earlier marriage and childbearing result in a great many women reaching middle age with time on their hands as the children leave home.[43] Shifting cultural norms regarding activities proper for women undoubtedly contribute to a long-range change in this direction.[44] Such factors, together with the shortage of male candidates during World War II, increased the number of women in the Connecticut House of Representatives from 22 in 1941 to 36 in 1945— an increase of 66 per cent in the proportion of lady members. Nor did the end of the war signal a female withdrawal to home and family; the 1961 House numbered 47 women among the members, an increase of 19 per cent over 1945 in the proportion of representatives. The indication is for a steady, long-range increase in the supply of unoccupied women and an accompanying increase in their Assembly representation.

Similarly, the number and proportion of retired people has increased radically. The percentage of the population over 65 has more than doubled since 1890, and this category is increasing more than twice as fast as the general population.[45] Changes in Connecticut's elderly population have been reflected roughly in the House, particularly in the last two decades, as the following figures show: [46]

	1930–40	*1940–50*	*1950–60*
Percentage change in proportion of population over 65	+31	+15	+10
Percentage change in proportion of members listing occupation as "retired"	+12	+15	+15

The physical health and financial security of the elderly population improve along with their numerical growth; they thus provide an expanding supply of potential nominees for the party recruiter.

Flexible Occupations

Fluctuations in the numbers employed in flexible occupations, such as law, insurance, and real estate, also affect the supply of candidates. For example, during the 1930s in the United States the "lawyers and judges" category grew from 161,000 to 182,000. In the same decade the number of insurance and real estate managers, officials, and pro-prietors actually declined, from 66,000 to 65,000. Presumably these statistics reflect the desperate business conditions of the depression years and the attractions of continued education. In the 1940s both trends were reversed; very few lawyers (about 2,000) were added to the population, while the insurance and real estate category increased by 80 per cent, to 117,000 in 1950. Comparable figures are not available for the 1960s, although the lawyers seem to have increased in that period faster than the general population.[47]

That these ups and downs can profoundly affect the supply of available candidates is evident from the Connecticut experience. The postwar real estate and insurance boom increased the proportion of managers of such enterprises in the state by 50 per cent from 1940–50. The proportion of House members who listed either or both these types of work as their occupations jumped upward in the same period by 79 per cent, from 17 to 31. Parallel changes in the lawyer category are even more striking: [48]

	1930–40	1940–50	1950–60
Percentage change in lawyer proportion in Connecticut population	+61	—2	+40
Percentage change in lawyer proportion of House membership	+36	—9	+40

The long-range implications of these figures are not clear; the wide swings may be attributable to peculiar conditions of depression and war which will not occur in the future. The numbers do indicate, however, how dependent the skills and attitudes available to the political order are on occupational changes among the general population.

At any given time, of course, these occupations are unevenly distributed throughout the state. Lawyers cluster in the big cities; of the sixty members who represented the ten largest Connecticut towns in 1941, 1951, and 1961, twenty-seven were lawyers. By contrast, the ten smallest towns sent only one attorney among their thirty-six representatives in the same years.[49]

The Organization Man

The third occupational category consists of those whose superiors permit or encourage them to seek legislative office in order to protect or enhance the enterprise. The proportions of those in such occupations appears to be on the rise; self-employment has been declining for some time in the United States.[50] Generally speaking, the larger the enterprise, the more likely it is to be affected in important ways by the operations of state government and thus to have an interest in legislation. More and more often, then, recruitment of candidates is going to depend on large-company policies regarding time off for politics.

Evidence from the interviews indicates that the process works in this fashion: a middle management person is released to run for the legislature with the explicit understanding that he is *not* to serve as company lobbyist, but rather to pursue an independent course. But once in the legislature, he is very likely to be assigned to a committee for which his occupational background suits him—that is, the insurance committee for the insurance man, the public utilities committee for the power-company man, etc. When the committee considers legislation affecting his company, the legislator's whole occupational orientation, his loyalties to his colleagues and employers, and his habitual preferences and styles of thought are naturally brought to bear. On difficult questions he is very apt to seek advice from those closest to him who know the subject best, namely his superiors in the company. Thus even without a conscious, cynical decision to infiltrate the legislature the enterprise gains, in practical effect, an inside voice in making the laws.

The interviews show that in numerous cases large-company decisions about releasing employees for candidacy are considered very carefully by several levels of management. The clearance process may take weeks or months. The evidence on the criteria employed is thin, but apparently the ideal company candidate is thoroughly indoctrinated with the company point of view (and thus "cooperative"), yet not so loaded with responsibilities that his absence would affect the work very adversely. Neither the maverick nor the busy office manager being groomed for an executive position is likely to be chosen. Company policies, then, probably eliminate from politics those in the enterprise with the best general talents—that combination of personal skills and independent judgment that characterizes the Lawmaker. Over the long run the supply of candidates will be increasingly affected by such practices.

These links between occupations and political recruitment illustrate how dependent the party recruiter's choices are on the supply of available potential candidates. Recruitment takes place at the margins of occupational groupings and must be adapted, at any given time, to employment conditions that are beyond the recruiter's control. The three trends identified here are:

(1) The increasing supply of available housewives and retired persons probably acts to increase the proportion of Spectators and Reluctants in the legislature.

(2) The large fluctuations in flexible occupations make their representation in the legislature highly variable, and mean that there will be a continual ebb and flow of talented members, reflecting not the current needs of the legislature but the current extrapolitical occupational distribution.

(3) Waning occupational independence indicates a long-run trend in selection which tends to remove from consideration the best talents and bring forth for candidacy the temporarily dispensable organization man.[51]

OPPORTUNITIES: COMMUNITY CHANGE AND
POLITICAL NOMINATIONS

However strong his motives, however ready he stands to serve, the potential candidate remains on the sidelines until and unless some practical opportunity presents itself. Here the role of the political recruiter is central, whether he seeks out candidates for nomination or merely selects from those who appear. At some stage of the game his (or their) support is necessary (at least in Connecticut), although it is not always sufficient.

Rational strategy for the party recruiter depends on the particular political goals he can hope to facilitate through the nominating process, in addition to the supply of potential candidates available as a means for these goals. Of key significance is the degree of uncertainty about the election outcome. We cannot posit "winning the election" as the universal goal of the party recruiter, because in very many situations the result of the election appears to him as a foregone conclusion. In such cases other political criteria tend to govern his strategy. Nor can we assume that the recruiter, once he has decided on his goals, has an unlimited choice of candidates to apply to them. In numerous cases the decisions are shaped by supply considerations: behind the name on the ballot may stand a long line of those who were asked and refused. The selection process is, in a sense, an economic one governed by the nature of demand and supply in a particular community.

Opportunities for Reluctants and Spectators

In the very smallest rural Connecticut towns, election-winning considerations rarely enter into the nominating decision. The political balance tends to reflect the degree of social variety in a constituency; the smaller the town, the more likely it is to be both socially and politically homogeneous. One party probably predominates. In these circumstances the recruiter has no particular reason to make close calculations regarding his candidate's chances for victory. He turns to other criteria: maintaining organization stability, presenting a respectable nominee who, because he personifies community values, can be counted on to represent them in the capitol. He faces also the sometimes difficult problem of finding a person who will undertake to serve a two-year term. A recruitment decision can be postponed for a long time by renominating the incumbent,[52] but eventually a replacement must be found. The recruiter then seeks a person who meets his criteria of selection (noncontroversial, respected, committed to community values) and who can be persuaded to serve.

The ideal candidate in this situation is the Reluctant. That he is the embodiment of community values—a sort of community patriot—works in two ways to facilitate his recruitment: the recruiter finds these qualities strategically useful and at the same time can use them as leverage in persuading the Reluctant to run. The appeal is to the Reluctant's overdeveloped social conscience, his feelings of duty to serve. By offering a mechanism for alleviating the discomforts such a person feels when he observes his current uselessness, the recruiter stands to gain a candidate who meets his political needs. Thus Reluctants are funneled into the system to represent the tight little cultures that have shaped their self-evaluations over a great many years.

But judging from the interviews, the task of persuading Reluctants to run can be a formidable one, and the recruiter may have to make do with a candidate who, while he lacks the Reluctant's positive virtues, is more easily persuaded. The Reluctant's resistance is the greater if he can point to some younger person who could as easily take the nomination. The supply of such substitutes depends to some extent on population trends; they are, of course, less likely to be available in communities which are continually losing their sons to the cities. But with some stability or slight growth the probability increases that a more youthful alternate will be present. The active go-getters in the younger generation have departed; those left behind are usually less ambitious, less talented, less personally sanguine. In short, they are Spectators—people for whom a legislative nomination is a step up, a flattering event in a rather dismal existence. For the recruiter they offer an easy out and a collection of negative virtues. Spectators are even more likely to be nominated from the minority party, where the political goal is simple survival by filling the ballot. In such circumstances, as we have seen,[53] the personal qualities of the candidates can be matters of indifference (within broad limits), and the nomination process degenerates into a lottery. Here the most easily persuasible among those at hand are likely to be chosen.

Opportunities for Advertisers and Lawmakers

Change and growth introduce uncertainties into the recruiter's calculations. The party balance begins to teeter as new residents arrive with their alien political habits. A steady stream of individual new-comers might be integrated into the system without much disruption, but nowadays they move in by the housing development. Increasingly the party recruiter must entertain the conjecture that the next election might be an upset. Concurrently, the supply of potential candidates expands. Nominating strategies will be organized differently as the goals and means change. Mere willingness to take a candidacy declines as an important criterion, while the salable characteristics of potential candidates gain significance. Political reputations are no longer spread widely by word of mouth but depend increasingly on the newspapers. The recruiter seeks "blue-ribbon" candidates who can impress the new people with their intelligence and energy.[54] Both Advertisers and Lawmakers can offer these qualities, the Lawmaker adding to his polit-ical competence an interest in and facility with issues. If our conclu-sions about the significance of Advertiser–Lawmaker distinctions are correct, the latter are more likely to be chosen from communities whose citizens have relatively high education and political sophistica-tion.

The interests of the recruiter and the Advertiser coincide at a num-ber of points. Both are affected by the increasing size and fragmenta-tion of the electorate-clientele; their common problem is to reach people (voters or clients) who are no longer reachable personally, as neighbors. The Advertiser's emphasis on the importance of impression-management—his stance as a self-salesman—fits nicely with the re-cruiter's desire to emphasize the candidate's personal qualifications. And the recruiter needs someone who will campaign energetically, something the hard-driving Advertiser does habitually. Personality politics in the increasingly competitive town thus offers opportunities for the young man seeking an indirect way to overcome a central problem, the flagging pace of his occupational advancement.

The Recruiter's Own Preferences

In the paragraphs above, the party recruiter appears as a rather hard-headed calculating type, cagily adapting means to ends in a highly rational way. This picture is undoubtedly distorted: the re-cruiter, like the candidate, is a person with needs and feelings and defenses—not a political computer. Little is known about the poli-tician's personal predispositions,[55] but it is probably true that the party boss's personality enters into the recruiter-candidate-community equation in more complicated ways. He is "always a bridesmaid, never a bride," continually backstage while the performer he has selected receives the applause. In a good many cases this dimension of the relationship no doubt gives rise to feelings of jealousy and a certain secret disdain for the candidate who thinks he knows so much and owes so little. Generally, the recruiter probably seeks the best man he can get. But the temptation to choose nominees who are not glaringly superior to him may also be a strong one. If he can find a man whose qualities are somehow flawed, who is dutiful but politically stupid, willing but hardly able, intelligent but internally harried, he is perhaps better able to retain a sense of superiority. Similar tendencies may affect the incumbent's choice of a successor in an inheritance situation. The classic propensity for strong leaders to surround themselves with mediocre talents (like the tendency for the sons of great men to turn out less than great) may operate here. The incumbent's self-image depends to some extent on his comparison of himself with his successor; unconsciously he may prefer to keep that comparison favorable by pushing the nomination of a person who will not do quite so good a job.

The electoral situation in the community, then, tends to shape the recruiter's strategy. In a variety of situations he may be motivated to choose candidates other than those best suited for the job. And his decisions depend not only on the particular community political structure but also on the supply of candidates available, factors that tend to be tied in with community size and rates of growth. And, we must hypothesize, the outcome is also likely to be shaped by the special personal needs of the recruiters and incumbents who take the main roles in the recruitment process.

RECRUITMENT FOR A PARTICULAR OFFICE: THE SPECIAL ATTRACTIONS OF LEGISLATIVE LIFE

No one ever participates in "politics." One "works in the Sixth District," "calls the names on this list," or "talks to Tom (or Dick or Harry) about the sidewalks on Parker Farms Road." Similarly, no one is ever recruited for "public office," but rather for a specific public office in a specific place at a specific time. Neglect of critical differences among offices can lead to bizarre conclusions; it is unlikely that the recruiter looking for a state legislator uses the same criteria he employs in finding a plumbing inspector. The motivation, resources, and opportunities we have reviewed come together in some peculiar ways in the first conversations between recruiter and potential candidate.

This is not to say, of course, that no generalizations are possible but only that major distinctions from office to office should not be passed over too lightly. It seems reasonable that many state legislative bodies, and perhaps even to some extent large city councils and the Congress, are like the Connecticut General Assembly in certain significant ways. They are collegial bodies, not individual offices. They perform a collection of similar functions and are organized in similar ways. These common factors may mean that legislatures tend to attract and recruit similar types of candidates for similar reasons.

The pattern of recruitment to the Connecticut House is affected by the ways candidates are introduced to it, by the alternatives against which it competes, and by the immediate interpersonal context in which recruitment takes place. Of particular importance in the first regard is the sequential nature of the recruitment process.

Step by Step to the Legislature

The candidate is introduced to candidacy progressively, step by step. His initial perceptions of it color his later ones. From phase to phase of this process, the ways in which he adds up the pros and cons of the office change and develop.

The fact that the initial recruitment steps take place, normally, before the potential candidate knows much about the legislature may be of special importance. The interviews show that many legislators accepted candidacy on the basis of very little information. Some did not know how long the session lasts; others had a few vague impressions left from visiting the chamber as students. The first encounter between recruiter and potential candidate thus takes place in highly ambiguous circumstances. Lack of information means that the candidate's personal needs are rather free to affect his perceptions, enabling him to select a need-satisfying image of the legislature. In addition, the recruiter is relatively unrestrained in the type of appeal he can make. Favorable aspects of the legislator's job can be stressed and the negative side played down. For example, several legislators commented in the interviews that they were surprised at the time the work takes; they had been assured that only part of a few days a week would be required. Commitment to candidacy undertaken in such circumstances is likely to reflect an attraction to the legislature on the basis of a strongly need-distorted image rather than an accurate weighing of many relevant facts.

Advantages over Competing Alternatives

The special characteristics of the legislature become especially relevant at this point. Both recruiter and potential candidate can stress those aspects of legislative life most attractive to the particular compensatory needs the person has. The fact that the legislature offers attractions quite different from other opportunities for organizational activity available in the home community facilitates the recruitment process. The recruiter's argument may stress the general desirability of taking some active role, but he can also stress those particular features of legislative participation that place it apart from the Rotary Club, the PTA, or the union local.

For the potential Spectator the legislature offers several comparative advantages in this regard. It is out of town, a way of escaping from a set of punishing relationships in the home community and starting out anew with strangers. It can be perceived as a higher-status organization than most home-town groups to which the Spectator can hope to belong. The legislature is much larger, more cosmopolitan than most clubs at home, offering better opportunities for maintaining a large collection of shallow social relationships. And the general aura of drama, fun, and excitement in the House can be stressed in contrast to the plodding pace of the usual local committee meeting.

The Advertiser can select other special features for attention. The legislature contrasts with the home-town arena in at least the following ways: (1) the effects of its decisions are more widespread and are enforced by a more powerful governmental machinery; unlike most organizations the legislature legitimizes and institutionalizes conflict among subgroups of members. (2) It offers more face-to-face opportunities for dominance; the legislator is the object of many pleas for help, many petitions for his favorable opinion. And (3) the Advertiser is especially attracted to the wider publicity, the broader political and business contacts accompanying the legislative role.

The Reluctant can make similarly favorable comparisons between home-town organizations and the legislature. The latter requires a good deal more work, takes up much more time and energy. It is linked in contrasting ways with values and symbols of patriotic public service. The questions the legislature handles are bigger than those the local planning and zoning board or town meeting or Grange chapter take up. The legislature is older, connected with a longer tradition, a link with the distant past. More than the local organizations the legislature is a place of formality, dignity, proper procedure.

The Candidate and His Audiences

Such special attractions, selected and emphasized in the initial encounters of recruitment, play upon particular needs and begin to define the legislature as a uniquely attractive alternative. But the suddenness with which many nominations are accepted indicates that long calculations about these factors are rare. At least equally important for the recruitment of persons with low self-esteem is the immediate relationship between recruiter and potential candidate at the time of the initial contact. Significantly, the recruitment process begins with an act of deference. The recruiter indicates to the candidate that after much thought on the subject the party leaders have decided that he is the best man for the job. He is made aware that he is being chosen, honored, preferred as an individual. Or, if he is requesting the job, he is given his way, allowed to proceed, admitted to candidacy. To the person with strong needs for reassurance about his value this is powerful medicine. The appeal can be so intense that the offer is accepted without much thought of the consequences. In many cases the matter seems to have been settled in one brief telephone conversation.

Deference continues to be received throughout the campaign and election. The risks and threats involved in campaigning—exposure, opposition, criticism—may be painful for the candidate with low self-esteem, but they are counteracted in some measure by the applause, the invitations, the new respect and attention given his opinions. Social relationships with three audiences are intensified during the campaign—with his sponsor, the party recruiter who selected him; with the inner circle of other candidates and party activists; and with the general electorate. The sponsor, having made his choice, acts in ways that will confirm that choice. Any previous doubts he had about the candidate's abilities now become dissonant with his decision, so his perceptions of the nominee's faults are dulled and those of his virtues sharpened. And in order to persuade the candidate to campaign, to perform strange political rituals, the sponsor must feed him a constant line of encouragement. Selecting those reassurances which best fit the candidate's needs, the sponsor contributes a steady flow of rewards.

The inner circle becomes a mutual admiration society during the campaign. Enmities left over from the nominations phase are suppressed; the demands of the common contest absorb criticism.[56] The candidates and canvassers trade campaign adventure stories; their experiences as well as their goals are shared. Each has an interest in the others' good favor (What is he saying about *me* as he visits from door to door?). The prevailing atmosphere among the inner party corps is similar to that of the locker room before a football game. To the person with strong needs for reassurance—not just during the campaign but at other times as well—this can be very rewarding.

The third important audience is the electorate, encountered at the doorstep and the shopping center and in the parlor coffee party. The meanings of these meetings for the candidate depend heavily on his initial expectations: if he is predisposed to anticipate a uniformly negative response, every pleasant experience is a surprise, an extra boost to his self-respect. The interviews show numerous reports of precisely this reaction. The candidate approaches the encounter uneasily, feeling somewhat threatened. He wonders whether he is intruding. He suspects he may be demeaning himself by acting like a house-to-house salesman. He hesitates to take advantage of old friendships or apparently purely social occasions to ask for votes. When these threats fail to materialize and in fact he receives politeness, attention, and respect, the attractions of politics are strengthened. Unpleasant experiences, on the other hand, tend to confirm his low self-estimate; such experiences add nothing new or different. They merely remind the campaigner that he is a somewhat inadequate political novice.

The response to these situations is ambivalent. Deep-seated feelings of inferiority are not washed away by a few contradictory experiences. The more basic feelings keep returning, marring the temporary glow one feels after a rewarding encounter. What is offered is only a series of brief respites from a nagging conscience, a sense of personal unattractiveness, or anxious doubts about one's powers. Nevertheless, these temporary compensatory rewards can be especially important because in the person's ongoing life they are so rare. Later on, when the more fundamental self-concept reasserts itself, the pleasures of campaigning may be denied or reinterpreted toward consistency with the self-concept. Thus the positive aspects are explained away as reflecting only the voter's self-interest or his pleasure at being flattered by a campaign visit, or some other reason different from a genuine respect or affection for the candidate. But, judging from the interviews, this explaining away is never complete; the memory of unexpected deference also recurs, reminding the legislator that for a few moments, here and there, he was thought to be quite a fellow.

The election returns are perceived in a similarly ambiguous way. The results themselves are precise statistics, but their meanings are indefinite when viewed by the winner. Did he win by an impressive margin? This may indicate either a gratifying vote of confidence in him personally or simply that he ran in a very safe district or at a time when electoral sentiments were changing radically without reference to him at all. Was he elected by a small plurality? Perhaps this means that he fought a good battle against high odds; perhaps it means he barely managed to squeak through to an uncertain victory. The mere fact of winning gives one reason for self-congratulation and is thus one more boost to the candidate's confidence. But as we have seen, the effect is never quite clear; some legislators report little or no pleasure at the news of their election. The continuing significance is perhaps this: he might have lost, and the fact that he did not remains with him as an encouraging sign. The election returns, by and large, probably stay on the plus side of his personal calculus, although in his blacker moments they fade in significance.

However the winning candidate may interpret the vote, those close to him are likely to communicate the most favorable interpretation possible. His family and friends, the party recruiter, the inner circle of other candidates and party workers—all will express congratulations. The whole process of nomination, campaign, and election thus culminates in a flood of approval. The contest is ended on a note of high optimism and gratitude. Again, this kind of event poses threats for the person accustomed to thinking of himself as inadequate. Part of him downgrades the whole business as meaningless hoopla. But the new element is the added prestige and respect and affection accorded him. Some of this sticks.

The candidate thus experiences, over a period of weeks or months, a series of events that tend to focus and intensify his political propensities. At the beginning he is made aware, in an immediate interpersonal context of deference, of selected aspects of legislative life that

are especially appealing to him. Then the campaign provides often unexpected increments of emotional compensation, albeit ambiguous
ones, from at least three new social sources: the recruiter–sponsor, the
party inner circle, and the electorate. Finally the election returns offer
opportunities for self-congratulation beyond the ordinary, opportunities which are grasped only hesitantly and uncertainly, but which remain in the winner's mind as signs of success.

COPING: ADAPTATION TO LEGISLATIVE LIFE

The newly elected legislator enters the House with certain expectations, and the consequent interplay between these expectations and
legislative realities give shape to his adaptation. Two sets of perceptions
affect these initial expectations: his deeper, more permanent self-
concept, developed over a lifetime, and his view of the current special
situation he finds himself in. These perceptions tend to conflict with
each other. The older personal ones draw him in pessimistic directions,
lead him to expect, if not the worst, more of the same punishment he
has experienced in a long past. The new political perceptions exert
an optimistic pull: the evidence seems to be piling up to indicate that
he is better than he had thought, and can expect, as a legislator, to
receive more of the favorable treatment he has been accorded as a
candidate. It is not surprising that he clings to these latter expectations,
since they offer pleasure rather than pain.

High Hopes and Shared Expectations

Based on his experience of politics so far, the new legislator begins
his first session with expectations which are both inaccurate and overly
optimistic. His information about the legislature and its work is
almost entirely second-hand and is conveyed to him by persons who
have an interest in stressing the brighter side of legislative life. He
interprets new information acquired after the nomination in the light
of his commitment; he tends to discount reports that are dissonant
with his public declaration that he wants the office. And to the extent
that he has exerted time and effort to win the election, he wants to
believe that this has been worthwhile. The inauguration ceremony
with all its symbolic dignity, public notice, and high oratory stimulates hopeful feelings. Lacking impartial knowledge, surrounded by
boosters, formally committed to the legislative office, having survived
a relatively severe initiation, and impressed by the rites of passage, the
beginner is encouraged to lay aside old doubts and expect the best.

At this stage new legislators probably share roughly the same expectations, or at least expectations with many common elements. The emphasis at first—in conversations and general meetings—is on unity: burying recent political enmities, telling one another about similar campaign experiences, looking forward to a common work. The new member finds others with similar backgrounds and opinions.[57] Furthermore, the pervasiveness of optimism, the air of encouragement, probably broadens the range of his interests and attention. That is to say, the encouraged Spectator tends to branch out into need-satisfaction areas other than those concerned with his desire for affection and approval, the Advertiser to take an interest in dimensions other than power, the Reluctant to reach beyond moral confirmation toward different, additional rewards. The influence of optimism here seems to be expansive; for a while the boundaries separating our types are compromised. The total effect is to increase the similarity of expectations.

Disillusionment and Differentiation

But when the real work begins, this orientational consensus starts to disintegrate. Most obviously, practical consideration of particular bills leads legislators into conflict with one another; one need only contrast the first few committee meetings with the fifteenth and twentieth, say, in order to see how continual arguing and voting corrode an initial sheen of harmony. Loyalties to party and constituency emerge and often supersede the newer loyalty to the committee. The differences between old and new members become evident.[58] The sense of shared hopes and purposes declines.

More significantly for the adaptation of legislators who suffer from low self-esteem, frustration and disillusionment create the conditions for a resurgence of doubts about the self, doubts that were temporarily palliated during the presession and introductory phases. The legislative process is essentially task-functional, that is, organized and scheduled so as to enable the institution to do its work effectively; it is not directly functional for the needs of the individual member, not aimed explicitly at making him happy.[59] Entering such a system with inflated ideas of the role he is to play, the good he can accomplish quickly, the honor he can expect, the freshman legislator soon learns that much of his effort is relatively trivial, slow to ripen into results which are themselves mixtures of good and bad—and in any case practically unnoticed by all but his closest colleagues.[60] The anxiety that accompanies this learning arouses the old special needs and their concomitant habitual defensive patterns. The person who had begun to make tentative investments in other patterns pulls in his horns and returns to a narrower, more familiar style.

This return has its rewards. For the person used to failure, high success can be threatening. An adaptive pattern that lasts into adulthood has behind it a history of hard times endured. It includes a way of perceiving and valuing objects that has served important personal purposes over the years. Even though it carries with it a burden of pain and failure, it has the advantage of familiarity: the pains are known ones, the failures are anticipated. In fact the negative, painful parts of the pattern are so interwoven with the rewards it brings that events which contradict the former tend to deny the latter. The man who has at last mastered the use of his crutches is uneasy when they suddenly become unnecessary. All that effort must have been to some purpose. It is a rare quality to be able to shuck off the no-longer appropriate defenses of childhood and adolescence and move into maturer ways.

The strategies that legislators use to cope with these problems have been detailed in the preceding chapters. Of central importance are the techniques for relating to others and to the task. For the Spectators and Advertisers emphasis is on the first of these problems; the legislative work appears secondary by far to their concern with interpersonal relationships. The Spectator who starts out to be an active advocate of issues soon finds himself embroiled in threatening circumstances that quickly divert his attention and call forth his defensive energies. The Advertiser who begins this process is continually hampered by others and by his own impatience and is loath to waste himself on matters without any direct bearing on his career. His attention is largely consumed with the scramble for position. Attempts to analyze the Spectators' and Advertisers' task orientations do not get very far.

Reluctants share with the Lawmakers a concern with issues or at least with legislative procedures. But the Reluctant style is still primarily determined by other people rather than by the task. His task concerns are derivative, a reaction of withdrawal from a confusing and uncomfortable social situation. It is only in the case of the Lawmaker that we find the issues taking first place, followed, to be sure, by attention to his colleagues.

The central significance of problems of social adjustment—a theme running through the interviews of the three less effective types—

becomes more readily understandable when we recall the processes of recruitment that brought these members to the legislature. The initial attractions involve a redefinition of one's personal relationships with others in his community. Potential candidates are those for whom such changes offer rewards—in other words, those whose present social environments are somehow deficient or incomplete and who have some need that might be met by a different set of relationships. The entire process is a markedly interpersonal one. There are no application blanks; one applies (or is applied for) in person. The entrance examination consists of a series of mutual face-to-face inspections. From the first orientation session to matriculation the candidate is immersed in social relationships of greater or less intensity. The complete introvert is as unlikely to be invited to enter this game as he is to want to do so. Potential candidates for elective offices, as a class, are very likely to be people whose rewards and punishments depend heavily on success or failure in relating to others.

But beyond this general common social focus and their common low self-esteem, the Spectators, Advertisers, and Reluctants seem to diverge from one another as they begin to cope with the legislative environment. Each type is likely to specialize in one style of adjustment, to the exclusion of other styles. This specialization reflects different underlying needs but also is made possible by the availability in the legislative environment of a wide variety of opportunities for different kinds of social behavior. The multifaceted character of the legislature makes it possible for one member to see it as an intense struggle for power while another sees it as a pleasant round of visits. The orator and the whisperer, the scholar and the back-slapper, the energetic and the lazy all can find some aspect of the House that suits them. Such matters are described in no organization chart. In fact, the norms of the place seem exceedingly permissive: tolerance apparently ranks near the top among the rules of the game. Persons whose styles are rooted in relatively intense needs thus find it fairly easy to maintain these styles in the legislature.

Impacts on Effectiveness

The end result of these processes, then, will be a legislature composed of persons expressing rather different styles. In some aspects these styles support and enhance the effectiveness of the body. As we have seen, the Spectator's behavior works to raise morale, an important concomitant of effective group work. The Reluctant contributes something to the sense of legitimacy and order in the House. Conceivably the Advertiser encourages rational conflict, although, as we have argued, this is highly questionable.[61] Against these partial and minor contributions we need to place in perspective the more general (and generally deleterious) effects on the process resulting from the presence in large numbers of the three types low in self-esteem. A major obstacle to the effectiveness of a task group consists of difficulties in solving its problems of social relations in such a way that the work is facilitated. Members must accept a system involving specialization, a degree of hierarchical organization, an incremental pacing, and extensive negotiation. All these features pose personal strains, are out of kilter to some extent with the personal needs of those filling the places. In brief, they require high adaptive abilities on the part of the actors; the problems do not solve themselves in some mysterious way but get solved or not solved by personal effort. The answer thus is not to dismiss such matters as irrelevant and hope they will disappear, but to face them directly and overcome them. This the Spectators, Advertisers, and Reluctants find difficult to do. Their needs distort and obscure the very recognition of such problems—an essential first step. They are sidetracked by habits of action that guard them against personal disaster but fall far short of freeing them for achievement.[62] Whenever we observe a legislature fumbling confusedly, fighting over trivia, drifting placidly toward a last-minute emergency, spending its energies irrelevantly, we have grounds for suspecting that, among other factors, frictions between the member and his office are affecting legislative production.

DEVELOPING AND RECRUITING THE LAWMAKER

The practical relevance of these findings can only be assessed in the light of certain political values. What distribution of the four types is desirable in a legislature? This depends on the view one has of the central functions a legislature is called upon to perform. At the extremes, two conflicting positions have been in continual tension in the theory of government.

Theories: Representation versus Effectiveness

At one extreme are arguments stressing the representative function. The legislature, it is said, ought to be a miniature of the larger society; the members should resemble closely the constituents they stand for.

Representative democracy is a "second best" solution, a less perfect substitute for direct democracy of the town-meeting variety. The more nearly similar a legislature is to the total representation of the town meeting, the better. From such a position the underrepresentation of various social groups in legislatures is a pathological sign, a dangerous tendency toward elitism. Perhaps even the irrationalities and prejudices typically found among the people ought to have their day in court. In this form, the representational argument opts for government acting not only of, by, and for the people but also *as* the people.

An opposing argument would stress the demands of rational decision-making, the efficiency or effectiveness of the legislature. The people are best served by a government that is better than they are. Considering the complexity and volume of decisions to be made, every effort should be expended to recruit the highest talents to office and to exclude the irrational and prejudiced. The electorate, according to this argument, should select not those who are like them but those who will best advance their real interests. The legislature should be not a microcosm of the larger society but rather a collection of the most rational, effective, emotionally sound leaders who operate in the interest of, but not in the manner of, their constituents.

The tension between these two value schemes can probably best be resolved by some compromise. As I have suggested in the four main chapters above, the less effective types, while they interfere with certain aspects of the legislative process, nevertheless may make some important contributions to that process. Lawmakers are generally found pressing for action on specific proposals. To gain the consent of the other legislators, they must shape their demands in certain ways. For the Spectator they need to surround the issue with color and drama in an attempt to stimulate the support of an apathetic citizenry. For the Advertiser the direct rewards and/or punishments involved in the measure have to be spelled out in some detail with the aim of helping to ensure the acceptability of the result to those with special interests. And for the Reluctant the Lawmaker would need to present a conventional moral justification for the action contemplated, thus enlisting those whose political decisions are heavily influenced by moral considerations. Each in his own way, legislators with different orientations mold legislation to fit the value scheme of the whole society. Acting in isolation from such influences, the Lawmakers—intelligent, sophisticated, energetic—might quickly agree on positions that the public at large would as quickly reject.[63]

The question is, however, one of balancing these good effects against the difficulties Spectators, Advertisers, and Reluctants introduce. In the end it is a matter of numbers: if the collection of legislators examined here is roughly reflective of the general category, and if the results of the deliberations of most state legislatures leave much to be desired, then we are probably correct in estimating that the balance is tilted too heavily toward the three less effective types. Granted that some of them should be included, the more pressing problem is to get a larger proportion of Lawmakers into more legislatures. It is the Lawmaker who possesses in unusual degree those qualities of spirit needed to make the legislature a more effective decision-making body. The chances are that the other types will continue to be recruited in sufficient numbers; the danger is that they will predominate.[64]

If it is evident that more Lawmakers are needed in politics, how are they to be developed and recruited? Two difficulties immediately confront the effort to answer this question. In the first place it is extremely unlikely and probably undesirable for the whole society to be mobilized for the production of good political leadership. Other things need doing, other uses for talents should not be forgotten. The system for nominating and electing public officials changes slowly and is often at the mercy of forces beyond the control of any manageable group. The party boss may some day be replaced by a board of psychiatrists or philosophers, but not soon.

In the second place, systematic comparative data on the life histories of Lawmakers in politics is practically nonexistent. Something more is known about the pathology of political leadership.[65] The interviews drawn upon here include only such information about the childhood and schooling of the respondents as they happened to volunteer. We can do no more than specify the central personal characteristics involved and then estimate how the party recruiter, also lacking intensive data, might identify those who have them.

The Central Lawmaker Characteristics

The Lawmaker enters politics from a position of personal strength, not as a compensation for personal weaknesses. His problem is less one of closing the gap between ideal self and perceived self than one of finding ways for putting to use his integrated self in some productive, meaningful way. The distinctive qualities the Lawmaker displays as

he discusses his reactions, his view of himself, and his strategies include
at least the following:

Confidence. This is perhaps the most deeply rooted quality underlying the Lawmaker's ability to move beyond his problems of personal
adjustment, to transcend himself and focus clearly on the real external
world. In contrast to mere optimism, this confidence means a fundamental conviction that one can be strong enough, good enough, and
knowing enough to manage the significant aspects of his experience
successfully. Not every time, not every aspect: genuine confidence
makes room for temporary, partial failure to be endured and accepted.[66] But if the adult is to be able to leave behind him the ways
of the child, he needs that basic expectation of success, that confidence
which allows him to step out into uncertainty. The person who knows
that there are things he has done well, other things he is coming to do
well, and still others he will be able to do well one day has discovered
the key to this sort of confidence.

Recognition. Successful adaptation is a far different thing from
passive conformity to a new environment. Such conforming is almost
always maladaptive, because it is based on the false premise that the
person is infinitely plastic, that he *can* lightly discard his past when
confronted with a new situation. This is a pretending that almost
inevitably leads to the disruptive appearance, in disguised form, of
the person's idiosyncratic needs and habitual strategies. Furthermore,
conformity involves the surrender of a whole class of strategies—
those involving action on the environment. The person fails to perceive
the possibilities for molding segments of the environment to his own
individual purposes. He tends instead to act as if all the important
questions had already been decided and he therefore has no choice but
to acquiesce. In fact this is almost never true.

On the other hand, adaptation is facilitated by a strong and realistic
sense of personal identity. The person who is aware of his individuality
and values large parts of it enough to retain them in difficult circumstances has a better chance for developing an explicit, productive congruence between self and situation. He is less surprised by frustration,
less apt to attribute it wholly to himself or wholly to others. He has
a basis for acting, a beginning point for working on the environment.
And he has a basis for realistic perception, because he is aware of his
special viewpoint. In short, the Lawmaker *recognizes* himself—in the
triple sense of awareness, acceptance, and respect.

Achievement. The Lawmaker style is marked by strong pressures to complete certain projects, to actually reach certain valued goals. This orientation is, it appears, peculiarly dependent on his consciousness of his own values and on his time perspective. The first enables him to distinguish between achievement and involvement, between production and expression, between excellence and efficiency. His approach is a discriminating one. Not everything but quite definitely some things are worth doing well. The ability to see in his activities the personal part he plays and to connect this part with his conscious value-choices is a primary Lawmaker resource.

The Lawmaker's time perspective, his sense of a developing self linked with a developing society, enables him to gain gratifications from achievement that other persons miss. He can act because he anticipates rewarding consequences of action. The reward does not need to be immediate. He can continue acting because he sees how the smaller steps cumulate toward real goals—but he need not invest these partial achievements with an all-or-nothing significance. He can take pleasure in completed action, because he is conscious that his contributions to its history were real ones—but he need not make a heroic myth of them. This special way of perceiving time and his place in it is perhaps the Lawmaker's one most significant characteristic.

Sharing. The Lawmaker's ways of relating to others reflect a fundamental respect for and empathy with persons unlike him, an expectation that others will return these feelings, a conviction that reasoning is effective in cooperative work, and an ability to work out personal guidelines for conducting such relations. These essentially *social* qualities mark off the Lawmaker from the creative artist or scientist. In order to play an effective part in politics he must be able to endure or enjoy social relations with a great variety of people who are related to him in a variety of ways. This requires the maintenance of a series of delicate balances. Lawmakers can listen to others without surrendering to them, hold back something in social intercourse without withdrawing to a quiet corner, and challenge an adversary without making him an enemy.

By defining his political roles, the Lawmaker forms some tentative sub-identities which cut his emotional costs in each encounter and link his social behavior with his political principles. These decisions involve a special technique: fundamentally, the ability to perceive the common problem of adjustment raised by a set of relationships, to determine a general, tentative stance toward the problem, and to employ with flexibility this orientation in particular circumstances.

Links to Political Issues

What features of the political world are likely to attract the Lawmaker?

The availability of Lawmakers probably depends more on the cultivation of the qualities surveyed above than on explicitly political training in the family.[67] The way the potential politician works out his childhood relations with his father—the first (or perhaps second) figure of authority he encounters—may have more to do with his political orientation than any indoctrination he receives at home.[68] The presence of a politician in the family may provide an example to be imitated or an embarrassment to be hushed up, depending on the intimate relationships family members define for one another.

The child probably develops an image of the political world indirectly, informally, by heeding the political cues he receives from his parents.[69] Party loyalties, interest in politics, sense of political efficacy, and even positions on specific issues appear to be strongly influenced by inheritance from one's parents.[70] Students in high school[71] and college[72] reflect to a marked degree the views of their parents.

The general picture emerging from much investigation is one of remarkable stability and consensus as the individual moves through the life cycle from group to group. In calm times, writes V. O. Key, "the modal values are so dominant that the educational system, like other institutions of society, dedicates itself to the assiduous affirmation of the status quo,"[73] and "it is safe to conclude that the major influence of the media upon political attitudes is by and large a reinforcement of the status quo," a tendency "to reaffirm existing values, to buttress prevailing institutions, and to support ancient ways of doing things."[74] And people who move from one community to another show little propensity to change their political attitudes.[75]

It would of course be unfortunate if the purveyors of political cues in the home, the school, the neighborhood, and the media world conveyed a picture of political chaos and conflict beyond reality, but the danger appears to lie in the opposite direction. The sense of givenness, of problems already solved by someone else far away, of impersonal events succeeding one another in an endless and unbreakable chain, of the irrelevance of alternative suggestions—such an image of politics dampens the interest of the active, intelligent citizen.[76] If somehow the molders of political opinion can communicate to him an awareness of the real choices to be made and the real opportunities for making

them, the Lawmaker will be attracted. Judging from the interest Lawmakers show in specific policy questions, they thrive on a political
curriculum that includes not only entertaining anecdotes, "realistic"
tales of corruption, and inspirational sermons, but also some discussion of important political issues—even controversial ones. The contemporary tendency to present a pat and finished image of politics
is hardly encouraging.

Recruitment: Finding and Keeping Lawmakers

Before the Lawmaker can be recruited, he must be found. What
identifying marks, visible to the party recruiter, set him apart? Probably the first place to look is among those already active in community
affairs, whether in the party itself or in organizations concerned with
some aspect of government policy. The larger the constituency, the
longer this list will be. Further selection might then proceed by asking
these questions:

(1) Has the individual been an *active* member of his organizations?
Does he throw himself into the work of the organization—or is it
merely one of a long list of his formal memberships? Even holding
office in an organization does not necessarily indicate a high level of
participation.

(2) Has he *persisted* in organizational work, seeing its tasks through
to completion? Or does his participation move by fits and starts? Temporary spurts of activity probably indicate a different orientation from
steady, responsible work.

(3) Has he shown an interest—including a personal, emotional
interest—in *political issues,* broadly defined? Here it is important to
recognize that participants in party affairs may be much less interested
in issues than are other community participants, that the individual's
interests cannot be accurately gauged from those of the organization,
and that high personal qualifications, such as advanced education, are
no sure guarantee of concern for the substance of politics.

(4) What is the potential candidate's *occupational situation?* Is he
well enough established to indicate that he is not using a political
opportunity to help solve a business problem? Does he show at least
some interest in the possibility of pursuing an extended political
career? Separating the Lawmaker from the Advertiser in this respect
may be exceptionally difficult. At least one other question may be
required:

(5) Insofar as one can judge, does the potential candidate appear to be *personally secure?* Does he seem confident of himself, have a flavor of individuality about him, seem willing to grow and learn? And can he laugh at himself as well as at others? When the choice is narrowed down this far, it should be possible to distinguish, after a long conversation or two, the healthy from the distraught, the puritanical cynic from the progressive activist.

Getting and keeping the Lawmaker will depend less on the recruiter's public relations skills and more on the nature of the job he has to offer. If he can realistically do so, the recruiter should stress the opportunity to act more effectively in resolving problems in which the potential candidate has already shown an interest, as well as other important issues likely to arise. This approach will be the more convincing if the party man can point to a local party organization that is open, broadly based in the electorate, and at least moderately programmatic, rather than a closed corporation of patronage brokers. In fact, in such circumstances Lawmakers are apt to recruit themselves.

More than twenty years ago Charles Hyneman wrote: "The state legislator must be made more happy in his career. . . . The key to rehabilitation of the legislative branch is in the nature of the legislator's job and his attitude toward it." [77] The central question becomes, "Can the legislature be made a place where primary attention is focused on the substantive work to be done?" If the government is so structured that special interests can block any important move, however necessary, if action by a persuaded majority is subject to veto by an entrenched rural minority, if the legislative time schedule or committee system is so constructed that only rubber-stamp action is possible, if the state government continually abdicates its responsibilities, or if the legislature is in reality so shot through with corruption and favoritism and logrolling that policy considerations have no relevance to the process—in such conditions the party recruiter might best begin by organizing a little reform movement of his own rather than by persuading others to attempt the impossible. Several states have shown what can be done to increase the ability of legislators to concentrate on their work: by providing research facilities, secretarial assistance, private offices, a reasonable salary, joint committees, special budget sessions, and other aids to the task. In general, any measure that pulls attention away from the trivia of legislative life and toward the main substantial questions will facilitate Lawmaker recruitment. [78] Such steps will do little for the other types but can do much to make the Lawmaker happy in his career.

Democracy bears no guarantee that the best will choose to run. Yet we have often acted as if throwing the rascals out would somehow elevate the excellent. There is little dispute any more that we live under a government of men as well as laws. Yet we have only begun to find out what public office means, in human terms, to those who govern. In a time of might and malaise such questions have a special urgency.

APPENDICES

Appendix A

Reflections in Research: Some Links to Other Studies

Quattor humores regnant in nostro corpore.

11TH-CENTURY POET

At a certain stage in the development of a typology, one experiences a peculiar intellectual seduction. The world begins to arrange itself in fourfold tables. The lines separating the categories get blacker and thicker, the objects near the margins move quietly toward the centers of the cells or fade into invisibility. Particularly in the speculative interpretation of interviews, the most resolute resistance to the wiles of simplicity is required. One's confidence in this effort is strengthened when other researchers, with different interests and methods, see similar clusterings.

I am tempted to begin with the ancient theory of the four humors. Does not the Lawmaker seem sanguine (hopeful, warm, and moist, like the air); the Reluctant melancholic (sad, cold, and dry, like the earth); the Advertiser choleric (irascible, warm, and dry, like fire); and the Spectator phlegmatic (apathetic, cold, and moist, like water)? Can it be an accident that through the centuries scores of thoughtful observers from Hippocrates to Pavlov have made use of these distinctions of temperament? [1] But the temptation must be resisted. Not everything comes in fours (else how shall we account for Freud?); not every quartet sings the same tune. What we may expect to find are some reflections, some common themes running through the accounts of those who have observed humans acting in similar circumstances. The reader is here referred to specific selections where relevant evidence or theory is presented.

1. See Gordon W. Allport, *Pattern and Growth in Personality* (New York, Holt, Rinehart and Winston, 1961), chap. 3. Pavlov applied the humors typology to his dogs, with some apparently striking results. See William Sargent, *Battle for the Mind* (Baltimore, Penguin Books, 1957), pp. 4 ff.

STUDIES OF LEGISLATORS

STATE LEGISLATORS

John C. Wahlke, Heinz Eulau, William Buchanan, and Leroy C. Ferguson, *The Legislative System: Explorations in Legislative Behavior* (New York, John Wiley, 1962), Table 4.7 and interview quotations on pages 104–29.

Oliver Garceau and Corinne Silverman, "A Pressure Group and the Pressured: A Case Report," *American Political Science Review, 48* (1954), note 8.

Robert S. Babcock, *State and Local Government and Politics* (New York, Random House, 1956), p. 198.

Robert M. Rosenzweig, "The Politician and the Career in Politics," *Midwest Journal of Political Science, 1* (August 1957), 165–66.

LOCAL PARTY ACTIVES SUPPLYING LEGISLATIVE CANDIDATES

Lester G. Seligman, "Recruitment in Politics," *Political Research Organization and Design, 1* (March 1958), 17.

Sonya Forthal, *Cogwheels of Democracy: A Study of the Precinct Captain* (New York, William-Frederich Press, 1946).

Louise Harned, *Participation in Party Politics: A Study of New Haven Committeemen* (Ph.D. dissertation, Yale University, 1956).

Dwaine Marvick and Charles Nixon, "Recruitment Contrasts in Rival Campaign Groups," in Marvick, ed., *Political Decision-Makers* (Glencoe, Ill., Free Press, 1961), p. 208.

Hugh Bone, *Grass Roots Party Leadership* (Seattle, University of Washington Press, 1952), pp. 30–31.

CONGRESSMEN

Robert A. Dahl, *Congress and Foreign Policy* (New York, Harcourt, Brace, 1950), pp. 10–11.

Donald R. Matthews, *U. S. Senators and Their World* (Chapel Hill, University of North Carolina Press, 1960), pp. 58–67.

Charles L. Clapp, *The Congressman: His Work as He Sees It* (Washington, Brookings Institution, 1963), pp. 430–37.

ADMINISTRATORS

Robert Presthus, *The Organizational Society* (New York, Knopf, 1962), chaps. 6–8.

STUDIES IN RELATED AREAS

PERSONALITY AND POLITICAL PREDISPOSITIONS

Robert E. Lane, *Political Life: Why People Get Involved in Politics* (Glencoe, Ill., Free Press, 1959), Part III.

M. Brewster Smith, Jerome S. Bruner, and Robert W. White, *Opinions and Personality* (New York, John Wiley, 1956), pp. 69–112, 189–96, 226–40.

RECRUITMENT AND ADJUSTMENT

Gabriel Almond, *The Appeals of Communism* (Princeton, Princeton University Press, 1954), pp. 235–94.

George G. Stern, Morris I. Stein, and Benjamin S. Bloom, *Methods in Personality Assessment* (Glencoe, Ill., Free Press, 1956), chap. 10.

Lotte Bailyn and Herbert C. Kelman, "The Effects of A Year's Experience in America on the Self-Image of Scandinavians: A Preliminary Analysis of Reactions to a New Environment," *Journal of Social Issues, 18* (1962).

POLITICAL STYLES

Harold D. Lasswell, *Power and Personality* (New York, Viking Press, 1962), pp. 65–88.

David Riesman, *The Lonely Crowd* (New York, Doubleday, 1955), chaps. 1, 8, and 11.

Elaine Graham Bell, *Inner-Directed and Other-Directed Attitudes* (Ph.D. dissertation, Yale University, 1955).

PSYCHOANALYTIC CATEGORIES

Karen Horney, *Neurosis and Human Growth* (New York, W. W. Norton, 1950), chaps. 8–11.

Erik H. Erikson, "Growth and Crises of the Healthy Personality," *Psychological Issues, 1* (1959).

THEORETICAL CATEGORIES

Talcott Parsons and Edward A. Shils, *Toward A General Theory of Action* (Cambridge, Harvard University Press, 1951), Fig. 8 and pp. 140–42; Fig. 10 and pp. 184–85; Fig. 11.

PATTERNS OF INTERACTION

Dorothy Stock and Herbert A. Thelen, *Emotional Dynamics and Group Culture* (New York, New York University Press, 1958), p. 242.

Arthur S. Couch, "Psychological Determinants of Interpersonal Behavior," *Proceedings of the XIVth International Congress of Applied Psychology,* Copenhagen, 1961.

David Krech, Richard S. Crutchfield, and Egerton L. Ballachey, *Individual in Society* (New York, McGraw-Hill, 1962), p. 114.

T. B. Lemann and R. I. Solomon, "Group Characteristics as Revealed in Sociometric Patterns and Personality Ratings," *Sociometry, 15* (1952) 220–43.

Robert F. Bales, "Task Roles and Social Roles in Problem Solving Groups," in Eleanor E. Maccoby, Theodore M. Newcomb, and Eugene L. Hartley, eds., *Readings in Social Psychology* (New York, Holt, 1958), pp. 446–47.

Appendix B

Contrasts at the Margins: Questionnaire Items on Which Legislator Categories Differ by Twenty-Five or More Percentage Points

The profiles and other questionnaire results cited in the main chapters contrast the particular category under consideration with all other new member respondents. Here contrasts between pairs of legislator categories are presented, to show those items which differentiated most markedly respondents who shared a common level of participation or a common position on the willingness-to-return variable. The items selected are those on which such differences amounted to at least twenty-five percentage points. The reader should keep in mind the small number of respondents in each category, as follows:

For presession questionnaire and items showing change during the session (both marked with an asterisk below), the N's are

Spectators	27
Advertisers	13
Reluctants	12
Lawmakers	31
TOTAL	83

For postsession questionnaire and data from official sources, the N's are

Spectators	30
Advertisers	16
Reluctants	17
Lawmakers	33
TOTAL	96

A. *High Participants: Advertisers vs. Lawmakers*

	Percentage Point Difference
More Advertisers:	
Have some contact with government through occupation	25
Have held appointive office *	30
Prefer spending leisure with others rather than alone	33
Lose interest in a bill once passed or defeated	29
Agree that "the ability to get along with people is more important than expert knowledge" in legislating	29
Agree that "every piece of legislation is a gamble—it doesn't make sense to hold back until you are certain you are right"	26
Agree that legislative "horse-trading" or "vote-swapping" are necessary, not morally wrong	27
More Lawmakers:	
Enjoyed campaigning "very much" or "a good deal" *	25
Attended many meetings during the campaign	44
Liked listening to legislative debate most	27
Took "an interest in the psychology of other legislators"	42
Agree that on most bills, "most legislators will need to take the word of the appropriate committee or caucus" rather than study every individual measure *	31
Are "definitely" interested in holding district or state party office *	35
Have considered seeking full-time elective office *	33

B. *Low Participants: Spectators vs. Reluctants*

	Percentage Point Difference
More Spectators:	
Agree that "my legislative work is probably about the most important activity I have ever been engaged in"	27
Found the session's first month neither "too fast and confusing" nor "too slow and boring"	26
Found legislative social affairs "very enjoyable"	31
In considering "moral implications" of legislation, bring to bear "general American ideas of liberty and justice for all" rather than "my own personal moral convictions"	32
More Reluctants:	
Have had public office experience *	30
Liked campaigning "very much" or "a good deal" *	27
Found the session's first month "too slow and boring"	48
Agree that "legislative work may be socially unpleasant, but the opportunity to accomplish something worthwhile makes up for this" rather than "legislative work has its enjoyable side: for one thing, it is an opportunity to get to know many new and interesting people" *	43
On roll calls, often decided at the last minute	34

C. *High Willingness-to-Return Categories: Spectators vs. Lawmakers*

	Percentage Point Difference
More Spectators:	
Are over forty years old	40
Come from towns with less than 5,000 population	51
Prefer spending leisure with others rather than alone	28

More Spectators:

With strangers, "reserve my trust until I know him better" — 27

Agree that "my legislative work is probably about the most important activity I have ever been engaged in" — 32

See the "principles of my party" as different from those of the other party — 26

Agree that "far too many legislators blindly follow their party leaders" — 25

Found "the excitement involved in some issues" "helpful, in that it stimulated my interest and attention" — 26

Attended more to "bills being developed slowly and carefully" than to "rapidly changing developments in some legislation" — 28

More Lawmakers:

Are attorneys — 30

Have more than high school education * — 39

Expect to be making more income in ten years — 45

Have occupational contact with government — 30

Originated action to get the nomination — 44

Had some competition for the nomination * — 25

Liked campaigning "very much" or "a good deal" * — 42

Attended many meetings during the campaign — 59

Feel legislators should get a higher salary — 41

Achieved leadership or important committee post — 36

In legislating, had to speed up their "customary working pace" — 28

Took an active part in major negotiations — 35

Were frequently sought for advice by other legislators — 25

Are interested in being committee chairman or party leaders * — 41

Have considered seeking full-time elective office * — 38

D. *Low Willingness-to-Return Categories: Advertisers vs. Reluctants*

More Advertisers:	Percentage Point Difference
Are attorneys	32
Make more than $8,000 a year income	37
Come from towns larger than 5,000 population	58
Have occupational contact with government	34
Have had appointive office experience *	29
Originated action to get their nominations	27
Saw election chances, at time of nominations, as "50-50"	46
Have "often" or "sometimes" "wished I were another person"	26
Were willing to be interviewed *	33
Agree that "I influence others more than others influence me"	34
Rate their own legislative performance "superior" or "excellent"	33
Liked "speaking in the legislature" most	25
Found session's first month neither "too fast and confusing," nor "too slow and boring"	32
Lost interest in bills once passed or defeated	26
Agree that "the ability to get along with people is more important than expert knowledge" in legislating	28
Agree that "every piece of legislation is a gamble—it doesn't make sense to hold back until you are certain you are right"	32
Feel that "most career politicians are mainly interested in what is in it for them" rather than in "trying to do a good job for the public" *	31
Achieved leadership or important committee post	54
Found they had to speed up their "customary working pace"	32
Took an active part in major negotiations	28

More Advertisers:

Were frequently sought for advice by other legislators	45
Agree that "many legislators experienced a great deal of pressure from their party leaders" during the session	35
Report they were personally pressured by the party leaders	25
Would be interested in holding district or state party office *	27
Would be interested in being committee chairman or state party leader *	35

More Reluctants:

Are over forty years old	34
Have had relatives active in politics	27
Have lived in their towns more than ten years	39
Have had elective office experience *	29
With strangers, "reserve my trust until I know him better"	28
Like "listening to debate" most	29
Found session's first month "too slow and boring"	27
See "political deals," "horse-trading," and "vote-swapping" as "morally wrong" and having "no place in a state legislature," rather than necessary *	52
Agree that "legislative work may be socially unpleasant, but the opportunity to accomplish something worthwhile makes up for this" rather than "legislative work has its enjoyable side: for one thing, it is an opportunity to get to know many new and interesting people"	42
Agree that "the conscientious legislator will not give his vote without first studying the measure voted on" rather than taking "the word of the appropriate committee or caucus" on most legislation *	25

Agree that "the legislator ought to vote the way he feels regardless of party considerations" rather than regularly go along with his party   43

Report "party labels" were more significant in the legislature than in his campaign   27

On roll call votes, often decided at the last minute   34

* Indicates presession questionnaire and items showing change during session.

Appendix C

Methodological Details

For a brief overview of the materials and methods employed, see Chapter 1, pages 15–17.

The aim of this study has been to interpret a large mass of data bearing on the recruitment and adaptation of new members to legislative life. The results are speculative generalizations, not verified hypotheses. Among the many sources of error the reader should be aware of the following: Only 27 of 150 freshman legislators were interviewed, and only 83 and 96 respectively returned presession and postsession questionnaires. When these responses were divided into subcategories, some very thinly populated cells resulted. Neither the interview questions nor those in the questionnaires were pretested. The interviews were conducted in an exploratory fashion; thus no two were precisely alike. On the other hand, most of the questionnaire items were of the forced choice, check-mark type which permit the respondent no way to express his interpretation of them. The session during which the study was conducted was obviously an unusual one (see Chapter 5 for some of its peculiarities), and the Connecticut General Assembly contrasts in important ways with many other state legislatures (generally, Connecticut is a high income, urban, Eastern, industrial state with a strong, competitive two-party system at the state level). The selection of passages for quotation involved the writer's judgment, which may have erred considerably in estimating the typicality of responses. Evidence is presented below that the more active new members are overrepresented in the data, and no information on more experienced members is used. The interpretations reported here, then, should not be taken by those unfamiliar with problems of questionnaire surveys, interviewing, statistical analysis, and the like as definitive empirical findings. There is little danger that the reader familiar with these arts will miss the methodological loopholes.

Procedures used to increase the probability that the results reflect reality can be summarized as follows:

1. Participation Index. Participation scores were calculated for each of the 150 new members of the House of Representatives for each of the four items. Counts were made of:

(1) The number of bills introduced. This includes both bills introduced jointly with other members and those introduced by the freshman alone.

(2) The number of comments in own committees. A comment is defined as any continuous remark in the committee transcript, i.e. the number of times the name appeared in the transcript margin is the total count.

(3) The number of comments in other committees. These were counted in the same way as (2) for remarks made before committees of which the legislator was not a member.

(4) The number of lines spoken on the floor of the House. This is simply the total number of lines attributed in the transcript to the new member. Transcripts were not available for ten legislative days.

These counts were then scored as follows, from 0 to 4:

(1) Bills introduced

Score	No. of bills	Legislators
0	0	15
1	1–5	57
2	6–10	40
3	11–15	22
4	16 or more	16

(2) Comments in own committees

Score	No. of comments	Legislators
0	0	43
1	1–10	43
2	11–40	29
3	41–80	15
4	81 or more	20

(3) Comments in other committees

Score	No. of comments	Legislators
0	0	12
1	1–5	43
2	6–10	31
3	11–20	38
4	21 or more	26

(4) Lines spoken on the floor of the House

Score	No. of lines	Legislators
0	0	32
1	1–20	35
2	21–100	38
3	101–250	29
4	251 or more	16

Then the scores were summed to produce a summary index of participation, dividing high and low participants:

Sum of scores	Legislators
0–7	79
8–16	71

2. Willingness to Return. For a description of the responses on which this variable was scored, see pages 19–20 above.

3. Categorization of responses. Interview transcripts were distributed among four categories as follows:

Willingness to return for three or more terms	PARTICIPATION	
	High	Low
High	Lawmakers	Spectators
Low	Advertisers	Reluctants

Assignment of interview transcripts to these categories was on the basis of the participation index and the answer to interview questions on willingness to return. No other criteria for categorization were permitted. Similarly, questionnaire responses were categorized by the participation index and the questionnaire question on willingness to return. Then comparisons of questionnaire responses were made (primarily as a check on interpretations of the interviews) by reference to the percentage choosing certain answers to common questions.

4. Selection of interview subjects. On the presession questionnaire, 94 first-term members indicated they were willing to be interviewed. These new members were divided into three categories: those answering "Definitely would"; "Probably would"; and "Definitely would not" or "Probably would not" to the questionnaire item on willingness to return. Ten potential interviewees were selected from each of these categories (numbering 37, 33, and 24 respectively) by random sampling within the category. Three of the prospective subjects were unable to arrange time for an interview, despite repeated efforts. In some cases, an interview was held after as many as four postponements. Insofar as possible, interviews were scheduled in series of three—one from each category—from late March through late June. In each of the four main chapters above, three interviews are explored in depth. These were selected by the writer to illustrate most clearly certain themes that appeared to typify the category. Quotations from the other interviews appear occasionally in the text or footnotes.

5. Interview methods. The approach followed in the interviews is described on pages 15–17 above. The interview guide is the final item in this Appendix. The questions were posed in neutral terms and each topic was pursued until connections between responses and the experiences which gave rise to them were specified. The interviews were confidential, tape recorded with the subjects' permission, and conducted away from the capitol.

6. Pre- and postsession questionnaires. Most of the questionnaire data utilized in the text are drawn from the postsession questionnaire, which was answered by 96 of the 150 new members. Of the 96, 83 had also answered the presession questionnaire. In order to avoid talking about two indeterminately different groups of members and yet to retain as much information as possible from the fuller second questionnaire, results of the first questionnaire are reported only for those who answered both the pre- and postsession questions. Thus the respondents whose presession replies are reported form a subgroup of those who replied after the session. And the thirteen new members who answered the second but not the first questionnaire are included in the reports of second-questionnaire results. Given the greater detail of the second questionnaire, it was thought to be worth losing the

advantage of discussing exactly the same members for both questionnaires in order to gain 13 more postsession respondents.

7. Overrepresentation of active members. Both the interviews and
the questionnaires appear to include a larger percentage of high participants than are found in the total grouping of new members. The
average participation score for all 150 new members was 7.14. The
average for the 8 new members who answered that they were not
willing to be interviewed was 4.88—or, if a single high score of 14 is
eliminated, 3.57. The three legislators who indicated on the questionnaire that they were willing to be interviewed, but later decided
against it, average 3.00 in participation.

Comparison of early respondents, late respondents (after a follow-
up letter), and nonrespondents to the questionnaires shows the following relationship to participation:

APPENDIX TABLE 1.

Participation Score, Time of Response and Nonresponse. Questionnaire #1

Participation Score	Early Response	Late Response	No Response
0–3	19%	27%	23%
4–7	27	33	36
8–11	33	27	27
12–16	21	12	14
Total	100	99	100
(Number)	(73)	(33)	(44)

APPENDIX TABLE 2.

Participation Score, Time of Response and Nonresponse. Questionnaire #2

Participation Score	Early Response	Late Response	No Response
0–3	16%	30%	25%
4–7	24	40	35
8–11	37	23	25
12–16	22	7	15
Total	99	100	100
(Number)	(67)	(30)	(53)

It thus appears that late respondents and nonrespondents are more
likely to be low participants than are early respondents. The active
members are over-represented. No information is available on the
willingness-to-return variable for nonrespondents, but a comparison
of early and late responses shows small and inconsistent differences.

Therefore, our best guess is that the nonrespondents included about the same proportions of those willing and not willing to return as were found among the respondents.

8. Interview guide. The following list of questions provided a guide for the conduct of the interviews. In some cases, questions had to be passed over because of time limitations. When the interview subject moved into a question area further down on the list, that question was discussed and then the interviewer returned to the intervening questions in order. Each of these questions was followed by probes aimed at eliciting connections between the legislator's feelings and his experiences. In the interview guide which follows, suggested probes are in parentheses:

Area I: General Reactions

1) What kind of an experience has this been for you so far—from a personal viewpoint?

   (How have things been going?)

   (Would you say that, all things considered, you have enjoyed it, or not?

2) What have been some of the things that have been (enjoyable, unpleasant, etc.—use his words) about it?

   (How do you account for it being a _____ experience so far?)

3) What is it about _____ that has made it _____ for you?

   (Why is it that _____ is _____?)

4) Most of the things you have mentioned so far have been on the (positive, negative) side. What about some of the (negative, positive) angles of it?

   (What have been some of the [not-so-enjoyable, more enjoyable] parts of it?)

Area II: General Role-definition and Self-rating

1) How would you describe the job of being a state legislator—that is, what are the most important things that you should be doing here?

   (What is the main duty or function of a state legislator?)

   (What approach should a member take to his legislative work?)

2) Thinking of these various points, how do you think you have done so far as a legislator?

(How would you rate yourself as a legislator?)

(Which of these things do you think you have been more successful in doing?)

(Which of them have given you trouble?)

3) What would you say has helped you, personally, in doing these things?

(What have been some of the things that have hindered you?)

Area III: Town Political Situation and Personal Situation before Nomination

1) Now let's think back to the summer of 1958, back before the nominations were made. Give me a general picture of the political situation in your town then.

(How would you describe [town] politics to an outsider unfamiliar with the town?)

(What was the state of organization of your party then? of the other party?)

(What were some of the groups that took part in town politics then?)

2) Now, again in the summer of 1958, what was your own personal situation then?

(What were you doing then?)

(What were your occupational activities?)

3) In general, how do you like your regular occupation?

(Have you ever considered changing your occupation, going into another line of work?)

Area IV: The Decision to Run

1) When did you first get interested in politics?

(Were you active then?)

(What were some of the things that interested you in it?)

2) Thinking back to last summer, give me a description of your first

conversation with someone in the party about your possible nomination.

(When was it that you first talked with a party official about the nomination? How did that conversation go?)

(What did he say?)

(What did you say?)

3) How did you feel about the idea then?

(How did the idea strike you then?)

(What was your viewpoint on running then?)

4) In making up your mind about running, what factors did you take into account?

(What were some of the pros and cons, as you saw it then?)

5) What were some of the attitudes of your family and friends about this?

6) Which of these factors that you have mentioned would you say had the most to do with your final decision?

Area V: Campaign and Election

1) Now, as to the campaign period: in the questionnaire you said that you liked campaigning_____(very much, etc.). What were some of the things that you (liked, disliked) about it?

2) What was it about _____ that you (liked, disliked)?

3) Now what were some of the things you (disliked, liked) about campaigning?

4) What was it about _____ that you (disliked, liked)?

5) Now how about election night last November—what were you doing then?

6) As the evening went on, the returns were coming in—how did you feel?

(What were you thinking about then?)

7) What was it that gave you this feeling of _____?

Area VI: Initial Legislative Experiences

1) Did you get to the ceremonies on inauguration day?

2) How did that strike you?

3) What particular parts of it led to this feeling of _____?

4) When you got into the regular sessions, what were some of your first impressions of the General Assembly?

   (What stands out in your mind about the early days of the session?)

5) What brought about this feeling of _____?

Area VII: Committee Work

1) Now let's turn to your work on committee(s). What is your general reaction to committee work so far?

   (How have things been going for you in the committee(s)?)

2) Concerning your committee activities, what is it about that that brings out this feeling of _____?

3) Let's see: you were assigned to the _____ committee(s). Was that your first or second or third choice, or what?

   (Did you get the committees you asked for?)

4) How did you feel about this assignment?

[Note: By about this time, the subject had got into the habit of specifying the sources of affects. Probes were used when necessary to make the link in what follows.]

5) Tell me about your first impressions at the first meeting of your committee(s).

6) How did that go? How did you feel then?

7) What differences are there in the atmosphere of an executive session as compared to a public hearing?

8) What accounts for these differences?

9) How would you say the members of the committee(s) get along with one another?

10) How do witnesses generally seem to feel about committee members?

11) What else about the committee(s) and its (their) work stands out in your mind?

Area VIII: Relationships with Party Leaders

1) What have been your own relationships with the party leaders in the General Assembly?

2) What sort of a job do you feel they are doing?

3) Have you felt pressured by the party leadership?

4) Is it your impression that others have or not?

5) What are some of the forms that pressure takes?

Area IX: General Sessions

1) Now let's move over to the floor of the House. How would you describe the atmosphere of the general session?

    (Give me your impressions of some of the others there.)

    (How do you think the members feel about the general sessions?)

2) Have you spoken in the House as yet?

3) How did you feel then? (or, what is your feeling about speaking in the House?)

4) What about before and after the session, out in the lobby—what is your impression of that?

    (What are you generally doing in the lobby there?)

Area X: Other Social Situations and Perceptions

1) Have you gotten together with other legislators outside of the regular sessions and committee meetings?

    (Have you been to any social events for legislators?)

    (Do you see other members outside of the capitol?)

2) How would you categorize the members of the General Assembly?

    (How would you go about classifying the legislators?)

    (What are some of the types of legislators you find there?)

    (Are there any groups in the legislature that act differently from other groups?)

3) In general, how would you rate the morale of the General Assembly?

4) What causes that, do you think?

(What would you say builds morale in the legislature? What hurts morale there?)

Area XI: Future Perspectives

1) What is your general feeling about politics in your own future?

2) What would you say are some of the more likely political possibilities for you in the future?

3) What are some of the less likely possibilities?

4) Now in making your decisions about these possibilities, what are some of the factors you will be taking into account?

5) How do these pros and cons add up to you now?

[If not covered—]

6) What about coming back here next time?

7) Do you think you would be interested in several more terms in the legislature?

8) How about appointed office—would you be interested in that?

9) Will you continue to be active in party activities?

Area XII: Other Reactions

1) Now, I've been asking a lot of questions. Why don't I stop for awhile and just let you talk about what all this has meant to you personally. (Allow long pause) (Anything else that stands out in your mind about this business of being a legislator?)

NOTES

Notes

Notes for Chapter One

1. Frank Kent, *The Great Game of Politics* (New York, Doubleday Doran, 1936), pp. vi, 217. Cf. the chapters entitled "The Lure" and "It's a Humbug World" in his *Political Behavior* (New York, Morrow, 1928). See J. H. Wallis, *The Politician* (New York, Stokes, 1935), a book dedicated to Machiavelli and beginning "The Only Goal.—The aim of a politician is the same as that of almost all other men. It is his own advancement and advantage."

2. "When Is a Candidate?" *New York Times Magazine* (November 1, 1959), p. 84.

3. Merlo J. Pusey, *Eisenhower the President* (New York, Macmillan, 1956), pp. 3–4.

4. Harry S. Truman, *Mr. Citizen* (New York, Popular Library, 1961), p. 49. After the election, Stevenson humorously reported an expenditure of $150 for "3-cent postage stamps to explain, mainly to the press, why I was not a candidate for the nomination." Adlai E. Stevenson, "A Funny Thing Happened to Me on the Way to the White House," in Lyman Jay Gould and E. William Steele, eds., *People, Power, and Politics* (New York, Random House, 1961), p. 705.

5. Paul T. David, Malcolm Moos, and Ralph M. Goldman, *Presidential Nominating Politics in 1952* (5 vols. Baltimore, Johns Hopkins Press, 1954), *1*, 35.

6. Cf. Robert A. Dahl, *A Preface to Democratic Theory* (Chicago, University of Chicago Press, 1956); Morton Grodzins, "American Political Parties and the American System," *Western Political Quarterly*, 13 (1960), 974–98; George Katona, "Economic Psychology," *Scientific American* (October 1954), 3–7.

7. Of course the *potentiality* of electoral competition is of immense importance, but is a very different thing from the continual *exercise* of competition.

8. In most studies competition is operationally defined in strictly statistical terms. Research correlating direct observations of campaign activity with the statistical measures is very rare (see first citation below). I know of no study in which politicians have been interviewed systematically to determine how they estimate their chances. Yet the pitfalls of inference from the statistical measures are evident. Imagine, for example, a community in which there are strongly insistent norms that everyone vote, yet the electorate is completely indifferent as to the outcome, and there is no campaigning whatsoever. The most probable result is a high turnout and a 50-50 split of the vote. Or conceive of a community in which 49 per cent of the voters are traditionally and irrevocably committed to the Democrats and 49 per cent to the Republicans. The election would be very close, but any campaigning would affect only 2 per cent of the electorate. Cf. Daniel Katz and Samuel J. Eldersveld, "The Impact of Local Party Activity upon the Electorate," *Public Opinion Quarterly, 25* (1961), 1–24: "Politicians often spend considerable time maintaining a running controversy with their opponents but the knowledge of the controversy is confined to the protagonists. It is often a private war carried on between the staffs of the rival candidates with little effect on the electoral outcome" (p. 20). In measuring competition, the use of averages, number of candidates, short and long time periods, alternation vs. vote margins, divisions of legislative

seats, votes for some offices and not others, etc., all involve conceptual difficulties which approach those of nonquantitative, impressionistic techniques. Besides the studies cited below, cf. Austin Ranney and Willmoore Kendall, "The American Party Systems," *American Political Science Review,* 48 (1954), 477–85; Joseph A. Schlesinger, "A Two-Dimensional Scheme for Classifying the States According to Degree of Inter-Party Competition," ibid., 49 (1955), 1120–28; V. O. Key, Jr., "A Theory of Critical Elections," *Journal of Politics,* 17 (1955), 3–8; William H. Standing and James A. Robinson, "Inter-party Competition and Primary Contesting: The Case of Indiana," *American Political Science Review,* 52 (1958), 1066–77; David Gold and John R. Schmidhauser, "Urbanization and Party Competition: The Case of Iowa," *Midwest Journal of Political Science,* 4 (1960), 62–75; Joseph A. Schlesinger, "Stability in the Vote for Governor," *Public Opinion Quarterly,* 24 (1960), 85–91; Robert T. Golembiewski, "A Taxonomic Approach to State Political Strength," *Western Political Quarterly,* 11 (1958), 494–513; John C. Wahlke, Heinz Eulau, William Buchanan, and LeRoy C. Ferguson, *The Legislative System* (New York, Wiley, 1962), pp. 40–46.

9. Warren E. Miller, "One-Party Politics and the Voter," *American Political Science Review,* 50 (1956), 707.

10. Duane Lockard, *New England State Politics* (Princeton, Princeton University Press, 1959), table 28, p. 232.

11. "The Structure of Competition for Office in the American States," *Behavioral Science,* 5 (1960), 197–210.

12. V. O. Key, Jr., *American State Politics* (New York, Knopf, 1956), chap. 3.

13. A look at congressional nominations in safe districts confirms this. Julius Turner shows that in 965 primary contests for congressional nominations in safe districts (i.e. where the stiffer fights would be anticipated) during 1944–50, 873 incumbents won, 57 incumbents did not run again, and only 35 incumbents lost. "Primary Elections as the Alternative to Party Competition in 'Safe Districts,'" *Journal of Politics,* 15 (1953), 197–210. In elections in "competitive" Connecticut, incumbency appears to be an important advantage: in 1,201 elections involving lower-house incumbents (1946–58), the officeholders won 982 times.

14. Norman C. Thomas, "Politics in Michigan: The Curse of Party Responsibility," *Papers of the Michigan Academy of Science, Arts, and Letters,* 47 (1962), 311–24; Key, chap. 7.

15. Lockard, chap. 12; John H. Fenton, "Two-Party Competition and Governmental Expenditure," paper presented at the 1962 American Political Science Association meeting. On the basis of rigorous statistical analysis of the question, Richard E. Dawson and James A. Robinson conclude that "inter-party competition does not play as influential a role in determining the nature and scope of welfare policies as earlier studies suggested. The level of public social welfare programs in the American states seems to be more a function of socio-economic factors, especially per capita income." "Inter-Party Competition, Economic Variables, and Welfare Policies in the American States," *Journal of Politics,* 25 (1963), 289.

16. James A. Robinson and William H. Standing, "Some Correlates of Voter Participation: The Case of Indiana," *Journal of Politics,* 22 (1960), 96–111.

17. Cf. Murray B. Levin and Murray Eden, "Political Strategy for the Alienated Voter," *Public Opinion Quarterly,* 26 (1962), 47–63; Stanley Kelley, Jr., *Professional Public Relations and Political Power* (Baltimore, Johns Hopkins Press, 1956), chaps. 5 and 6, and *Political Campaigning* (Washington, D.C., Brookings Institution, 1960), chap. 4; William G. Carleton, "The Revolution in the Presidential Nominating Conventions," *Political Science Quarterly,* 72 (1957), 224–40; Robert Bendiner, "Chotiner Academy of Scientific Vote-Catching," *The Reporter* (September 20, 1956), p. 28; Sidney Hyman, "What Trendex for Lincoln?" *New York Times Magazine* (September 25, 1960), p. 26; Roger Eddy, "Why I Won't Be Governor of Connecticut," *Harper's* (November 1962), p. 48.

18. Morris Janowitz and Dwaine Marvick, "Competitive Pressure and Democratic Consent," *Public Opinion Quarterly*, 19 (1955–56), 381–400.

19. "The virtues of competition as an incentive have been extolled so often that it may seem like sentimentality to talk about its drawbacks from the standpoint of efficiency. Actually, these drawbacks can be very great. Basically, it is a simple matter of the direction of attention. If the attention of group members is focused mainly on where they stand as individuals, it cannot be focused on the goals of the group. In many situations, a status orientation is the enemy of a problem orientation. The experimental evidence on this point is overwhelming." Ralph K. White and Ronald Lippitt, *Autocracy and Democracy* (New York, Harper, 1960), p. 285. Cf. Jane Srygley Mouton and Robert R. Blake, "The Influence of Competitively Vested Interests on Judgments," *Journal of Conflict Resolution*, 6 (1962), 149–53; D. C. S. Williams, "Effects of Competition between Groups in a Training Situation," *Occupational Psychology*, 30 (1956), 85–93; M. Deutsch, "An Experimental Study of the Effects of Cooperation and Competition upon Group Process," *Human Relations*, 2 (1949), 129–52. On the other hand, see Robert C. North, Howard E. Koch, Jr., and Dina A. Zinnes, "The Integrative Functions of Conflict," *Journal of Conflict Resolution*, 4 (1960), 256–74; George A. Theodorson, "The Function of Hostility in Small Groups," *Journal of Social Psychology*, 56 (1962), 57–66. The situation and the phase in the decision-making process in which competition occurs are probably prime determinants of its positive or negative effects. See below, pp. 113–14. Theodore Lowi suggests that too close interparty competition suppresses innovation. "Toward Functionalism in Political Science: The Case of Innovation in Party Systems," *American Political Science Review*, 57 (1963), 575.

20. Key, p. 271. Cf. Herman Finer's opinion: "On the whole . . . in a country with well-organized and purposive parties, the constituencies do not cause much damage in returning mediocrities, but so far as such qualities are lacking—as in France and the United States (especially in the South)—their choice may be very damaging not only to their civilization but to the very notion of parliamentary government." "The Tasks and Functions of the Legislator," in John C. Wahlke and Heinz Eulau, eds., *Legislative Behavior* (Glencoe, Ill., Free Press, 1959), p. 284.

21. Cf. Angus Campbell, "The Passive Citizen," *Acta Sociologica*, 6, fasc. 1–2 (1962 special issue, "Approaches to the Study of Political Participation," ed. Stein Rokkan); Morris Rosenberg, "Some Determinants of Political Apathy," in Heinz Eulau, Samuel J. Eldersveld, and Morris Janowitz, eds., *Political Behavior* (Glencoe, Ill., Free Press, 1956); David Riesman and Nathan Glazer, "Criteria for Political Apathy," in Alvin W. Gouldner, ed., *Studies in Leadership* (New York, Harper, 1950); Murray B. Levin, *The Alienated Voter* (New York, Holt, Rinehart, and Winston, 1960).

22. Robert E. Lane, *Political Life: Why People Get Involved in Politics* (Glencoe, Ill., Free Press, 1959), pp. 20–22. Voting turnout reached a new high of 64.3 per cent of estimated adults in 1960. See Philip E. Converse and others, "Stability and Change in 1960: A Reinstating Election," *American Political Science Review*, 55 (1961), 269–80.

23. American statistics often equate the "eligible" voting population with the civilian population of voting age. Consequently Americans turn out to be apathetic in comparison with Europeans, because in many European countries eligibility is estimated from registration of one sort or another. Elmo Roper estimates that in 1960 some 19,590,000 Americans of voting age cannot realistically be considered "eligible" voters. These include 8,000,000 adults unable to meet state, county, or precinct residence requirements, as well as the ill, those who travel, southern Negroes, illiterates, citizens of the District of Columbia, prisoners, citizens living abroad, and 225,000 adult preachers of the Jehovah's Witnesses whose religion forbids voting. Elmo Roper, "How to Lose Your Vote," *Saturday Review* (March 18, 1961), p. 14. The University of Michigan Survey Research Center found 74 per cent of their sample in

1952 and 73 per cent in 1956 voting, and attributes the differences between these figures and the percentage of the voting age population (63 and 60 respectively) in part to the exclusion from their samples of the above categories. Cf. Angus Campbell, Philip E. Converse, Warren E. Miller, and Donald E. Stokes, *The American Voter* (New York, Wiley, 1960), p. 94.

24. Lane, p. 54.

25. Ibid., p. 61.

26. Ibid., p. 53; and Campbell et al., p. 91 n.

27. National Opinion Research Center, "Jobs and Occupations: A Popular Evaluation," in Reinhard Bendix and Seymour Lipset, eds., *Class, Status and Power* (Glencoe, Ill., Free Press, 1953), pp. 412, 414.

28. Cf. Lane, pp. 48, 76.

29. Cf. William C. Mitchell, "The Ambivalent Social Status of the American Politician," *Western Political Quarterly, 12* (1959), table III, 689. Cf. Lane, p. 207. In 1962, the present writer asked 85 elected local government officials the standard question, "If you had a son just getting out of school would you like to see him go into politics as a life work?" Sixty-eight per cent said "no." For a more detailed discussion of this question see below, p. 222. For evidence that negative attitudes toward government are not sharply differentiated by class or other demographic variables see Donald E. Stokes, "Popular Evaluations of Government: An Empirical Assessment," in Harlan Cleveland and Harold D. Lasswell, eds., *Ethics and Bigness* (New York, Harper, 1962).

30. Lane, p. 75. Cf. Wendell Bell, Richard J. Hill, and Charles R. Wright, *Public Leadership* (San Francisco, Chandler, 1961), p. 131: "In general, persons from low-status or low-class segments of the population attached greater prestige to public employment than did those from higher status and class positions. Possibly more significant is the consistent finding of a negative relationship between formal education and the prestige accorded to public employment."

31. Robert A. Dahl, *Who Governs?* (New Haven, Yale University Press, 1961), pp. 287–93.

32. Ibid., p. 290.

33. William F. Whyte, Jr., *The Organization Man* (Garden City, N.Y., Doubleday, 1956), pp. 325–26.

34. Cf. Robert K. Merton, *Social Theory and Social Structure* (Glencoe, Ill., Free Press, 1957), chap. 10; Norton E. Long, *The Polity* (Chicago, Rand McNally, 1962), chap. 9; Robert O. Schulze, "The Bifurcation of Power in a Satellite City," in Morris Janowitz, ed., *Community Political Systems* (Glencoe, Ill., Free Press, 1961), p. 71; Harry Scoble, "Leadership Hierarchies and Political Issues in a New England Town," ibid., p. 139; James S. Coleman, *Community Conflict* (Glencoe, Ill., Free Press, 1957), p. 7; and Edward G. Janosik, "Report on Political Activity of Philadelphia Businessmen" (Committee on Economic Development, 1963). The last-mentioned report concludes, p. 18: "Although half of all executives said their firms favored political activity, in fewer than 10% of these firms was an atmosphere created which would encourage management to participate in politics." Cf. Peter B. Clark, "Civic Leadership: The Symbols of Legitimacy," paper presented at the 1960 Annual Meeting of the American Political Science Association. Corporations have invested a great deal of time, effort, and money in political training programs, but few corporation executives run for office. See Andrew Hacker, "The Corporation and Campaign Politics: Power and Legitimacy," paper presented at the 1961 Annual Meeting of the American Political Science Association. For an inadvertently amusing explanation of this phenomenon, see Perrin Stryker, *The Character of the Executive* (New York, Harper, 1960), chap. 11, "Loyalty, Dedication and Integrity."

35. Cf. Solomon Barkin, "The Decline of the Labor Movement," a report of The Center for the Study of Democratic Institutions (New York, Fund for the Republic, 1961), p. 63;

C. Wright Mills, *The New Men of Power: America's Labor Leaders* (New York, Harcourt, Brace, 1948), especially chaps. 9, 12, and 15.

36. Seymour Martin Lipset, *Political Man* (Garden City, N.Y., Doubleday, 1960), chap. 10; Sebastian de Grazia, "Politics and the Contemplative Life," *American Political Science Review, 54* (1960), 447–56; William A. Glaser, "Doctors and Politics," *American Journal of Sociology, 66* (1960), 230–45.

37. For a more detailed analysis of occupational changes and their effects on recruitment, see below, pp. 233 ff.

38. Donald J. Bogue, *The Population of the United States* (Glencoe, Ill., Free Press, 1959), table 7–4, p. 126

39. Ibid., list 2, "Slowly-Growing or Declining Occupations, 1940–1950," pp. 479–82.

40. *Bulletin of the American Association of University Professors, 44* (March 1958), 247.

41. Cf. Avery Leiserson, *Parties and Politics* (New York, Knopf, 1958), p. 99.

42. For a review of literature on legislatures, see Norman Meller, "Legislative Behavior Research," *Western Political Quarterly, 13* (1960), 131–53.

43. Belle Zeller, *American State Legislatures* (New York, Crowell, 1954), p. 62. For a more recent discussion of this problem see *The Book of the States, 1958–59* (Chicago, Council of State Governments, 1958), *12, 32.*

44. Vernon A. McGee, "The Vitality of State Legislatures," in *State Government, 31* (1959), 9.

45. *The Book of the States, 1962–63* (Chicago, Council of State Governments, 1962), *14, 56.*

46. Ibid., pp. 35–37.

47. Ibid., p. 37.

48. Each member has a two-room office suite and a full-time secretary, and earns approximately $120 per legislative day. Cf. Wahlke et al., *The Legislative System,* pp. 50 ff.

49. Robert S. Babcock, *State and Local Government and Politics* (2d ed. New York, Random House, 1962), p. 183. Cf. George S. Odiorne, "So You've Been Elected," *National Municipal Review, 47* (June 1958), 271–74.

50. Zeller, pp. 61, 65; John M. Swarthout and Ernest R. Bartley, *Principles and Problems of State and Local Government* (New York, Oxford University Press, 1958), p. 87.

51. Cf. Charles S. Hyneman, "Tenure and Turnover of Legislative Personnel," *Annals of the American Academy of Political and Social Science, 195* (1938), 21–31; Babcock, p. 174; Oliver Garceau and Corinne Silverman, "A Pressure Group and the Pressured," in Eulau, *Political Behavior,* p. 256; Arthur B. Langlie, "Stronger States in the Federal Union: Why and How," *State Government, 28* (December 1956), 268; David A. Bingham, "Public Personnel Selection and Value Theory," *Political Research Organization and Design* (PROD), *2* (1958), 27–32. The problem is neither new—see John A. Lapp, "Making Legislators Lawmakers," *Annals, 14* (1916), 172—nor strictly American—see "Wastage in Politics," *Manchester Guardian Weekly* (December 7, 1961), p. 9.

52. Hyneman, pp. 23, 25. Based on a study of ten state legislatures in ten sessions, 1925–35.

53. Ibid., p. 26. This figure is for eight state legislatures in the period 1925–35.

54. Legislators were asked, via a questionnaire: "To your knowledge, is there a tradition or practice in your town or district that most state legislators serve one or two terms only?" Fifteen per cent of those responding said yes. Pre-election turnover in their towns was slightly higher than in other towns. However, if such agreements exist, their terms must be vague: in only three cases did *both* representatives from a two-member town agree that this practice exists, while there were seven cases in which one member answered yes and his colleague no. One respondent replied: "Formerly but not now," apparently meaning that the rule would not apply to him. It should be noted that the question is not entirely free of

ambiguity. The results, however, tend to confirm Hyneman's finding: "Such pass-it-around understandings are much less common than is ordinarily believed. An extensive correspondence with persons who ought to know, in several states, supports that conclusion." Hyneman, p. 28.

55. Ibid., pp. 30–31. Cf. Renate Mayntz, "Oligarchic Problems in a German Party District," in Dwaine Marvick, ed., *Political Decision-Makers* (New York, Free Press of Glencoe, 1961), p. 149: "An organization, like an institution or profession (e.g. the police force or the priesthood), may unintentionally attract a particular type of person; subsequently, this type of person in turn may leave a distinctive mark on the organization."

56. Cf. Ezra Stotland, "Determinants of Attraction to Groups," *Journal of Social Psychology, 49* (1959), 71–80.

57. Cf. Robert A. Dahl's comment: "The variation among different individuals in capacity for 'rational' adaptation to reality, as against compulsive behavior, indicates a problem of crucial importance to the role of Congress in foreign policy. . . . A solution of the problem of how Congress is to act rationally on foreign policy questions must finally depend upon the extent to which the American political process recruits the more rational, noncompulsive personality types into Congress, rather than the more compulsive, irrational types." *Congress and Foreign Policy* (New York, Harcourt, Brace, 1950), p. 22. Cf. Alexander L. George, "Comment on 'Opinions, Personality, and Political Behavior,'" *American Political Science Review, 52* (1958), 21–23; Andrew Hacker, "The Elected and the Anointed: Two American Elites," ibid., *55* (1961), 539–49; Lewis A. Froman, Jr., "Personality and Political Socialization," *Journal of Politics, 23* (1961), 348–50.

58. V. O. Key, Jr., *Politics, Parties and Pressure Groups* (4th ed. New York, Crowell, 1958), p. 442.

59. William G. Carleton, "The Revolution in the Presidential Nominating Convention," *Political Science Quarterly, 72* (1957) 224–40.

60. Donald R. Matthews, *The Social Background of Political Decision-Makers* (New York, Random House, 1954), pp. 30–32.

61. Cf. Joseph A. Schlesinger, "Lawyers and American Politics: A Clarified View," *Midwest Journal of Political Science, 1* (1957), 26–39.

62. Herbert Jacob, "Initial Recruitment of Elected Officials in the U.S.—a Model," *Journal of Politics, 24* (1962), 703–16.

63. Rufus P. Browning, "Businessmen in Politics: Motivation and Circumstances in the Rise to Power," unpublished doctoral dissertation, Yale University, 1960. Cf. Bernard Hennessy, "Politicals and Apoliticals: Some Measurements of Personality Traits," *Midwest Journal of Political Science, 3* (1959), 336–55; and John B. McConaughy, "Certain Personality Factors of State Legislators in South Carolina," *American Political Science Review, 44* (1950), 897–903; Lester W. Milbrath, *The Washington Lobbyists* (Chicago, Rand McNally, 1963), chap. 5.

64. Extensive bibliographies are presented in Bell et al., *Public Leadership;* Marvick, *Political Decision-Makers;* and Matthews.

65. Cf. George A. Kelly, "Man's Construction of His Alternatives," in Gardner Lindzey, ed., *Assessment of Human Motives* (New York, Grove Press, 1958), pp. 49–50. See also Kelly's *The Psychology of Personal Constructs* (New York, Norton, 1955).

66. Theodore M. Newcomb, *Social Psychology* (New York, Dryden Press, 1950), p. 79.

67. The formulation which follows is similar to that of Lucian W. Pye in his *Politics, Personality, and Nation Building* (New Haven, Yale University Press, 1962), p. 211.

68. Cf., for example, Harold D. Lasswell, *Power and Personality* (New York, Viking, 1962), p. 37. See also Lucian W. Pye, "Personal Identity and Political Ideology," in Marvick, *Political Decision-Makers,* for an elaboration of Lasswell's repeated insistence on the significance

of situational variables. Cf. Alexander and Juliette George, "Some Uses of Dynamic Psychology in Political Biography," mimeographed draft, April, 1960, p. 11; Samuel A. Stouffer, "Intervening Opportunities: A Theory Relating Mobility and Distance," *American Sociological Review,* 5 (1940), 845–67; Kurt Lewin, "Defining the Field at a Given Time," *Psychological Review,* 50 (1943), 292–310; Bernard R. Berelson, Paul F. Lazarsfeld, and William N. McPhee, *Voting* (Chicago, University of Chicago Press, 1954), pp. 277–80. For an elegant empirical demonstration that the social situation within which motives operate is highly significant, see Arthur S. Couch, "The Psychological Determinants of Interpersonal Behavior," *Proceedings of the XIV International Congress of Applied Psychology* (Copenhagen, 1961), pp. 111–27. See also Daniel J. Levinson, "The Relevance of Personality for Political Participation," *Public Opinion Quarterly,* 22 (1958), 10; J. Milton Yinger, "Research Implications of a Field View of Personality," *American Journal of Sociology,* 68 (1963), 580–92; Robert E. Lane, "Political Character and Political Analysis," *Psychiatry,* 16 (November 1953), reprinted in Eulau, *Political Behavior.* Cf. David Easton, *The Political System: An Inquiry Into the State of Political Science* (New York, Knopf, 1953), pp. 206–18; Lester G. Seligman, "The Study of Political Leadership," *American Political Science Review,* 44 (1950), 904–15.

69. Robert K. Merton, Marjorie Fiske, and Patricia L. Kendall, *The Focused Interview* (Glencoe, Ill., Free Press, 1956). Cf. M. Brewster Smith, Jerome S. Bruner, and Robert W. White, *Opinions and Personality* (New York, Wiley, 1956), pp. 280–84.

70. Cf. George, *American Political Science Review,* 52 (1958), 21.

71. For striking evidence on the perils of neglecting the respondent's explanations, see Gordon W. Allport, "The Trend in Motivational Theory," *Journal of Orthopsychiatry,* 23 (1953), 107–19.

72. Cf. Robert E. Lane, *Political Ideology* (New York, Free Press of Glencoe, 1962), pp. 8–10, and Pye, *Politics, Personality, and Nation Building,* p. 160.

73. Karl Bosworth, "Lawmaking in State Governments," in *The American Assembly, The Forty-Eight States* (American Assembly, 1955), p. 99.

74. For an excellent analysis of Connecticut politics in elections and the General Assembly, see Lockard, Chapters 10 and 11.

75. They are probably best considered as being in an initial or trial stage of a political career. Cf. William H. Form and Delbert C. Mitchell, "Occupational Career Pattern as a Sociological Instrument," *American Journal of Sociology,* 54 (1959), 317–29.

76. Cf. Merton, *Social Theory and Social Structure,* p. 309.

77. David B. Truman, *The Governmental Process* (New York, Knopf, 1960), pp. 139–55. Cf. Herman Finer, *Theory and Practice of Modern Government* (rev. ed. New York, Holt, 1949), p. 379.

78. This translation from expressed intention to commitment or attraction is familiar from sociometric studies. See A. Paul Hare, *Handbook of Small Groups Research* (New York, Free Press of Glencoe, 1962), chap. 5. In psychological terms, "one can infer the cathexis from the disposition to re-experience the affect." Daniel R. Miller, "Personality and Social Interaction," in Bert Kaplan, ed., *Studying Personality Cross-Culturally* (Evanston, Ill., Row, Peterson, 1961), p. 285.

79. Dorwin Cartwright and Alvin Zander, eds., *Group Dynamics: Research and Theory* (2d ed. Evanston, Ill., Row, Peterson, 1960), p. 72.

80. On nominations, I have found the following of special help: Arthur J. Vidich and Joseph Bensman, *Small Town in Mass Society: Class, Power, and Religion in a Rural Community* (Princeton, Princeton University Press, 1958); V. O. Key, Jr., *Southern Politics in State and Nation* (New York, Knopf, 1949); Lockard, *New England State Politics;* Oliver P. Williams, "A Typology for Comparative Local Government," *Midwest Journal of Political*

Science, 5 (1961), 150–64; James Q. Wilson, *The Amateur Democrat* (Chicago, University of Chicago Press, 1962); Dahl, *Who Governs?;* Edward C. Banfield, *Political Influence* (Glencoe, Ill., Free Press, 1960); Eli Ginzberg et al., *Occupational Choice: An Approach to a General Theory* (New York, Columbia University Press, 1951); Donald E. Super, *The Psychology of Careers* (New York, Harper, 1957); Morris Rosenberg, *Occupations and Values* (Glencoe, Ill., Free Press, 1957); Howard S. Becker and Anselm L. Strauss, "Careers, Personality, and Adult Socialization," in Maurice R. Stein, Arthur J. Vidich, and David M. White, eds., *Identity and Anxiety* (Glencoe, Ill., Free Press, 1960).

81. This and the following two topics are familiar ones in social psychology. See, for example, David Krech, Richard S. Crutchfield, and Egerton L. Ballachey, *Individual in Society* (New York, McGraw-Hill, 1962), chapters entitled "Cognition," "Motivation," and "Interpersonal Response Traits." In deriving needs and adjustment problems from reactions to the environment, I have found much assistance in the following: Lane, *Political Life* and *Political Ideology;* Smith, *Opinions and Personality;* Daniel Katz, "The Functional Approach to the Study of Attitudes," *Public Opinion Quarterly,* 24 (1960), 163–204; David Riesman, *The Lonely Crowd* (New Haven, Yale University Press, 1953); Leon Festinger, *A Theory of Cognitive Dissonance* (Evanston, Ill., Row, Peterson, 1957); Lewis A. Dexter, "The Representative and His District," *Human Organization,* 16 (1957), 2–13; Edward A. Shils, "The Legislator and His Environment," *University of Chicago Law Review,* 18 (1950–51), 571–84; Kurt Lewin, *A Dynamic Theory of Personality* (New York, McGraw-Hill, 1935), pp. 74–79 and chap. 4.

82. On the inner dynamics of personality I have found the following most useful: Karen Horney, *Neurosis and Human Growth* (New York, Norton, 1950) and *The Neurotic Personality of Our Time* (New York, Norton, 1937); C. H. Patterson, "The Self in Recent Rogerian Theory," *Journal of Individual Psychology,* 17 (1961), 5–11; Calvin S. Hall and Gardner Lindzey, *Theories of Personality* (New York, Wiley, 1957), chap. 12, "Rogers' Self Theory"; George Herbert Mead, "The Social Self," *Journal of Philosophy, Psychology and Scientific Methods,* 10 (January–December 1913), 374–80; S. I. Hayakawa, *Symbol, Status, and Personality* (New York, Harcourt, Brace, 1953), chap. 4; Erik H. Erikson, "Identity and the Life Cycle," *Psychological Issues,* 1 (1959), Monograph 1, and *Childhood and Society* (New York, Norton, 1950); Lasswell, *Power and Personality* and *Psychopathology and Politics* (New York, Viking, 1960); Alexander and Juliette George, *Woodrow Wilson and Colonel House: A Personality Study* (New York, John Day, 1950), especially the "Research Note"; Ernest R. Hilgard, "Human Motives and the Concept of the Self," *American Psychologist,* 4 (September 1949); Tamotsu Shibutani, *Society and Personality* (Englewood Cliffs, N.J., Prentice-Hall, 1961), especially chap. 13, "Self-Esteem and Social Control." Cf. T. V. Smith, *The Legislative Way of Life* (Chicago, University of Chicago Press, 1940), p. 16: "The first obstacle to the legislative way of life . . . is the self with its natural egoism and its utopia-building reveries."

83. Besides the references already mentioned, the following have been of help in assessing strategies of adjustment: Franklin J. Shaw and Robert S. Ort, *Personal Adjustment in the American Culture* (New York, Harper, 1953); James C. Coleman, "Types of Adjustive Reactions," in Leon Gorlow and Walter Katkovsky, eds., *Readings in the Psychology of Adjustment* (New York, McGraw-Hill, 1959); Robert K. Merton, "Social Structure and Anomie," in *Social Theory and Social Structure;* Erving Goffman, *The Presentation of Self in Everyday Life* (New York, Doubleday, 1959); Nathan Leites, "Psycho-Cultural Hypotheses about Political Acts," *World Politics,* 1 (1948), 102–19.

On the analysis of adaptation through reactions, self, and strategies, see H. A. Witkin et al., *Personality Through Perception* (New York, Harper, 1954); and Harriet B. Linton, "Relations between Mode of Perception and Tendency to Conform" (dissertation, Yale University,

1952), and "Rorschach Correlates of Response to Suggestion," *Journal of Abnormal and Social Psychology*, 49 (1954), 75–83. "The previous findings of Witkin et al. and Linton suggested that the significant personality tendencies underlying individual differences in mode of perception and in social conformity were in the areas of *attitudes toward the self*, the quality of *coping* with the environment, and the degree of emotional responsiveness to the environment" Elaine Graham Sofer, "Inner-direction, Other-direction, and Autonomy: A Study of College Students," in Lipset and Lowenthal, *Culture and Social Character*, p. 329).

84. On the interplay between personal needs and strategies and group tasks, see especially Harold D. Lasswell, "Political Constitution and Character," *Psychoanalysis and the Psychoanalytic Review*, 46 (1960), 3–18; Lane, "Political Character and Political Analysis," and Dahl, "Hierarchy, Democracy, and Bargaining in Politics and Economics," both in Eulau, *Political Behavior*; Truman, *The Governmental Process*, chap. 11; Donald R. Matthews, *U.S. Senators and Their World* (Chapel Hill, N.C., University of North Carolina Press, 1960), chaps. 4 and 5; Seymour Martin Lipset, Martin A. Trow, and James S. Coleman, *Union Democracy* (New York, Doubleday, 1962), chaps. 10 and 11; Chris Argyris, "The Individual and Organization: Some Problems of Mutual Adjustment," *Administrative Science Quarterly*, 2 (1957), 1–24; William C. Mitchell, "Occupational Role Strains: The American Elective Public Official," ibid., 3 (1958), 210–28; and Edward A. Shils, "The Legislator and His Environment," *University of Chicago Law Review*, 18 (1950–51), 571–84. Cf. David Riesman and Nathan Glazer, " 'The Lonely Crowd': A Reconsideration in 1960," in Lipset and Lowenthal, *Culture and Social Character*, p. 438: "We emphasized the price paid by the character types that fitted badly, as against the release of energy provided by congruence of character and task." On legislative procedures and their functional significances see especially Roland Young, *The American Congress* (New York, Harper, 1958) and Bertram Gross, *The Legislative Struggle* (New York, McGraw-Hill, 1953).

NOTES FOR CHAPTER TWO

1. See below, Chap. 4.
2. Cf. Lester G. Seligman, "Political Recruitment and Party Structure: A Case Study," *American Political Science Review*, 55 (1961), 77–86.
3. From 1946 to 1958, Connecticut House incumbents won 982 times and lost 219 times.
4. This is nicely illustrated by contrasting observations on the same session of Congress, as quoted by George W. Galloway, *History of the House of Representatives* (New York, Crowell, 1961), p. 35 Cf. Charles L. Clapp, *The Congressman* (Washington, Brookings Institution, 1963) pp. 17–20.
5. *The Lonely Crowd*, p. 214.
6. Glamour "is not only a veneer for apathy but also a sign that people crave a political leadership that, by dispelling their apathy, would allow them to become excited, committed, and related to politics. That is, glamour has an ambivalent effect: it reinforces apathy by invoking consumership motivations, while at the same time people look to glamour as a way of altering their motivations" (ibid., p. 215).
7. For detailed analysis of conflicts underlying placidity, cf. Anna Freud, *The Ego and the Mechanisms of Defense* (New York, International Universities Press, 1946), chap. 8; Harry Stack Sullivan, *The Interpersonal Theory of Psychiatry* (New York, Norton, 1953), pp.

55–57; Otto Fenichel, *The Psychoanalytic Theory of Neurosis* (New York, Norton, 1945), pp. 185–86; Ralph Greenson, "The Psychology of Apathy," *Psychoanalytic Quarterly*, 18 (1949), 290–302; Nathan Leites, "Trends in Affectlessness," in Clyde Kluckhohn and Henry A. Murray, eds., *Personality in Nature, Society, and Culture* (New York, Knopf, 1956), chap. 40.

8. For the approval-seeking person, Horney writes: "The timidity serves as a defense against exposing one's self to rebuff. The conviction of being unlovable is used as the same kind of defense. It is as if persons of this type said to themselves, 'People do not like me anyhow, so I had better stay in the corner, and thereby protect myself against any possible rejection.'" Horney, *The Neurotic Personality*, p. 137. This protective device decreases the person's chances for gaining affection, because the need remains concealed. For further evidence of the relation of concealment and low self-esteem, see Leonard I. Pearlin, "The Appeals of Anonymity in Questionnaire Response," *Public Opinion Quarterly*, 25 (1961), 644.

9. On anxiety and company-seeking, cf. Stanley Schacter, *The Psychology of Affiliation: Experimental Studies of the Sources of Gregariousness* (Stanford, Stanford University Press, 1959).

10. Cf. Alexander L. George, "Some Uses of Dynamic Psychology in Political Biography," p. 14: "The usefulness of the technical literature to the biographer will be enhanced if the distinction is kept in mind between the question of the *origins* of compulsiveness and compulsive traits, about which there are various views, and the *dynamics* of such behavior, about which there is less disagreement." Cf. Erik H. Erikson on "orinology," *Young Man Luther* (New York, Norton, 1958), pp. 18–19.

11. Cf. Karen Horney on "moving toward people," "moving against people," and "moving away from people," in *Our Inner Conflicts* (New York, Norton, 1945).

12. This is not to say, of course, that no significant changes take place after one reaches adulthood, or that personality becomes permanently fixed in the early years, though evidence of the latter appears inconclusive. See Ian Stevenson, "Is the Human Personality More Plastic in Infancy and Childhood?," *American Journal of Psychiatry*, 114 (1957), 152–61. On adult consistency, E. Lowell Kelly found considerable stability in some variables (e.g. attitudes toward marriage, rearing children) among 446 subjects after twenty years of adult life: "Consistency of the Adult Personality," *American Psychologist*, 10 (1955), 659–81. D. P. Morris, E. Soroker, and G. Buruss, "Follow-Up Studies of Shy, Withdrawn Children. I. Evaluation of Later Adjustment," *American Journal of Orthopsychiatry*, 24 (1954), 743–54. Cf. G. W. Allport, J. S. Bruner, and E. M. Jandorf, "Personality under Social Catastrophe: Ninety Life-Histories of the Nazi Revolution," in Clyde Kluckhohn and Henry Murray, eds., *Personality in Nature, Society and Culture*, p. 443: "Very rarely does catastrophic social change produce catastrophic alterations in personality. . . . On the contrary, perhaps the most vivid impression gained by our analysts from this case-history material is of the extraordinary continuity and sameness in the individual personality." For evidence that ability to dispense with minor habits is strongly related to childhood experience, see Charles McArthur, Helen Waldron, and John Dickinson, "The Psychology of Smoking," *Journal of Abnormal and Social Psychology*, 56 (1958), 267–75. On the meaning of "habit" or "habit potential" as "the probability of evocation of the response," rather than a fixation, compulsion, or obsession of some kind, see John W. M. Whiting and Irvin L. Child, *Child Training and Personality* (New Haven, Yale University Press, 1953), pp. 18 ff.

13. Cf. Horney, *Neurosis and Human Growth*, pp. 185–86. Newcomb notes that "threat-oriented behaviors are commonly rewarding, and hence persistent, because they are perceived as defending the ego—perhaps imperfectly, but nonetheless in the best way in which the person knows how." *Social Psychology*, p. 462.

14. This is probably as good a place as any to assert categorically that I do not consider the

subjects of this study "psychotic," "neurotic," or even especially troubled in comparison with the theoretically normal population. Such terms represent overlapping categories. The use of clinical language implies only that certain concepts have an applicability to the generally well-adjusted as well as to those under treatment. For evidence of such continuities see, for example, Gerald Gurin, Joseph Veroff, and Sheila Feld, *Americans View Their Mental Health* (New York, Basic Books, 1960), especially chap. 11; Raymond B. Cattell, *Personality* (New York, McGraw-Hill, 1950), especially chap. 1 and 17; William Schofield and Lucy Balian, "A Comparative Study of the Personal Histories of Schizophrenic and Nonpsychiatric Patients," *Journal of Abnormal and Social Psychology*, 59 (1959), 216–25. For a good introductory discussion of such matters, see Fenichel, *The Psychoanalytic Theory of Neurosis*, or Newcomb, *Social Psychology*, pp. 392 ff.

15. "In a typically self-effacing person, feeling abused is an almost constant undercurrent in his whole attitude toward life. If we wanted to characterize him crudely and glibly in a few words, we would say that he is a person who craves affection and feels abused most of the time." Horney, *Neurosis and Human Growth*, p. 230.

16. For links between conforming behavior and personality variables, see Richard S. Crutchfield, "Conformity and Character," *American Psychologist*, 10 (1955), 191–98; James E. Dittes and Harold H. Kelley, "Effects of Different Conditions of Acceptance upon Conformity to Group Norms," *Journal of Abnormal and Social Psychology*, 53 (1956), 100–07; Hans L. Zetterberg, "Compliant Actions," *Acta Sociologica*, 2 (1957), 179–201; John W. Thibaut and Lloyd H. Strickland, "Psychological Set and Social Conformity," *Journal of Personality*, 25 (1956), 115–29.

17. Horney, *Neurosis and Human Growth*, p. 320.

18. Cf. Samuel C. Patterson, "The Role of the Deviant in the State Legislative System: The Wisconsin Assembly," *Western Political Quarterly*, 14 (1961), 463.

19. Cf. Stimson Bullitt, *To Be a Politician* (Garden City, N.Y., Doubleday, 1959), p. 63. The ambiguity involved in such encounters is probably a general source of strain in American politics, a strain that is ameliorated in more formally conventional environments. See Matthews, *U.S. Senators*, p. 69, and Margaret Mary Wood, *Paths of Loneliness* (New York, Columbia University Press, 1953), chap. 5, "Men in Great Place." Graham Wallas describes the protective function served—"Light chatter, even among strangers, in which neither party 'gives himself away,' is very much less fatiguing than an intimacy which makes some call upon the emotions"—and notes that London clubs "are successful exactly because it is an unwritten law in almost every one of them that no member must speak to any other who is not one of his own personal acquaintances." *Human Nature in Politics* (3d ed. New York, F. S. Crofts, 1921), pp. 73, 71. See Georg Simmel, "The Sociology of Sociability," *American Journal of Sociology*, 55 (1949), 254–61.

20. Truman, *The Governmental Process*, chap. 6; Paul F. Lazarsfeld, Bernard Berelson, and Hazel Gaudet, *The People's Choice* (New York, Columbia University Press, 1948), chaps. 6, 7, and 15.

21. The elaborateness of experimental designs for creating conflict situations gives perhaps some indication of how infrequently scuh situations arise in natural settings. Cf. Edward L. Walker and Roger W. Heyns, *An Anatomy for Conformity* (Englewood Cliffs, N.J., Prentice-Hall, 1962). And there is much evidence that many people do not see their conflicting memberships or contradictory opinions as either conflicting or contradictory. Cf. Martin Kriesberg, "Cross-Pressures and Attitudes," *Public Opinion Quarterly*, 13 (1949), 5–16; Festinger, *A Theory of Cognitive Dissonance*. In an elegant article, Wilder Crane examined differences between Wisconsin representatives and their constituents on a "daylight time" issue. Ten of the fifteen whose votes were inconsistent with their constituency majorities (as later revealed in a referendum) explained that they were uncertain what their constituents felt. And "only a

minority of assemblymen were faced with the problem of feeling compelled to vote contrary to their own preferences. Frequently the assemblymen could vote what were simultaneously their own opinions and majority opinions in their district. However, when there were conflicts, most assemblymen made clear that they were willing to disregard their own preferences in order to represent their constituents." "Do Representatives Represent?," *Journal of Politics*, 22 (1960), 295–99. Cf. Lewis A. Dexter, "The Representative and his District"; William C. Mitchell, *The American Polity* (New York, The Free Press of Glencoe, 1962), p. 86; Warren E. Miller and Donald E. Stokes, "Constituency Influences in Congress," *American Political Science Review*, 57 (March 1963), 56.

22. "The feeling of powerlessness of the other-directed character is, then, the result in part of the lack of genuine commitment to work. His life is not engaged in a direct struggle for mastery over himself and nature; he has no long-term goals since the goals must constantly be changed. At the same time, he is in competition with others for the very values they tell him are worth pursuing; in a circular process, one of these values is the approval of the competing group itself. Hence, he is apt to repress overt competitiveness both out of anxiety to be liked and out of fear of retaliation. In this situation, he is likely to lose interest in the work itself. With loss of interest, he may even find himself little more than a dilettante, not quite sure that he is really able to accomplish anything." David Riesman, *Individualism Reconsidered* (Glencoe, Ill., Free Press, 1954), p. 110. Cf. Harold D. Lasswell, *Political Writings* (Glencoe, Ill., Free Press, 1951), p. 499.

23. The disturbing effects of tasks on interpersonal relations has been noted in small-groups research. Cf. Robert F. Bales and Fred L. Strodtbeck, "Phases in Group Problem Solving," in Cartwright and Zander, *Group Dynamics Research and Theory*, 2d ed., p. 630.

24. Cf. William C. Mitchell, "Reduction of Tension in Legislatures," *Political Research Organization and Design*, 2 (January, 1959).

NOTES FOR CHAPTER THREE

1. American Bar Association, *Canons of Professional Ethics of the American Bar Association* (Boston, American Bar Association, 1953), p. 24.

2. Cf. A. B. Crawford and S. H. Clements, eds., *The Choice of an Occupation* (New Haven, Yale Office of Counseling, Placement, and Research, 1958), p. 116: "Among the occupations that have been found particularly compatible with political and especially legislative careers are the practice of law, insurance, real estate, farming, and journalism. The activity compatible with politics is likely to have some of these characteristics: usefulness of political candidacy in getting one's name before the public as a person available for performance of the non-political occupational service (law, insurance, real estate) . . ." Cf. Heinz Eulau and David Koff, "Occupational Mobility and Political Career," *Western Political Quarterly*, 15 (1962), 507–21.

3. No implication is intended here that lawyers as such are more likely to display the particular characteristics described in this chapter. For a quite different cluster of characteristics shared by a number of lawyers, see below, Chapter 5. On the pervasiveness of (and personal strains involved in) the search for "contacts" in American entrepreneurial life, see Francis X. Sutton and others, *The American Business Creed* (New York, Schocken Books, 1962), pp. 342–43. On the same thing in bureaucracies, see Robert Presthus, *The Organizational Society*

(New York, Knopf, 1962), p. 187. Merton finds the "localists" exhibiting this pattern more often than the "cosmopolitans": *Social Theory and Social Structure,* p. 399.

4. Population change is, of course, only one factor affecting the local political system over time, although it is apparently an important one. Cf. Christian T. Jonassen and Sherwood H. Peres, *Interrelationships of Dimensions of Community Systems: A Factor Analysis of Eighty-Two Variables* (Columbus, Ohio State University Press, 1960); Charles R. Adrian, *Governing Urban America* (New York, McGraw-Hill, 1961), chap. 1; Norman F. Washburne, *Interpreting Social Change in America* (Garden City, N.Y., Doubleday, 1954); George Peter Murdock, "How Culture Changes," in Harry L. Shapiro, ed., *Man, Culture, and Society* (New York, Oxford University Press, 1960); Maurice Stein, "The Eclipse of Community," in Warren G. Bennis, Kenneth D. Benne, and Robert Chin, eds., *The Planning of Change* (New York, Holt, Rinehart, and Winston, 1961); Edward C. Banfield, "The Political Implications of Metropolitan Growth," *Daedalus, 90* (Winter 1960), 61–78; Seymour M. Lipset and Reinhard Bendix, *Social Mobility in Industrial Society* (Berkeley, University of California Press, 1962), chap. 8.

5. For an account of connections between community change and a newcomer's election see David A. Booth and Charles R. Adrian, "Elections and Community Power," *Journal of Politics, 25* (1963), 107–18.

6. Bullitt, *To Be a Politician,* p. 37.

7. See Harry Stack Sullivan, "Psychiatric Aspects of Morale," in Alfred H. Stanton and Stewart E. Perry, eds., *Personality and Political Crisis* (Glencoe, Ill., Free Press, 1951), p. 49. Cf. Edmond Rostand, *Cyrano de Bergerac,* Act V:

> Do you know, when a man wins
> Everything in this world, when he succeeds
> Too much—He feels, having done nothing wrong
> Especially, Heaven knows!—he feels somehow
> A thousand small displeasures with himself,
> Whose whole sum is not quite Remorse, but rather
> A sort of vague disgust.

8. Cf. another Advertiser's comment explaining his motives for seeking office: "I think maybe the main reason was to get out and, you know, to be a public figure doing something constructive and all that sort of thing. And try and do an excellent job up here and receive credit for it. It was something—I suppose somebody might say it's sort of selfish, or something like that—but after all I have to earn a living, or try to."

9. Cf. this explanation by another Advertiser: "I think I've done all right. I—I'm a man with a—my parents endowed me with a very strong conscience, and when I do something wrong it bothers me for a long time. And I don't—I haven't done anything in the legislature yet that I really regret, that I think has been basically wrong. . . . But you still wonder, is it right to do this? And as I say, I've tried to justify these cases to myself and I see this, I don't know whether I've talked myself into this, or whether they're really right, but you never know, I don't think. You want to believe that what you've done is right. Maybe you argue yourself into it, you know?"

10. It is unnecessary here to take a stand on whether aggression springs *only* from frustration, or whether frustration *always* leads to aggression. Cf. John Dollard and others, *Frustration and Aggression* (New Haven, Yale University Press, 1939); Arnold H. Buss, *The Psychology of Aggression* (New York, John Wiley and Sons, 1961), chap. 2; Robert R. Sears, "Effects of Frustration and Anxiety on Fantasy Aggression," in Irwin G. Sarason, ed., *Contemporary Research in Personality* (New York, Van Nostrand, 1962); White and Lippitt, *Autocracy and Democracy,* pp. 66–78, and chaps. 9–11; Bjorn Christiansen, *Attitudes towards Foreign Affairs as a Function of Personality* (Oslo University Press, 1959).

11. Bob begins to identify himself with this category, but then steps off: "Maybe sometimes I can classify myself that way, too. No, I'm talking about, oh, the farmer type of guy."

12. Cf. Mike's comment in another connection: "And what does human nature do? When somebody else can do something better than another? You try to tear it down. You belittle it. Because you are not of—say, you cannot do what the other one can do and you're trying to do it, and you can't, and you fall on your face, so you resent it. It's human nature!—even if you didn't want to, even if you won't admit it to yourself, you become resentful, you try to tear it down."

13. Another Advertiser comments regarding campaigning that "with a lot of people you'd like to be able to tell them to go to hell and break off—but you can't do it."

14. Another Advertiser shows this pattern: "I'm going to do something about it. I probably won't succeed very much, but at least I'm going to feel free to argue about it."

15. Mike much more than the other two Advertisers interviewed seems to have a strong preference for tangible accomplishments, and there may be a somewhat compulsive element in his work. Cf. this uninterrupted passage: "I like—I like to paint my house. I like to mow my lawn. I like to make things. I like to build up places. I like to build things. I like to make things—I like to, I don't care what it is, I like to make things, construct it from nothing, and make it."

16. Cf. above, pp. 42–45.

17. Cf. Gordon W. Allport's distinction between "activity" and "participation." Allport would ask, "Does he, in a psychological sense, *participate* in what he is doing? Although constantly *task-involved*, is he ever really *ego-involved?*" "The Psychology of Participation," *Psychological Review*, 53 (1945), 121–22. Victor H. Vroom presents evidence suggesting that "participation in decision-making has a definitely favorable effect on the attitudes toward the job of low authoritarians who have a strong need for independence. On the other hand, high authoritarians with low need for independence are apparently unaffected by participating in making decisions." *Some Personality Determinants of the Effects of Participation* (Englewood Cliffs, N.J., Prentice-Hall, 1960), p. 37.

18. Emphasis added.

19. Cf. this passage from another Advertiser interview: "Some of the decisions you have to make bother you sometimes. For various reasons—because you're kind-hearted and you hate to turn somebody down, or you do something that leaves some doubt in your mind as to whether you've done the right things or not. But it—I know it's—I'm *exhausted*, I'll tell you that. When I get home at night I am really dragged out."

20. Cf. Mike's image of the legislators at the first of the session: "Did you ever see a herd of cows? They're waiting around there, you have the chief bull around. They're just munching on the grass and basking in the sun—you know, like contented cows. They're—a nice sunny day, and life is easy. Of course, you have a few stragglers that are—not stragglers, but, you—the apprehensive ones. Those that are impatient—maybe the young bulls around, want to go free. That was the general routine." In a similar way, Mike develops a picture of the life of the judge (see above, p. 84), the professor, and the congressman; he begins with an idealized image of safety and comfort, and then adds the contender, the upward mobile person. Compare his description of home-town politics: "Just personalities. Individual in there wanted to be kingpin and the other wanted to be kingpin. And the natural bickering and fighting between them—like animals. You get a bull that's in charge of the herd and then you get another bull that comes along and he wants to be in charge of the herd. Or you get a bull that grows up in a herd and then he wants to take over."

21. Cf. above, p. 94.

22. Cf. above, pp. 42–45.

23. Cf. Tom Burns, "The Reference of Conduct in Small Groups: Cliques and Cabals in Occupational Milieux," *Human Relations*, 3 (1955), 467–86.

24. Cf. E. E. Schattschneider, *The Semi-Sovereign People* (New York, Holt, Rinehart, and Winston, 1960). Conflict within a group may in the long run solidify the group. See Robert C. North et al., "The Integrative Functions of Conflict," *Journal of Conflict Resolution, 4* (1960), 355–74. And the expression of hostility at a certain stage of decision-making may aid the process. See George A. Theodorson, "The Function of Hostility in Small Groups," *Journal of Social Psychology, 56* (1962), 57–66; E. Paul Torrance, "Function of Expressed Disagreement in Small Processes," *Social Forces, 35* (1957), 314–18. On the other hand, in the wrong circumstances, competition can be destructive. Herman Finer puts the matter succinctly when he writes, "The good in dialectic is not only that it causes one person or party to triumph over another, but that it sometimes causes truth to triumph over both by provoking the explanation of self to self." "The Tasks and Functions of the Legislator," in Wahlke and Eulau, eds., *Legislative Behavior*, p. 282.

25. For evidence that some kinds of silence are more conducive to effective decision-making than some kinds of expression, see Andie L. Knutson, "Quiet and Vocal Groups," *Sociometry, 23* (1960), 36–49.

NOTES FOR CHAPTER FOUR

1. Quoted in Ralph Volney Harlow, *The Growth of the United States* (New York, Henry Holt, 1943), 2, 310.

2. Root, *The Citizen's Part in Government* (New York, Scribner, 1907), pp. 30–31. From one of the Yale "Lectures on the Responsibilities of Citizenship" for that year, "upon the foundation established by the late William Earl Dodge." Cf. Charles H. Cooley, *Social Organization: A Study of the Larger Mind* (New York, Schocken Books, 1962, 1st ed. 1909): "Ours, then, is an Age of Diffusion. The best minds and hearts seek joy and self-forgetfulness in active service, as in another time they might seek it in solitary worship" (p. 175 of Schocken ed.).

2. On the impacts of community change, cf. Chap. 1, note 80 above.

4. Robert Wood supplies a quote from Sherwood Anderson which expresses these themes precisely: "You have to go on living with people, day after day, week after week. You can't just ignore your brother-in-law, forget him as you might in a city. Tomorrow you will meet him in the street. You will be meeting him in the stores and in the post-office. Better make it up, start over again." "A Re-examination of Local Democracy," in Oliver P. Williams and Charles Press, eds., *Democracy in Urban America* (Chicago, Rand McNally, 1961), p. 114. Cf. S. F. Nadel, *The Theory of Social Structure* (Glencoe, Ill., Free Press, 1958), pp. 70–72.

5. Above, p. 29.

6. Nominating a newcomer "isn't according to Hoyle, the way I see it, in my old-fashioned way of thinking," a Reluctant comments.

7. See Whiting and Child, *Child Training and Personality*, pp. 32–38.

8. Above, pp. 117–18.

9. Cf. Vidich and Bensman, p. 122: "It is more difficult to find a qualified person willing to stand for election, not because such persons are not flattered by being considered, but rather because they do not want to appear to be eager 'to seek public office.' The potential candidate is coaxed to run, finally accedes and is elected to office." And Ruth Benedict, *Patterns of Culture* (New York, New American Library, 1948), p. 91: "The 'ideal man of the Pueblos'

avoids office. He must have it thrust upon him, but he does not seek it. When the kiva offices must be filled, the hatchway of the kiva is fastened and all the men are imprisoned until some-one's excuses have been battered down. The folktales always relate of good men their unwill-ingness to take office—though they always take it. A man must avoid the appearance of leadership."

10. Below, pp. 140 ff.

11. "Social and Psychological Needs of the Aging," in Gorlow and Katovsky, eds., *Readings in the Psychology of Adjustment.*

12. Ibid., p. 441.

13. Cf. Frank A. Pinner, Paul Jacobs, and Philip Selznick, *Old Age and Political Behavior: A Case Study* (Berkeley, University of California Press, 1959), p. 267.

14. Havighurst, p. 440. Cf. Edmund H. Volkart and Stanley T. Michael, "Bereavement and Mental Health," in Alexander Leighton, John A. Clausen, and Robert N. Wilson, eds., *Explorations in Social Psychiatry* (New York, Basic Books, 1957); Elaine Cumming and William F. Henry, *Growing Old: The Process of Disengagement* (New York, Basic Books, 1961); Faina Jyrkilä, "Society and Adjustment to Old Age," *Transactions of the Wester-marck Society*, Vol. 5; Merton, *Social Theory and Social Structure*, pp. 188–90.

15. These names are not the same ones the subject listed, but are approximately equal to them in "Yankee-ness."

16. Pressed to specify the differences among nationality groups, Dan reluctantly says that the Italians "get up and express their opinions in a little more—aggressive way, you know," while the Irish are "very well organized and all that" and "more smooth in their talking."

17. Cf. another Reluctant's comments on "a young lawyer, for example, who is there for a very specific purpose—either that purpose is because he wants to become a judge, or be-cause he wants experience, or because he wants to make connections. I don't know—but it is unimportant: the fact is he is in a different position than I am at my stage of life."

18. Cf. above, pp. 136 ff.

19. Cf. Richard F. Carter, "Stereotyping as a Process," *Public Opinion Quarterly*, 26 (1962), 77–91.

20. Reluctants focus on shared attributes cutting across party lines, as one does when he says, "Republicans or Democrats—there isn't much difference between us. We all have the same amount of gray matter more or less."

21. One Reluctant gives an interesting justification for his town-first orientation: "You have your state offices and commissioners and everybody else that's fighting for the state, and we're here to fight for the towns."

22. Above, p. 139.

23. Above, p. 141.

24. Cf. Jim's explanation: "There couldn't anything happen to me, because I wasn't looking for anything, and I didn't promise anybody anything, and I wasn't expecting anything—so what could happen to me? I was—I'm different from a man at your age, who's looking to, perhaps, go along and make something in there. But at my age, I'm not looking to come again, you see? And they can't promise me anything, because I don't want to."

25. Above, p. 133.

26. Above, p. 143.

27. Cf. Matthews, *U. S. Senators and Their World*, chap. 5; Wahlke et al., *The Legislative System*, chap. 7; Truman, *The Governmental Process*, pp. 512–24; and Smith, *The Legislative Way of Life.*

28. Of the four state legislatures surveyed by John Wahlke and colleagues, only Tennessee failed to give top priority to rules of the game stressing "performance of obligations; keep your word; abide by commitments." Wahlke et al., p. 146.

NOTES FOR CHAPTER FIVE

1. See, for example, the quotations in Campbell et al., *The American Voter,* chap. 10, and the data in chap. 8.

2. Cf. Francis Carney, *The Rise of the Democratic Clubs in California* (New York, Holt, 1958); Stephen B. and Vera H. Sarasohn, *Political Party Patterns in Michigan* (Detroit, Wayne State University Press, 1957); Wilson, *The Amateur Democrat;* Robert S. Hirschfield, Bert E. Swanson, and Blanche D. Blank, "A Profile of Political Activists in Manhattan," *Western Political Quarterly,* 15 (1962), 489–506; Tom Wicker, "The Political 'Pros' Give the 'Ams' a Nod," *New York Times Magazine* (June 9, 1963), p. 28. Charles R. Nixon concludes from a review of demographic projections that "we should expect that in the period 1965–70 there will be a more active electorate, a more informed and a more articulate electorate, one which has a higher percentage of people participating in political affairs and voluntary political organizations than is the case at the present time." "The Coming Electorate: 1965–1970," *Western Political Quarterly,* 13 (1960), 632.

3. Campbell et al., pp. 172, 174. Cf. V. O. Key, Jr., *Public Opinion and American Democracy* (New York, Knopf, 1961), 332–36.

4. Campbell et al., table 8-3, p. 182. The issues are titled "economic aid to foreign countries," "send soldiers abroad," "leave electricity, housing to private industry," "government aid to education," etc.

5. Ibid., pp. 91–92.

6. The phrase is Edward C. Banfield's. See *Political Influence,* p. 251.

7. By way of contrast, a lady Lawmaker relates that when another person told her she was "doing too much" in community activities and asked "What thanks do you get for it?", she answered, "I'm not doing it for thanks."

8. Cf. F. C. Redlich, "The Concept of Health in Psychiatry," in Leighton et al., *Explorations in Social Psychiatry.*

9. Cf. Erikson's comment that "humor marks the moment when our ego regains some territory from oppressive conscience." *Young Man Luther,* p. 169. Jacob Levine, "Response to Humor," *Scientific American* (Feb. 1956), p. 29. Periods of relaxation appear to be essential to creativity. See Eliot D. Hutchinson, "Varieties of Insight in Humans," "The Period of Frustration in Creative Endeavor," and "The Nature of Insight," all reprinted in Patrick Mullahy, ed., *A Study of Interpersonal Relations* (New York, Grove Press, 1957). Frank Barron finds that creative people "have exceptionally broad and flexible awareness of themselves. The self is strongest when it can regress (admit primitive fantasies, naive ideas, tabooed impulses into consciousness and behavior), and yet return to a high degree of rationality and self-criticism." "The Psychology of Imagination," *Scientific American* (Sept. 1958), p. 9.

10. The Lawmaker interviews abound with activist imagery: a demand that others "wake up and see"; those who "pitch in and do what has to be done." Conversely, there are many phrases of irritation with the "do-nothings," those who "follow and follow and follow," the "seat-warmers," those who "want to be ruled," the "rubber-stamp legislator," the "status-quo guy," the "man that can't think for himself," those in whom "there's no rebellion." "What a waste!" one of them comments, "all those lawmakers milling around" in the lobby, "not paying any attention," "not in there doing what they're supposed to be doing."

11. "This self-esteem, confirmed at the end of the major crises, . . . grows to be a conviction that one is learning effective steps toward a tangible future, that one is developing a defined personality within a social reality which one understands." Erik H. Erikson, "Growth and Crisis of the 'Healthy Personality,'" in Kluckhohn and Murray, eds., *Personality in Nature, Society, and Culture,* p. 216.

12. "To be adult means among other things to see one's life in continuous perspective, both

in retrospect and in prospect. By accepting some definition as to who he is, usually on the basis of a function in the economy, a place in the sequence of generations, and a status in the structure of society, the adult is able to selectively reconstruct his past in such a way that, step for step, it seems to have planned him, or better, he seems to have planned *it*. In this sense, psychologically, we *do* choose our parents, our family history, and the history of our kings, heroes and gods." Erikson, *Young Man Luther*, pp. 111–12.

13. Time perspectives may be linked in significant ways with cultures, classes, and motivational patterns. Robert E. Lane's working-class American subjects seemed to focus primarily on "the day after tomorrow." See his *Political Ideology*, chap. 18. David F. Ricks and D. Epley found that subjects with high "need for achievement" have longer time perspectives in the imaginative stories they write. See their "Foresight and Hindsight in the TAT," paper read at the Eastern Psychological Association meeting, New York, 1960. Cf. also David C. McClelland, *The Achieving Society* (Princeton, N.J., Van Nostrand, 1961), pp. 324-29, and Georges Poulet, *Studies in Human Time* (Baltimore, Johns Hopkins Press, 1956).

14. The term "role" is especially slippery. See Edgar F. Borgatta, "Role-Playing Specification, Personality, and Performance," *Sociometry, 24* (1961), 218–33. For some of the difficulties in defining "role" see Daniel J. Levinson, "Role, Personality, and Social Structure," *Journal of Abnormal and Social Psychology, 58* (1959), 170–80, and Theodore R. Sarbin, "Role Theory," in Gardner Lindzey, ed., *Handbook of Social Psychology, 1* (Reading, Mass., Addison-Wesley, 1954), especially 224–26. "Role" has been taken to mean the behavior normatively expected of an individual who occupies a certain formal position or status. See Wahlke et al., *The Legislative System*, pp. 7 ff., and Ralph Ross and Ernest Van Den Haag, *The Fabric of Society* (New York, Harcourt, Brace and World, 1957), p. 139. But the word is often used ambiguously to refer to the position itself, the values observers or occupants hold about the position, average or typical performance of individuals in the position, etc. See Ralph H. Turner, "Role-Taking, Role Standpoint, and Reference Group Behavior," *American Journal of Sociology, 61* (1956), 316–17.

I use "role" here to refer to special problems of orientation which members typically encounter *insofar as they attempt to take part in political and legislative tasks.* Nonmembers, as well as members who are relatively unconcerned with these tasks, feel these problems less intensely if at all. Role in this sense is a special category of adjustment problems: orienting oneself to the tasks which define the position. See Alex Inkeles, "Personality and Social Structure," in Robert K. Merton, Leonard Broom, and L. S. Cottrell, Jr., eds., *Sociology Today: Problems and Prospects* (New York, Basic Books, 1959), pp. 249–76; Howard Baumgartel, "The Concept of Role," in Bennis et al., eds., *The Planning of Change.*

I would agree with Alexander L. George: "The fact that a person's behavior *can* be interpreted in terms of role theory . . . does not relieve the investigator from considering the possibility that aspects of basic personality are also expressing themselves in such behavior. It is incorrect, therefore, to define the problem as some proponents of role theory tend to do in terms of 'role *vs.* personality.' Rather the interplay of role and personality needs to be considered." "Some Uses of Dynamic Psychology in Political Biography," p. 22. Cf. Richard E. Neustadt, *Presidential Power* (New York, John Wiley, 1960), p. viii.

15. Above, pp. 187–88.

16. Cf. Newcomb: "Learning to take roles and learning to differentiate oneself go hand in hand." *Social Psychology*, p. 456.

17. See the tables showing a wide range of role orientations among state legislators and within the same legislature, in Wahlke et al., chap. 16.

18. Although it is not stressed in the discussion to follow, Lawmakers appear to see themselves as concerned with a greater variety of political and legislative roles than do the other types. This greater "breadth of role conception" may be related to their more extensive political and organizational experiences before coming to the legislature. Cf. Edwin J. Thomas,

"Role Conceptions and Organizational Size," in S. Sidney Ulmer, ed., *Introductory Readings in Political Behavior* (Chicago, Rand McNally, 1961), p. 403.

19. Bullitt, *To Be a Politician*, p. 31.

20. "The very essence of the legislative process is the willingness to accept trading as a means." Truman, *The Governmental Process*, p. 368. For indications that the three roles mentioned above have been significant ones for some time, see Lily Ross Taylor, *Party Politics in the Age of Caesar* (Berkeley, University of California Press, 1961), especially pp. 6–9, 62–75.

21. See above, p. 116.

22. White and Lippitt write of "the kind of pride or self-confidence that makes it possible to arrive at an individual 'point of view' in the first place. Listless self-distrust is as inimical to creative thinking as arrogant self-assertion. However, the paradox is more apparent than real, since it is clear that *genuine* self-acceptance and self-confidence lead not to a decreased but to an increased ability to listen to others. The fully self-confident person can pass easily from enthusiastic presentation of his own ideas to an appreciative, open-minded listening to the ideas of others." *Autocracy and Democracy*, p. 229. For an account of the "kind of inner detachment" a good Senator needs, see William S. White, *Citadel: The Story of the U.S. Senate* (New York, Harper, 1956), p. 118. Cf. Jerome S. Bruner, "The Conditions of Creativity," in Howard E. Gruber, Glenn Terrell, and Michael Wertheimer, eds., *Contemporary Approaches to Creative Thinking* (New York, Atherton, 1963), p. 12.

23. Above, pp. 187 ff.

24. On the persistence of individual leadership behavior from one social environment to another, see E. F. Borgatta, A. S. Couch, and R. F. Bales, "Some Findings Relevant to the Great Man Theory of Leadership," *American Sociological Review, 19* (1954), 755–59.

25. Cf. George H. Mead, *Mind, Self and Society* (Chicago, University of Chicago Press, 1934), pp. 260–73.

26. Above, pp. 196 ff.

NOTES FOR CHAPTER SIX

1. See above, pp. 13 ff.

2. See, for example, Lane, *Political Life*, pp. 154–55; Campbell et al., *The American Voter*, pp. 515–19; Morris Rosenberg, "Self-Esteem and Concern with Public Affairs," *Public Opinion Quarterly, 26* (1962), 201–11; Heinz Eulau and Peter Schneider, "Dimensions of Political Involvement," *Public Opinion Quarterly, 20* (1956), 128–42; Robert E. Agger, Marshall N. Goldstein, and Stanley A. Pearl, "Political Cynicism: Measurement and Meaning," *Journal of Politics, 23* (1961), 477–506.

3. See especially Lasswell, *Power and Personality*, chap. 3, and *Psychopathology and Politics;* Alex Gottfried, "The Use of Socio-Psychological Categories in a Study of Political Personality," in Eulau et al., eds., *Political Behavior*, p. 129; George, *Woodrow Wilson*, pp. 317–22; Louise Harned, "Authoritarian Attitudes and Party Activity," *Public Opinion Quarterly, 25* (1961), 393–99. The assessment of interview responses as indicating low or high self-esteem remains a matter of inference, particularly as to the degree to which they show deep-seated, persistent or superficial, temporary feelings. That some low-self responses are due to challenges of a new environment is evident. In judging the relative importance of these situational elements,

however, the reader should take into account (1) the respondent's own generalization of his self-estimate, (2) his tendency to react similarly to many environmental facets, (3) the apparently habitual character of his defenses, (4) the lack of tight correspondence between objective features of past social milieus and reactions to the new one, especially in Advertiser-Lawmaker comparisons, (5) findings from other research indicating persistence of personality and especially self-concepts through the life cycle. I am indebted to Philip Converse for noting this problem.

4. Research by James E. Teele casts doubt on the validity of cumulative indices of "social participation." "Measures of Social Participation," *Social Problems, 10* (1962), 31–39. Cf. Arnold M. Rose, "Attitudinal Correlates of Social Participation," *Social Forces, 37* (1959), 202–06.

5. Cf. Theodore Caplow, *The Sociology of Work* (Minneapolis, University of Minnesota Press, 1954), chap. 6, "Occupational Ideologies." On "legitimizing characteristics" see Robert S. Weiss, "Factors Determining the Adoption of Decision-Making as a Role Behavior: A Study of Scientists in a Government Organization," in Albert H. Rubenstein and Chadwick J. Haberstroh, eds., *Some Theories of Organization* (Homewood, Ill., Irwin, 1960); Lewis M. Terman, "Are Scientists Different?," *Scientific American* (Jan. 1955), p. 25. On "occupational-role identification" see Robert F. Winch, *Identification and Its Familial Determinants* (Indianapolis, Bobbs-Merrill, 1962), pp. 102–04. On the distinction between general and special norms in small groups see Richard Videbeck and Alan P. Bates, "An Experimental Study of Conformity to Role Expectations," *Sociometry, 22* (1959), 1–11.

6. Cf. Key, *Public Opinion and American Democracy*, Pt. IV; Herbert H. Hyman, *Political Socialization* (Glencoe, Ill., Free Press, 1959), chaps. 4 and 5. That a good deal of this takes hold is evident. See Lane, *Political Life*, pp. 157–62. Gabriel A. Almond and Sidney Verba, *The Civic Culture* (Princeton, Princeton University Press, 1963) indicates that Americans put exceptional stress on "the obligation to participate." See pp. 146–47 and chap. 6.

7. Campbell et al., *The American Voter*, pp. 101–06.

8. Lazarsfeld et al., *The People's Choice*, chart 16, p. 48; Angus Campbell, Gerald Gurin, and Warren E. Miller, *The Voter Decides* (Evanston, Row, Peterson, 1954), p. 39.

9. Campbell et al., *The American Voter*, table 5–7, p. 106.

10. Cf. Lane, *Political Life*, p. 93, and *Political Ideology*, pp. 343–45.

11. Relationships among three dichotomized variables from the 1956 Survey Research Center election study support this interpretation. "Personal competence" is significantly related to "sense of citizen duty" (chi square $p < .001$) and the latter is significantly related to "political involvement" (chi square $p < .01$). I am indebted to Arthur Goldberg for this analysis. Cf. Morris Rosenberg, "Self-Esteem and Concern with Public Affairs," *Public Opinion Quarterly, 26* (1962), 201–11; Jeanne Clare Ridley, "Status, Anomie, Political Alienation, and Political Participation," *American Journal of Sociology, 68* (1962), 205–13. See also Wayne E. Thompson and John E. Horton, "Political Alienation as a Force in Political Action," *Social Forces, 38* (1960), 190–95.

12. Cf. William C. Mitchell, "The Ambivalent Social Status of the American Politician," *Western Political Quarterly, 12* (1959), 683–98.

13. Research on public attitudes toward elective office careers leaves a great deal to be desired. The questions asked often refer vaguely to "going into politics" or "entering politics," thus introducing an obviously pejorative term. As Mitchell suggests, p. 695, this is much like asking "whether they would like to see their sons become 'shysters' rather than lawyers, or 'quacks' rather than physicians." Fewer than half the Connecticut legislators agreed with a questionnaire item, "I am a politician." And of 85 *elected* local *government officials* I surveyed for another study, 68 per cent were against political careers for their sons. Other effects of wording are evident in the following results: In November 1945 a national sample was

asked: "If you had a son just getting out of school, would you like to see him enter politics as a life work?" 65 per cent said no. A year later (December 1946) another national sample was asked: "Suppose a boy or girl asks your advice about entering politics. Would you advise him or her to plan to enter politics or keep away from politics?" The negative responses dropped to 45 per cent. Explanations are speculative, but the second form differed in at least three ways: (1) an anonymous child rather than one's son is referred to; (2) the inappropriate timing of entry is dropped; and (3) the second-choice nature of politics (not "life work") is allowed for. The questions and figures are in Hadley Cantril and Mildred Strunk, *Public Opinion 1935–1946* (Princeton, Princeton University Press, 1951), pp. 534, 538. It is interesting to note that far more Germans (76 per cent) and almost as many Englishmen (43 per cent) responded in negative terms about political careers for their children. For a useful review of literature on "Attitudes toward Public Leaders" see Bell et al., *Public Leadership*. For critiques of simple interpretations of such questions as indicative of occupational "prestige," see the following: Joseph A. Gusfield and Michael Schwartz, "The Meanings of Occupational Prestige: Reconsideration of the NORC Scale," *American Sociological Review, 28* (1963), 265–70; Albert J. Reiss and others, *Occupations and Social Status* (New York, Free Press of Glencoe, 1961); William A. Gamson and Howard Schuman, "Some Undercurrents in the Prestige of Physicians," *American Journal of Sociology, 68* (1963), 463–70; Kingsley Davis, "Reply," *American Sociological Review, 18* (1953), 397; Paul K. Hatt, "Occupation and Social Stratification," *American Journal of Sociology, 55* (1950), 533–43.

14. The evidence on Eisenhower and Stevenson is from Campbell et al., *The American Voter*, pp. 55–59.

15. Elihu Katz and Jacob J. Feldman, "The Debates in the Light of Research: A Survey of Surveys," in Sidney Kraus, ed., *The Great Debates* (Bloomington, University of Indiana Press, 1962), p. 198.

16. Philip E. Converse et al., "Stability and Change in 1960: A Reinstating Election," *American Political Science Review, 55* (1961), 269–80.

17. In 1939 a national sample was asked to specify the "youngest age at which a man should become President" and the age at which "a man becomes too old for the presidency." Medians were 40 and 65 respectively. Cantril and Strunk, p. 590. For a review of evidence on the variability of criteria applied by the public, see Bell, pp. 135–43.

18. Super, *The Psychology of Careers*. See also Robert E. Agger, Marshall N. Goldstein, and Stanley A. Pearl, "Political Cynicism: Measurement and Meaning," *Journal of Politics, 23* (1961), 501.

19. It is at least worth suggesting that for some of the more effective politicians, the period between school and entry to politics is one of cumulative experimentation and cogitation in which a strong personal identity is slowly being forged, while for the less effective types the period is one of relatively aimless drifting, reflecting an inability to come to grips with identity problems. Cf. Erikson, *Young Man Luther*, pp. 43, 176.

20. Everett C. Hughes, "Institutional Office and the Person," *American Journal of Sociology, 43* (1937–38), 413. Cf. Leiserson, *Parties and Politics*, pp. 202–03. On the other hand, it is wise not to exaggerate the contrast with other occupations: many business careers seem to proceed in mysterious fits and starts. See Melville Dalton, "Informal Factors in Career Achievement," *American Journal of Sociology, 56* (1951), 209–18; Fred E. Katz, "Occupational Contact Networks," *Social Forces, 37* (1958), 52.

21. C. Wright Mills notes that "From 1789 right up to 1921, generation after generation, the proportion of the political elite which has *ever* held local or state offices decreased from 93 to 69 per cent. In the Eisenhower administration, it fell to 57 per cent." Mills presents evidence that recruitment of the "political elite" from the House and Senate is on the wane, *The Power Elite* (New York, Oxford University Press, 1959), pp. 229 ff. Of the United

States Senators who served between 1947 and 1957, Matthews classifies 34 per cent as "Amateur Politicians," 60 per cent of them having been over forty when they achieved their first public offices. A quarter of the amateurs had no prior public office experience. Matthews, *U.S. Senators and Their World,* p. 62.

22. Of the 932 governors who served between 1870 and 1950, 86 had held no previous public office, and another 154 had spent only one to four years in public office. Joseph A. Schlesinger, "Lawyers and American Politics: A Clarified View," *Midwest Journal of Political Science, 1* (1957), 29. See also his *How They Became Governor* (East Lansing, Mich., Governmental Research Bureau, 1957).

23. The following percentages of state legislators in four states reported that they had "no party office or work" prior to their legislative service: New Jersey, 41 per cent; Ohio, 62 per cent; California, 52 per cent; Tennessee, 66 per cent. Wahlke et al., *The Legislative System,* p. 97. Of the Connecticut legislators responding to the questionnaire (a group over-representing the more active members), 55 per cent reported no previous elective public office, 58 per cent no appointive office, and 45 per cent no political party office. Derge reports that 51 per cent of the Missouri legislators responding to a questionnaire reported "no prior political experience." David R. Derge, "The Lawyer as Decision-Maker in the American State Legislature," *Journal of Politics, 21* (1959), 416.

24. Of 59 local government officials in Louisiana, 28 per cent reported that they first participated in politics by "campaigning for oneself." Herbert Jacob, "Why Men Seek Political Office: Motivation and Social Status in the Recruitment of Locally Elected Officials," a paper delivered at the 1961 Annual Meeting of the American Political Science Association, p. 14. Samuel C. Patterson reports that "more than 40 per cent of the county chairmen in Oklahoma have not run for public office, do not intend to run, and do not desire to run; and in this Democratic and Republican chairmen do not differ significantly. "Characteristics of Party Leaders," *Western Political Quarterly, 16* (1963), 345.

25. Cf. Riesman, *The Lonely Crowd,* chap. 12.

26. This hypothesis is consistent with some findings reported by Lester W. Milbrath on the political activities of 98 North Carolinians who made monetary contributions to their parties. Milbrath develops a scale of "sociability" which appears to have a strong self-esteem dimension and is related significantly (.05 or better) with a variety of political activities, but *not* with holding public office or making a political contribution. "Predispositions toward Political Contention," *Western Political Quarterly, 13* (1960), 5–18. William Buchanan's "purposive voters"—"a tolerant, educated, experienced, active minority in community affairs" —"who see their vote as a tool for shaping their environment do not prefer the political to the social techniques; in fact, they are more likely to use the latter." "An Inquiry into Purposive Voting," *Journal of Politics, 18* (1956), 295.

27. The following discussion has been facilitated by Arthur R. Cohen's chapter, "Some Implications of Self-Esteem for Social Influence," in Irving S. Janis et al., *Personality and Persuasibility* (New Haven, Yale University Press, 1959); Carl R. Rogers, "Some Observations on the Organization of Personality," *American Psychologist, 2* (1947), 358–68; Hall and Lindzey, *Theories of Personality,* chap. 12, "Rogers Self Theory." Cf. Jacob Tuckman and Robert J. Kleiner, "Discrepancy between Aspiration and Achievement as a Predictor of Schizophrenia," *Behavioral Science, 7* (1962), 443–47, for a simple technique, using demographic variables, for estimating such discrepancies.

28. Hall and Lindzey, p. 47, describing identification in Freud's psychoanalytic theory. Cf. Nelson N. Foote, "Identification as the Basis for a Theory of Motivation," *American Sociological Review, 16* (1951), 14–21; Shibutani, *Society and Personality,* chap. 7 and Pt. IV; Helen Merrell Lynd, *On Shame and the Search for Identity* (New York, Science Editions, 1961), chap. 5; White and Lippitt, *Autocracy and Democracy,* pp. 209–22; Winch, *Identi-*

fication and Its Familial Determinants; James C. Davies, *Human Nature in Politics* (New York, Wiley, 1963), pp. 37 ff.

29. For purposes of illustration I focus on identification with individual leaders, but similar things could be said about identification with political groups. Cf. Franz Neumann, "Anxiety and Politics," in Stein et al., eds., *Identity and Anxiety*, p. 276. On "positional" as contrasted with "personal" identification see Winch, p. 147. On "proximal" and "distal" groups in politics, see Davies, *Human Nature in Politics*, chaps. 5 and 6. The identification concept has its ambiguities, which are analyzed effectively by Nevitt Sanford, "The Dynamics of Identification," *Psychological Review*, 62 (1955), 106–18.

30. Cf. Leon J. Saul, *The Hostile Mind* (New York, Random House, 1956), chap. 6, "Hostility and Politics."

31. Cf. Fred I. Greenstein, "The Benevolent Leader: Children's Images of Political Authority," *American Political Science Review*, 54 (1960), 934–43.

32. Erikson, *Young Man Luther*, p. 102. Cf. Winch, pp. 13–14.

33. See above, pp. 78–82.

34. Lane, *Political Ideology*, chap. 17. This view is confirmed by Russell Middleton and Snell Putney, "Political Expression of Adolescent Rebellion," *American Journal of Sociology*, 68 (1963), and by Philip Nogee and Murray B. Levin, "Some Determinants of Political Attitudes among College Voters," *Public Opinion Quarterly*, 22 (1958–59), 449–63.

35. Harold D. Lasswell, "Psychology Looks at Morals and Politics," in Ulmer, ed., *Introductory Readings in Political Behavior*, p. 26. Cf. William H. Sewell and A. O. Haller, "Factors in the Relationship between Social Status and the Personality Adjustment of the Child," *American Sociological Review*, 24 (1959), 511–20.

36. E. J. Cleveland and W. D. Longaker, "Neurotic Patterns in the Family," in Leighton et al., *Explorations in Social Psychiatry*, p. 171; Manford H. Kuhn, "Self-Attitudes by Age, Sex, and Professional Training," *Sociological Quarterly*, 9 (1960), 39–55.

37. Cf. Robert A. Dahl, "Who Participates in Local Politics and Why," *Science*, 134 (Oct. 27, 1961), 9. At another level, Lasswell writes, "A general proposition is that *the accent on power rather than some other value in the social process has come because limitations upon access to other values have been overcome by the use of power.*" "The Selective Effect of Personality on Political Participation," in Richard Christie and Marie Jahoda, eds., *Studies in the Scope and Method of "The Authoritarian Personality"* (Glencoe, Ill., Free Press, 1954), p. 206 (emphasis in the original).

38. Cf. above, pp. 116–18.

39. Cf. Vidich and Bensman, *Small Town in Mass Society*, pp. 111–12.

40. Cf. Anne Roe, *The Psychology of Occupations* (New York, John Wiley, 1956), chaps. 21, 22. Relatively few occupational aspirations are fulfilled in fact. And apparently many people drift into careers for which they may or may not be suited, rather than making a definite, conscious occupational choice at some definite moment in time. Fred E. Katz and Harry W. Martin, "Career Choice Processes," *Social Forces*, 41 (1962), 149–54. Cf. Lamar T. Empey, "Social Class and Occupational Aspiration: A Comparison of Absolute and Relative Measurement," *American Sociological Review*, 21 (1956), 703–09; and Russell R. Dynes, Alfred C. Clarke, and Simon Dinitz, "Levels of Occupational Aspiration: Some Aspects of Family Experience as a Variable," *American Sociological Review*, 21 (1956), 212–15. The latter two articles are reprinted in Stoodley, ed., *Society and Self*.

41. Joan W. Moore, "Social Deprivation and Advantage as Sources of Political Values," *Western Political Quarterly*, 15 (1962), 217–26. Cf. Robert K. Merton and Alice S. Kitt, "Contributions to the Theory of Reference Group Behavior," in Merton and Paul F. Lazarsfeld, eds., *Studies in the Scope and Method of "The American Soldier"* (Glencoe, Ill., Free Press, 1950).

42. Duncan MacRae, "The Role of the State Legislator in Massachusetts," *American Sociological Review, 19* (1954), 188.

43. The median age at marriage has declined from 26.1 for husbands and 22.0 for wives in 1890, to 22.8 for husbands and 20.1 for wives in 1950. "The average woman who married in 1950 will be about 48 when her last child leaves home. By comparison, the average woman of her grandmother's day was about 55, if she lived that long, when her last child got married." Paul C. Glick, "The Life Cycle of the Family," in S. M. Lipset and Neil J. Smelser, eds., *Sociology: The Progress of a Decade* (Englewood Cliffs, N.J., Prentice-Hall, 1961), pp. 256–57. "Today the postparental couple can look forward to an average of about twenty years of life together after their last child has left home, whereas in 1890, the average couple could not expect to survive jointly even to the end of the parental stage." Marguerite F. Levy, "The Joint Survival Years," *American Behavioral Scientist, 6* (May 1963), 8–9.

44. Matilda White Riley, Marilyn E. Johnson, and Sarane S. Boocock, "Woman's Changing Occupational Role—A Research Report," *American Behavioral Scientist, 6* (1963), 33–37.

45. In 1890, 3.9 per cent of the population were over 65; in 1959, 8.8 per cent. Projections indicate that 9.1 per cent of the population will be in this category by 1975. In the decade 1940–50 the general population increased 14.5 per cent, while those over 65 increased 36.6 per cent. The same figures for 1950–60 are 7.0 per cent and 16.9 per cent respectively. Joseph T. Drake, *The Aged in American Society* (New York, Ronald Press, 1958), pp. 48–49.

46. Table derived from *U.S. Census of Population, 1950; Statistical Abstract of the United States, 1962* (83d ed., Washington, D.C., GPO, 1962) and official state records. House figures are for members elected in the given year.

47. Cf. "Detailed Occupation of the Economically Active Population: 1900 to 1950," U.S. Bureau of the Census, *Historical Statistics of the United States: Colonial Times to 1957* (Washington, GPO, 1960), p. 75, Series D 123–572. "Total lawyers reporting" to the American Bar Foundation increased from 204,111 in 1951 to 252,385 in 1960: "Legal Profession—Selected Characteristics of Lawyers: 1951–1960," *Statistical Abstract of the United States, 1962*, p. 157, table 205. Enrollment in ABA-approved law schools increased from 41,499 in 1961–62 to 49,552 in 1963–64. *American Bar Association Newsletter*, January 15, 1964.

48. Figures for House and for number of lawyers in the state in 1930 and 1960 are derived from *Connecticut Register and Manual*. Others are from the *U.S. Census of Population, 1950*, Vol. 2.

49. David R. Derge, "The Lawyer in the Indiana General Assembly," *Midwest Journal of Political Science, 6* (1962), 42–47.

50. Lipset and Bendix, *Social Mobility*, p. 102. See Edward Gross, "The Occupational Variable as a Research Category," *American Sociological Review, 24* (1959), 640–49; William A. Glaser, "Job Mobility between Government and Other Social Structures," *Political Research Organization and Design* (PROD), 3 (Nov. 1959).

51. Another trend poses no particular problem in Connecticut, but may in other states. Albert D. Biderman reports Defense Department estimates that military retirement pay recipients will increase from 231,000 to 405,000 in 1965, to 753,000 by 1973. Fifty-five per cent of the officers will be eligible for retirement in the next ten years. The average length-of-service (i.e. not disability) retirement age is 45.8, and the average nondisability pay $3,000 per year. Almost half the retired officers are concentrated in California, Florida, New York, Texas, and Virginia. "The crest of these retirements will coincide with . . . a vast increase in the numbers of persons seeking employment." Biderman supposes that "occupations in which the seniority system does not play an important role would be favored; those which involve highly general rather than very specific skills." "The Prospective Impact of Large Scale Military Retirement," *Social Problems, 7* (1959), 84–90.

52. In Brunswick, Maine, the same two men were elected moderator and treasurer for

half a century. Lincoln Smith, "Political Leadership in a New England Community," *Review of Politics,* 17 (1955), 392–409.

53. See above, Chap. 2.

54. Robert T. Daland found that urbanization was accompanied by increasing nomination of newcomers and the better educated in a rapidly growing Alabama community. *Dixie City: A Portrait of Political Leadership* (University of Alabama, Bureau of Public Administration, 1956).

55. Cf. Key, *Public Opinion,* "A Missing Link of the Puzzle," pp. 536–43.

56. Cf. Kent, *Political Behavior,* "The Instability of Political Enmities," pp. 294–98.

57. Edward A. Shils, "Primary Groups in the American Army," in Merton and Lazarsfeld, eds., *Scope and Method of "The American Soldier,"* pp. 30–31. Cf. Theodore M. Mills, *Group Structure and the Newcomer* (Oslo University Press, 1957); Kullervo Rainio, "A Stochastic Model of Social Interaction," *Transactions of the Westermarck Society,* 7 (1961), 116 ff.

58. See Robert C. Ziller, Richard D. Behringer, and Mathilda J. Jansen, "The Newcomer in Open and Closed Groups," *Journal of Applied Psychology,* 45 (1961), 55–58; Garland C. Routt, "Interpersonal Relationships and the Legislative Process," *Annals,* 195 (1938), 129–36.

59. Chris Argyris, "The Individual and the Organization: Some Problems of Mutual Adjustment," *Administrative Science Quarterly,* 2 (1957), 1–24; Presthus, *The Organizational Society;* Victor A. Thompson, *Modern Organization* (New York, Knopf, 1961). For a sophisticated theory regarding how group task demands affect personal relations and satisfactions, see Robert F. Bales, "The Equilibrium Problem in Small Groups," in Talcott Parsons, Robert F. Bales, and Edward A. Shils, *Working Papers in the Theory of Action* (Glencoe, Ill., Free Press, 1953). On the pathologies of "personalization of role," see Scott A. Greer, *Social Organization* (New York, Random House, 1955), pp. 63–64. Cf. Daniel Katz, "The Motivational Basis of Organizational Behavior," and Abraham Zaleznik, "Managerial Behavior and Interpersonal Competence," *Behavioral Science,* 9 (April 1964).

60. "From a prominent place in the public eye in his own community, he sinks into comparative insignificance. Many legislators never recover fully from this blow to their ego." Harvey Walker, *The Legislative Process: Lawmaking in the United States* (New York, Ronald Press, 1948), p. 161. Such effects are apparently especially strong for people with low self-esteem. See James E. Dittes, "Attractiveness of Group as Function of Self-Esteem and Acceptance by Group," *Journal of Abnormal and Social Psychology,* 59 (1959), 77–82.

61. Cf. above, pp. 113–15.

62. "Emotional tension does not always produce reversion to earlier types of behavior; what it does always produce, apparently, is a reduction in the complexity of the psychological field that determines behavior at a given moment. The more tense and frustrated a person is, the more his thought processes are reduced to their simplest and crudest elements. Creative thinking tends to disappear, imaginative understanding of another person's viewpoint tends to disappear, remote goals tend to disappear, inhibitions based on an appreciation of remote consequences tend to disappear, intelligent weighing and choosing between various alternatives tends to disappear; and, as a result, the behavior that occurs is likely to be not the most intelligent or adaptive behavior, but the most 'available' behavior—the behavior that comes most quickly into one's mind." White and Lippitt, *Autocracy and Democracy,* pp. 171–72. Cf. James E. Dittes, "Effect of Changes in Self-Esteem upon Impulsiveness and Deliberation in Making Judgments," *Journal of Abnormal and Social Psychology,* 58 (1959), 496–500; Edgar F. Borgatta, "Role-Playing Specification, Personality, and Performance," *Sociometry,* 24 (1961), 218–33; Marjorie E. Rees and Morton Goldman, "Some Relationships between Creativity and Personality," *Journal of General Psychology,* 65 (1961), 145–61; Ezra Stotland and Nicholas B. Cottrell, "Self-Esteem, Group Interaction, and Group Influence on Performance," *Journal of Personality,* 29 (1961), 273–84; Richard D. Mann, "A Review of the Relation-

ships between Personality and Performance in Small Groups," *Psychological Bulletin, 56* (1959), 241–70.

63. James S. Coleman, *Community Conflict* (Glencoe, Ill., Free Press, 1957). This seems to be the way some significant political crises arise in local communities governed by professionalized administrators. I am indebted to Robert Lane for calling this to my attention. See Harry Eckstein, *A Theory of Stable Democracy,* Research Monograph 10, Center of International Studies (Princeton University, April 10, 1961), p. 32. Cf. Wallas, *Human Nature,* 3d ed., Pt. I, chaps. 2 and 4; Pt. II, chap. 2; and Berelson et al., *Voting,* pp. 314–15.

64. The recruitment focus is essential here. High standards of selection might be used simply to weed out the less talented. But "if a society waited to have its statuses filled by individuals with special gifts, certain statuses might not be filled at all," as Ralph Linton puts it. "Status and Role," in Parsons et al., eds., *Theories of Society, 1, 207.*

65. See above, 217 ff.

66. Joachim M. Furster, S.J., "The Self Concept Approach to Personal Adjustment," *Journal of Social Psychology, 59* (1963), 239–46.

67. Wahlke et al., *The Legislative System,* p. 84: "Ties with a political party, consciousness of public issues, knowledge of both the serious and pleasurable aspects of political behavior, or sense of public responsibility, appear as by-products of political socialization in the most intimate form of primary group life. What strikes one in reading some of the comments is the casualness of the socialization process when the agents are friends or associates."

68. Robert E. Lane, "Fathers and Sons: Foundations of Political Belief," *American Sociological Review, 24* (1959), 510. See William C. Schutz, *FIRO: A Three-Dimensional Theory of Interpersonal Behavior* (New York, Holt, Rinehart, and Winston, 1960), chap. 5, "The Postulate of Relational Continuity," and pp. 69–72; see also C. W. Wahl, "The Relation between Primary and Secondary Identifications: Psychiatry and the Group Sciences," in Eugene Burdick and Arthur J. Brodbeck, eds., *American Voting Behavior* (Glencoe, Ill., Free Press, 1959).

69. See Greenstein, "The Benevolent Leader: Children's Images of Political Authority," *American Political Science Review, 54* (1960), especially pp. 940–41; and Greenstein, "Sex-Related Political Differences in Childhood," *Journal of Politics, 23* (1961), 353–71; Lewis A. Froman, Jr., "Learning Political Attitudes," *Western Political Quarterly, 15* (1962), 304–13; David Easton and Robert D. Hess, "The Child's Political World," *Midwest Journal of Political Science, 6* (1962), 229–46; Lester W. Milbrath, "Latent Origins of Liberalism-Conservatism and Party Identification: A Research Note," *Journal of Politics, 24* (1962), 679–88.

70. Key, *Public Opinion,* chap. 12.

71. See H. H. Remmers, "Early Socialization of Attitudes," in Burdick and Brodbeck, eds., *American Voting Behavior.*

72. See Rose K. Goldsen, Morris Rosenberg, Robin M. Williams, Jr., and Edward A. Suchman, "Political Apathy, Economic Conservatism," in Stoodley, ed., *Society and Self.*

73. *Public Opinion,* p. 320.

74. Ibid., p. 396.

75. See Campbell et al., *The American Voter,* pp. 458–59.

76. Cf. Riesman and Glazer, "Criteria for Political Apathy," in Gouldner, ed., *Studies in Leadership.*

77. Charles S. Hyneman, "Tenure and Turnover of Legislative Personnel," *Annals, 195* (1938), 31.

78. There is evidence that persons high in need for achievement are more attracted by the excellence a role demands than by its prestige. Eugene Burnstein, Robert Moulton, and Paul Liberty, Jr., "Prestige vs. Excellence as Determinants of Role Attraction," *American Sociological Review, 28* (1963), 212–18. Cf. Chris Argyris, "Employee Apathy and Noninvolvement," *Personnel* (July–August, 1961), pp. 8–14.

Index

Achievement: as motivation, 11; and Spectator, 55; and Advertiser, 85–86, 97–98, 105–06, 111; and sense of time, 189; and Lawmaker, 191, 205, 253–54

Activity in legislature, 18–20; Spectator's, 24–25; engaged, 100; Advertiser's, 100, 102, 165; Reluctant's, 118–19, 150–51; Lawmaker's, 164–65; pattern of, 212; as political measurement, 218; nature of political, 219

Adams, John, 1

Adaptation: patterns of, 18–19, 213; and Spectator, 45, 48, 177, 248 f.; and Reluctant, 145–47, 156–59, 177, 248–49; and Lawmaker, 174, 183, 248; and Advertiser, 177, 248–49

Advertiser, 20, 140, 196, 206; and lawyers, 67–69; occupational type, 68; integrity of, 89; social ideals of, 100–01, 103; and Spectator, 105; and environment, 107, 109–10, 183; legislative role of, 111–12, 250; and legislative conflict, 114; future of, 115; and Lawmaker, 166–69, 251, 265; and adaptation, 177, 248–49; satisfactions of, 182; and sense of time, 189–90; role of, 191–92, 195; as public figure, 198; as campaigner, 200–01; and compromise, 203; and self-concept, 214, 217, 229; summary of type, 215; and power, 231–32; and candidacy, 239, 242; as new legislator, 247; and Reluctant, 268–69. *See also* Jackson, Mike; Muldoon, Bob; Rossini, Charles

Affiliation motivation, 11. *See also* Motivation

Aggression, 199; and Spectator, 54–56; and Advertiser, 91, 96–97, 100, 102–03, 104–08 passim, 110–11, 114; and Reluctant, 133, 157–58; and Lawmaker, 206

Amateurism and legislature, 109, 155

Ambition, 1, 52, 115; and Spectator, 25–26; and Advertiser, 70–71, 84, 89; and Reluctant, 119–20; and Lawmaker, 166–67

American Bar Association, 67

Anxiety, 89–90, 102

Approval, need for, 30, 35–36, 38, 43. *See also* Self

Availability, 27–28, 57, 126–29, 172–74

Baker, Ray Stannard, 116

Baker, Russell, 2

Bennis, Don, 174–77, 183 f., 186, 189 ff., 195 ff., 198 f., 200–01, 203

Bullitt, Stimson, 77, 197

Businessmen and politics, 6, 11

California, perquisites of state legislators, 7

Campaigns, 5, 131, 136–37, 165, 180, 197–202, 243–45

Candidacy, 57; motives for, 2, 11–13, 21, 223; and recruitment, 5, 10, 237–41, 243; and occupational availability, 6, 233–36; interaction of factors determining, 13–14; and Spectator, 76, 238, 242; and Lawmaker, 197, 227, 239; attitudes toward, 222; appeal of, 224–25; illustrative example of, 225–26; and self-estimates, 229; and identification, 230; and Reluctant, 238, 242; and Advertiser, 239, 242; and electorate, 244; and relation to others, 249; and identification of Lawmaker, 256–57. *See also* Competition and political candidacy; Motivation; Recruitment

Cartwright, Dorwin, 19

Committee system in legislature, 22, 178, 180

Competition and political candidacy, 2–4, 72–74, 124–26

Compromise, 197, 202–05

Conflict: in legislature, 113; in small towns, 125–27; and Reluctant, 143, 148–49, 153; impersonality in, 160–61; and Lawmaker, 192; and Advertiser, 250

Conformity: pressures for, 60, 62, 83; as adaptation, 253